SHARK AMONG DOLPHINS

SHARK AMONG DOLPHINS

Inside Jimmy Johnson's Transformation of the Miami Dolphins

STEVE HUBBARD

BALLANTINE BOOKS / NEW YORK

Grateful acknowledgment is made to Hyperion for permission to reprint an excerpt from
Turning the Thing Around by Jimmy Johnson, as told to Ed Hinton.
Copyright © 1993 Jimmy Johnson and Ed Hinton. Reprinted with permission of Hyperion.

http://www.randomhouse.com

Library of Congress Cataloging-in-Publication Data
Hubbard, Steve (Steve A.)
Shark among Dolphins : inside Jimmy Johnson's transformation of the Miami Dolphins / by Steve Hubbard.—1st ed.
p.   cm.
ISBN 0-345-41204-4 (alk. paper)
1. Johnson, Jimmy, 1943–   .   2. Football coaches—United States—Biography.
3. Miami Dolphins (Football team)   I. Title.
GV939.J613H83   1997
796.332'092—dc21   97-23129
[B]

Manufactured in the United States of America

First Edition: August 1997
10   9   8   7   6   5   4   3   2   1

To Julie, the best wife a writer could ever ask for.

ACKNOWLEDGMENTS

The secrets of writing and coaching are in the details. To go beyond the superficiality of the sound bite, to give the reader vivid examples why many experts consider Jimmy Johnson to be football's best coach, personnel man, and motivator, I needed uncommon cooperation from the coach. I needed to go behind the scenes, to meetings and places that are almost always off-limits to reporters. I needed rare access, and I needed Jimmy's candor.

Paranoia runs deeper than the pockets in the NFL, and Jimmy had to be sold on why he should concur when he could not control what I wrote. He would have preferred to wait until the Miami Dolphins were better, their controversies fewer, but the most telling examples of how he molds a team in his image would come in 1996, his initial year replacing Don Shula. *Sports Illustrated*'s Peter King, whose friendship we both value, helped convince Jimmy of this author's and this book's merits. But ultimately, I think Jimmy agreed because he truly has, as he once bragged, brass balls. He is that rare NFL coach willing to take bold risks, and that is essential to why he allowed this inside story, why he has a yacht and a restaurant named *Three Rings*.

How does a coach win three championship rings? How does a person become the best at what he or she does? I wanted to go beyond Xs and Os to see if Jimmy's techniques transcended football, if all of us, whether in our business or personal lives, could learn about motivating, molding, and picking people, and I hope that you, too, will find the answer is yes. Jimmy Johnson wound up giving more time and access than he would have preferred, and the book and the author are the better for it.

I am indebted to Jimmy for his remarkable candor and insights. This book truly could not have been written without the cooperation of Jimmy and the entire Dolphins organization. I constantly sought and received help from Harvey Greene and his media-relations staff: Mike Hanson, Seth Levit, and Gayle Baden. I cannot thank them enough. Jimmy's right-hand man, Bob Ackles, spent hours detailing the Dolphins' draft process for me. Players such as Zach Thomas, Larry Izzo, Terrell Buckley, Keith Sims, Fred Barnett, and even the media-wary Dan Marino gave freely of their time. Jimmy's friends, Bears coach Dave Wannstedt and attorney Nick Christin, were great helps. Photographer Dave Cross bailed me out more than once.

My nine-month voyage in uncharted waters would have been much rougher without the insights and friendships shared by so many South Florida media members, in particular Pat McManamon and Dan Graziano of the *Palm Beach Post*, Joe Frisaro of the *Tampa Tribune*, Rick Weber of the Fort Myers *News Press*, Jason Cole and Dave Hyde of the Fort Lauderdale *Sun-Sentinel*, Armando Salguero and Edwin Pope of *The Miami Herald*, and Jody Jackson and Joe Rose of WQAM radio.

I could not have survived the whirlwind of negotiating, researching, writing, and publishing this book without the guidance, patience, and encouragement of my agent, Scott Waxman, and my editor, Doug Grad.

And finally, I could not have endured endless hours of anxiety and seemingly non-stop work without the unfailing support of my wife Julie, who raised two small children practically alone while I was off chasing what I thought was sports' most compelling story of 1996. I hope all of the forenamed—and you, the reader—will find the efforts worth the while.

Steve Hubbard
June 1997

1
"THREE RINGS" CIRCUS

Fifty-eight players, fifteen assistant coaches, six trainers and equipment men, the director of football operations, the media relations director, and the security investigator filtered into the auditorium, each man arriving at least five minutes early for the 9:30 A.M. start. Eight months before, in their introduction to their new coach, two Miami Dolphins players had straggled in maybe a minute late, and Jimmy Johnson caustically warned them the next misdemeanor would cost them money—or maybe even their jobs.

These survivors knew the threat had been real and hoped they had endured the worst of the ordeal. They had been pushed beyond what they thought possible ever since Jimmy's not-so-voluntary "voluntary" workouts had begun in March, had pounded on each other's bodies twice a day since the National Football League's most physical training camp opened in July, and they had the bruises to show for it. Every blessed day, in the unrelenting summer heat and humidity that turns South Florida into the world's largest steambath, they had practiced the demolition derby that is the "middle drill," with runner after runner charging between the tackles at full speed. "Two-a-days . . . in pads . . . every second!" cornerback Terrell Buckley exclaimed. "I didn't think I could make it through."

The exhaustion was as much mental as physical. The rookies were struggling to comprehend a new system, a new league, a new lifestyle. Even the veterans were struggling with the complexities of a new defense, a new coaching staff, and a demanding new head coach who seemed to relish trashing the Dolphins' history and Don Shula's legacy. They had seen revered starters, stars with big reputations and big salaries, lose half or all their pay, lose their starting jobs or their jobs, period. Only thirty of Don's Dolphins had survived what the NFL calls the final cutdown, and still they knew the roster is never final when Jimmy Johnson

1

is the boss. If he didn't think they could help him win the Super Bowl in the next two or three years, they weren't going to last long. It didn't matter what they had done yesterday for Shula or even JJ. When he cut one of his all-time personal favorites, Jimmy warned, "A guy can be my best friend and if he's got someone behind him who I can't stand but performs better, I've got to make the change."

He was ruthless and heartless, selfish and devious—and those were the adjectives Jimmy and his friends used. When the Raiders' Darth Vader had trumped his bid to hire an assistant coach, Jimmy had said, "Fuckin' Al Davis, only fucker in the league more devious than me." When he was asked whom he'd like to kick back with on his boat, he named Hannibal the Cannibal, the *Silence of the Lambs* killer. "Hannibal Lecter was able to make the guy in the next cell kill himself by talking to him and making him swallow his tongue," Jimmy said. "That's a pretty influential speaker. You think that guy could get a team to play?"

Shula, like his seventies contemporaries Tom Landry and Chuck Noll, didn't think a coach needed to motivate his players. He figured they were professionals and their motivation should come from within. Jimmy had a psychology degree and a 162 IQ, and his motivational techniques earned him hundreds of thousands for his business speeches and three championship rings for his football talks. He figured, "Everybody needs motivating, from the vice president of IBM to a professional football player to a head coach. This old bullshit about 'They're paid a lot to do a job and they've got to be self-motivated,' that doesn't hold water with me. We all need to be motivated at one time or another."

And so here sat the 1996 Miami Dolphins, four days before their season opener, eager to hear how the master motivator, the coaching genius, planned to beat the New England Patriots. Most of them were here because he wanted them here, and the rookies, especially, felt beholden to him. The veterans were wiser and warier, yet just as anxious to see what lay ahead. Shula had won more games than anyone in NFL history ever had or likely ever will. But he hadn't won a Super Bowl since the 1973 season, hadn't taken the Dolphins to one since the 1984 season, and his last Miami team had disintegrated: selfish, undisciplined, overpriced, and underachieving.

Jimmy had followed local legend Howard Schnellenberger at the University of Miami and won a national championship. He had followed the legendary Landry at Dallas and taken the Cowboys from 1–15 to back-to-back Super Bowl titles in just four years. When he walked away—or was shoved away—from the dynasty in the making, his legend only grew as NFL owners, television executives, and corporate CEOs all wooed him.

He was supposed to be the best coach, best motivator, best talent evaluator of the nineties. What were his secrets? What could Jimmy do that Don could not? The 1995 Dolphins had made the playoffs despite all their problems. The 1996 Dolphins certainly had holes in their lineup, but what American Football Conference team didn't? With Jimmy as coach and Dan Marino as quarterback, how good they could be?

The "experts" had all sorts of answers. *Sports Illustrated* predicted the Dolphins would finish second or third in the AFC East. *The Sporting News* and *ESPN Pro Football '96* magazine forecast fourth in the East, ahead of only the perennially grounded Jets. ESPN's Chris Mortensen wrote Jimmy had "no real chance of making the playoffs, let alone the Super Bowl. He's got no running game. No pass rush. No speed on defense. In short, not much except No. 13 and a lot of fat contracts."

The beat writers for the three major South Florida newspapers figured the Dolphins would win somewhere between seven and nine games, the most optimistic forecasting a wild-card playoff spot. But two players turned commentators, Mike Ditka and Bob Trumpy, predicted in *Inside Sports* magazine that the Dolphins would win the AFC East and advance to the AFC title game before losing. TNT analyst Randall Cunningham forecast a Dolphins-Packers Super Bowl, while counterpart Mark May said, "I don't think Jimmy Johnson's impact will be that great."

So what would it be? Even the veterans who didn't automatically accept Jimmy as Jesus were enthused by the real season starting, if only because that's when the real money began. And so on Wednesday, August 28, they gathered in the 2,950-square-foot auditorium, just off the lobby of the Dolphins' gleaming $10 million complex.

The players reclined in the ninety cushioned chairs, some leaning forward onto the tables in front of them. The assistant coaches and various staffers stood along the back wall. Jimmy stood down in front, a lectern but no notes in front of him. As much as he believed in motivational talks, he saw little use in rah-rah speeches right before the game. Even the best Knute Rockne talk tended to last only a few minutes, and most players were ready to play on Sundays anyway. No, they needed motivation not on game day but on the weekdays. Jimmy thought these Wednesday-morning talks were his most important of the week because they not only laid out the game plan but set the tone for the workweek. The Wednesday, Thursday, and Friday practices were his longest, most physical, and most vital. He wanted his players to get better, his plays sharper, in each of those practices. If any of them went poorly, he fretted about losing on Sunday.

"Before we break up into offensive and defensive meetings, let me go into more details as far as what we're doing this week," Jimmy began. "We've spent a lot of time preparing for New England already. I think that's obvious to you. We've practiced for them on and off for the last couple of weeks. We've studied them. We feel like we have a hell of a game plan. We feel like in all three phases that we're in really good shape to prevent the stuff that could really hurt us.

"I talked to Norv Turner [the Redskins' coach and Jimmy's former offensive coordinator] this morning. He played the Patriots last week. He said they're not a physical team. You look at the tape, you'll see that. You'll see the things we'll be able to take advantage of. You look at some of the things we can do against them.

"First of all, the way we have picked it up running the football, we're gonna be able to do some things. You look at the matchups, and they've got a 250-pound kid over there on you, Richmond!" One minute into the morning's work and already Jimmy had stirred his players out of any lethargy by singling out his Pro Bowl left tackle, Richmond Webb. Players lifted their chins off their necks and turned and looked at each other. Why, Shula never challenged his linemen like this. Jimmy wasn't done. He turned to his Pro Bowl left guard, Keith Sims, and his emerging center, Tim Ruddy: "They've got a rookie on you, Keith!" he said, sharply.

And then his words turned louder, slower, more emphatic, more profane, just in case anybody missed the message. Publicly, he does not curse; he talks the language of the boardroom. Privately, Jimmy can swear like a sergeant; he speaks the language of the locker room: "And we can wear their ass down! Just running the football! Dooowwwnhill! At their ass! The whole balllll game!"

Slight pause. Press the challenge: "If a 250-pound kid can beat you, Richmond . . . or if that *dammmnn* rookie is going to handle you, Keith—or Tim—then we've got problems.

"And I don't think we have problems.

"They're gonna have a big-assed problem.

"Because we're gonna come at their asssssses runnnnninn' the football.

"They don't cover the damn seam. They play a lot of Cover Two [a zone pass defense with each safety covering one half of the field deep]. If we get down the field and stretch that damn thing, we're gonna be able to hit the tight end down the middle. So we can do some things offensively. We're *gonna* move the football. We're *gonna* score points."

Players turned and looked at each other with upraised eyebrows. When was the last time the Dolphins went into a game focusing this much on the run? Certainly not since Marino arrived in 1983. Maybe not since the days of Larry Csonka and Jim Kiick and Mercury Morris. When was the last time Shula called out players' names, challenged individuals so openly? Webb and Sims had arrived in 1990, drafted back to back in the first and second rounds to fortify the weak left side of the offensive line, and they had. They were terrific pass protectors. For years, they had been begging, like almost all linemen do, to run the ball more. But Don's Dolphins hadn't averaged even four yards a carry since 1987. They hadn't had a thousand-yard rusher since 1978.

1978!

Think how long it had been.

Disco and velour were in.

VCRs and PCs, cell phones and faxes were not.

Jimmy Johnson was an assistant coach at Pitt.

Dan Marino was at Catholic Central High.

Karim Abdul-Jabbar wasn't even in kindergarten.

Backs had run for a thousand yards 178 times since 1978, an average of six times per team. Every team in the league had done it. Every team except the two expansion teams born in 1995 . . . and Miami.

The Dolphins had relied on Dan Marino, and that tactic was hard to argue with because who wanted to take the ball out of the hands of the most prolific passer in NFL history? And yet when the Dolphins needed to hold on to the ball at the end of the game to assure victory, they could not. When they needed a tough yard on the goal line or third and one, they could not. When they needed to keep a hot offense off the field, they could not. When they needed to avoid the inevitable interceptions, they could not. They owned all these glittery passing records, but they had not recorded more takeaways than giveaways since 1984, and turnover ratio is the most important statistic in football. It wasn't just coincidence that 1984 had been their last Super Bowl season.

As much as Jimmy was the Coach of the Nineties, his offensive philosophy was decidedly old-fashioned. He didn't have Emmitt Smith here, but still, his Dolphins were going to run, and run, and run some more. Even if his running game got stuffed, as it frequently had in preseason, the Dolphins would keep pounding away. They weren't going to give up on it the way Shula had. They were going to be *persistent*. They had heard him say the word a hundred times already, and they'd hear it another hundred before the year was over.

The offensive game plan obvious, Jimmy turned toward his defenders. He told them the Patriots had some offensive players with big names and talents, and publicly, he would spend the week telling the media about how wonderful Drew Bledsoe and Curtis Martin and Ben Coates and even Shawn Jefferson were. But privately, here among his players, he would attack every hint of weakness. His words would not be too different from what every coach has said for decades: Harry the quarterback into sacks and interceptions. Swarm the star running back. Hit the backs and receivers and force turnovers. But Jimmy would do it with his unique touch, with a tug on his players' psyches. He challenged his Pro Bowl stars. He subtly stabbed at one of the Dolphins' major motivators—money—a point further emphasized on the bulletin board in their locker room, where Bledsoe's photograph was surrounded by fake, green million-dollar bills, Bledsoe's face superimposed on each one, underneath large letters blaring, "$Six Million Dollar Man." Bledsoe, a sack-prone, interception-prone twenty-four-year-old, was making more money than any of them. Drew Bledsoe was worth more than Dan Marino?

"You get after his assss," Jimmy said, voice rising, "and the way he stares down those receivers, hey, we'll *get* some picks! We'll *get* some turnovers, and we'll sack his *assss*! You get after him, and we'll be in pretty damn good shape. They ain't played a defensive line as physical as ours is.

"Now, Curtis Martin is a damn good player. Their number one play, the play they're able to make yards on, is a little draw. He goes all over the place. Now, what stops him from getting big yards? It's swarming their *asss*! He had two fumbles last week. So let's get after him.

"Let's look at who Bledsoe's throwing to. His number one receiver, Vincent Brisby, is out. The guy they were counting on to be opposite Brisby, Terry Glenn, is doubtful, probably not gonna play, and, if he does play, he's a damn rookie who's only practiced half a dozen times. So who's he gonna throw to? Shawn Jefferson? Puhhhh-lease!"

When most people used the word, it was a one-syllable show of good manners. Please. When Jimmy used the word, it was a two-syllable form of dismissal. Jimmy used "Puhhhh-lease" the way other people used "Give me a break" or "You've got to be kidding."

Jefferson had been traded by Houston and cut by San Diego. He had a reputation for good speed and bad hands. Will Moore was a refuge from the Canadian Football League. Jimmy told his defenders the New England receivers would lay the ball on the ground if they got hit hard, would throw short-arm passes that were high or wide, and would not block the way the Dolphins' receivers do.

"You know how we like to be a physical team?" he asked. "You watch our receivers. They'll knock you on your assss! You watch O.J. [McDuffie] go back and crack back on a fuckin' linebacker or hit one of those safeties. Our receivers *block*! You watch the tape, you DBs, and after watching the tape a couple of days, you tell me; you tell me how physical their receivers are. They ain't gonna block anybody! And if our safeties and corners get on their ass, that ball *will* be on the ground. They'll be going across the middle feeling gun-shy, using alligator arms. So that's what they've got at receiver.

"Okay, now what else they got? They got Ben Coates. Damn good tight end. Damn good player. Now, you swarm his ass, he'll drop the ball, too. We've got some good shit in the defensive game plan for him. We'll keep his ass out of it. Their big deal is to run screens and draws. We blitz on him, his ass has to stay right inside to block those people. That eliminates him. Then we can clamp down on Coates. That takes his ass away. Now we can adjust to those damn wide receivers. So we've got some good shit on them.

"Special teams, hey, guys, you looked at it this morning. Hey, we put this wedge together that we've worked on in practice but we haven't shown in preseason games, and we're gonna return 'em.

"We're gonna have a shot to change momentum. You're going to see that all year long we're gonna have two or three things designed for every ball game when we want to change momentum. We get ahead and they start to creep back, we're gonna do things to get back our way.

"Now, the other thing, special teams, is Dave Meggett. He's damn good. He hasn't done a whole lot in preseason, but that's planned. He'll be there Sunday. Cover those damn punts, guys! We need to swarm his ass and *tackle*! On their kickoffs, they like to run that wedge, put Meggett behind them and let him pick his spots. If our kickoff coverage people do a nice job when they're blocking on you, if you pop 'em across the face, we're gonna be fine the way Joe Nedney is kicking the ball. They're gonna be starting deep.

"Their kicker, you see him in preseason, he's spraying kickoffs all over the damn place. That's one reason I'm giving us a chance for a return. They just let their best deep snapper go and signed a new guy. The ball's going all over the place. We've got a chance to get after his ass. So we're gonna have some things ready."

The overview of the game plan complete, Jimmy turned and looked at John Gamble. The top-ranked power lifter in the world for three straight years, Gamble wasn't some gargantuan player. He was the team's strength and conditioning coach, and he had put everyone through grueling workouts ever since those so-called voluntary workouts had begun in March.

"You remember, John, when we started working toward this year?" Jimmy asked. "How many months ago was that, John?"

"Six months," Gamble replied.

"Six months ago," Jimmy repeated, and he scanned the room, looking into his players' eyes. "How hard did you work in that period of time, getting ready for this? You look at what we did in preseason, starting out with the middle drills. How hard did we work then? How hard did we work the whole damn preseason? How did we prepare? The coaching staff has been up here at all hours, up until one o'clock in the morning, getting ready with the scripts [for each day's practice] and game plans.

"We've done everything possible," Jimmy said. "You," he said, pointing to the players. "Me," he said, jabbing a finger in his chest. "Him," he said, pointing to the coaches along the back wall. His voice was growing steadily louder. "We've all done *everything possible* to get to this point. We've got a hell of a plan. We're gonna have a hell of a team. And it starts Sunday. Now it's up to you. If . . . *you* . . . approach it . . . like a job."

He had measured each of these seven words for effect. Jimmy had studied the techniques of the world's best motivational speakers, and he doesn't get $30,000 (for in-town talks) or $40,000 (for an out-of-town speech) for nothing. Even at those prices, he rejects more speeches than he accepts, so he can focus on football and fun.

Now he wanted to hammer home the season-long game plan. It was his first year with these Dolphins, and he wanted to emphasize the ground rules again.

"See, you approach it like a job. If your mind is somewhere else, if you're not doing everything possible to do the best you can . . . It's up to you now. Get into your playbook. Study your game plan. Study your assignments.

"If I'm Richmond, I'm gonna study that 250-pound defensive end. Because this group right here"—he pointed to the offensive linemen—"we're depending on you, Richmond. We're depending on you, Keith. When we have to have it, we want to *rrrrrooccckkk that damn rookie.*

"We're depending on you rookies. Karim, we're depending on you. Jerris McPhail, we're depending on you. Watch those tapes! And not just when the coach shows it to you! Study that playbook! Start working your mind, guys!"

Jimmy knew he had inherited a lot of late-night carousers. O. J. McDuffie had been arrested at 4 A.M. on a Saturday before a game. Four Dolphins had flown to Cleveland and back for the World Series, returning at 4 A.M., just five hours before practice. He already had cut party animal Eric Green, and he again reminded them of his expectations.

"I can't force you to *want* to play. It's dumb for me to say, 'Okay, we've got all these curfews, we've got all these damn rules, and we've got all these fines, and I'm gonna make you want it. *You've gotta want it!*

"Hey, thirty-two years I've been doing this. I can tell you this. John Gamble and Kevin O'Neill [the trainer] will be the first to tell you this: In preparing for any contest, your body is going to have a carryover effect from the days leading up to that contest. The forty-eight hours prior to the game are critical! So Friday, when we finish our practice and you're done, you could say, 'Friday night! All right! I've got a night off! I don't have to get up that early Saturday morning. I'm going out! I'm gonna have myself a good time!'

"Men, be accountable. Take the responsibility to be the best you can be. You may say, 'I'm a backup, I'm not gonna play.' Hey, you might be in there the second play. If you're in there five plays, those five plays might be the difference in this team winning or losing.

"Be the *best* that you can be!" he said, voice booming again. "So Friday night, hey, have a great night, have a little relaxation, be with your family, do whatever. If you want to go out to dinner, that's fine. But hey, listen up, guys: I haven't done my job if I hear about guys at some honky-tonk at two o'clock in the morning. I haven't done my job if that's going to have a carryover effect to the game. You may say, 'It's Friday night, not the night before the game.' But it has a hell of an effect on the body, doesn't it, Kevin?"

"Yes, sir!" O'Neill said, quick as could be.

"A hell of an effect on your body," Jimmy repeated, and motioned toward his coaches. "Like I said, we've done our best. We're gonna coach our asses off all week long, but we can't force you to want it. *You* have got to want it. And I mean everybody—everybody in here, from the oldest guy to the youngest guy, from first-teamers to second-teamers to the inactive players to the practice-squad guys. Practice-squad guys will go out there today, and your whole thought process is to get this team ready to play. Go as hard as you can go. That in itself will give you an opportunity to make the regular roster."

He clapped once.

"If a guy's inactive, hey, maybe you're inactive this week, but next week you're probably going to be active. At some time, you're going to have an opportunity. Stay positive! Stay together and get ready to go out there and kick their ass on Sunday! Let's get this thing started off the right way! Do everything possible to be the best you can be come Sunday at four o'clock. Let's start building up toward Sunday. Let's have a hell of a time and then start getting ready for Arizona!"

And with that, the eighteen-minute monologue was over and players broke into meetings with their coordinators and position coaches to start learning the details of the game plan.

Jimmy addresses the team in some manner every day, but these Wednesday speeches are usually the longest and most prepared, though rarely as long as this season-opening trendsetter. In a normal week, the coach will talk to the players for just a couple of minutes after a Sunday game, then review the positives and negatives during Monday's film review, then talk briefly before and sometimes after Monday's light workout. The players are off Tuesday while the coaches critique the opponent and formulate the game plan. Wednesday, Jimmy is back in front of them again, laying out the basics of the game plan, usually adding a message such as this take-care-of-your-body-and-brain theme. Often, he'll discuss the division race, or tweak their pride, or tell them how they can improve. The rest of the week, he will call them together spontaneously. "Whenever the time is right," he explains. "I don't meet just to meet."

This opening sermon seemed like a rousing speech, one that should have gotten the guys fired up and working hard 102 hours before game time. But, as Jimmy suspected, practice did not go well that afternoon. Guys had worked frenetically to make the team, and, now that they had, the letdown was inevitable. Veterans were relieved and ready to relax. Rookies were excited, busy informing all their friends and family, busy rearranging their lives. Most of them had been living in the team hotel. Some didn't even have cars yet and still took the shuttle bus to practice and hitched rides with friends. Now they were scrambling to lease or buy cars, to rent apartments and furnish them. They'd tried to get everything done Tuesday, except a big hunk of their day was spent traveling to and attending the Greater Miami Chamber of Commerce's meet-the-Dolphins luncheon. The distractions were understandable yet unacceptable to Jimmy.

Wednesday's practice stretched on for two and a half hours, well past Shula's norm, and when it mercifully ended, Jimmy, as always, was engulfed by a sea of print, radio, and television reporters. The routine was simple: Jimmy opened with his daily update on any roster moves, position changes, and how practice went. Then the electronic media asked questions. Then they were dismissed, and the print reporters fired away. If a newspaperman had a question he didn't want the competition to hear, he would request a "sidebar" alone with Jimmy after that. Jimmy took these many demands good-naturedly at first. His answers had been expansive virtually every day of training camp. He knew not much else was going on in the sports world, and reporters were setting scenes and gathering extra information for all their preseason guides.

No NFL coach better understood the media, and how to use them, than Jimmy. This was true even before his two-year sojourn at HBO and Fox TV, true even before he had joined the Cowboys. He had a politician's sense for spin control, a publicist's sense for damage control. He knew he could influence the media, knew the media influenced millions of readers and listeners, and he wanted everyone always to have a positive spin on the Dolphins. Even more important, he knew his players read the papers and listened to the talk shows, and so he always used the media to send messages. The wonder, really, was not that Jimmy was so good at media relations but that his peers, including his predecessor, were so mediocre.

The media had been barred from all but the final moments of practice since the regular-season preparations had begun, but Jimmy had seen plenty. The offense giving blitzers free shots at Marino. The defense blowing coverages and arm tackling. Mental mistakes. Physical mistakes. Jimmy was annoyed, and he could assure his anger would be portrayed if he were short with the media. Give them gruff answers and they would have nothing to air, nothing to write about, other than his anger. Easy story for them, easy way for him to hammer home his point to the players. This wouldn't work every day with either the media or the players, but he would do it three or four times this year—and every time it would get the desired results.

He walked briskly off the field, waited for the horde to gather around and the camera lights to come on, and instantly launched his attack. "We weren't as sharp in practice as I'd like," he griped into the microphones. "We were pretty ragged at times. We'll have to practice much better tomorrow if we're gonna expect to have any success on Sunday."

It was no full-scale blowup, but when half a dozen follow-up questions brought ten terse sentences in reply, some just a single word, the media surrendered. Media members walked away, grumbling among themselves, but they did just as Jimmy expected. The next morning, the players went to their doorsteps, retrieved their papers, and were greeted with the headlines:

"RAGGED" PRACTICE HAS J.J. SOMBER
POOR PRACTICE LEAVES COACHES IRRITATED

Just in case the players missed the headlines, the coaches reiterated them before Thursday's practice. "I didn't need to meet with them," Jimmy said afterward. "They knew."

They can read.

"And they can listen," he said.

He was smiling, happy with them, happy with himself.

"It's obvious to me that our guys are not only hungry to get the season started but they're spending time away from the complex thinking about the game and their assignments," he told the horde. "That's a big key. We can only talk to them so much and coach them so much. This is the type of practice we like."

Still, Jimmy was counting upon an awful lot of rookies, and rookies are notoriously undependable, and Jimmy wants to control everything.

The Dolphins had never started more rookies in an opener.

First-round pick Daryl Gardener was starting at defensive tackle, fifth-round pick Zach Thomas at middle linebacker, third-round pick Karim Abdul-Jabbar at halfback, fourth-round pick Stanley Pritchett at fullback.

Sixth-rounder Shawn Wooden was starting in the nickel and dime pass defenses. Fifth-rounder Shane Burton was in the defensive line rotation. Seventh-rounder Jeff Buckey was helping out on the offensive line and special teams. Undrafted Larry Izzo was a key in the kicking game.

Fifth-rounder Jerris McPhail was the nickel back and kick returner. "I played before eighty-five thousand at Auburn and eighty thousand at Tennessee," he said. "That won't be a big deal. I'll be nervous, but I'm nervous before every game. After the first lick, I'll be all right."

Or would he?

Terrell Buckley, the fifth pick in the country in 1992 and as confident a man as you will ever meet, remembered what happened in his first game as a pro, for the Green Bay Packers.

"My first game was my most embarrassing," the cocky cornerback said. "We're playing Cincinnati. I'm guarding Tim McGee in our nickel package. I'm running across the field, I'm excited, I'm twenty-one, I'm playing my first game. We have a blitz on and David Klingler throws the ball up. I make a nice break on the ball and there's nothing between me and the goalpost but seventy-five yards of green grass. The ball is coming right to me! I see it! I put my hands up and . . ."

T-Buck started laughing. He held both hands a couple of feet apart, above his head, then swung one to his forehead.

"And the ball goes right between my hands and hits me right in the helmet!"

The ball caromed so high in the air, McGee almost caught it before T-Buck knocked it away.

"You *know* my teammates were on me," T-Buck said. "This was after I'd held out [and missed the first two games], and they're going, 'First-round pick? You'd better make a play.' When we watched films the next day, they showed it probably four or five times. Everybody laughed."

He turned and looked at Wooden. "It was all nerves," T-Buck said.

"Trust me," Wooden said. "I know. I already did my T-Buck interception. I dropped the first ball that came to me the first series against Tampa Bay. I'm over that. I got it out of the way the first preseason game. Of course, right now, I can say that. Check back with me after the game."

Would he overcome the rookie jitters—or would they overcome him? "I'm as much up in the air as anybody," Jimmy told his weekly Thursday radio show. "We're gonna throw our rookies into the fire and we're gonna have to live with them. They'll give us a plus as the season goes on."

Ah, but who could wait?

Instant gratification is expected in the NFL, not only from rookies but from Jimmy the Genius. The national spotlight is shining upon him again, and, as much as he revels in it, well, he'd rather it return in a year or two, when he's assembled the club he really wants.

Sorry. Jimmy's return to coaching is The Story of NFL '96. Most of the TV networks and several large newspapers had already trekked to South Florida to do stories on Jimmy. This week, the media frenzy had kicked off Sunday afternoon with Jimmy sitting down with TNT. The next morning, Jimmy spent half an hour with a pair of local sportscasters and another half hour with sportswriters on a national conference call. Wednesday, he did another half-hour conference call with the New England media and a one-on-one with the *Boston Herald*. Thursday, he met with ESPN and NBC, then did his local radio show in the morning and his TV show in the evening. And, of course, he still did his daily skull sessions with the local media.

Friday, he did one-on-ones with Ron Borges of the *Boston Globe* and Peter King of *Sports Illustrated* and CNN. Craig Sager of TNT arrived for the end of practice. Phil Simms of NBC *tried* to watch practice to prepare for Sunday's broadcast, but Jimmy tethered Simms to the complex and practiced at the far edge of the field, more than a hundred yards away.

"How'd you like that practice, Phil?" Jimmy asked.

"Yeahhh," Simms grumbled. "I saw a lot of big people's butts."

Jimmy just laughed. Got 'em again.

What Simms couldn't see, but Jimmy could, was another sorry practice. When the final horn blew, he called his players together.

"Guys," he said, "it seems like everybody was pressing so hard out here today. Everybody was straining, trying extra hard. When you're afraid to fail, then a lot of times you *do* fail because you get so nervous you don't do your job the right way.

"Say I put a two-by-four on the ground. You'd have no problem walking twenty yards across it. But if I raise that two-by-four off the ground to ten feet, a lot of times you'll fall off just because of the fear of falling. You'll be saying, 'Oh, no! I'm gonna fall!' What I'm trying to tell you is, don't be afraid to fall. Don't be afraid to make mistakes during a game. Because mistakes are gonna happen— and you make big plays when you just play recklessly and free of any fear.

"You know, a few years ago, I was going through a bad time. I had a bunch of things going on in my life that just made me miserable. And so my girlfriend, Rhonda, got exasperated with me and tried to snap me out of it. She said, 'Jimmy, relax! They can kill you, but they can't eat you!' "

Everyone laughed.

"And to this day," Jimmy said, "I have no idea what she meant!"

They roared. He had cited a problem, had made it easy to understand with an example, had hammered it home with humor. Think it worked? Two weeks later, one player cited the story when asked how Jimmy had helped him. Four months later, asked the same question, another player repeated that story virtually verbatim.

The next day was just a ten-minute walk-through, usually a nothing day as far as the media were concerned, but you would have never known judging by the circus gathered next to the practice field. Thirty-seven people were waiting to talk to Jimmy. Eleven NBC staffers joined Jimmy for a forty-five-minute production meeting; normally, it's five. And that didn't count *Sports Illustrated* photographer Bill Frakes, snapping away in the background. Media relations director Harvey Greene said the Dolphins never had received this much attention for regular-season games. Not even when Shula broke the record for victories. Not even when Marino shattered the four biggest passing records.

After practice, Jimmy gave a little time to everyone, but he was in a hurry. His sons, Brent and Chad, were in town, and he wanted to spend the afternoon with them before heading to the Bonaventure Hotel and Spa Resort, where the team stays the night before every home game.

We hustled through the team complex on the way upstairs to Jimmy's office. I told him the latest Barry Switzer story. Earlier this week, Barry got lost on the way to the team preview luncheon. He's in his third year in Dallas, trying to replace Jimmy, and still doesn't know where he's going. The same day, Barry was asked about the upcoming matchup with the Chicago Bears and their $13.2 million middle linebacker, Bryan Cox.

"We've looked at a lot of film this week," Switzer replied. "He's a guy playing a new position. He's playing middle linebacker and . . ."

Wrong.

Cox moved to middle linebacker *three years ago*. He was a Pro Bowl middle linebacker each of his final two years in Miami. Most everyone who recruited him in the off-season wanted him at middle linebacker. Three years in the league and Barry Switzer still didn't know who the hell the league's best players were or where they played.

Jimmy put his head down, shook it, and mumbled something about Barry still not having a clue.

Oh, if only Dallas-Miami would come down to purely a battle of wits . . .

The game was eight weeks away, and already people were talking about it. People asked Jimmy about it from the day the schedule came out in April. And not just the sports groupies. Why, this week's issue of *TV Guide* was breathlessly promoting the "inside dish on this year's biggest game," with an "NFL Pullout Section" headlined MIAMI-DALLAS: THE GAME OF THE YEAR. Jimmy appeared on the covers of *TV Guide*, *ESPN Pro Football '96*, and *South Florida* magazine. He'd shared the cover of *Sports Illustrated* and *Inside Sports* with Marino.

And it wasn't just media hype. The public was fawning over him, too. When he'd hit the streets near the Dolphins' complex for his daily three-mile jog with Kevin O'Neill, his trainer and right-hand man, fans drove by and shouted compliments. One day, a mom stopped alongside them and nudged her son out of the car. The boy jogged with Jimmy and Kevin for maybe a quarter of a mile, the car crawling beside them. Finally, the car passed them, pulled over, parked, and the mom jumped out and snapped a photo.

That night at the Bonaventure—a world-famous spa since renamed the Registry—Jimmy had wrapped up the team meal and meeting and was talking with Peter King when safety Gene Atkins walked by. Jimmy enveloped Atkins in his arms and castigated him for missing the team meal. It was going to cost him $1,000.

Atkins pleaded with Jimmy: He didn't know the meal was mandatory. He never ate at night. Jimmy stared into his eyes.

"Okay," he said. "Half."

"No, coach!" Atkins said. "Don't fine me. Let me make it up to you."

"Tell you what," Jimmy said. "You make some great plays tomorrow and I'll think about it." "Okay," Atkins said. "You see that big grin on your face? That's what you'll have on your face after you see how I play. I'll make big plays. You'll see."

Atkins left, and Jimmy turned toward the writer.

"They'd better be *really* big plays," he said.

And with that he was off to his hotel suite.

THE MAKEOVER BEGINS

When Jimmy Johnson coached his first regular-season game as Miami Dolphins coach on September 1, 1996, fourteen starters were new or playing new positions since Opening Day 1995:

POSITION	'95 STARTER	'96 STARTER
WR:	Irving Fryar	Scott Miller
LT:	Richmond Webb	Webb
LG:	Keith Sims	Sims
C:	Tim Ruddy	Ruddy
RG:	Chris Gray	Gray
RT:	Ron Heller	James Brown
TE:	Eric Green	Keith Byars
WR:	O. J. McDuffie	McDuffie
QB:	Dan Marino	Marino
RB:	Bernie Parmalee	*Karim Abdul-Jabbar*
FB:	Keith Byars	*Stanley Pritchett*
LE:	Jeff Cross	Trace Armstrong
DT:	Chuck Klingbeil	*Daryl Gardener*
DT:	Tim Bowens	Bowens
RE:	Marco Coleman	Daniel Stubbs
LLB:	Chris Singleton	Dwight Hollier
MLB:	Bryan Cox	*Zach Thomas*
RLB:	Dwight Hollier	Chris Singleton
LCB:	Troy Vincent	Terrell Buckley
RCB:	J. B. Brown	Calvin Jackson
SS:	Michael Stewart	Louis Oliver
FS:	Gene Atkins	Atkins

Italics denote rookie.

Sunday, September 1, Miami. Jimmy woke up two or three times in the middle of the night. It wasn't nerves, he said. "I wake up every night."

Or was it? "Every time I turned on the TV or read the paper, somebody was picking New England. I didn't see a bunch of folks picking Miami, and that kinda scared me because, you know, sometimes you [media] guys are right. So I got nervous. I haven't been with a team recently that everybody was picking against us. I admit I was nervous."

The off-season changes and preseason games hadn't gotten him jumpy.

But now the Jimmy Johnson Era was to begin for real. Kickoff for the long-awaited, much-anticipated debut wasn't until 4 P.M., but Jimmy was up early, as always. Too early to anesthetize the bundle of neurons with his trademark Heineken on ice. He opted for a 7:30 A.M. jog with Rhonda, and not even then could he escape the public infatuation—Frakes clicked away as Jimmy surged ahead of Rhonda.

The jog calmed him and the shower cooled him, and Jimmy looked CEO cool and dapper in his dark blue suit as he taped an interview for CNN's preview show and another for Fox's preview show.

The media attention was unbelievable. At 10:30, ESPN opened its *Sports Reporters* show talking about Jimmy. Tony Kornheiser said the best game of the day was Jimmy's debut, that a lot of people thought "he was the best coach or manager of his time" while he was in Dallas, and now we'll see. Mike Lupica chimed in, "I'm not saying he's the football coach Vince Lombardi was, but this will be the most-viewed comeback since Lombardi." At eleven, CNN opened with Jimmy's earlier interview, and a few minutes later Vince Cellini swiped, "You ever notice Barry Switzer's initials are BS?" At 11:30, Jimmy's local show aired and ESPN teased Mark Malone's live report from Miami and Chris Mortensen's feature on Jimmy and his quarterback. Malone said the Patriots could test the Dolphins' "suspect corners." ESPN's Tom Jackson concurred. "If the Dolphins have a problem, it's the defensive backfield. Drew Bledsoe has to be The Man today."

So desperate were the networks for anything on Jimmy, NBC showed him arriving at the stadium and walking through a deserted locker room. And then there was brief mention of his counterpart, who was entering the final year of his Patriot contract. "Bill Parcells said New England would be his last coaching job, and he still means it," Simms reported.

Puhhhh-lease.

As if NBC weren't hyping the game enough, Miami affiliate WTVJ-TV breathlessly broke into the network coverage with its own update. At 12:30, Cris Collinsworth, who had worked with Jimmy at HBO, launched their interview with a laugh: "Are you *nuts*? Why are you back?"

"Sometimes I ask myself that," Jimmy replied, grinning. He insisted he wasn't rebuilding, claimed he had "not made a single move thinking it'll help us down the road and hurt us this year. We're not sacrificing anything here."

It was a little white lie, and Jimmy knew it. He could not confess this to his public or his players until season's end, but *every* move he had made or would make in 1996 was about winning in '97 and '98 and '99—and not in '96.

But Collinsworth knew, or at least guessed at, Jimmy's secret. He said some moves would hurt the team in '96—for instance, releasing slothful Eric Green left the Dolphins desperate for a tight end—but it was more important to build a team with Jimmy's kind of players.

"He's going to keep disciplined guys," Mike Ditka concurred. "If he can get Terrell Buckley to tackle, he's got it made."

Only he pronounced it TIE-rel, not Ter-REL. Ditka disliked Buckley, and the feeling was mutual. Ditka wasn't the only T-Buck doubter. Jimmy had criticized Buckley as both a commentator and coach, had forced him to take a pay cut, but then had encouraged him and shown confidence in him and had seen his faith—or was it desperation?—rewarded in preseason. But how long would it last?

Ditka had no faith in T-Buck but great faith in Jimmy. He predicted the Dolphins would make the Super Bowl. But among the eight NBC and ESPN experts polled this day, he was alone in this viewpoint. The rest believed the AFC would be represented by Buffalo, Pittsburgh, or Denver (none forecast New England), the NFC by Green Bay, San Francisco, or Dallas.

By now, the press box was filling with reporters. TNT, Fox, ESPN, CNN, and NBC were there. *Sports Illustrated*, *Football News*, *USA Today*, the Associated Press, *The Washington Post*, the *New York Post*, *The Sun* in Baltimore, *The Dallas Morning News*, and virtually every Florida newspaper was there. An on-line service, Sportsline USA, was there. Why, even *The Times* of London—yes, London, England—breathlessly awaited JJ's debut.

The Dolphins normally issue three hundred media credentials for a national television game. They did five hundred for this one. "That record will be broken for our Dallas game, I'll guarantee you right now," Harvey Greene said.

The glare of the spotlight has cracked many a police suspect and even a few football coaches. Not Jimmy. The more they said he could not follow Shula's legend, the more they said he could not repeat his Dallas success, the more it drove him. His ego craved the challenge and the spotlight.

But as game time approached, he retreated into his own world. Ninety-four minutes before the game, he paced the Dolphins' sideline. Three feet away, no one near us, I nodded to him, and if he even noticed, he did not show it. Every game would not be like this, but, for big games, he put the blinders on and nobody or nothing else mattered.

Rhonda had tried to shock him out of his zone several times. "Jimmy, I'm going to a club to watch some nude male dancers," she would say.

"Uh-huh," he'd say.

"I'm gonna stuff dollar bills down their G-strings," she'd say.

"Uh-huh," he'd say.

"I'm gonna bring one home with me," she'd say.

"Okay," he'd say.

Most weeks, maybe ten or twenty players would have been on the field loosening up by now. But not today. A few left the locker room, stepped outside, felt the blast furnace smack them in the face, and quickly fled. It would be ninety-three degrees at kickoff, the second-warmest home game in history, just one degree behind the 1995 Jets game. On the field, the temperature would be measured at 104 degrees, the humidity at 40 percent. Stand there—don't play, don't move, just stand there—and sweat oozed out within a minute. Kevin O'Neill told the players to gulp down at least two drinks of water every time they came off the field.

Not wishing to sap any energy, the Patriots halted their warm-ups early. The Dolphins loosened up only briefly before retreating to the air-conditioned comfort of the locker room twenty-five minutes before kickoff. Marino buried his head in his playbook. During games, the cameras showed him screaming at coaches and players, the stereotype of the emotional Italian. But before the game, he quietly visualized the game plan.

Jimmy paced rapidly, rubbed his chin with his hands, and told the players they would win because they deserved to win. He talked no more than two minutes, surprising some players, even one who had played for him before. "Maybe he's saving his classic motivational speeches for the Dallas game," wide receiver Lamar Thomas thought.

The locker room went silent.

"I got afraid because it seemed like a morgue, like someone just died," Aaron Jones said later.

Too silent for Daniel Stubbs, another veteran defensive end, sitting next to Jones in the middle of the locker room. Stubbs used to love it when he was with the 49ers and All-Pro safety Ronnie Lott would start screaming just before game time. Trash talk got Stubbs wired. He had started hollering when he walked through the door. Now he was really rolling.

"It's Opening Day!" he began, in that deep voice and tone that sounds as if it emanates from God on high—except his motivational monologue included a string of epithets that would make God blush.

"If you fuckin' people don't make plays, you won't be here! Shiiiit! If you aren't fuckin' ready to play, no need for you to even fuckin' go out there! God-damnit! If you're fuckin' scared, keep your big ass home!"

On and on Stubbs went. Across the room, Zach Thomas couldn't suppress his impish Texas grin.

"I thought Danny had lost his mind," Zach said later. "I love that."

It is just before four o'clock. The Dolphins reemerge from the tunnel. The public address announcer at pick-a-name stadium—last game it was called Joe Robbie Stadium, this game it's called Pro Player Park, next game it'll be called Pro Player Stadium—introduces each starter on offense. Dan Marino earns the loudest cheers . . . until Jimmy surpasses him. One hundred children hold an American flag stretching fifty-three yards across midfield as the national anthem is sung. One fan embraces a sign reading, "JJ, I LOVE YOU, MAN." Another clasps one reading, THE JOHNSON ERA BEGINS.

The Patriots win the coin toss and send in Dave Meggett to receive the kick-off. Just as Jimmy warned Wednesday, Meggett hides behind a four-man wedge, and it swallows up Larry Izzo, Robert Wilson, and O. J. Brigance. Kicker Joe Nedney pushes Meggett out of bounds at the New England forty-eight, and soon the Patriots have a first and five at the Miami thirty-two and the Dolphins are not looking good.

But then Zach Thomas stuffs Curtis Martin at the line of scrimmage, Louis Oliver rocks him for another no-gainer, and it's third and five. The Patriots come to the line with three wide receivers, and Oliver, who has studied all the Patriots' preseason games and diagrammed all their routes, instantly recognizes this is the same third-and-short formation they have used throughout preseason. Three times in practice he has seen this play, broken to the ball, intercepted, and run it back all the way.

He has promised his wife he will score today and give her the ball. He thinks this might be his chance. He lines up, points to receiver Will Moore, and tells nickel back J. B. Brown, "If he runs that slant, I'm going to hit it. Catch me over the top if he runs the slant-and-up." When Bledsoe drops back just three steps, Oliver is sure this will be a quick slant. But Bledsoe makes it even easier by doing just what Jimmy predicted: He stares down the receiver. Oliver sees him looking, looking, looking, breaks to the spot before Bledsoe even throws, and arrives long before the receiver. He bobbles the ball momentarily before latching on. Jump a sideline "out" pass, intercept it cleanly, and you've got a good chance to score. All the preparation is paying off as Oliver sprints for the end zone.

But Oliver is slow for a safety, and Meggett chases him down at the ten and swipes the ball away. But Providence is not in New England today. The ball bounces directly to Dolphins safety Sean Hill, who cavorts into the end zone untouched. Oliver streaks toward the stands and cups his hand to his ear as the fans scream their trademark "Loooouuuu!" Later this year "Loouuu" will turn to "Booooo." But now Hill runs to the stands and high-fives fans and it is 7–0 Dolphins and Dan Marino hasn't touched the ball yet.

This time, Nedney aims toward Troy Brown and Hill stops him at the twenty-two. First play, Moore runs a curl route, and Bledsoe fires toward him. T-Buck has seen this play so often on videotape that he jumps it hard. Too hard. He runs a bit past the ball, and the would-be interception clangs off his right arm and shoulder pad. Next play, Bledsoe fakes a handoff to fool the Dolphins' pass rush and coverage. Doesn't help. Calvin Jackson knocks the ball away. Third down. Bledsoe rolls right to try to buy time. Doesn't help. Under pressure, he reverts to a very bad habit. He throws off his back foot, Tim Bowens clobbers him, and Atkins gets *his* hands on the ball. The game isn't even five minutes old and the twenty-four-year-old quarterback is acting fourteen.

The Patriots punt, and the first offensive play of the Jimmy Johnson Era arrives with a rush, as promised. Four Karim carries produce twenty yards and set up a field goal to make it 10–0 less than ten minutes into the game.

Bledsoe looks, looks, double-clutches, and earns a Zach sack. J.B. almost steals another Bledsoe ball. Coates short-arms a pass while turning to look for defenders and drops the ball. He catches one on third and six, but, sapped by the heat, gets just five yards. "He's running so slow, he looks like Paul," Phil Simms says up in the NBC booth, jabbing the corpulent Maguire.

Fourth and one. Martin bounces off linebacker Dwight Hollier and earns a first down at the Miami four before Atkins wrestles him down.

Zach and Atkins stuff Martin for no gain. Then Zach chases down the speedy back along the sideline after a gain of one. Jimmy's newest draft-day steal is having a splendid game.

"He's the Tasmanian devil," Simms says of Zach. "He's everywhere."

Adds Dick Enberg: "Playing on his twenty-third birthday, in his first NFL game, he has been superb!"

Zach was just the 154th pick in the 1996 draft, and the scouts didn't rate him even that highly. But he seemed to make every tackle at Texas Tech, so Jimmy drafted him and his eye for talent is already paying off.

Steve Emtman forces Bledsoe to throw the ball away on third down and the Patriots settle for a field goal. Karim squirts for twenty-one yards on back-to-back plays, but with three downs to get one yard, the Dolphins can't do it, and after a delay-of-game penalty on fourth down forces a punt, Marino slams the ball in frustration.

Gardener stuffs Meggett after a yard. Jefferson uses his quickness to get past J. B. Brown for a first down, but J.B. tugs on his jersey with his left hand and punches the ball loose with his right hand. Oliver falls on the turnover. The Patriots steal the ball back, but their next offensive play is almost identical to the previous one: Jefferson grabs a pass, runs around J.B. again, slashes toward the middle of the field, gets crushed by Emtman, and fumbles to Bowens. "Shawn Jefferson used to catch the ball and drop it," Maguire says. "Now he catches it, holds it a while, and then drops it."

Jimmy promised to stick with the running game, even when it wasn't going well. He promised to run behind Webb and Sims. He keeps his promises. Karim scoots nine yards off left tackle, then eight up the middle. Bernie Parmalee bursts seventeen yards up the middle, then three behind Pritchett's wham block on 285-pound Mark Wheeler. Now the Patriots have to respect the run, and how often have the Dolphins made opponents do that in the past decade? The Patriots begin to stack the line with eight men, daring the Dolphins to throw. What are the odds of *that*?

Marino zips a quick slant for one first down, then dinks over the middle for another. It's only a seven-yard gain, but it's a play maybe only Marino makes. He is about to throw when a Patriot jumps, arms up, in front of him. Marino somehow stops his motion, pulls back, and all in the same motion fires a sidearm bullet with just his wrist, as if it's a yo-yo and not a football at the end of his hand. A frustrated Ferric Collons gets up and swipes Marino's face with his foot. No foul is called, but it's first and goal at the five. Karim powers behind Keith Sims to the three, then sprints off the right side for a 17–3 lead.

"It's hard to believe this is the Miami Dolphins," Phil Simms gushes. "Running is an attitude. Jimmy brought that attitude to the Dolphins."

The Dolphins run eighteen times and Marino throws just seven times in the half—and yet they lead by fourteen. What are the odds of that? Says Collinsworth: "There are a lot of defensive coordinators around the league going, 'Dan Marino with a running game? Uhh-oooh!' "

The rookie jitters get McPhail on the second-half kickoff. He had caught the ball smoothly throughout preseason, but this one he misjudges and fumbles. The ever-present Oliver comes back and recovers, but the Dolphins are stuck at their own four.

Offensive coordinator Gary Stevens wants to run, wants to play it safe. Jimmy isn't big on safe. Especially when the Patriots are expecting safe.

"Throw the ball!" he tells Stevens on his headset.

Stevens orders a nice, safe pass, a little flare in the flat to Pritchett, who just gets back to the line of scrimmage.

Second down. "Okay," Stevens says. "We'll come back with a run up the middle."

"Throw the *damn* thing again!" Jimmy commands.

He knows the Patriots are expecting a run because that's what every coach does down here, because that's what Miami has done near the goal line throughout preseason, because Jimmy is hardheaded and wants to prove the Dolphins can run. It's a crucial time. If the Dolphins don't get out of this hole, they'll have to punt, and the Patriots will get the ball at midfield with a chance to pull within 17–10, right back in the game. Jimmy fools them. It's time for a play designed specifically for the Patriots. Remember back on Wednesday, when Jimmy said their Cover Two defense left them vulnerable to catches deep down the seam by the tight end? The coaches have since opted to design the play for Pritchett instead of slowpoke tight end Keith Byars. So they send Pritchett streaking down the right hash, Marino hits him in stride, and Pritchett is fifty-two yards downfield before slow-footed safety Willie Clay stops him. It's the longest catch by a Dolphins back since 1990.

McPhail, the fastest Dolphin, blows by linebacker Todd Collins for twenty-one yards. Pritchett sprints by linebacker Dwayne Sabb and takes a Marino bullet fifteen yards to the one before Clay sticks his helmet on the ball and it pops into the end zone. But Scott Miller, a six-year veteran making a surprise start—the first of his career—falls on the ball in the end zone for a 24–3 lead.

Imagine that! Even when the Dolphins screw up and fumble, the ball bounces directly to some totally unknown scrub for a touchdown! It's happened twice in three quarters! Does Jimmy have an angel looking over his shoulder? Or is this the hustle of the young and driven?

His three rookie backs are responsible for ninety-five of the ninety-six yards on the drive. With the Patriots expecting the run, the Dolphins have passed on seven of the eight plays.

The game's not quite over. Meggett and the wedge bust the Dolphins again. He takes the kickoff to the Miami thirty-eight, and, four plays later, on fourth and one, the Patriots expose the slooooowwwwww, overaggressive Miami safeties. Bledsoe's fake to Martin should fool no one, but Oliver and Hollier bite anyway and Coates breaks wide open. Atkins arrives late, tries to strip the ball, and Coates pulls away and dives into the end zone.

The Patriots can pull within a touchdown early in the fourth quarter when Jefferson takes a reverse on second and one. He gets the first down, gets past midfield, and looks downfield for more. He does not look back toward the middle of the field.

Bad mistake.

Zach realizes Jefferson doesn't see him and decides not to just wrap his arms around the receiver but to wallop him. He sticks the crown of his helmet into Jefferson's earhole, and Jefferson's world goes black. Arms above his head, legs crossed, he lies supine and motionless, unconscious for a full minute or more. When he finally wakes up, he asks for his coach by name. Except it's his high school coach, and Jefferson left high school in 1987.

Zach hasn't knocked him into next week, as the tough guys like to brag. No, he's knocked him into last decade!

Doctors, trainers, and frightened Patriots huddle around Jefferson. After six or seven minutes, even a few Dolphins wander over to see if he's okay. "I started shivering," T-Buck says later. "It was scary." Nearly ten minutes pass before Jefferson is strapped onto a stretcher, immobilized, and wheeled off the field. An ambulance takes him to the hospital, and he stays the night.

The collision is so violent, Zach momentarily loses his hearing. He does not hear the hit, but he does hear the crowd go, "Ooooooh." He tries to see the replay on the scoreboard but does not. He does not approach Jefferson. He stays in the middle of the field, near the line of scrimmage, trying to concentrate. Off the field, he is as nice a guy as you will find, but on the field, nice guys lose. Joe

Walton put it best when he was coaching the Jets. "Football," he said, "is for thugs."

The next play, Zach makes another tackle so vicious that, he recalls, "I was trying to figure out where *my* coach was. I lost it there for a second." But not for long. Four plays later, he busts through the line and forces Bledsoe to throw the ball away on fourth and two. Next series, Bledsoe, totally shaken, throws the ball up for grabs. Oliver tips it, and T-Buck holds on to this one for an interception.

Karim spins around left end for five yards, up the middle for six, off left guard for six more, giving him 115 yards in his pro debut. Jimmy lifts him so the crowd can applaud, and the ovation is thunderous, but Karim doesn't even realize it's for him. Jimmy slaps his palms and says, "Great going!" Karim, ever humble to Allah, simply, softly, says, "Thanks." Sweat and sand cake his uniform, all over his numbers, his butt, his left arm. But look closely and you can see the name on his jersey is misspelled: Adbul, not Abdul, Jabbar.

There's a party goin' on 'round here, a celebration to last throughout the year . . . er, well, it would turn out, just the day.

Up in Suite 226A are Jimmy's two closest friends in South Florida, his girlfriend, Rhonda, and his agent/attorney, Nick Christin. His two sons and two favorite bartenders are here. So are the guy who built the bar in his house in the Florida Keys, the guy who helped put in his pride-and-joy aquariums, and, all told, more than a dozen friends from the laid-back life he left behind in Tavernier. A bunch of them had piled into a stretch limo on the way here, but the suite life is not really their style. They stopped for beer on the way and admonished the driver when he tried to hold doors open for them. "Jimmy's Hobo Friends," they call themselves. Heady with boozy victory, they are giddy as kindergartners on Christmas.

"To Jimmy!" one says, and hoists a Heineken. "Undefeated!"

Don Shula has a suite here, too, but he's nowhere to be found. Didn't want to be here. Didn't want to be anywhere near here when someone else coached the Dolphins for the first time since 1970. The legend who had been synonymous with the Miami Dolphins, with all of South Florida, is getting jabbed repeatedly in his famous jaw. His ego is bruised.

Don Shula is in North Carolina.

He might as well be Napoleon, exiled in Elba.

Back down on the field, Zach breaks up a pass on first down and Bowens tips one away on fourth down. All that's left is for Marino to kneel on the ball until time expires.

Father Leo Armbrust, Jimmy's team chaplain with the Hurricanes and now the Dolphins, high-fives Zach. Zach sits down, chugs down a cup of Gatorade, and shucks it away, the ice tumbling all over. He's exhausted but too excited to sit. He bounces back up and high-fives T-Buck and a parade of people along the sideline. The scoreboard shows Miami 24, New England 10, as the clock strikes 0:00 and everyone swarms the field.

Jimmy runs across the field, and the first player he finds is Atkins. He pulls him tight and whispers in his ear, "I'm lifting the fine."

Both men break into big grins.

Within weeks those grins will turn to sneers, but this is a time for cheers. Television cameramen and still photographers chase after Jimmy as he shakes hands with Parcells. They encircle him as he makes his victory jog to the locker room. They're trying to backpedal and film at the same time, and they're so crowded and chaotic that one, moving backward, stumbles and lands hard on his butt, the big TV camera crumpling against him. Jimmy instantly leans over, gives him a hand up, and jogs on. He smiles that famous smile. He pumps his fist into the air. Sunlight glints off the huge chunks of gold and diamonds on one of his Super Bowl rings. He looks like a man who is right where he wants to be . . . and not all that far from where he is headed.

Lounging on his forty-eight-foot yacht, trolling for fish, drinking Heinekens, eating chips and salsa with Rhonda and his crew, following the Bahamian winds and his own whims . . . all that was fun and relaxing. But this is fun and reward-ing. This is what all the hours, all the sweat, all the anguish were about. Maybe being rich and semiretired and living the easy life was the stuff of dreams for other people, but Jimmy Johnson needs more than Margaritaville. From the time he was in grade school, 'rassling a brother three years his elder, he had always craved the challenge, sought it out, fought it out, overcame it, and moved on to the next one. Take away life's challenges, he figures, and he'd lose his ambition, his sense of achievement. And then what would be the purpose of living?

He was a coach, he would always be a coach, and now he has shown himself and all the critics that his legend was no lie. Jimmy Johnson can flat-out coach. Why, just look how far, how fast, this club had come. The Dolphins were humili-ated in the playoffs in December. They were $5 million over the NFL spending cap with four of their best players unsigned in January. They were a sorry, ragged wreck in July. But now the transformation is in full flower. "Oh yeah," Jimmy says later, Heineken in hand, "I'm having fun."

His draft picks were making him look like a genius. Gardener, goaded like never before, overcame a sprained ankle to collect a sack and help hold New En-gland to 2.1 yards a carry. Karim, finally responding to Jimmy's challenges, was the game's leading rusher. Pritchett, quickly replacing Byars, was the game's leading receiver. Zach, ably replacing Pro Bowl veterans Bryan Cox and Jack Del Rio, was the game's leading tackler. There was nothing Cox, the $13.2 million linebacker, could have done that this kid didn't. There was no play Del Rio, the eleven-year vet, could have diagnosed quicker. Most every other coach would have waited until the end of preseason, the middle of the regular season, or even next preseason to replace Cox and Del Rio. Why risk their reputations replacing name players with no-name rookies? But Jimmy decided instantly, gave Pritchett and Zach all the work in preseason, and they had learned from their mistakes and were ready to shine by Opening Day.

Everything he had said would happen did. He said they would run down the Patriots' ass, and they did for 146 yards. He said they would run behind Webb and Sims, and they did. He said they would burn the Patriots' Cover Two defense for a big play, and they did, for the game's longest offensive play. He said they would swarm Martin, and they held the reigning Rookie of the Year to twenty-three yards. He said they would intimidate the wideouts, and they forced two fumbles from Jefferson alone. He said his receivers would knock people down, and the best block Karim saw all day was not from a lineman or fullback but when McDuffie cracked back on a big defensive end. Jimmy said his defense would be better than the experts forecast, and it was, limiting New England to 230 yards. He said the Dolphins would harry Bledsoe into mistakes, and they forced four sacks and two interceptions. He wanted the most physical, best-conditioned team in football, and the heat from the Miami pass rush proved as relentless as the Miami sun.

Every change seemed perfect, every Wednesday prediction prophetic, converting even the staunchest Dolphins disbelievers.

"They'd come out in formations and we'd be screaming out the play before they ran it," Oliver says.

"I guess there's a method to what Jimmy does. Guys were complaining in preseason that we were running too much and not getting enough rest. Now we're glad he worked us this hard because they were sucking air by the third and fourth quarter and it was like we'd just started. Our guys weren't fatigued. We pounded them the second half."

"Today," Trace Armstrong adds, "validated everything we did in the off-season."

The Dolphins are clapping and cheering and celebrating as Jimmy gathers them 'round him in the locker room.

"Y'all remember Wednesday, when we said we were gonna run right at their ass?" he asks.

"Wooooo!" they holler.

"Well, where's Richmond? Way to go!" Jimmy hollers, and applauds.

"Where's Keith? Remember we said we were gonna run right behind your big butt? Great game!" Jimmy says, and claps again.

"This game was about making plays. Making plays and winning the fourth quarter. There was a little scare, but the fourth quarter, our guys were getting after their *ass*! They couldn't complete a pass!

"Hell of a job, fellas!" he continues, still clapping. "Hell of a job! But that's only one! And we've got a looooonnng journey. A looong journey. That's only one.

"For the first one, I want to give one game ball . . . to Wayne Huizenga."

The players salute their owner for ten seconds, and just as the applause dies down, Marino steps forward. He's not a storyteller or motivator like Jimmy, and he's certainly no ass kisser, but he is the players' leader. Jimmy can't give himself a game ball, but Danny can.

"I got something for ya, all right?" Marino says. "Way to fuckin' kick ass! That's a team effort, fellas. First win as Dolphins coach, game ball goes to Coach Johnson."

Everyone claps for another ten seconds.

"I've had big wins before. But I'll treasure this one as much as any win I've ever had in my life," Jimmy says, his voice and face filled with emotion. The game ball for his first victory should come as no surprise—why, an assistant coach actually suggested it to Marino beforehand—but Jimmy seems genuinely touched. The players clap some more.

But enough of the revelry. He who celebrates too long does not last long in the NFL. "Two o'clock," Jimmy says, reminding them of Monday's schedule. "Get your weight lifting in and report for two o'clock meetings."

The whole scene lasts just ninety seconds. Then it's time to meet the press. Harvey Greene leads Jimmy into a room off the dressing room. Fifteen television cameras encircle the podium, and the rest of the room is crammed with reporters.

"Well," Jimmy begins, "that was a nice win, but I don't want the guys to get too ecstatic because it's only one win."

But clearly, he *is* ecstatic. He enumerates all the good things. The entire team's progress and effort. The big plays on defense. Oliver's big interception and two fumble recoveries. T-Buck's pick. Zach's big hit and all those tackles. Pritchett's blocks and catches. Karim's carries.

The performances leave Jimmy so excited, he will not "sleep worth a damn." They leave Parcells so disgusted, he broods deep into the night as the Patriots' plane hurdles homeward. He had been confident of victory, of unmasking the Dolphins' defense, only to see New England's holes exposed. "If that's our best effort," he grouses, "we're in trouble."

One of these teams is bound for the Super Bowl. Which will it be? The one with the confused quarterback and lame-duck coach? Or the one with the Hall of Fame quarterback and the clairvoyant coach?

2
GOOD-BYE, DON

Out of the limousines and into the lobby of the Broward County Convention Center unfold men in black tuxedos and women garnished in gowns and jewels. Violins serenade them on every floor. Aqua-gowned, cleavage-accentuated cheerleaders escort them to every door. Black-tie waiters ply them with champagne and Russian caviar and lobster hors d'oeuvres. Even the parking-garage attendants wear tuxes.

Inside the gigantic ballroom is a tribute worthy of royalty. The largest ice sculptures ever created. Enough trophies and awards to fill a museum—except all the honors are dedicated and all the visiting dignitaries are celebrating one man's career. The orchestra plays as the powerful mingle amid Don Shula's treasure trove:

Four presidents' congratulatory letters. Four Coach of the Year plaques from *The Sporting News*. Three Coach of the Year plaques from the Pro Football Writers of America. Two Coach of the Year awards from the Touchdown Club. Two Super Bowl trophy replicas. Two LeRoy Neiman paintings. One silver football. The Horatio Alger Award. The NFL Lifetime Achievement Award. The Jim Thorpe Pro Sports Award for career achievement. The Pete Rozelle Award for outstanding service. The Golden Helmet Award. The All-Madden team. The cover of *Sports Illustrated* as Sportsman of the Year. The cover of *Time* magazine. The front page of the *Los Angeles Herald Examiner* heralding BEST TEAM EVER in world war–sized type. Team photos spanning decades. Game balls galore honoring milestone victories. Even a Coke can imprinted with his image.

It is September 12, 1996, or, as the NFL has proclaimed it, "Don Shula Day." Dolphins owner Wayne Huizenga invests a million bucks and nine hundred luminaries invest an evening in this "Tribute to a Legend." A videotape highlights his record 347 victories and career. A parade of people march to the podium and brag about Don Shula in words as sweet as the violins' notes. Players like Dan Marino, Bob Griese, and Larry Csonka. Friends like Raymond Floyd, the PGA star and neighbor, and Art Donovan, the Hall of Fame player and raconteur. Even Jimmy Johnson interrupts their feud to say, "You'll always be remembered as the greatest of all time."

The president appears via videotape. The governor appears in person and gives Shula a gold-framed resolution. The NFL commissioner gives him a painting depicting Shula as a player and coach. "Wayne Huizenga throws a hell of a party, doesn't he?" says the emcee, ESPN's Chris Berman. "I've never seen a thousand tuxes. Does Wayne own a tux rental business, too?"

Nope, but the billionaire owns just about everything else, including the stadium where two of his three sports franchises play. Wayne says he's putting up a statue of Shula in front of the stadium and unveiling Shula's name to the Ring of Honor during a halftime ceremony on *Monday Night Football*. And he says Shula is so huge, the NFL will make an exception it hasn't permitted for anyone: He gets Tiffany duplicates of the Super Bowl trophies, for victories in Super Bowls VII and VIII. Shula shakes his head, turns to his family, and mouths, "Unbelievable." He kisses his wife and squeezes his cheeks, eyes glistening, as Natalie Cole sings a personalized version of his favorite song, "Unforgettable."

"Don, that's what you'll always be to everyone in this room: Unforgettable," Huizenga says. "All of my memories are fantastic."

All his memories are fantastic? Uh, well, not exactly. Hate to spoil the party, but this was a *farewell* party, and Shula said farewell only after he took Huizenga's hint—some would say shove—and retired. Huizenga spent $18 million buying stars in 1995, and Shula was supposed to deliver a Super Bowl. But a 4–0 start turned into a Miami meltdown of such humiliating proportions that the Buffalo Bills ran for 341 yards on them and somebody named Tim Tindale averaged seventeen yards a carry, and the so-called superstars limped home 9–8 and wild-card losers. In a few months, Shula had gone from legendary hero to the old man who'd stayed too long. Fans and media clamored for change, and they got it.

Now it was September, and the Dolphins were 2–0, and the team and the town belonged to Jimmy Johnson. South Florida hailed Jimmy as a hero who could do no wrong. The Dolphins' start was simply proof of his genius—and of Don Shula's descending star. Shula should have been secure in his own accomplishments, but he was a vain man who let criticism bother him far more than it should. A gold watch wouldn't be enough. This million-dollar gala was to salve his wounds and soothe his considerable ego.

To understand what Don Shula and now Jimmy Johnson mean to South Florida, the Miami Dolphins, and the National Football League . . .

"You've got to go back with me, back to the early days of the Dolphins B.S.—before Shula—to realize what it was like," said Larry Csonka, the Hall of Famer whose nickname—Zonk—perfectly described his brutish running style. Zonk arrived in 1968, two years after the Dolphins debuted as an American Football League expansion franchise. They won three games that first year, four the second. This, remember, in a league that everyone considered inferior to the NFL. They were coached by some guy named George Wilson.

"Let me take you back to my first experience with the Miami Dolphins, the first time anyone ever said to me, 'Miami Dolphins,' " Csonka continued. "I was a senior at Syracuse University, looking forward to going into the pros because they were paying a lot of money.

"I hailed from a little small town in the Midwest. River workers, ironworkers, a lot of tough people. They made me humble in the years I grew up there. My mother put me on a school bus in first grade at the age of five with a bouquet of flowers in my hand. Put you on a school bus when you're five and you've got flowers in your hand and your name is Larry and it rhymes with fairy, you're in a hell of a lot of trouble.

"And I wanted one time to go back to my hometown with the intensity, with the macho awareness of the NFL plastered on my chest. I wanted to go home with a T-shirt that said Rams or Vikings or Bears. On draft day, I walked in and looked at my attorney, and he put down the phone and smiled and said, 'Congratulations, Larry, you have been selected in the first round.' And I said, 'Tell me, am I a *Raaammmm*?'

"He said, 'No.'

"I said, 'A *Viii-king*?'

He said, 'No.'

"I said, 'A *Bearrrr*?'

"No," he said, "you're a Dolphin."

"I said, 'Isn't a dolphin a fish?'

"He said, 'Yes, there's a new team in Miami. You said you wanted to play where it was warm.'

"And I thought to myself, 'Who in the world owns this team? They're gonna put a picture of Flipper on my head?' You think Johnny Cash, when he sang the song 'A Boy Named Sue,' knew what he was talking about? You run around the NFL with a picture of Flipper on your forehead and see what happens! It cost me seven thousand dollars to straighten my nose out! Carl Eller busted my nose all over my face because he hated Flipper!"

Csonka's eyes bugged out of their sockets, and his voice resonated with machismo as he used the words Rams, Vikings, and Bears; with wimpiness as he mentioned Flipper, the star of a warm-and-fuzzy TV show that was big in the late sixties and early seventies. At fifty, Zonk is still a big, imposing man. But his is a nose that only a mother could love. It looks like something out of a Picasso painting. The top half veers hard left; the bottom half covers half his face, like somebody splattered a ripe tomato. If that nose job cost $7,000, the surgeon earned about $6,995 more than he deserved.

Miami won just eight games in Zonk's first two years, and the Dolphins spawned a nickname: The Fish That Couldn't Swim.

They needed a drawing card and a winner to survive the NFL merger, and they got both February 18, 1970, when owner Joe Robbie lured Shula away from the Baltimore Colts. Shula had become the NFL's youngest head coach at thirty-three, had taken Baltimore to the NFL title game his second year, to the Super Bowl his sixth year.

He inherited a Miami club that had gone 15–39–2 in the AFL. Some of the pieces were in place: Griese, Csonka and fellow running backs Jim Kiick and Mercury Morris, wide receivers Paul Warfield and Howard Twilley, offensive linemen Larry Little and Norm Evans, defensive lineman Bill Stanfill, linebacker Nick Buoniconti, and safety Dick Anderson. Still, these Dolphins didn't know what it took to win in the AFL—and now they were supposed to win in their first year in the NFL?

Shula set out to show them.

By practicing four times a day.

"Remember my attorney said I'd like to play in Miami because it was warm?" Csonka asked. "In 1970, I realized just how *hottt* it could get in Miami. In August of that year, it was about 103 degrees. When you have twenty-two pounds of equipment on and a heavy jersey, and you're diving up and down in wet, freshly mowed grass because your head coach wants you to do the grass drill, you realize Miami is not warm, it's *hottt*. It's *damn hottt*.

"I looked at this guy and thought, He's possessed. Four-a-day practices! We got up before the sun, had our regular two practices, and then we had a thing called evening entertainment, where we just stood around in shorts and bumped into each other in the twilight. In one of those little run-around deals, we lost Mercury Morris for six weeks. And I thought, How can I get out of here?

"He talked about the will to win. He talked about the winning edge. He talked about sacrifice. And frankly, we thought he was on *druuuggggggssss*."

Zonk shook his head back and forth like a Rich Little parody of Richard Nixon as he elongated the word "drugs," and the audience rocked with laughter. Zonk was joking; he loves Shula and what he has done for him.

The Dolphins improved by seven games in one year despite tougher competition. Shula took them to the Super Bowl the next three years, winning the final two. They went 17–0 in 1972 and 15–2 in 1973. Nobody else has ever gone unbeaten in a season, or 32–2 in two seasons.

"That first year as coach was as fine a coaching job as has ever been done," said Tim Robbie, Joe's son and successor. "Many people refer to the years that immediately followed as the glory years. When you have the best record in sports over twenty-six years, I don't think you can confine the glory years to two years. In hindsight, damn near every year was glorious."

Shula took over a 3–10–1 Miami team and went 10–4. Jimmy Johnson took over a 3–13 Dallas team and went 1–15. Shula taught a young team how to win. Jimmy tore apart an old team and built a young one.

They would hate to admit it, but in their heyday, they shared some remarkable similarities. Johnson fired the guy who holds the cord to his headset on game day in Philadelphia because he saw the guy laughing with the Eagles. Shula fired a player who challenged an assistant coach on the plane ride home.

Johnson fired Curvin Richards, his only backup halfback, when he fumbled twice in the meaningless final minutes of a blowout victory. "Shula kept a bus ticket in his back pocket, and when it was third and one, he'd say, 'It's time for you to go in' . . . and he'd pat that bus ticket," says Don Nottingham, his short-yardage fullback. "I think he was serious."

Johnson raged at his players on the plane ride home after losses, in the meeting rooms after victories. Shula became famous for his iron jaw as he screamed at officials and players alike. "Intensity bred out of a desire to win," Csonka says. "We're in the middle of a meeting and Shula's going on and on and finally Kiick turned to me and said, 'Didn't we win this game? What the hell's going on? I thought when you won, the coach was happy.' But Shula wasn't. He was possessed."

When Joe Robbie offended him in front of friends, Shula threatened to punch out his boss. When Dallas owner Jerry Jones paraded Prince Bandar bin Sultan, Saudi Arabia's ambassador to the United States and one of the world's richest and most powerful men, onto the Texas Stadium turf with the Cowboys ahead 27–0 and clinching their first division title, Jimmy chewed out his players, coaches, and boss.

When George Bush attended a Marlins game, Shula sent his security man, Stu Weinstein, down to suggest the ex-president come to his skybox. Bush said he'd love to meet Shula but stipulated, "Get him to come to me." No, let him come here, Shula said. No, let him come to me, Bush said. Back and forth the emissary went, but neither man budged. Shula's *cojones*—or was it ego?—were too big. Jimmy Johnson uses the words egotistical and arrogant and gloat to describe himself.

Both demanded total control over coaching and personnel matters, and both chafed on the rare occasions they did not get it. Johnson never coached any college or pro team for more than five years. He left a two-time defending Super Bowl champion when he became frustrated with Jones, part bored and part burned out. Shula thought about leaving Joe Robbie for another team—he came very close to leaving for Donald Trump's USFL New Jersey Generals—but never did.

And that's one of the big differences between Shula and Johnson. Or, for that matter, everyone else. Shula coached against his own son, David, and against the NFL's founding father, George Halas. Only twice in thirty-three years did he have a losing season. Hell, Jimmy had a losing record twice in his first *two* years. Jimmy lost fifteen games his first year in Dallas. Shula lost sixteen games in his first *six* years in Miami.

Shula won 347 regular-season and postseason games. The only active coaches with even a hundred victories are Dan Reeves (148), Marv Levy (135), Marty Schottenheimer (128), and Bill Parcells (119). To catch Shula, even if they average ten wins a year (a feat none has achieved), Reeves would have to coach until he's seventy-three, Schottenheimer until seventy-six, Parcells until seventy-eight, Levy until ninety-one.

The other twenty-nine clubs employed 201 coaches while the Dolphins employed Don. In fact, only Levy and Schottenheimer joined their current clubs before 1992. Twenty-five have enlisted since 1993, twenty-four since 1994, twenty since 1995, ten this year.

Check out the NFL's annual group photo of coaches.

"I keep all those pictures, and every year I look to see how the faces have changed," Shula told me back in 1993, the year he broke Papa Bear Halas's record of 324 victories. "I have one with me, George Halas, Norm Van Brocklin and Allie Sherman. That's what really makes you feel it's been a long time. But I feel good, I feel young, no health problems at all."

Oh, once he had arthroscopic surgery on his knee. "I missed the morning practice," Shula said.

He was sixty-three and working sixty-three hours a week, not counting Saturdays and Sundays. He jogged daily and was perpetually tanned but never raisin-wrinkled. He didn't sleep in his office or burn out on the job. He schooled his teams to commit few penalties or foolish mistakes. Too many coaches fell in love with their "system" and were too proud to change it. Shula had an ego as big or bigger than any of them, but he willingly changed systems rather than players. Because plays don't win; players do.

"I don't dictate or jam a system down anyone's throat," Shula said. "It's evident by the quarterbacks. When I had Johnny Unitas, I threw the ball. When I had Griese, I also had Csonka and utilized ground control. With Marino, it's a whole new philosophy. Same thing defensively. I've always been willing to adapt."

Yes, he won with two Hall of Fame quarterbacks and a third who's a lead-pipe cinch, but he also went to the Super Bowl with Earl Morrall and David Woodley.

He coached his first game the day Marino turned two. He won his record 325th with Doug Pederson, who was unemployed until Marino went down for the year.

Shula's impact stretched beyond the NFL and into society. He became as synonymous with Miami as white loafers, gold chains, and pastel-colored linen blazers. A golf course, café, health club, two hotels, a chain of steak houses—why, even a highway—are named for him. He put Miami—not just the team but the city—on the map. South Florida's population has doubled, its pro sports teams quadrupled, and many experts credit Shula for creating a winning, world-class image.

Air-conditioning and Don Shula might be the two biggest reasons for South Florida's growth spurt. Certainly, image is not everything. But people want to be associated with winners, and Don Shula was a winner. Think that doesn't mean something? Ever seen the excitement and energy in a Super Bowl city—or the heartbreak and mourning after a Super loss? When kids are growing up, or adults are thinking about leaving the Rust Belt for the Sun Belt, think they want to root for the Tampa Bay Buccaneers or the Miami Dolphins? People around the world wear Dolphins colors and read *Dolphin Digest*.

Dolphins victories drew big crowds, which helped pay for a new stadium, which helped attract a baseball team. That success fueled expansion basketball and hockey teams and three new arenas. Shula's success—and optimism for more—helped turn around the town the way it turned around the team. South Beach and Miami Beach were in the doldrums of decay. But now glittering high-rises and refurbished Art Deco bars have replaced dilapidated motels. Now they're the toyland of the rich and beautiful.

Shula helped the community by donating time and money to countless churches, charities, colleges, and construction drives.

"People measured this man by whether he went to the Super Bowl or not," said Cesar Odio, a former Miami city manager. "But that simply isn't enough."

And yet . . .

For all his victories on and off the field, Don Shula hadn't won the ultimate game since the 1973 season, hadn't even appeared in it since the '84 season. The only other NFL coach to last that long without winning a title was Chuck Knox. In fact, in all of pro football, baseball, basketball, and hockey, only baseball's Gene Mauch had a longer drought. He hadn't won a playoff game on the road in twenty-two years.

And ultimately, that wasn't good enough.

What happened? In many ways, Shula was a victim of his own success. Because he routinely won ten games a year, he rarely got the high draft choices and franchise players. He never picked higher than seventh. Because he had the game's most prolific passer, he relied on Marino and never built a strong running game and defense around him. Because he and Marino were always in contention, he never tore the team apart and started over. Making the playoffs today eclipsed winning it all in the future.

And subtle changes began to take place with the man himself. He was the iron man with the iron will to match the iron jaw, but somewhere in his sixties, the iron became pliable.

Shula liked to say he was as subtle as a punch in the mouth, that he didn't get ulcers, he gave them. He was so focused on football, he didn't know who Don Johnson or Kevin Costner were when they met, didn't know how to operate the VCRs or microwave in his home. On their honeymoon, Don asked Dorothy to backpedal. She thought he was kidding; he wasn't. He wanted to see her moves, so he could see if his unborn sons would be football players some day. His competitiveness at football, golf, even jogging were the stuff of legend. He was John Wayne tough and gruff. Even his own children never saw him cry . . . until the day his wife of thirty-two years died of cancer.

Dorothy's death changed him. She had soothed him when he was down, had kept him humble when he was too high on himself. She had been unpretentious, the mother of five children and den mother to hundreds. Without her, he was empty, lonely, grieving. To fill the void, he finally let down the guard of all-powerful leader, showed his vulnerability, and joined his children's and grandchildren's lives. He roughhoused with the grandkids, taught them tennis, even attended their plays. If Dorothy couldn't fulfill her dream, he'd do it instead.

The immortal became mortal.

He began to date Mary Anne Stephens, a socialite divorcée well connected to old money (her ex was worth $1.7 billion) and big politics (Bill Clinton attended her wedding). She taught Don about fine art, explaining that "the ugliest picture" he'd ever seen was a Picasso. She took the workaholic and homebody to museums and charities, to ball games and black-tie events. She replaced his plain golf shirts with $2,500 suits and tropical-print silk shirts, white slacks, and Italian loafers, with the designer duds matched by number and computer printout so Shula could figure out which shoes to wear. Why, he wore a turquoise sequined dinner jacket with matching bow tie to an Elvis theme party. The previously private Shula held hands and smooched in public.

They married during a bye week in 1993, and he moved from his longtime home in Miami Lakes to her twelve-thousand-square-foot mini Versailles on Indian Creek Island. Indian Creek Country Club, with its initiation fee of $45,000 and yearly dues of $6,650, dominates the center of the island, which is rimmed by thirty-two extravagant waterfront estates, each secluded by high walls decked with exotic gardens. Neighbors have included Raymond Floyd, Julio Iglesias, former Eagles owner Norman Braman, and a Saudi prince. Care to mingle? Home prices start at $2.95 million.

Mary Anne made Don less guarded and more human, which is wonderful for a man but maybe not for a demanding boss in a brutal business. Don Shula, the hard-nosed Hungarian famed for The Look of lasers and The Jaw of granite, was becoming "Shoes." It would be an exaggeration to say he became as soft and comfortable as old shoes. But age, money, and contentment have a way of taking the edge off even the most competitive of coaches and players.

Even his body betrayed him in 1994. In a freaky coincidence, Shula suffered the same injury as his star quarterback had the year before. Surgery to repair the torn Achilles' tendon forced him to watch practice and games from a golf cart. He became more removed, less imposing, than ever. He couldn't pull players aside during practice, couldn't walk through the locker room afterward, and, the players snickered, couldn't board the team plane without being carried on and off like some Egyptian pharaoh.

Ron Jaworski, a longtime NFL quarterback who played under Shula as a backup in 1987 and 1988 and stayed in touch because of his friends on the team and his job as an ESPN analyst, could not believe how much the discipline had slipped. He said Shula was letting players get away with stuff that he never would have allowed before. Players begged out of practice, claiming they were hurt. They showed up late to meetings. They slept in meetings. One Shula draft bust even masturbated during a meeting. They partied too much, worked too little, and thought way too highly of their individual abilities.

Louis Oliver returned from a one-year stay in Cincinnati to find the 1995 Dolphins "too comfortable and too complacent. We thought we looked like Super Bowl champions on paper, and that was good enough." Buckley arrived from Green Bay thinking he'd play cornerback and felt betrayed when he was moved inside, mismatched against bigger slot receivers, in the nickel defense. Oliver, Buckley, and other defenders seethed about the passive, soft schemes that robbed them of their aggressiveness.

The offense was soft, too. Those four-a-day physical practices of 1970 had evolved into walk-throughs and finesse football. Trying to ensure a crisp passing game and fresh bodies at playoff time, Shula leaned toward San Francisco 49ers–style workouts and didn't make players practice as hard, if at all. Trying to do too much, he made too many poor draft choices. Trying for one last desperate grab at a Super Bowl, he imported too many me-first mercenaries. Trying to balance the offense and keep his defense off the field, he started every season pledging allegiance to his running game and ended every crunch time relying upon Marino's arm. The running game and defense crumbled. Teamwork tumbled. Discipline diminished. The Dolphins dove.

"Going for the gusto backfired," said Joe Rose, a former Shula tight end turned Shula critic for WQAM radio and Channel 6. Rose faulted Shula's personnel decisions, poor motivational skills, soft defensive philosophy, and paying big money up front to unmotivated players who made more than better, harder-working players.

"Front-loading contracts was a big mistake. It left a bad taste in a lot of players' mouths, and it caused problems even before camp started. There was friction all year. In the eighties, if someone were benched or not making enough, no one ever stormed off. We didn't like it, but we knew who was running the show. We swallowed our pride. We had guys who didn't like each other, but they never moved their lockers to get away from each other. Forget hanging around together afterward; these guys couldn't even get along in the locker room. They were taking advantage of Shula. He still loved the game, but he didn't want to argue anymore. Shoes didn't deal well with character issues."

When Jimmy left the Cowboys within days of Huizenga's earning approval to buy the Dolphins, Shula endured disquieting questions in 1994. Would he finish the final year on his contract and be booted out? Would he move upstairs with Jimmy taking over on the field? Could those egos coexist? But the speculation was suppressed, at least for a while, when Shula signed a contract extension to coach in '95 and '96. Huizenga gave him partial ownership of the club and said he could coach as long as he wanted and also that he'd only talked to Jimmy once in his life, back when Jimmy was coaching the University of Miami.

Shula's '94 club went 10–6 and won the AFC East. But even amid the success were signs of trouble. The Dolphins were 6–2 when Mark Ingram, a marginal wide receiver who'd won a Super Bowl with the run-happy New York Giants, thought he was the Super answer for the Dolphins. He went to Shula and complained that defenses were double-covering Irving Fryar and Keith Jackson and the Dolphins still weren't throwing to him or O. J. McDuffie. Shula's strategy didn't change. The Dolphins pounded the Patriots by twenty points. Only one pass was aimed toward Ingram. Was he happy to win? Not exactly. He skipped practice in protest. Shula could have sent a lasting message to everyone by cutting the selfish bum on the spot. He did not. The cancer spread.

Marino and Miami doused Joe Montana and Kansas City in the first round of the playoffs, then traveled to San Diego and led, 21–6 at halftime. Marino was one half away from returning to his hometown of Pittsburgh for the AFC championship game and, at long last, the storybook ending to his Super dream.

Then came the collapse, one that foretold Don's downfall. Shula's failure to emphasize the run came back to bite him. If you don't practice smash-mouth football, you can't succeed when it's imperative. You won't be able to grind out yards on third and one, the goal line, or the game's end. And you won't be able to escape the shadows of your own goal line.

On first down from his own one, Bernie Parmalee was tackled in the Dolphins' end zone for a momentum-swinging safety. The rejuvenated Chargers, a power team with big linemen and a big back playing against a defense missing two starting linebackers, marched fifty-four yards in eight plays. The Chargers didn't take the lead until thirty-five seconds remained. Even then, Miami could have won with a forty-eight-yard field goal.

Miami had made Pete Stoyanovich one of the league's richest kickers for just such moments.

He missed. Wide right.

San Diego was going to Pittsburgh.

Shula was going to waste more money on guys with better reputations than performances.

That off-season, Huizenga told Shula and financial gurus Eddie Jones and Bryan Weidmeier, "Do whatever it takes." He gave them an unlimited expense account, and they exceeded it. They spent $18 million on signing bonuses alone.

They fell for what agent Drew Rosenhaus later admitted was a lie, a con. They got involved in a bidding war—mostly with themselves, it would turn out—and vastly overpaid for Eric Green, who talked about becoming the best tight end ever, then went out and partied so much, he tested positive for drugs twice and was suspended the second time for six games. He dragged down not only himself but one or two Pittsburgh teammates. The Steelers pleaded with him to work harder, but he refused to increase his workouts or decrease his pig-outs, and he got open less and got hurt more often, partly because his weight— Eric's ass was fatter than Rhode Island—kept stressing out his joints. The best way to motivate Eric was to give him a small salary and big incentives. The worst way was to give him a big signing bonus and a long-term contract. The Dolphins gave him a $3.5 million signing bonus and a six-year, $12 million deal. You wonder who was on drugs here.

Shula signed Gary Clark and Ricky Sanders, two receivers past their prime. He signed Randal Hill, a receiver with a big ego and speed and nothing else. He traded second- and third-round picks for Trace Armstrong, an average but over-paid defensive end with a reputation as a clubhouse lawyer. He brought back Oliver, even though he was a liability in pass coverage. He traded away Mark Ingram and Keith Jackson and dealt promising rookie tight end Pete Mitchell to Jacksonville for Mike Williams, another wideout who thought he was better than he really was. Williams caught just two passes, played poorly on special teams, and was resented by teammates and coaches alike for his lax habits. Mitchell ended 1995 with forty-one catches, two fewer than Green, and finished 1996 with fifty-two receptions, or fifty-two more than Green gave the Dolphins.

Shula's 1995 draft had so many slugs, only one would survive Jimmy Johnson's first year: third-string defensive tackle Norman Hand.

Yet not many people saw the fall coming. Seduced by Shula, Marino, and the rest of these names, a lot of "experts" picked the 1995 Dolphins to go to the Super Bowl. One of those experts was Jimmy Johnson, and, knowing his nature, it's hard to believe it wasn't a cold and calculating prediction. If Shula got his ring, he'd get the storybook ending to a glorious career and Jimmy would be proven right, with a chance to take over if Shula decided it was a good time to retire. If Shula didn't live up to these Super expectations, why, what was wrong with him? Couldn't Jimmy do better?

Jimmy was omnipresent, lurking nearby, waiting to swoop in, like a shark among dolphins.

Shula downplayed speculation about Jimmy and his own "last chance." He thought he had nothing left to prove. But the NFL is a now game in a now world. Huizenga didn't become a billionaire by accepting less than the best. The owner said there could be "no excuses" for failure and "this has to be our year." Added Oliver: "Everybody knows anything less than getting to the Super Bowl is a tragic season."

And then the Shakespearean tragedy unfolded:

• The day the Dolphins improved to 4–0, Keith Byars flung his helmet and stomped to the far end of the bench. The Dolphins were inside the Cincinnati ten, and yet he was too angry to watch. He said Miami was struggling to score inside the twenty, "and it's only because I'm not in the game."

• The next week, the Dolphins blew a 24–3 halftime lead and lost, 27–24, in overtime to the Colts. Jim Harbaugh, whose reputation had been in tatters, left the defense in tatters, completing twenty for twenty-four for 275 yards and three touchdowns in the second half alone. Jeff Cross second-guessed the much-maligned defensive boss, Tom Olivadotti. Marino tore cartilage in his knee and damaged his hip.

• Without Marino, the Dolphins lost to the Saints and Jets, who were 1–11 combined. Bernie Kosar was intercepted five times and fumbled two more in the losses. Oliver complained he should be starting, and high-priced free agent Gene Atkins stood up in a defensive meeting and said if Michael Stewart were benched for Oliver, he might walk out. But Shula didn't cut Atkins because Olivadotti still liked him and Miami would have to swallow $2.4 million of his signing bonus against its salary cap.

• The Dolphins ended their three-game losing streak and climbed into a tie for first with a win over the Bills, but, several boycotted the media, including the four players who traveled to Cleveland on Tuesday, their day off. *Miami Herald* sports editor Edwin Pope, South Florida's most influential sports voice, had ripped them for failing to focus. Terry Kirby wanted to watch brother Wayne, and Indians outfielder, play in the World Series, and Huizenga let them use his private plane. They got home at 4 A.M. but were on time for Wednesday's meetings. Shula said the trip didn't bother him. You think Jimmy would have felt the same way? Only one of the Cleveland Four survived Jimmy's first season.

• A 34–17 thumping by New England led to more controversy. Atkins gave up a deep touchdown pass, then stomped around the sideline, angrily confronting Olivadotti and Shula and waving away Troy Vincent, who was trying to calm him. Atkins claimed he played the coverage correctly, but Shula said he'd never heard of a three-deep zone where the free safety wasn't responsible for the deep middle. Atkins walked out of a team meeting the next day and was benched for Oliver.

• By the time Elvis Grbac left the building, he had thrown for 382 yards and four touchdowns, the 49ers had blown out the Dolphins, 44–20, with their backup quarterback, and many in the biggest crowd ever at Joe Robbie Stadium were chanting, "We want Jimmy."

"We showed no heart," said Bryan Cox, who missed a tackle and gave up San Francisco's first touchdown. Miami wasted one time-out when it had ten men on the field and another when nobody on defense knew who should cover Jerry Rice. Coaches called a play they hadn't practiced since training camp. Players anonymously lamented the lack of a coherent, week-to-week plan, saying Stevens sent in plays that seemed to come out of the air.

The three big South Florida newspapers asked fans whether Shula should stay or go. More than thirteen thousand fans called the papers, and the unscientific polls were almost identical: between 75 and 80 percent said he should go. Columnists called for his tenure to end. Even ex-Dolphin Nick Buoniconti asked Shula why he didn't discipline modern-day players the same way he did the undefeated team. Sources told the papers that Shula's close friends were advising him to retire. Other sources said Shula could save his job by offering to clean out his staff, especially Stevens and Olivadotti.

Shula called it the worst week of his career.

It got worse.

• After a third straight loss dropped the Dolphins to 6–6, Oliver claimed the defense wasn't prepared for formations the Colts used and added that not all the defensive players knew the defensive calls.

Sports Illustrated came to town and put Shula on the cover with Miami Heat coach Pat Riley. The headline read, "Hot & Not." Shula was the Not. Inside, one story raved on Riley. The other, headlined "The Waning of a Legend," called Miami "the league's biggest flop" and questioned Shula's future. Huizenga told the magazine, "Right now Shula's got my vote of confidence, and we're going to go through the rest of this season and try to remain positive. Now, at the end of every year, every person in America gets reviewed. Don will review his coaches, the coaches will review the players, and I'll review Don."

• Earlier in the year, Atkins had taken a running start and knocked down Jason Cole of the Fort Lauderdale *Sun-Sentinel*. Then, after the last-second win over Atlanta, Cox also blamed the media, in an expletive-filled tirade that ESPN ran in its bleeping entirety. The Friday before that game, when the Dolphins were supposed to observe an 11 P.M. curfew, O. J. McDuffie was arrested for a nightclub scuffle at 4 A.M. And, oh yeah, the whining tight end let a touchdown pass go through his hands for an interception.

• When Thurman Thomas drove through Cox for a first down, Cox fought Buffalo's Carwell Gardner. Cox and Gardner were ejected, and as Buffalo's fans threw trash at him, Cox spit toward the fans.

The Dolphins lost by three points, and Green complained they'd never win until their running game got more physical. Maybe they'd have been more physical if Green hadn't missed thirty-nine practices.

• The 1995 Dolphins earned a trip to the playoffs—and a third meeting with Buffalo—only when Denver came back from an eleven-point deficit and beat Oakland the last week of the regular season. And then they were humiliated, giving up an AFC playoff record of 341 yards rushing.

"We never challenged," Shula said, "and that's the way this team will be remembered."

A week before, Huizenga had said Shula could complete his contract, but after this debacle, he strode briskly, angrily to his car, refusing to answer questions about Shula's future. Shula sidestepped the questions, too.

Cross and cornerback J. B. Brown called for change. Little did they know they'd be part of it.

Vincent said some of his teammates quit when it was 24–0 in the second quarter. Cox said selfish players ruined the season. Marco Coleman said the Dolphins never were a true team because of "all this money-hungry crap. Nobody started playing football for money. Now all of a sudden it's money, money, money, money."

A few months later, Vincent, Cox, and Coleman would leave for money, money, money, money. A season in which Dan Marino broke the NFL's four most significant career passing records, a season in which Dan and Don were supposed to be fitted for Super Bowl rings, ended with Don being fitted for a noose.

The season ended Saturday, December 30. The next day, Shula met briefly with his players. They didn't know it would be the last time he'd address them as coach. As Shula was about to leave, Huizenga walked into his office, unannounced. For an hour, they talked about the disappointment, about the future, and Shula said he planned to complete his contract and coach in 1996.

But Huizenga wanted changes on the staff, and they agreed to meet again at 4 P.M. Wednesday. Shula had some soul-searching to do. He did not want to make anyone into a scapegoat. He called some friends, including three general managers: George Young of the Giants, Bobby Beathard of the Chargers, and Bill Polian of the Panthers.

The general managers and Shula agreed: It would be difficult to hire good assistants when they knew he had only one year left on his contract. Huizenga told Shula if that were a problem, he'd extend Shula's contract. That response "took me back some because that was the furthest thing from my mind," Shula said. "I just wasn't prepared to make any further commitment at this stage of my life." He needed to think some more. The meeting broke up after two and a half hours, with the promise of another to come.

Huizenga knew Shula did not plan to coach beyond 1996 and did not want to fire loyal aides and start over. He also knew Jimmy was taking his time deciding on Tampa Bay's offer—delaying to see if the Miami job came open—but if this decision dragged on, or if Shula returned as a lame duck in 1996, he risked losing Jimmy for good.

Wayne Huizenga did not want to lose Jimmy Johnson.

The billionaire was driven by a fierce desire to win but also by business: The licenses on most of the two hundred-some skyboxes and ten thousand-plus club seats were coming up for renewal in the next year or two, and the best way to sell them, especially for the hefty increases he wanted, would be selling the sizzle of Jimmy Johnson, not the apathy and outright hostility toward Shula.

But Huizenga did not want to be seen as a ham-handed ogre firing a legend, the way Jerry Jones was portrayed in dismissing Tom Landry. Untenable demands and a sweet going-away present could shove Shula into retirement with dignity and without bloody fingerprints.

As late as Wednesday afternoon, Shula was talking to agents about players and telling offensive line coach Monte Clark to assemble a list of prospective new assistant coaches. But the meeting changed everything. Shula went home and agonized with his wife, who told him he didn't need the aggravation of coaching.

Thursday, January 4, 1996, Shula celebrated his sixty-sixth birthday, "if you can call that celebrating," Shula said. He left to play golf, only to be greeted by his secretary at the eighteenth green. She told him various reports were coming out that he was resigning. Huizenga was coming to Shula's birthday party on Indian Creek. They met at 7:30 P.M.

Recalled Huizenga: "The first thing he said was, 'I don't want to do anything that's going to restrict your ability to bring in the best possible person. And if you pick a person that needs to and wants to consult with me, than I'm available as much as you want. If you bring in a person that doesn't want me around, then I'm all for that. I'm not going to be the reason we don't bring the best person into this organization.' "

Jimmy had angered Don Shula when he demoted David Shula in Dallas. The animosity grew when Don thought Jimmy was campaigning for his job. Just a few weeks before, he stared into a TV camera and seethed, "Jimmy Johnson is sitting there talking about how much he would enjoy to coach the Dolphins. That's adding fuel to the fire."

But now, in so many words, he was telling Huizenga, if you want Jimmy so badly, go ahead. Not that Huizenga needed Shula's blessing to do what just about everyone in South Florida was expecting and coveting, but it made both feel better.

That night, Shula confirmed he was quitting, personally calling a few media friends. A media conference was scheduled for 4 P.M. Friday. Shula arrived at the Dolphins' facility around 11 A.M., went straight to his office, and bade farewell to his assistants. He talked with players such as Marino, Kosar, and Cox. He thanked the front-office staffers and wished them well. Then he headed downstairs to the auditorium with wife Mary Anne, daughters Anne and Donna, Raymond Floyd, and a bunch of past and present players. Why, even his accountant attended the public farewell—perhaps because Huizenga had thrown in a lucrative going-away present.

As thirty-two cameras recorded every word, Shula gave his spin on what happened, insisted it was totally his decision, and said as the new vice chairman of the board, he'd help in any way he was needed.

He turned to face his wife.

"Today, Mary Anne, is the first day of our new life. And we're looking forward to that. We're going to make this a happy time. It's tough to leave. When I get up in the morning the car's going to automatically head out of the driveway up this way, and I'm going to have to . . . find other things to do. But when you make a decision, you do everything in your power to make it the right decision."

Someone said he seemed in great spirits. "I'm putting on a hell of a front," Shula confessed.

Huizenga insisted he hadn't talked to Jimmy, that Jimmy was just one candidate to consider. But as he left the auditorium, the billionaire finally confirmed everyone's suspicion: "Obviously, he's at the top of the list."

3
HELLO, JIMMY

Wednesday, January 10, 1996. The Old West heroes rode to the rescue on white stallions, punching ponies and outlaws. Jimmy Johnson punched the 345 horses in his red Corvette, then punched Butch Davis's number on his cell phone.

Jimmy was speeding up U.S. 1 from his home in Tavernier, near the northern tip of the Florida Keys, past Coral Gables, where his former defensive line coach now worked as the University of Miami's head coach.

"Whatcha doing?" hollered Jimmy, talking as fast as he was driving.

"It's seven-thirty in the morning. What are *you* doing?" Butch wondered.

"Well, I'm going up to see Wayne Huizenga," Jimmy said, and over the roar of the road, Butch could hear the ecstasy in his old boss's voice.

Jimmy had told Rhonda Rookmaaker, his longtime girlfriend, and Nick Christin, his agent, attorney, and close friend, that he would not agree to a contract that day. It would be hard to say no to the Dolphins, but if he did, he did not think he would ever coach again. He had left Nick uncertain as to what he would do. They had gone through this mating ritual before, and Jimmy had always listened, been intrigued, then said no. But this was different. This was *home*. This was the job Jimmy had coveted and campaigned for.

What a whirlwind two weeks it had been. Tampa Bay had fired Sam Wyche and offered Jimmy total control. Art Modell had not even left Cleveland or fired Bill Belichick yet, but made the same offer. Miami had said good-bye to Shula on Friday, January 5. The next day, while working as a Fox analyst, Jimmy had said he was interested but had not talked to Huizenga yet. But that didn't stop the rumors. Nick had eaten lunch with his son Saturday at a little Miami restaurant, where the TV was tuned to ESPN, which reported Nick was negotiating with the Dolphins. "The only thing he's negotiating now," the owner said to the cook, "is what to have on his cheeseburger."

Reporters had tried everything to get to Jimmy and Nick. Two television stations, a reporter, and a photographer were waiting for Jimmy when he returned from Los Angeles at ten-thirty Sunday night. Three television crews camped outside his home Monday, "like *Hard Copy*," he complained. A fourth camera crew arrived by helicopter and borrowed a neighbor's phone to call Nick and beg that Jimmy come outside and talk to them. A TV station, a newspaper reporter, and a magazine writer showed up Tuesday, and though Jimmy said he didn't want to talk, he eventually relented, talked to *Sports Illustrated*, and told *The Dallas Morning News* he would meet Huizenga the next day. Other reporters camped out in the reception area of Nick's offices, even asking receptionists what kind of car he drove so they could tail him, until he finally kicked them out.

Sunday, Dolphins general manager Eddie Jones and vice president of administration Bryan Wiedmeier had compiled a list of candidates with background information. Jimmy Johnson and Florida coach Steve Spurrier topped the list, followed by NFL coordinators such as Pete Carroll and Tony Dungy. Monday morning, Jones had called Huizenga, who approved the list and suggested Jones start with the obvious first choice. Jones looked up Christin's phone number in the bar registry that morning and scheduled a meeting for Wednesday morning.

The much-awaited marriage—or at least the courtship—was about to begin.

As soon as Jimmy pulled in front of Nick's office, a TV reporter and cameraman popped in front of the Corvette, filming away. Jimmy wheeled around them and they scrambled for their Bronco and gave chase. Jimmy and Nick joked it was like the O.J. Bronco chase, only a whole lot faster.

The Channel 6 crew followed them all the way to the Dolphins offices in Davie. They had a 10 A.M. appointment with Huizenga, Jones, and Wiedmeier. Half of South Florida wondered why the deal hadn't been done by the fourth quarter of the Buffalo blowout, but when the Dolphins didn't call Friday, Saturday, or Sunday, Nick wondered if they had someone else in mind, and if this interview was just a sham to appease the public. More likely, Huizenga didn't want to appear too eager to dance on Shula's grave or give away his negotiating leverage. Huizenga and Jones had compiled a two–page list of twenty–some issues to discuss. They didn't plan to talk money that day, either.

So much for plans.

Jimmy and Nick arrived early and got a brief tour of the complex from Jones and backup quarterback Bernie Kosar, whom Jimmy had coached at the University of Miami and Dallas. Then everybody convened in the second-floor conference room, Jimmy and Nick on one side of the table, Wayne, Eddie, and Bryan on the other. By now, it was about ten-thirty, and after a little chatting, Wayne said, "Nick, where do we start?"

"Why don't I talk to you about how I feel a pro football team should be run?" Jimmy answered, and laid out his philosophies on building a team. Eddie and Wayne asked questions and offered a few details about the salary cap and free agency, but it wasn't the typical Q&A job interview, and Jimmy did most of the talking.

"I want a coach I can enjoy winning with," Huizenga said. "I want to be your friend. There's no money in sports, so I have to have other reasons to be in it. I'm not Jerry. I'm not a hands-on owner. I'm not going to bug you a lot—we might talk once or twice each week during the season—but I have to have a relationship with the man running my team, or it's not going to work."

I'm not Jerry. Those were the exact words Jimmy wanted to hear. He wanted total control, not daily skirmishes. He wanted all the credit—or blame, though he didn't think it would come to that.

Huizenga wanted to hear if Jimmy still had the raging desire to win. "Why don't you take the easy road, Jimmy?" he asked. "You're a hero, with two Super Bowl rings. You have the credentials to second-guess everybody, work a couple of days a week, and do almost as well financially as you could in coaching. Why take a job where, immediately, you'll be under so much pressure?"

It was a damn good question, one that even Rhonda, Nick, and his family and friends asked. They had seen the stress gnaw at him in Dallas, seen it melt away in the Keys. They liked this Jimmy a whole lot better. But they couldn't feel his fire inside. Wayne could. He looked at Jimmy and listened.

"I have a passion for the game," Jimmy said. "I want to win. I *need* to win."

Those were the words Wayne wanted to hear. This man had started with one garbage truck and wound up with the world's largest waste-management firm. He bought into Blockbuster Entertainment when it had nineteen video stores. It had 4,400 when he sold it within the decade. Now he had launched Republic Industries and Huizenga Holdings, with enterprises ranging from garbage to auto rentals to auto dealers, and he was flying all over the country, doing deals almost daily, working as hard as ever. He had a spectacular waterfront home, a helicopter, a jet, and too many cars to count. He could have retired a billion bucks ago, but he, too, had a passion for the game, albeit a different game.

Between noon and twelve-thirty, Huizenga walked out of the room with Jones and Wiedmeier and said he wanted to talk to Jimmy privately to discuss money. While the others broke to use the rest room and order sandwiches from a local deli, Wayne called Jimmy aside. They stepped into Eddie Jones's office and closed the door.

Wayne told Jimmy he wanted him to be his coach, and they began to discuss money. Wayne had heard the rumors that Philadelphia (in 1994) and Tampa (in 1995) had offered more than $3 million a year. He said he'd make Jimmy the NFL's highest-paid coach, but he didn't want to embarrass Shula by paying

Jimmy a lot more, and the relationship wouldn't work if one guy felt he'd been taken advantage of. He said Shula made $1.85 million a year and he'd give Jimmy $8 million for four years, with a chance for more in side deals. Jimmy said that wasn't exactly the number he was looking for, but he wanted to talk with Nick. The whole conversation didn't take more than thirty minutes, the negotiation stage more than ten or fifteen minutes.

Nick had no clue of Huizenga's plans until the billionaire emerged and said they had just discussed money and Jimmy wanted to talk with Nick. Then Huizenga went to call Shula and said he thought he'd offer Jimmy the job. Shula told him if he felt good about it, go ahead.

Jimmy had told Nick he would not accept that day. And yet when Nick came in, Jimmy said, "I want to call Rhonda."

That told Nick that Jimmy was serious. They went over Wayne's offer. Nick thought the money could have been better, but everything else was perfect. Wayne's hands-off management and commitment to win it all "swept us off our feet," Nick said later.

"I don't even want to ask for anything else," Nick told Jimmy.

"Yeah," Jimmy said, "you're right."

They asked Wayne back into the room to restate the terms, compromised on a few details, and shook hands.

"I've done hundreds of acquisitions and business deals, but I've never had one like this," Huizenga said later. "I can't explain it. Jimmy was charming, easy to be with. I felt I had to have him."

And Jimmy felt he had to have this job.

"The negotiations were not hard," he said. "Wayne understood I was making pretty good money with all my television and outside income, and he'd have to pay what would be considered top dollar in coaching circles."

Jimmy was making about $1.5 million a year and had turned down coaching offers of $3 million to $4 million. He could have made more coaching elsewhere, and money does matter to Jimmy. It's another way of keeping score. But Jimmy was already a rich man. Money couldn't buy him as much happiness as his dream job could.

"It's easy for someone who's secure and making the money I'm making to say, 'I'm not money-driven,' " Jimmy said. "But there are people who have a lot of money who continually want more, so in that light, I can say I'm not money-driven. I wasn't looking to break the bank.

"There'd been so much conversation for so long about me being the Dolphins' coach that when it came available, I would have been second-guessing myself for the rest of my life if I hadn't said yes. Just to satisfy my own drive, I had to say yes."

Wayne sent his helicopter to pick up Rhonda in Tavernier, and Jimmy could look out the wall-length picture window in his new office and see her land on the practice field below him. Jimmy started to hand out assignments to the staff while Nick huddled with Bryan and a Huizenga attorney to put a contract on paper.

At 2:40 P.M., Jimmy and Wayne strolled down the stairs, out of the lobby, and down to the base of the steps in front of the complex. South Florida's media had been camped out inside and outside, yet they were momentarily stunned when their prey came to them like that. No one moved for a few seconds until Wayne said, "Okay, come on." And then the circus bolted toward them, shredding a beautifully manicured hedge and flower bed into tossed salad. "There goes the landscaping." Jimmy laughed.

Jimmy and Wayne said they had had good talks but more to work on. Like what?

"Jimmy has to agree to shave his head," Wayne said, and everyone laughed as the sunlight bounced off Wayne's bald dome and Jimmy's famous coif.

"That's a big hang-up," Jimmy said.

Actually, Jimmy confessed later, "Everything was ninety-nine percent decided. Obviously, either one of us could have slept on it and changed our minds."

But neither Jimmy nor Wayne wanted that. Wayne left in his black Mercedes. Jimmy went back upstairs, straight to work. He gathered all the assistant coaches together and told them he'd make some changes and talk to them individually no later than the Senior Bowl the following week.

Jimmy called Butch Davis again. "It went great," he said.

A little after 6 P.M., Jimmy headed to the Eden Roc hotel for the evening, his mind racing faster than his Corvette. He had a wish list of coaches, and he had to figure out what he was going to say to the staff and media and Marino and the rest of the players. As they drove along, Rhonda gushed about the neat helicopter ride and the kind secretary, and Jimmy reacted not a whit.

"Okay, I'll shut up now," she said, and smiled. She'd been spoiled for two years, living the easy life in the Keys, but now she'd lost him again, to that all-consuming mistress called football.

Four Eden Roc valets greeted them at the door. A cluster of fans applauded as Jimmy walked past. One rushed over, placed a hand on his shoulder, and said, "Super Bowl!"

The place was so crazy, security cordoned Jimmy, Rhonda, and Nick in a corner of the hotel's candlelight restaurant, where they had dinner and drinks with Father Leo Armbrust, Jimmy's past and future team priest, and Dr. John Cunio, who would become his diet doctor.

It was not the wild celebration you would suspect. Jimmy's friends flashed back to Jimmy's long hours and high stress as a coach, and fretted about him.

Finally, Nick asked, "Jimmy, is this something you really want to do?"

Jimmy turned and looked him in the eye.

"This is something I *have* to do," he said, and Nick could see the old determination and fire in his eyes.

Jimmy called his mom and told her he was taking the job. She told him to take it easy, and he replied, "You know I can't do that."

Nick called Edwin Pope and WQAM's Hank Goldberg, spoon-feeding the scoop and currying even more favor with the media members he considered the most important in South Florida. Ever the master media manipulator, Jimmy talked briefly with both and let Nick dismiss the rumors of $3 million–$4 million a year. Other media members eventually got the news that night, but from more distant sources with fewer details. Nobody got too angry. Jimmy was so smooth, so persuasive, that only the most cynical could suggest he'd been hatching this scheme with Wayne as far back as July 1994, before Wayne signed Shula to a contract extension.

"Truly," Jimmy said, "I had met Wayne once or twice, but nothing more than 'Hi, how ya doin'?' A year earlier, Nick and I thought we were dealing with someone speaking on Wayne's behalf, Hugh Culverhouse, Jr. [a lawyer whose father owned the Tampa Bay Buccaneers before his death in August 1994].

"Hugh Jr. talked to Nick and indicated he had talked to Huizenga and Huizenga had interest in me. Hugh Jr. said he also had interest in us going to Tampa. Nick had numerous visits with Hugh Jr. So that's when a lot of publicity came out that Huizenga had contacted me. As it turned out, I asked Wayne about this after our interview. He said he'd never talked to Hugh Culverhouse, Jr., about any kind of interest in me."

Thursday, January 11. Cyclone Jimmy returned to Davie at 8 A.M. He'd already met with the assistant coaches. Now he met with the support staff. He realized their tension, their fear. The day before, when Eddie Jones and Bernie Kosar were showing him around, Eddie introduced Anne Rodriguez as "Coach Shula's secretary." She got all flustered and nervous, and Bernie came up with a saving "Oh, she's everybody's secretary."

As Jimmy spoke Thursday morning, the beeper of Scott Chait, a young community relations assistant, went off. Cystic fibrosis was destroying Chait's lungs, simply breathing was a struggle, and if he did not get a lung transplant soon, he would die. He was high on the lung donor list, and the beeper was supposed to alert him when a suitable match was found so he could rush to the hospital for the operation. But when his beeper sounded, he was as petrified by the prospect of Jimmy ending his career as excited by the prospect of saving his life.

Chait turned off the beeper as fast as he could, and if Jimmy heard it, he chose to ignore it.

This time.

"I want you all to know I'm sensitive to the way you're feeling," Jimmy told the staffers. "A coach with a long tradition with this team has been replaced, and you're wondering about your jobs. I went through this same thing when Jerry Jones hired me to replace Tom Landry with the Dallas Cowboys. Jerry Jones said, 'This is just like Christmas.' Well, to a lot of people in that room, that was not Christmas!"

Jimmy promised no staffers would get fired.

"I don't know who you are now, but I will," he said. And he kept his word. For instance, Joe Curbelo had spent four years as the Dolphins' system analyst, and yet if Shula knew his name, he never showed it. If they passed each other in the hallway, Shula never gave more than a "Hey" or a harrumph, whereas Jimmy would always address him by name, even if it were just "Hey, Joe, how's it goin'?" The computer guru helped Jimmy and Rhonda with their laptop computers, and while Jimmy could be cold and ruthless, he thought it was important to show all Dolphins—players or not—he was interested enough to know their names. Jimmy tries to say something to all the people he cares about, every time he goes by them, to let them know he's thinking about them.

He especially wanted to let the Dolphins' biggest name know he was thinking about him. He called a team meeting for Friday morning, but first he wanted to talk with Marino privately. He told Dan he didn't want to fall into the trap of relying on the great passer too much. He explained his philosophy and said passing less would lead to championships for the team and a longer career for Marino. He was hoping for blind loyalty and seemed to get it. The most prolific passer in history said he'd set all the records already, and he didn't care if he threw ten times a game if it meant the Dolphins would win a championship.

And if Marino had balked?

Jimmy says he would have traded him.

Jimmy signed his contract and met the media at 4:30 P.M., the start delayed half an hour so the local stations could air Bill Clinton's live news conference about the national budget. When the president of the United States ran long, six local TV stations decided what was more important. They turned off Bill and turned on Jimmy.

Jimmy turned toward Rhonda. "We've had a nice vacation for two years. It's over now," he said. She already knew.

Jimmy told the media masses that the defense would emphasize zone coverages and zone blitzes, the offense would feature the I formation and a running game, and the dependence on Marino and high-priced free agents would be reduced. Jimmy said everyone would be evaluated, including players, coaches, and scouts.

Every move would be based on winning the Super Bowl as soon as possible. He dismissed the Dolphins' severe salary-cap bind, saying Dallas ranked in the top third in salaries when he got there and in the bottom fourth when he left. Among the reasons he chose the Dolphins over the Buccaneers, he said, were Marino's presence, Huizenga's commitment, and the talent level.

He said they did not need "a major overhaul at all. That was one of the big pluses of coming to the Miami Dolphins. I'll be very guarded to make it as little a transitional period as possible. There will be changes. That comes with the territory. I will try to make it a situation where it is not a rebuilding time."

A lot of people bought it. His former players did not.

"Shakedown," Dallas running back Emmitt Smith predicted. "Total shakedown."

"He's going to rebuild," Dallas guard Nate Newton said. "He's going to say he ain't, but watch that revolving door. You're going to think you're at Dillard's.

"I'll bet you two thousand dollars he'll rebuild. I know it's against the NFL rules to bet, but I bet you it won't be a veteran club after the second year. I got cash money on that. He won't have to clean house. Those guys will be trying to get out of there."

J. B. Brown was not trying to get out then. "I think it'll be a different attitude," the cornerback told reporters. "I don't think we'll have the type of problems we had last season. It won't be an 'I' thing."

Within months, J.B. would develop an "I" problem. He would be so desperate to get out, he would sell his house and move into an apartment.

Don Shula cleaned out his office the day Jimmy's interview was arranged. He left the state, even the time zone, the day Jimmy was announced as coach. He was going golfing in Arizona and Hawaii. He was getting as far away as possible from the scene of the crime.

Friday morning, January 12. The Miami Dolphins were less than two weeks into their winter vacation when their new coach called his first meeting. Jimmy gave one day's notice and started a minute or two early. Thirty-two players showed. Troy Vincent and Michael Stewart appeared as the first words tumbled from Jimmy's mouth.

And that is how long the vacation lasted.

"Hey," Jimmy said. "Everybody's got to understand: Once I start a meeting, don't ever, *ever* walk in that door. If you're ten seconds late, you stand outside the door until the meeting's over."

Then you will lose some money—and maybe your job.

Miami's message—and makeover—had just begun.

Jimmy delivered several messages that first day. Practices will be physical.

The main workdays of Wednesday, Thursday, and Friday will emphasize running and tackling with rapid-fire, all-out hitting. Everyone will not be treated the same; the hardest workers and best producers will earn special privileges. Those who do not work or produce will earn unemployment.

Bernie Parmalee's beeper went off. No more beepers, cell phones, or interruptions, Jimmy commanded. No more half-speed, two-hand-touch sessions. No more missing practice with nagging little pains. No more excuses about injuries or weather. No more bitching about contracts. No more lounging around your hometowns getting fat in the off-season.

I want to see you here, showing me you are working, showing me you are part of a team, when workouts begin March 1. The league says I cannot force you to be here, but I want you here. I want you in shape. When training camp starts, if you miss a workout in the weight room, it will cost you $1,250. When camp starts, you will be measured in sixteen 110-yard sprints.

Sound easy?

"After those drills, some guys can't breathe," Dallas fullback Daryl "Moose" Johnston said. "We called it the asthma field."

His advice to the Dolphins?

"Be fit," Moose said. "Be very fit."

Marino liked and respected Shula enough that he was careful not to trample on his feelings, but when asked if he thought he had a better chance to win the Super Bowl, he replied, "I'd like to think so. I thought coming into [1995] that we were going to be in the Super Bowl and have a chance to win it, and it didn't work out.

"But that's the past, so hopefully we can fulfill those expectations of winning a Super Bowl. That's all Jimmy wants to do, that's why he took the job, and that's what I want to do."

Ah, yes, the Super Bowl. The words were never far from Jimmy's mind . . . or hand. When he wanted to make an impression, Jimmy made sure everybody saw his Super Bowl ring.

Louis Oliver saw it and said, "I want one."

And Jimmy said, "That's why I'm here."

Oliver grinned. He had seethed under Shula.

"It's like a new breath of air. It's a new era," Oliver said. "Everybody's been waiting for JJ, and now he's finally here. As I drive up on I-95, I'm seeing all these cars with signs saying JJ FOR PRESIDENT and stuff like that. It's just exciting. I mean, you'd think President Clinton was inside, with all these cars and TV trucks out here."

The excitement wasn't just momentary, either. The 1996 Dolphins would sell seven thousand more season tickets than they had in 1995, surpassing sixty thousand for the first time since opening their opulent stadium in 1987. They would finish fifth in the league in attendance, and rarely would be heard a discouraging word. The entire season would be one long JJ love fest.

But even the best honeymoons don't last forever. History was filled with Super Bowl coaches who couldn't win it all elsewhere: Vince Lombardi, Forrest Gregg, Hank Stram, Tom Flores, Sam Wyche, Bill Walsh, and now Dan Reeves and Bill Parcells.

What could Jimmy Johnson do that they could not?

What could he do that Don Shula could not?

Could he turn Dan Marino into a Super Bowl champion for the first time?

Could he motivate a team that had too little discipline and too much selfishness?

Could he turn around the Dolphins the way he did the Cowboys?

Or would he be doomed without a Herschel Walker heist, buried by free agency and the salary cap, his magic reduced to myth?

All these questions confronted Jimmy in the months ahead. But when he left Davie Thursday with Rhonda, his only question was "Where do I get gas?"

When they stopped, somebody said, "It's Jimmy!" and instantly people began to encircle his Corvette. Finally, he had to get out and do a lap around the car to sign all the autographs.

Everyone was acting as if he were Jesus Christ reincarnated. Except for one man.

"Jeez, he's only human," the guy said. "He can't raise the dead. He can't heal the sick."

No, but he would try. He would try.

4
THE FIRE INSIDE

James William Johnson was born July 16, 1943, the second son of C. W. and Allene Johnson. C.W. toiled for the Gulf Oil refinery and later Townsend Dairy in Port Arthur, Texas, a hardscrabble port town on Sabine Lake, just off the Gulf of Mexico, just across the river from the Louisiana border. Jimmy grew up poor, staring at the sea, a siren beckoning him all the days of his life, granting him an almost mystical serenity as the perfect antidote for the fire that raged within.

He competed with his buddy Jimmy Maxfield, casting fifty-yard nets into the water and seeing how many crabs, sharks, stingrays, and whatever else they could dredge up. He played full-contact football on the grassy median in front of his home on DeQueen Boulevard, no pads, no helmets, crash-landing onto the curb and pavement so hard, so often, that "Max" called him "Scar Head" for all the cuts on his scalp. He competed to choose the best pickup baseball team, to excel in Little League, to outwrestle a brother three years his elder. Jimmy and Wayne imitated the leaps and dives and death grips of the fake wrestlers of the fifties.

"Only ours weren't fake moves," Jimmy said, grinning. "Back then, there was a wrestler who was always the bad guy by the name of Bull Curry. Wayne would always be the bad guy. I would be Ricki Starr, who was the crowd favorite, who supposedly had had ballet lessons, who did all these moves on the mat."

From such simple starts came a lifelong drive not just to compete, but to win. He earned all-state honors as a two-way lineman for Jefferson High, developing such a wicked forearm shiver he could put big dents in car doors. He won the 1964 national championship as a 195-pound defensive lineman for the University of Arkansas. Playing for a freshman coach named Barry Switzer and a varsity coach named Frank Broyles, and rooming on the road with a guard named

Jerry Jones, Jimmy was quick and nasty enough to make the Razorbacks' All-Decade team.

He majored in psychology because he enjoyed the classes—and because he could play cards or skip class if he wanted. Years later, he would conclude this spur-of-the-moment decision would make the difference between a good, solid Xs-and-Os coach and a Super Bowl coach. But even as he neared graduation, he was thinking about going to grad school and becoming an industrial psychologist, helping companies make employees more efficient and motivated. Then Louisiana Tech offered a three-month coaching assignment. He had no intentions of making coaching a lifelong career, but he had a wife and a baby, and they sure could use the money, and he could always start grad school a semester late.

Jimmy Johnson never went to grad school. In three months, he got so hooked on coaching and competing, he was willing to coach in the worst place on earth. Which is just about what he did next: He became an assistant high school coach in Picayune, Mississippi.

He was there half a year before Switzer called and said his buddy Larry Lacewell had become Wichita State's defensive coordinator and was looking for a young, cheap defensive line coach. Jimmy jumped . . . for $6,000 a year. Jimmy, Barry, and Larry would be linked for thirty years.

The U-Haul life had just begun. Jimmy and "Lace" joined Johnny Majors's Iowa State staff in 1968, and when Lace left for Oklahoma in '69, Jimmy became defensive coordinator and hired Jackie Sherrill in his spot. The next year, Barry and Larry convinced Oklahoma coach Chuck Fairbanks to hire Jimmy. But when Fairbanks left in 1973, Jimmy split to become defensive coordinator at his alma mater. When Broyles retired in 1977 and hired Lou Holtz instead of Jimmy, Jimmy bolted to become Sherrill's assistant head coach and defensive coordinator at the University of Pittsburgh.

He was developing a reputation for the same smart, attacking style and vicious competitiveness he had displayed as a player. Why, even when the coaches were supposed to be having fun at an ice-skating party, he was still competing. The Texas kid who had never skated in his life took lessons for three or four days, and looked like Dick Button compared to his peers.

When he played racquetball, he got all red in the face and literally bounced off walls. "You can't turn competitiveness on and off," Jimmy reasoned. "Even at shuffleboard and ice skating, I wanted to win and was willing to work to get there."

When Oklahoma State sought a coach in 1979, his old road roommate Jerry Jones recommended Jimmy. Initially, Jimmy was not interested. Oklahoma State was a perennial Big Eight doormat competing against perennial national powers Oklahoma and Nebraska, the program was on probation, another NCAA investigation had begun, and the Cowboys had just fifty-five scholarships instead of ninety-five.

But Jimmy liked nothing better than a challenge, and he cajoled seven victories out of the 1979 Cowboys and was voted Big Eight Coach of the Year. They were struggling through a 3–7–1 record the next year when Jimmy took his best coaching buddies, Dave Wannstedt and Tony Wise, to a Stillwater watering hole called the Ancestor Inn. To drink beer, most certainly, but not to drown their sorrows in the brew. For a pep speech.

"We'd been winning national championships at Pitt, and now we'd been hit on the head pretty good," Wannstedt remembered. "Jimmy looked at us and said, determined as ever, 'We've got the plan. If we stick together, if we stay committed, and work this thing through, we'll win a national championship some day. If we go to the pros some day, we'll win a Super Bowl.' "

Oklahoma State had never even won a conference championship outright, let alone a national championship.

"There wasn't a guy at the table who doubted him," Wannstedt said. "Heck, we may have just gotten beat by West Texas the week before. It wasn't like we'd just trounced Nebraska. But there was just that confidence that hey, it *will* happen."

Wannstedt laughed. "Now, it didn't happen at Oklahoma State," he said, "but Jimmy reminded me of that night when we won the national championship at the University of Miami."

They won seven games in '81 and eight in '83, and they recruited Thurman Thomas and had a chance to do more in '84, but Oklahoma State was never going to win a national championship, and that's what Jimmy wanted. Not to be the underdog, but the top dog, the very best.

Howard Schnellenberger had rescued the University of Miami football program from being disbanded, had turned nonexistent crowds into Orange Bowl bedlam, and had won the 1983 national championship. But when he resigned to coach in the United States Football League, Jimmy's coaches and friends asked aloud, "Who in the world would want to take that job?" UM's top players were graduating, Miami was a crime-infested city, and it would be impossible to follow Schnellenberger's legend.

Another challenge. Jimmy wanted to prove he could succeed a legend. He wanted to prove he could win a national title. He hated landlocked small towns and cold weather; he wanted the big city and the beach and the heat. Miami was perfect. Except for one thing. It was June, and Jimmy would have to keep every Schnellenberger assistant who wanted to stay. That caveat almost killed the deal, but Lace convinced Jimmy to go. Three assistants had been contenders for the head coaching job, and they resented losing their dream to some backwater hick.

Jimmy lost five games that year with a seething, splintered staff and vowed never to let that happen again. The next year, he brought in "his guys"—and they went 44–4 the next four years. They turned a short-term winner into a perennial powerhouse while Schnellenberger's new league folded and his Louisville and Oklahoma programs foundered. The Hurricanes lost two games by a combined five points Jimmy's final three years, or they might have gone 36–0 and won three national championships in a row. But his most talented team lost a championship—when a flustered Vinny Testaverde threw five interceptions against Penn State in the Fiesta Bowl.

Ask Jimmy where his raging desire came from, and he cites his Port Arthur competitions—and his Fiesta Bowl loss thirty years later.

"It wasn't so much getting out of Port Arthur as getting beyond Port Arthur," he said. "It's just an attitude that I want to see and do things that are pleasurable, that give me pleasure above and beyond. When I had a thirty-foot boat, I wanted a forty-foot boat. When I got a forty-foot boat, I wanted a forty-eight-foot boat.

"I was always involved in some kind of competition. The real crowning blow was when we had the first undefeated team in University of Miami history and what I felt like was the most talented team in college football, not only that year but probably most years. Not only did we lose the game to Penn State—in a game where we had about 450 yards and they had about 150, with one first down the second half—but I was severely raked over the coals for a full year because of the perceived misconduct when our players wore fatigues and walked out of a steak-fry dinner after the other team had made some racist comments.

"I mean, to this day, my biggest disappointment in football has always been that one game. And as glorious a year as it could have been, as much as we achieved that year, being 11–0 in the regular season, the year was absolutely misery because we lost the bowl game. And that in itself instilled in me that I didn't want to be just good, I had to be the best."

The following year, he was the best, a perfect 12–0. And then after going 11–1 in 1988, it was time for an even bigger challenge, time to follow an even bigger legend.

He replaced America's Coach on America's Team.

Some would view this as a burden. Jimmy saw only challenge.

"Is this what you really want to do?" his wife asked.

"It's not a matter of what I want to do," he replied. "It's what I *have* to do."

The skeptics said how dare the Dallas Cowboys replace the legendary Landry with this college coach? Jimmy was compared to a cockroach and a vulture "waiting for the body to quit twitching." His parents got harassing phone calls. And when he traded his only star, Herschel Walker, and called it "The Great Train Robbery," one Dallas columnist complained that the "Cowboys got nothing more than a handful of Minnesota smoke" while another wrote they got "five players named Joe and an assortment of draft choices." Even two assistant coaches hated the trade.

But that trade—coupled with what Jimmy parlayed from it—made Dallas a dynasty. Dallas got a first-round pick, five players, and six conditional picks in the first three rounds. Jimmy chose the picks over the players, and, after a lot of convoluted wheeling and dealing, wound up drafting Emmitt Smith, Kevin Smith, Russell Maryland, and Darren Woodson, among others.

He inherited a pathetically old, slow, and overpaid team. Ed "Too Tall" Jones, Randy White, Danny White, Everson Walls, and Michael Downs were Texas legends, but they were washed up. The Cowboys were so short on talent, they held auditions every week, and often, castoffs who didn't know the Cowboys' system were better than the incumbents.

"We'd bring players in on Tuesday and work 'em out and if they looked or sounded like they were better than what we had, we signed 'em and coached 'em up Wednesday, Thursday, and Friday, got 'em ready on Saturday, and played 'em on Sunday," Wannstedt said. "I mean, it was a true nightmare."

A 1–15 nightmare. Nobody took the losses harder, yet Jimmy kept stoking his coaches. At one of their near weekly drinking runs at Bennigan's, Jimmy reminded them of his previous vow.

"He reflected back on that night at Oklahoma State and said it shouldn't be any different now: If we stick to the plan and get good people and keep determined, then one day we'll win the Super Bowl," Wannstedt said. "Three years later, it happened."

Winning was Jimmy's single-minded obsession. He divorced his wife of twenty-six years, partly to avoid the distraction of family life and chit-chatting with coaches' wives. Losing was an affront to his ego, to all his effort. He took losses harder than his divorce. Long before Bill Clinton said he could feel your pain, Jimmy demanded his players to feel *his* pain. A loss—or even sloppy performance—could send him into the blind rage of a lunatic's mental breakdown.

The most famous episode came after a 1992 loss at Washington, when an incomplete pass was erroneously ruled an Aikman fumble and the Redskins returned it for the winning touchdown. The loss prevented Jimmy's Cowboys from winning their first NFC East title, and that was stewing in his gut along with maybe ten Heinekens on the flight home when, the plane grounded maybe half an hour by weather problems, he demanded the pilots "get this fuckin' plane off the ground." He thought he heard someone chuckle. He got up, found offensive coordinator Norv Turner standing in the aisle, and ordered him to sit down. He stormed back to the players' section of the plane and reamed out three backup players. He cussed his coaches. He forced the flight attendants to quit serving dinner.

"He was upset. We were all upset," recalled Turner, now the Redskins' coach. "Jimmy has a stronger way of showing when he's upset. He feels if someone sees him not being hurt, not being upset, then it's easier for them not to be upset. He made sure everyone understood, 'Don't be satisfied. It doesn't matter how well you played, we lost the game. You might have had a great game, but you might have done something on one other play to help us win.' "

Did that attitude carry over to greater success?

"Absolutely," Norv answered. "If you lose and guys slough it off, if it quits hurting and you start accepting losing, then at some point in any game, you're willing to accept defeat. And that's wrong. If it hurts and you're miserable, you're gonna do everything you can to make sure you win the next one. No question it helps you get focused."

The next week, the Cowboys trounced Atlanta, 41–17, and won the division title, but Jimmy still seethed about sloppy play late in the game. And the final regular-season game, he blew up again when, ahead 27–0 and all the scrubs in, Curvin Richards fumbled twice and the Bears closed to 27–14 in the final minutes. The next day, he cut Richards, a flashy fourth-round pick and his only backup halfback.

He wanted to send a message to his players. "When we get into the playoffs, you get no second chances," Jimmy told them. "I didn't want to go into the playoffs with a guy I couldn't depend on and you couldn't depend on." The players grumbled among themselves. Has Jimmy gone mad? We're 13–3. What does he expect? Perfection?

Yes.

"The success came so fast at Dallas," Wannstedt said. "One year you're winning one game, and three years later you're making a run for the Super Bowl. It would have been very easy for human nature to take over and the players, coaches, and owners to be patting themselves on the back, to be toasting and saying, 'This was good. We got into the playoffs this year.' That's where Jimmy's experience and drive kicked in for the league's youngest team. He wasn't happy just to get to the playoffs or the championship game. He wanted the ring."

He got it. They all got it, except Curvin Richards. The Cowboys committed just one turnover in the postseason until the final moments of Super Bowl XXVII. The Buffalo Bills committed a record nine turnovers.

Dallas 52, Buffalo 17.

It was human nature to get complacent, so Jimmy worked the Cowboys harder than ever in 1993, and they demolished San Francisco for the NFC title and a rematch with the Bills.

Before the team flew to the Super Bowl, each player was handed his ticket allotment. Backup defensive tackle Chad Hennings, the nicest, straightest guy on the team, set his tickets on a table, walked away to do something, came back—and his tickets were gone. The Cowboys landed in Atlanta Monday, and Jimmy told them they had the night off and they could get the partying out of their system because they would have no curfew that night. But they did have to catch a team bus at six-thirty the next morning to attend Media Day interviews. Then it was No More Mr. Nice Guy:

"Chad Hennings's sixteen tickets are missing," Jimmy told the Cowboys. "Only teammates were in the room at the time they disappeared. I want those tickets in my hands by six A.M. tomorrow, before we get on the bus. I don't care who you are, I want them in the hands of Ben Mix [Dallas's security chief] and then ultimately in my hands."

Jimmy's voice grew loud, and he bit off each word.

"No questions will be asked if you return them. But if you don't, Ben and the league and I will use every bit of security to find out who did it. When I find out, I'll do everything in my power to make sure you *never* play for this team *or any team in this league*. So help me God."

Jimmy had the tickets in his hands at 6 A.M., and he bragged to everybody, "Hey, look—I got the tickets." Half an hour later, his mood soured. Just about every player had gone out the night before, and a few had gotten totally wasted. When six-thirty came, four players were late for the bus, and Jimmy was steamed.

"Fuck it! Let's go! Send the buses!" he commanded, and sent trainer Kevin O'Neill and director of operations Bruce Mays to roust the laggards while Jimmy waited outside.

O'Neill returned and said, "Coach, Erik Williams must have just gotten in. He's still got his clothes on, he's laying facedown, and you couldn't get him off that bed with a crane."

The three other Cowboys caught cabs and made it to Media Day. Williams, a shy guy who broke into a cold sweat whenever he faced the media anyway, skipped the session and was fined $10,000 by the league. Jimmy turned the distraction into "an excuse to talk to the players that night."

He asked the players who had won Super Bowl rings the year before to raise their hands. Then he asked which newcomers had never won a Super Bowl ring. Bernie Kosar, Eddie Murray, Matt Vanderbeek, and a few young backups raised their hands.

"Okay," Jimmy said, "hands down. Bernie Kosar, we just got you here. How long you been in this league?"

"Ten years, Coach," Bernie said.

"Ever been to the Super Bowl?" Jimmy asked.

"No, sir," Bernie said.

"Ever been close?"

"We made it to three AFC championship games, and they beat us, and we never made it. But we came close," Bernie said.

"Is it *special* to you?" Jimmy asked.

"Coach," Bernie said, "it's a dream."

"Eddie Murray," Jimmy called out. "All those great years kicking with Detroit. Ever made the Super Bowl?"

"No, sir," Eddie said.

"Ever come close?" Jimmy asked.

"Not even a sniff," Eddie answered.

"Kinda special, isn't it?" Jimmy said.

He pointed to Matt Vanderbeek, a kamikaze cover guy who had never even made the playoffs in his three years in Indianapolis.

"How many of you guys like watching Matt Vanderbeek run down on kickoffs?" Jimmy asked his players, and every single one raised his hand.

"All of you guys who were here last year got a ring," Jimmy said. "Think back to a year ago, how good you felt when you achieved something you always dreamed about. Now, you're not playing for just yourself. You're playing for these guys who haven't won. If you're gonna go out, go out, but take some responsibility. If you cut it short, if you don't give every effort you've got, then you're cheating a lot of people.

"Just imagine how you'd feel a month from now if for a few hours of hee-hee haw-haw, you threw away something that would be special to you for a *lifetime*! We're here for ourselves, for selfish reasons, but we're here to win for these guys, too. We're here for your mama and daddy."

Then he wrapped Erik Williams in a headlock, and the players laughed. But the rest of the week, they stopped partying and started focusing.

Dallas 30, Buffalo 13.

Jimmy had basked in the glow of a ticker-tape parade. He had reveled as the biggest names in sports applauded as he accepted an ESPY as the best coach or manager in all of sports. He had gone to the White House and shaken hands with the president of the United States after one NCAA and two NFL championships.

He had lost a Port Arthur girl because her parents didn't think he was good enough. Now Port Arthur named a boulevard after him. The skeptics had said he could not follow Schnellenberger and Landry. He not only succeeded them, he did better.

But once he had done all that, what more was left? He could not work himself into a frenzy again. He had never lasted more than five years at any one place, and he was bored. His battles with Jerry Jones were getting more frequent and more heated, and neither ego could take it any longer. And he was burned out.

"It doesn't matter if it's coaching, if you're out having a couple of beers, or if you're out on his boat, he's gonna do everything a hundred miles an hour, full speed," Norv Turner said.

Washington's Joe Gibbs worked even longer hours during the season, then took a break while his personnel department handled all the scouting. But Jimmy had to be out on the road, scouting, scheming, grinding. It took its toll.

"He keeps his hand involved in everything," Wannstedt said. "That gives him a lesser chance to make an error. But maybe that's why he hasn't been any one place more than four or five years. I don't know how long you can do that before it truly just wears you out. That's what happened in Dallas. That's a shame. Because you should be able to get it in place and use that old biblical verse of reap what you sow.

"For Jimmy, it was a twelve-month-a-year, seven-day-a-week job. Some guys can walk away from it for two or three months and come back and be ready to go. It was only until the last year or two in Dallas before he'd even consider taking a vacation. He would get away at times, but he had very few hobbies and very few places he liked to go other than the sunshine in Florida."

Relaxing on Jimmy's boat after that second Super Bowl victory, Wannstedt noticed the difference. "I knew that the flame wasn't burning like I had seen it."

Two months after Super Bowl XXVIII, Jimmy and Jerry agreed to separate. Jerry gave him a $2 million parting gift. HBO and Fox gave him hundreds of thousands more to work two or three days a week during football season. Corporations gave him $30,000 to $40,000 for half-hour speeches.

Jimmy had money and time to enjoy himself. He could wake up whenever he wanted and his toughest decision was choosing what he wanted to do that day. Take his yacht *Three Rings* to the Bahamas? Up the Intracoastal? Go fishing or just sightseeing? Sunbathing or snorkeling? Ride the waves on his Jet Ski? Or just stay home and crank up his killer sound system? Watch a laser disc or a boxing match on his big-screen TV? Play computer games? Stare at the ocean or the tropical fish and real, live coral in his many aquariums? Lounge by the pool and pound down a few Heinekens?

It was the good life that most of us dream about.

"It was the first time in his life he ever had a good time," his son Brent said. "He was joking around, laughing, not in a rush. What could be wrong?"

"It was too easy," Wannstedt said.

Jimmy discovered he was addicted. His drug of choice was not so much Heineken as adrenaline. After two years of semiretirement, he craved another fix. C.W. and Allene didn't want to see him go through all that stress and frustration. Allene was afraid he'd have a heart attack some day. Rhonda was afraid she'd rarely see him. But it was like he'd told his wife in 1989. He did not just want to coach, he needed it.

Why coach when losing tears you up so much? If you are only happy when you win it all, why bet against thirty-to-one odds every year?

"If you're not challenged, the inactivity causes depression," Jimmy said. "The lack of achievement and challenge, you lose a lot of things. You lose drive. You lose pride. You get to the attitude that you don't care anymore.

"So I think we have to continually challenge ourselves. And that's one reason why, after you win a national championship, you challenge yourself to be a successful pro coach. You go out and win a Super Bowl and that's not a challenge anymore. Then you're successful in television and you've got plenty of money and it's not a challenge to go out there and catch a bunch of fish.

"So you accept a challenge that most people say you can't do, that a lot of them don't *want* you to accomplish. I'm not necessarily talking about people in football. I'm talking about people working eight to five, fifty hours a week down at the mill. A high majority of people enjoy hearing about other people's failures and misery more than they want to hear about the success story because it makes their life bearable."

This was not a decision made lightly. In those two years off, Jimmy spent a lot of time reflecting on what he wanted out of life. He still does. A copy of his favorite book, *Flow*, by University of Chicago psychology professor Mihaly Csikszentmihalyi, rests on top of his desk, the only book in a spotless office. It is as difficult to read as Mihaly Csikszentmihalyi is to pronounce. But ever since Jimmy first read it in 1992, *Flow* has had a profound influence on the old psychology graduate. Csikszentmihalyi says "flow," which he defines as "optimal experience" and what we laymen usually define as true happiness, comes when people are so involved in an activity that nothing else seems to matter.

In *Flow*, Jimmy found ways to motivate his players. In *Flow*, he found why he needed to coach again and why so many millionaires and retirees reached their goals, only to discover they were unfulfilled.

They need passion.

"*Flow* talks about the difference between pleasure and being truly happy," Jimmy explained. "Certain things bring you pleasure, but they don't make you happy. A good meal is pleasurable, but it doesn't make you happy. So I can experience some pleasurable things, but to be happy, I've got to be challenged, I've got to accomplish things, I've got to have some sense of satisfaction and achievement."

He needed the highs and, yes, even the lows, of coaching.

"And I guess the other thing is, a lot of people have a high opinion of my abilities. To them and to myself, I want to prove my accomplishments were no fluke." He chose Miami even though Tampa Bay offered more money, salary-cap room, good youngsters, and draft choices. Tampa offered sun and water, too. But it also offered less stable ownership, one that was negotiating to move to California while talking with Jimmy. Its quarterback was Trent Dilfer, not Dan Marino, and Jimmy didn't know if he could ever win with Dilfer, let alone as fast and as much as he wanted to win.

"Miami has such great memories for me, the success at the University of Miami. I love the year-round weather. Other places have warm weather but they also have cold weather, and I *don't* like cold weather. And when in your mind you've got the best, why search for something else? In my mind, I set it up to where I enjoyed things so much that I wasn't going to live anywhere else but here."

And if the Miami job had not come open in 1996, would the urge to coach have been so great that he would have gone to Tampa or somewhere else?

"It's hard to say what you would or wouldn't have done. Because of my affection for Miami and South Florida, I don't think I would have said yes to anybody other than Miami. I would have redirected and tried to become the best football analyst. I was nominated for an Emmy. I was a finalist for the cable Ace awards for the HBO show. But I didn't *win* either one of them."

And Jimmy Johnson *needs* to win.

"I don't know if I ever would have been happy with myself if I had turned this job down. I'm at home. I won't coach forever, but I think I'll live here forever.

"I've got to win it again. It's the only reason I came back. If we win it all, then Miami is the dream job everybody seems to think it is for me. If we don't, then it's a nightmare. And a mistake."

5
OFF-SEASON?
NOT EXACTLY

Jimmy began assembling his Dolphins staff even before he was named coach. To the fans, they were anonymous names. To Jimmy, they were indispensable to victory and sanity. What did he demand from them? "You've got to like Mexican food," Dave Wannstedt said. A love of salsa, chips, and beer did help, but more than that, Wannstedt added, "He demands a loyalty to himself number one, a loyalty to the job and the game."

Loyalty. Interesting word to choose. When asked the difference between Jimmy and Barry Switzer, Jerry Jones had said, "Barry is loyal down to his toes. Jimmy doesn't know the meaning of the word."

When he heard that, Miami's director of football operations, Bob Ackles, shook his head. "Disloyal?" Jimmy's right hand said. "That's the last thing Jimmy is." Barry was so loyal, he slept with his best friend's wife.

Some coaches hired cronies whether they could coach or not. Example: Rich Kotite. Result: Jets 4–28. Jimmy hired people he could count upon to teach, communicate, work hard, and above all instill his philosophy. They could be brilliant coaches, but if they did not share his beliefs, they flirted with disaster.

Jimmy had been there. In his 1993 autobiography, Jimmy wrote that the worst year of his coaching life came his first year at the University of Miami, where he was forced to keep his predecessor's assistants. Three of them had interviewed for the job—including defensive coordinator Tom Olivadotti and offensive coordinator Gary Stevens—and they resented Jimmy for getting it. This was how he described that first staff meeting in *Turning the Thing Around*:

> The whole time I was talking, Olivadotti was sitting there with a set of keys in his hand, continually dropping the keys on the table, picking them

up, and dropping them. Picking them up . . . And dropping them . . . picking them up . . . and dropping them. Clink . . . clink . . . clink . . . clink . . . as he, and every other coach, just sat there, staring down at the table . . .

Finally, Olivadotti spoke up and said, "I've seen your teams play, and I really don't think our philosophies could coexist. I can't coach defense the way your teams play defense." He picked out a game where we'd played poorly and been upset a couple of years before by a weak opponent, and threw it in my face. He said, "I saw the film of that game, and your teams don't play the way we want to play."

He might as well have said, "I think you're a horseshit coach from out on the range, with cowshit stuck to your boots, and I just got through coaching a national championship defense in the big time in a big town. And how you got this job over me, I have not the slightest clue."

And some guys in my shoes might have just lost it then and there and said, "Look, asshole: the Selmon brothers were making All-America in an upfield-pressure defense at Oklahoma while you were coaching at some place called Salesianum Prep School in fucking *Delaware*. Did you ever happen to wonder who might have thought up the Oklahoma upfield-pressure defense that got the football world's attention, all the way to Salesianum Prep School in fucking *Delaware*?"

Olivadotti took his salary and sat out the season, but enough hostilities and disparate philosophies remained that it made for an 8–5 record and downright misery, and Jimmy vowed to never again work with a staff that did not bond.

Now, in a strange twist, Jimmy was returning to coach Miami—and inheriting Olivadotti and Stevens again.

Olivadotti's Dolphins defenses had finished in the top ten in total defense just twice in nine years, and South Florida—not to mention a few Dolphins and Bills and one Dolphins owner—blamed Coach Uh-O.

Hello, Jimmy. Uh-oh, Uh-O. Good-bye, Uh-O.

Stevens had wound up working well with Jimmy at the University of Miami, but when Jimmy went to Dallas, he instead hired David Shula to run his offense and incorporate some of the famous Shula passing game. But the Cowboys' offense struggled, and David did not gel with Troy Aikman. Jimmy called Don to tell him things weren't working out and he wanted to demote David to receivers coach and hire a new offensive coordinator/quarterback coach. The Shulas were incensed. David left to coach the Bengals' receivers (and later was hired and fired as head coach). Jimmy offered his coordinator's job to Stevens, who accepted, only to renege the next day after talking with Shula. Now it was Jimmy's turn to be furious, and he barely spoke to Stevens for the next five years. Stevens was "one of three men I have written off in my life, all for failing to be men of their word," Jimmy wrote. "That was the end of my relationship with Gary Stevens . . . and that's the way it will always be."

Never say never. "I ran into Gary in the Bahamas, and Gary made some overtures to patch things up, and so you might say he broke the ice," Jimmy said. "Then Gary called a time or two when I was at Fox TV. Gary probably realized I could help him down the road. He mentioned he wanted to come and have a beer and one time [in the summer of '95] he drove down to the Keys and we had a few beers and pretty well patched up our relationship. I knew he realized he'd made a big mistake. Him knowing he'd screwed up, without me telling him, was sufficient enough for me to let the past be past. He stayed at Miami because he thought he'd get a head coaching job, but after that decision, I had three leave my staff to become head coaches and no one left the Dolphins."

So the Wednesday he interviewed with Wayne Huizenga, Jimmy spent a good bit of the afternoon with Gary, and the next morning, Dan Marino lobbied to keep Gary. Jimmy decided he had a veteran quarterback and offense that had performed well, and he would keep the offensive scheme and coordinator. By the following week at the Senior Bowl, Jimmy and Gary seemed joined at the hip, conferring as they watched practices during the day, joshing as they drank in the hotel bar at night.

Jimmy decided some coaches—and players—deserved second chances. "At one time, Gary Stevens was written out of my life, and now he's my offensive coordinator," he said a few months later. "I was mad at him because he jilted me. No one likes to be jilted. Now he's my confidante. He's my buddy."

He went looking for more buddies. Ackles had been one of the few front-office gurus to survive the purge when Jimmy and Jerry arrived in Dallas in 1989, and Jimmy wasn't happy when Jerry fired Bob as the Cowboys' personnel director in 1992 because Jerry wanted the job for himself and his twenty-something son, Stephen. Jimmy stayed in touch with Bob, called Philadelphia owner Jeffrey Lurie and recommended him highly, and when the Tampa and Miami jobs came open, Jimmy asked Bob to follow him wherever he went. The day he accepted the Miami job, he called Lurie to ask permission to hire Ackles to be his director of football operations. Lurie wanted compensation but eventually agreed.

Eddie Jones runs the business end as team president, Jimmy handles all football decisions as coach and general manager, and Ackles serves as his second in command, grinding away on the films and phones, overseeing personnel, contracts, and even the equipment and video departments. Kevin O'Neill, another Jimmy buddy from the UM and Dallas days, came in to reduce the number of games and practices missed because of injuries. Probably the NFL's most influential trainer, he treats injured players and oversees other administrative areas, and he has taken Wannstedt's place as Jimmy's jogging partner. A lot transpires on those jogs because Jimmy values Kevin's opinions on the players' mental and physical state. The trainers spend a lot of time with the players, and the players know Kevin is Jimmy's confidante, so a lot of messages are sent back and forth through the trainer.

When he still was debating between Tampa and Miami, Jimmy also called Bill Lewis, his secondary coach and next-door neighbor at Arkansas in the mid-seventies. Their sons were nearly the same age, and the families and fathers did a lot together, including late-night frog-gigging forays, with Jimmy chest-deep in the water spearing frogs and Lewis in the boat looking for water moccasins. Jimmy tried to hire him twice before but Lewis regretfully declined. "Well, maybe some day," Jimmy said.

Some day came seven years later when Jimmy asked if Lewis would join him with the Bucs or Dolphins. "This time, yes," Lewis said.

Pat Jones had coached with Jimmy and Bill at Arkansas, and again with Jimmy at Pitt and Oklahoma State. He had succeeded Jimmy as OSU's head coach and stayed eleven years, but he was looking for a job when Jimmy called the night he joined Miami. Jones canceled plans to go to the Hula Bowl and joined Jimmy at the Senior Bowl.

Before Jimmy could complete his staff, he had to fulfill his obligations to Fox. After his first meeting with his players, he left Friday for, of all places, Dallas, which was hosting the NFC championship game. He shook hands and congratulated Jerry Jones. Was Jimmy trying to make up—or steal Jerry's spotlight? Was Jerry interested in détente—or proving he could win without Jimmy? Both had their suspicions; the greeting lasted only seconds.

Jimmy flew to Miami Sunday night and to Mobile Monday morning on the team plane with the incumbent assistant coaches and scouts. The same day, he told Olivadotti and another Shula loyalist, Monte Clark, to use the trip as a chance to look for new jobs. He fired Mean Joe Greene and Tony Nathan on the practice field in front of hundreds of their peers, who grumbled about Jimmy's cruelty. He hired six new coaches and retained eight.

But he was struggling to find two key coaches.

He couldn't hire his two former Dallas defensive coordinators, Dave Wannstedt and Butch Davis, because they were head coaches now. He knew Art Modell planned to fire Bill Belichick, and he talked to Belichick about philosophy, but it took Modell a month to can Belichick, who opted for his old boss, Bill Parcells. Jimmy settled for promoting linebacker coach George Hill to defensive coordinator.

The most vital hire, though, was an aggressive line coach who could teach a finesse line how to get physical, and after Jimmy's efforts to hire the Raiders' Joe Bugel and the Cowboys' Hudson Houck were rebuffed, he settled for the Oilers' Larry Beightol.

Jimmy flew to Phoenix and set yet another Super Bowl record: 200 media people attended a Super Bowl press conference for a coach whose team wasn't playing in the Super Bowl. Or were those Jimmy's Cowboys out there? "Well, the guys winning the games haven't changed since I left. Maybe the ones chasing down the kickoffs have, but . . ." Jimmy said, and smiled. Jerry and Barry screamed vindication: Dallas was winning without Jimmy.

Next the new coach/general manager turned to personnel. Counting the minimal salaries due to transition players Troy Vincent and Marco Coleman, he was $5 million over the 1996 salary cap—and that didn't count a batch of key unsigned players. When Vincent (five years, $16.5 million), Coleman (three years, $9.6 million), and Bryan Cox (four years, $13.2 million) got enormous offers from Philadelphia, San Diego, and Chicago, respectively, Jimmy decided he could not keep any of them. He tried to move money around to keep Vincent, and maybe if he had shown interest sooner, Vincent would have stayed. Too late.

The returning coaches didn't think Irving Fryar had had a good season, Fryar would turn thirty-four in 1996, and a study by a scouting service the Dolphins used showed almost every wide receiver's production fell off or was nonexistent at that age, so they let him sign with Philadelphia. Jimmy spent his wide receiver money instead on Philadelphia veteran Fred Barnett and Green Bay speedster Charles Jordan. He signed cheap free agents Daniel Stubbs, Robert Bailey, Mike Buck, and Cal Dixon. He re-signed Keith Sims when Sims found the big free agent money went to tackles, not guards.

And then he started asking many of his overpaid players to take pay cuts. He asked Keith Byars to take a $992,000 cut to $500,000. Byars balked. Jimmy cut him. Byars shopped around the NFL and discovered nobody else thought he was worth big money, either. Jimmy re-signed him . . . for $200,000 less than his original offer. Another starter, Chuck Klingbeil, wouldn't take a pay cut and took the ultimate cut. Nobody signed him. Other guys got the hint. Terrell Buckley, J. B. Brown, Steve Emtman, Gene Atkins, Michael Stewart, Louis Oliver, and a few no-names accepted big pay cuts.

When the rest of the league's coaches, GMs, and owners flew in for the annual March meetings at the opulent Breakers Hotel in ritzy Palm Beach, Jimmy couldn't resist cruising up the Intracoastal in his new forty-eight-foot version of *Three Rings*, and just in case anybody didn't see it or hear about it, why, lookee here: He just happened to have this big blown-up photo. Some people show off baby pictures; Jimmy shows off boat pictures. He stood in the lobby, Rhonda by his side, attracting reporters as if he were magnetized, and loving it all.

At these same meetings two years earlier in Orlando, Jimmy and Jerry had gotten into their famed late-night spat that led to their divorce. Now Jimmy was back, reveling in the attention. When all the coaches gathered at big round tables for interviews, the biggest horde of reporters swarmed to Jimmy, almost elbowing Jacksonville coach Tom Coughlin out of his chair. Nobody knew Coughlin would be the Sunshine State coach taking his club to the AFC championship game.

When *Dallas Morning News* reporter Ed Werder asked who was the team to beat in the AFC this year, Jimmy said, "I want our guys to have the attitude that we are the team to beat. So if you write for *The Dallas Morning News*, you can tell Dallas we are the team to beat."

He wanted Jerry and Barry and all the 'Boys to read that.

Hell, maybe they heard it. Behind Jimmy's back, Barry sat at a table kitty-corner from Jimmy. Jimmy had won over the doubting Dallas media; Barry had not. After Werder sat at Barry's table, Barry's eyes narrowed, his brow wrinkled, and his answers wore icicles. I asked if winning the Super Bowl had quelled the critics and allowed him to celebrate.

"It was a relief," Barry said. "That's all it was. I felt tremendous pressure for Jerry, and obviously myself, too, but I wanted to win it for Jerry and our organization and players because of the confidence he showed in me. You don't get to enjoy it. That night, maybe. But the next day, everybody says, 'Let's do it again.' I've had close friends say, 'Why subject yourself to all this pressure and abuse?' I do it because I enjoy it."

He didn't sound as if he enjoyed it. He complained about free agent defectors and his frosty relations with Dallas's quarterback and press. "The only part I don't like is dealing with the media," Barry said. "That's constant pressure."

Where Barry saw pressure, Jimmy saw a pulpit.

The Gospel of Jimmy would be printed in newspapers and magazines across the land, read by fans, foes, and friends alike.

And so he preached about practice habits. Eric Green, the high-priced, low-production tight end, missed thirty-nine practices in 1995. He wasn't alone.

"We had players miss as many as twenty, thirty, forty practices," Jimmy huffed. "I was astonished by the numbers. When you consider there are three main practices a week, that's missing thirteen weeks of practice. If you miss thirteen weeks, you're not going to get a whole lot better. I made a book with a history of every single player: I've got my notes, the trainer's notes, the strength coach's notes, the previous coach's notes. I'm keeping a record, and the guys who've continually slacked off, who've continually had problems, that's a red flag for me not to put up with this mess."

Another message: Everyone will be treated differently. "If Troy Aikman was late to a meeting, I'd probably say, 'Troy, come in.' But if it was a backup guard who'd been late before and didn't play very well, I'd say, 'Hey, you're cut.' If they're good players and work their ass off and set an example, I'll be very enjoyable to work for. If they don't play hard and they don't play good, they better not make a mistake because they're out the door."

Another message: The Fish will learn to run. "It's going to be a thing where I say, 'I'm the head coach and we *will* run the ball,' " he said. "You've got to have the people, but it's also an attitude. Sometimes it's just being stubborn. It's a total commitment to physical training."

But not a total overhaul of the offense. "The thing I was conscious of was Dan Marino is going to have two, three, optimistically four more years," Jimmy said. "It would have been a tragedy for me to completely restructure the offense with a bunch of new players."

There was no such reluctance to restructure defensively partly because of the loss of Cox, Vincent, and Coleman. "People would say we lost the three best players on our defense," Jimmy said. "I don't know. How good was the defense? We're going to have to completely redo the scheme and structure of the defense anyway, so I might as well start off with guys fresh from college who can fit into what I want. I want to draft speed and teach them a new defense. We won our first Super Bowl with a rookie middle linebacker. You can win with rookies. You just can't have too many of them."

And have no doubt, he planned to win.

"As much as I'd like to have Dan get a ring, I want a third one, and I guess selfishly I want it more for me than I do for him," Jimmy said. "I'm just being honest. I could say I want it for Dan Marino. The hell with that, I want it for Jimmy Johnson."

The last transplanted coach to brag so much was Buddy Ryan. Buddy arrived in Phoenix proclaiming, "There's a winner in town," and departed Phoenix a loser of twenty games in two years.

But then, Buddy didn't have Jimmy drafting for him. Neither did Don Shula, which, more than Xs and Os, was his downfall.

In five drafts with Dallas, Jimmy drafted sixty-three players, and twenty made the starting lineup and eight made the Pro Bowl. In that same span, Don drafted only thirteen starters and three Pro Bowlers. Of Jimmy's twenty-two picks in the first three rounds, only four didn't contribute significantly. Shula's eleven picks in that span included Sammie Smith, Alfred Oglesby, Randal Hill, Aaron Craver, Eddie Blake, and Larry Webster. If you say "Who?" or "Ugh," that's the point.

Many NFL teams were afraid to trade; they rested in their draft spots as if they had been ordained by God himself and they accepted the best athlete available. Jimmy and his people ranked all the players on their draft board, then called around the league, trying to see who would choose whom. Jimmy targeted four or five players he thought he could get in each round, and he moved around to assure he got them. He made an incredible fifty-five trades. He wanted Emmitt Smith instead of Rodney Hampton; he traded up to get him. He wanted Moose Johnston and Darrin Smith, but they weren't worth first-round picks; he traded down and got them, plus extra draft picks. Twelve of his twenty starters and six of eight Pro Bowlers were acquired in draft deals.

Jimmy was wired on Diet Coke and adrenaline on draft day. He loved to gamble on blackjack because he could count cards. He loved to gamble on draft day because he did his homework. He watched more videotape, scouted more players in person, studied and memorized more scouting reports, than maybe any coach. Some coaches had no or minimal input in the draft; Jimmy had total input. He immersed himself in "grinding" out information. His entire coaching and scouting staffs would grind away, talking to everyone going back to a player's high school teachers, looking for an edge.

Once they had evaluated players, most teams had all their scouts sit down with the personnel director and/or general manager and/or coach and debate and rank players at every position. On teams that involved the assistant coaches, they might join these sessions or have a separate one where the grades might be revised a bit.

Jimmy did it differently. The first week of April, each scout spent half a day giving evaluations and rankings to Jimmy, Bob Ackles, and incumbent personnel bosses Tom Braatz and Tom Heckert. "I want each scout to tell me exactly what he thinks," Jimmy explained. "I don't want one scout to be intimidated or change what he says because another scout has a stronger personality. The scout did the majority of the talking, and I did all the asking."

Then they determined a final scouting department grade. The next week, they repeated the process with the coaches. One by one, the coaches reported on prospects at their positions, and everyone in the room hashed out a final coaching grade. Finally, they put both grades together, hashed out any differences, and assigned a final Dolphins grade for players overall and at each position. Then they called around the league, digging for insider clues. They read reports by draftniks such as Mel Kiper and Joel Buchsbaum and even paid attention to reporters' mock drafts because they knew those people were working the phones, too.

Jimmy talked to Will McDonough of NBC and *The Boston Globe* and discovered even though Bill Parcells liked Daryl Gardener, the Patriots no longer were likely to select him seventh. In fact, so many teams were leery of Gardener's work ethic and inconsistency, it appeared he could slip to the Dolphins' twentieth spot. Jimmy had been focusing on linebackers John Mobley and Reggie Brown. He'd never talked with Gardener, let alone made him one of the twenty players brought into Miami for final interviews and workouts.

Three days before the draft, he broke the scouts and coaches into small groups and told them to recheck Gardener and twenty-five other players. He saw some scared looks at the mention of Gardener's name. Why, Buchsbaum had labeled Gardener and Lawrence Phillips as the draft's two biggest boom-or-bust picks, and Braatz said Gardener was the draft's biggest question mark. "His ability is not a question; his motor is the question," Braatz said. "He doesn't drive the scouts crazy; he'll drive the coach that gets him crazy."

Call Jimmy crazy.

He started watching tapes of Gardener. The day before the draft, he watched him play against North Carolina State. "He's getting double-teamed, and he's throwing guys right and left," Jimmy recalled. "The more I watched this player, the more excited I got."

Jimmy thought the big defensive lineman had the size and strength and quickness to be another Reggie White or Leon Lett. As much as any coach, Jimmy detested lazy players wasting their potential. They were coach killers. But Gardener scored perfect tens on confidence and competitiveness on the Dolphins' psychological test, scored an impressive twenty-six on the Wonderlic intelligence test, and Jimmy decided he would have made more plays if Baylor had let him do more and if he had been in better shape. And so he debated whether he should gamble on greatness, gamble on his own ability to instill intensity.

He called Wannstedt, who had coached Gardener in the Senior Bowl, and asked if he should be scared off. He said Wannstedt replied, "Jimmy, there are so many people in this league who are afraid to take him. You're one of the few guys in this league who's got enough security in your own position and your own mind that you're not going to be afraid for your job."

It was almost a dare. Jimmy loves dares.

On Day 101 of the JJ Era, Jimmy didn't bet on Daryl Gardener so much as on himself. "If I wanted something safe," he said, "I would have stayed in Tavernier. Maybe it's my own ego. Maybe it's my confidence in my staff. But I believe we can make this guy special. I'm never afraid of controversy. Yeah, it's a risk. But it gets down to your philosophy. Do you want to be safe and good or do you want to take a chance and be great?"

Gardener was 6'6" and 320 pounds, with the V-shaped torso of a swimmer and the 4.75 speed of a fullback or middle linebacker. He could bench-press nearly five hundred pounds and dunk a basketball from a flat-footed start. And yet in three years as a Baylor starter, he averaged just four sacks and never forced a fumble.

"This was the twentieth pick, so if you're going to get a guy of this talent, you're going to have to take a little risk," Jimmy said. "People might want to use the phrase 'boom or bust,' but I feel we have either a real good player or a great player. I coached defensive line for all the years prior to becoming a head coach. I saw him do things I can only relate to the great defensive linemen.

"This guy is strong as a horse. You slap him on the shoulder and you about break your hand. He's like a piece of rock. But I haven't seen a 320-pounder yet who likes to run. We have to get him in this Miami heat and make sure we get him running. And run and run and run some more."

Daryl Gardener, meet Jimmy Johnson, human cattle prod.

Jimmy was just getting warmed up. Next, he pulled off a trade with Jerry Jones and another with Tom Coughlin, turning one second-round pick into five picks in rounds three through five.

"We picked up four extra picks," he said. "If you pick up four extra picks for four years, you're going to have sixteen extra picks in the critical rounds. And if half of those sixteen make your team, you've got eight more good players than your opponent. And you never can tell: One of those eight might be a Leon Lett or someone special.

"There's such a difference of opinion once you get into the third, fourth, fifth rounds. The first round, everybody from your personnel director to *Inside Sports* to *Sports Illustrated* has the same guys picked. You may shuffle them around three or four spots, but they're the same guys. Once you get to the second round, then the opinions start changing. And then you get in the third round and they're all over the board. So obviously, you're taking more chances in those rounds. Now, I've always felt if I'm trying to catch a fish, I'd be much better with a big net than a hand net, so the more fish I catch, the more chance I might get a big one."

He already had problems at cornerback, and when the other four AFC East teams used first-round picks on wide receivers, Jimmy used the first of a pair of third-round picks and the first of his trio of fourth-round picks on Dorian Brew and Kirk Pointer, who were supposed to be cover cornerbacks.

Then he used third-, fourth-, and fifth-round picks on running backs Karim Abdul-Jabbar, Stanley Pritchett, and Jerris McPhail. Karim had first-round production but not first-round speed. That had been the knock on Emmitt Smith, but Jimmy didn't listen to the scouts or his running back coach and took Emmitt anyway because he saw he made a lot of runs of twenty-five yards or more. That was an important measuring stick to Jimmy. "You don't get caught up in how fast he is. You say, 'Can this guy play?' " Karim ran for 2,646 yards his final two years at UCLA. He could play. He was such a bargain with the eightieth choice that four teams called Jimmy within minutes of Karim's selection. "They said, 'You got a pretty good player.' I said, 'I know.' "

Pritchett caught the ball well and Jimmy thought he could learn to block well, the two things he wanted in a fullback. And while McPhail had bounced between receiver, runner, and injured, Jimmy loved his speed and big-play potential as a third-down back.

With his last of three picks in each of the fourth and fifth rounds, Jimmy took Southwest Conference linebackers LaCurtis Jones and Zach Thomas. What they lacked in size, they made up in heart and instincts. Jimmy didn't mind small linebackers if they were fast because big bodies up front like Gardener and fifth-round pick Shane Burton were supposed to tie up the offensive linemen.

He chose yet another cornerback in the sixth round. Notre Dame's Shawn Wooden had a history of neck and knee problems, but he'd held Keyshawn Johnson and Terry Glenn without a catch in man-to-man coverage. Wooden and Stanford lineman Jeff Buckey scored well on the intelligence test. The final pick, wideout Brice Hunter, was overweight and only ran a 4.6 forty, but "he's got as good hands as anybody in the draft," Jimmy said.

When the draft was done, the Dolphins were not. They spent the night on the phone, signing five players who'd gone undrafted. Two, Anthony Harris and Larry Izzo, would emerge as rookie playmakers. And this rookie class would emerge as the league's finest and the Dolphins' best hope for the future.

The draft ended Sunday, April 21, 1996. On April 23, the Dolphins announced Dan Marino had signed a contract extension. Under Shula, Miami had come close to rewarding Marino with six years. Jimmy chopped that in half for an average of $5.91 million a year. If Marino had signed a long deal only to fade quickly, the Dolphins would have been stuck counting the rest of his signing bonus against their salary cap. If he still had a lot left after two years, then Jimmy would extend him again.

On April 24, the NFL announced Fox had won the right to broadcast the Hype of the Year, the Jimmy-Jerry Grudge Match, Dallas at Miami, October 27. "I just happen to have a red pen with me," Jerry said. "Had Jimmy been sitting with me, he would have seen me circle it."

On April 26, Jimmy launched a three-day minicamp. All eighty-four players arrived at least ten minutes early for *this* meeting. You might say Jimmy was a little wired. He chased Irving Spikes, grabbed his jersey, and got carried downfield in the ball-stripping drill. He lined up and jammed 245-pound tight end Frank Wainright. He backpedaled with cornerbacks Terrell Buckley and Rodney Ray. He sprinted forty-five yards to congratulate J. B. Brown after the cornerback stripped Fred Barnett of a catch.

That night, 1,100 suits and skirts paid $100 a head to devour filet mignon and grilled salmon at the Dolphins' annual awards banquet. Many bid hundreds more at a silent auction of memorabilia from the Shula glory years. Speakers lauded, fans applauded, and players accepted congratulations and awards. Marino thanked Shula for all this glorious tradition.

And then Jimmy walked to the podium. "I'm supposed to say congratulations to all the people in the past. To all the great tradition. To all the people who laid the groundwork." He waved his hand in the air, dissing Shula, dismissing twenty-six years of memories. "But I only care about one thing. The present. The people who are here now to win now."

The convention center vibrated with applause. All hail the savior. And forget the legacy. A local Ford dealership ran a barrage of ads on TV celebrating Don Shula Appreciation Month—and endured one of its slowest Aprils ever.

A record number of players took part in an off-season conditioning program and minicamps so physical that the players' union filed a complaint. Even Dan Marino grunted through wind sprints, and Marino hadn't run since he was a rookie, ostensibly because of his knees but actually because Shula wouldn't make him. Jimmy would. Not even Dan Marino would challenge Jimmy Johnson.

6
CAMP GUILLOTINE: MOLDING WITH MESSAGES

June 1. First day the NFL allows rookies to report to their teams, save those quick three-day minicamps after the draft. A few are not ready for running endlessly in a sauna. Their muscles seize up and burst into spasms. Whether the diagnoses are cramps, dehydration, heat exhaustion, or heat stroke, they miss workouts. So Jimmy sends his sympathies.

"You rookies, I feel bad for you. You cramped up," he says, his voice soft with compassion. "These vets are in shape, ready to go, and you just got here."

And out come his rattlesnake eyes and stinging tongue.

"Listen, guys," he says, "this is not college. It's a job. We get to training camp, your ass has cramps, I'll cut you in a minute. On your waiver papers, I'll say 'He tried, but he had cramps. He tried, but he had an excuse.' Hey, there are no excuses. You better prepare yourself to be the best. We expect you to be the best. Dan Marino, Bernie Kosar, Zach Thomas, me—I don't care who you are—we don't cut anybody any slack. Because once we do, it filters in to everybody."

July 1. Two weeks before training camp can begin. But why waste a morning of camp? Let's hold the speed and conditioning tests today. Let's see if everybody got the messages.

They did. Jimmy calls it "the best-conditioned team going into a training camp that I've been around."

Daryl Gardener, the supposed sloth who hated to run, "was thirty yards ahead of everybody else," Jimmy brags. Jerris McPhail, the draft sleeper, covered forty yards in 4.31 seconds, fastest on the team. Even Dan Marino, the gimpy legend, did the conditioning test until Jimmy waved him off with a simple explanation: "I'm not a complete fool."

July 9. Another message. Eric Green, the $12 million tight end signed just one year ago, is cut. Big E missed thirty-nine practices in 1995. He caught forty-three passes and dropped nine, according to Stats Inc., and that wasn't even counting four more in the playoff humiliation. He symbolized the 1995 Dolphins: fat, arrogant, underachieving.

Jimmy made it clear in the off-season that he wasn't happy with Big E's work habits, but people figured he couldn't cut Big E because it would cost him $583,000 against his salary cap this year and $2.3 million next year, because Big E would file an injury grievance that would tie up another $750,000 and could cost as much as $1.5 million. Jimmy cut him anyway, saying he didn't warrant his salary. But asked if he'd want Green back at a reduced salary, Jimmy replies, "I didn't want him on our team."

July 15. Rookies report. But Karim Abdul-Jabbar, the third-round pick Jimmy wants to be his feature back, is holding out for more money. Holdouts are typical for rookies, but within three days, Jimmy can take it no more. "If he doesn't get in here pretty quick, he's going to start at number five [on the depth chart] and have to work his way back up," he snarls.

The next day, Karim signs.

July 17. Johnny Mitchell turns down nearly $1 million more from the Bengals to sign with the Dolphins. He might be the league's most athletic tight end, but he is an enigma. The Jets' 1992 first-round pick has earned criticism for his blocking, dropped passes, selfishness, laziness, and forgetfulness. In short, he's a lot like Eric Green. But he comes cheap, and Jimmy had been told Johnny will work hard. The coach thinks the tight end just needs direction and positive reinforcement.

Incumbent Ronnie Williams, promoted to starter when Big E was axed, gets cut when Johnny signs. Another message. Williams missed a week of off-season workouts and returned only after Jimmy warned him sternly. And he had not completed the July 1 conditioning test. Williams claims he had a nagging hamstring injury; Jimmy says he doesn't like excuses. Good-bye.

"Life is beautiful," Johnny says, beaming about working just thirty minutes from his home in Boca Raton, the glitzy mecca for rich retirees. "This is a marriage here and I'm committed to giving one hundred percent of myself to this organization."

July 18. Just in case Johnny's marriage doesn't last, the Dolphins agree to a two-year deal with Kerry Cash, another tight end more adept at catching than blocking. Cash will sign his contract and report with the rest of the veterans the next day.

They will not ease into work in shorts, as in the past. Two-a-day practices will begin immediately, at 10 A.M., in full pads, at full speed, with full-contact seven-on-seven inside running drills in the morning and afternoon blitz drills.

"I want contact," Jimmy warns. "I want our guys to feel when we walk on the field that they can dominate the line of scrimmage, they can run the football, they can stop the run, they can dominate the opponent. You do that through physical play."

Jimmy is a vast change from Shula, who ran physical practices most of his career but let up in the final years, as he tried to work on the mental and finesse games and safeguard his aging players' bodies. Jimmy had heard and dismissed those arguments long ago.

"When we first went to Dallas with our physical practices, there was a lot of skepticism about running out of gas. People said the team would fall apart the end of the season. Well, even in our horrible year [1989's 1–15] and our not-so-good year [1990's 7–9], we still finished fairly strong. The last three years, we lost one game in December and one game in the playoffs. That's a pretty good record in December and January."

But the Buffalo Bills had a pretty good record in December and January, too, and seventy-year-old Marv Levy is taking a kinder, gentler approach. They will have but one week of double sessions, will break camp August 10. Workouts will last no longer than ninety minutes and will not be particularly physical.

"There is a great and erroneous tendency to make a player prove every day how tough he is," Levy explains. "If you have to prove how tough you are every day by taking a haymaker on the chin, pretty soon you don't even care to be tough anymore. Too many coaches are 'real tough' with somebody else's body."

July 19. Eyes narrow, eyebrows pinched together, accenting the flaring cheeks, Jimmy storms toward the Dolphins defenders.

"Get back in the huddle!" he commands.

Momentarily puzzled, they hesitate.

"Get back in the huddle!" he shouts again.

He isn't angry about the preceding play. He is angry about the way they have left the huddle.

"Let's break out of a damned huddle like we're gonna stomp their ass!" he booms.

So they gather in a circle again and break with a resounding clap. Brawny forearms folded, Jimmy nods.

He is introducing Football 101, the JJ Way, and, just in case they miss it, he makes sure the media chronicles it. Normally, Jimmy keeps the media at a distance. They are forbidden from practice during the regular season, and even during the preseason they are restricted to the patio off the Dolphins' complex, maybe fifteen yards from the nearest end zone. He doesn't want the media hearing the coaches' criticisms and corrections. He is paranoid about tipping off even preseason opponents; when the *Sun-Sentinel's* Charlie Bricker broaches etiquette and notes the Dolphins practiced a fake field goal, Jimmy rails and doesn't trust Bricker the rest of the year.

But he makes an exception for his beloved "middle drill." This is basic but brutal football: Five offensive linemen, a tight end, fullback, and halfback face four defensive linemen and three linebackers, using only running plays between the tackles. The drill combines Jimmy's love for hard running and hard hitting, and he wants to emphasize it so much, he not only allows the media to watch, he has his P.R. people usher the media to the nearest sideline so they can view it up close and personal. He wants them to write about it, and they do.

The offense breaks the huddle. "Let's see who can play," Jimmy yells.

Steve Emtman arm-tackles Jerris McPhail and the rookie scoots free. "Don't give me that 'I would have had him.' The only way you have him is if his ass is on the ground!" Jimmy hollers. Emtman makes a punishing hit on the drill's last play.

Aubrey Beavers misses a tackle. "Aubrey, damnit!" Jimmy bellows. "You gotta fight through that block." Beavers doesn't get it, just like he doesn't get a lot of things. He will be cut in four days.

Karim tries to juke out a would-be tackler. "You gotta run *through* somebody!" Jimmy corrects.

Linemen are criticized for missing blocks, backs for missing holes and fumbling, defensive linemen for trying to dance around blocks or waiting to see where the play was going. Jimmy stops practice, lines up opposite an offensive lineman, and drives him backward.

"It's a simple game!" he barks. "Hit him as hard and as fast as you can. I don't want you running around blocks or slipping blocks. Knock his ass back!"

Three defensive linemen jump offside the next play. You were expecting miracles?

Jimmy will run the middle drill every morning of every practice. "We do enough middle drills," he says, "we'll find out who the best players are."

Jimmy repeats his message about injuries more than once this first day. Aaron Jones, a former first-round bust for the Pittsburgh Steelers, starts at defensive end instead of Trace Armstrong. Trace angered Jimmy when he rehabilitated his injured wrist and ankle at home in Gainesville, Florida, and not in South Florida. He says he couldn't have done anything more in Miami and shrugs off the initial depth chart. He isn't reading Jimmy well.

Neither is third-round pick Dorian Brew, who skips workouts complaining of a strained hamstring. "It's a waste of my time talking about people who don't have pads on," Jimmy seethes.

"I'm hurt," Brew says. "What am I going to do about that?"

Get healthy in a hurry, that's what. Jimmy can not feel their pain, so he does not believe their pain. The brilliant psychologist can be a Neanderthal about injuries. If his trainers do not think an injury is that serious, he expects his players to practice and perform one hundred percent. Anything less is just an excuse, and he doesn't permit excuses.

Charles Jordan sprains his ankle today, but Jimmy doesn't think it's serious. "I hope it's not real serious," he says, "because he's a guy we're counting on." Jordan thinks it's serious. Jordan is not a guy they can count on.

July 20. Another bad break. Defensive end Jeff Cross, the Dolphins' most accomplished pass rusher, has a degenerative disk in his lower back and is placed on the active/physically-unable-to-perform list. He had seen Dr. Robert Watkins, and the specialist prescribed a series of strengthening exercises and cortisone shots, but Cross's back was throbbing after the very first day of workouts. He will have surgery July 23 and is projected to miss two months.

July 23. Four practices, and Aubrey Beavers is gone. That's all it takes to convince Jimmy the guy can't play for him. Beavers was a terrific athlete, as evidenced by his 20.5 sacks in two years as an Oklahoma starter, as evidenced by the second-round pick Don Shula invested in him, as evidenced by the eleven starts and All-Rookie honors he won in 1994.

But Beavers just doesn't get it. Take the time he was scheduled to appear live on Shula's TV show, which ran from 8:30 to 9 P.M., just before *Monday Night Football*. Players always showed up early in coat and tie, or at least a fancy shirt. Beavers arrived in a Marlins jersey, untucked, five minutes before the show was to go off the air—the first player in history to miss his appointment on the *Don Shula Show*.

Long before, when Jimmy analyzed why some of his draft picks turned out to be busts, he realized they just weren't smart enough to learn his systems, which really are not all that complicated. He will waste zero time teaching Don's dunce.

July 24. Jimmy can put the fear of God in players, but he believes even more in the power of positive reinforcement.

And so here the Dolphins are, finishing another long day in the summer heat, and guys are dragging through the goal-line drill. As they line up for the final play, Jimmy eyes his offensive and defensive units.

"Whoever wins," he says, "doesn't have to run any conditioning drills."

Twenty-two players slam into each other with every last bit of effort, and Jerris McPhail scores from the three. The offensive players roar and head for the air conditioning.

The defenders run wind sprints.

July 25. Double trouble. Johnny Mitchell leaves the morning workout with the visiting Washington Redskins holding his back, grimacing, and heads for a bone scan.

In the afternoon, Fred Barnett plants his right leg to make a cut, the same move he's made a million times, only this time his knee gives way and floods instantly with pain. Fred holds his leg in the air. He's already missed one year of his career when he tore the anterior cruciate ligament, the most vital of the four ligaments that crisscross the knee and give it stability, and he doesn't want to endure that again. He limps off the field and is taken for an MRI.

Jimmy says the Dolphins think Mitchell just has muscle spasms and Barnett might have some cartilage damage. Several others are out with various nicks and bruises, and practices are not going nearly as smoothly as Jimmy had foreseen back in March. It's time for a little revisionist history. "My comment was *eventually* we are going to be the team to beat," he says. "That's the way I want our players to think. I want them to think that *eventually* we will be the team to beat. Obviously, we're not the team to beat right now because we've got a long way to go."

July 26. When doctors make a tiny incision in Barnett's knee and insert the arthroscope, they don't see cartilage damage. They see the ACL is shredded. ACL injuries used to end careers, especially for players who needed to twist and turn and put as much pressure on the knee as a wide receiver does. But medical science and rehabilitation has advanced so far that hardworking players can typically come back in a year, sometimes even nine or ten months. Oh, but this is the second time Barnett has torn his, and who comes back from two tears of the same ACL? Jimmy just invested $8.5 million in Barnett to be his big-play receiver, and now this? Argggghhh!

Jimmy's passing game is in serious trouble. Already, it has looked ragged in practice, and now two of his three top targets—Barnett and Mitchell—are hurt, and the only one left, O. J. McDuffie, has some quick moves but no breakaway speed. Jimmy believes in speed, but Barnett is gone and Jordan is limping. Marino admits he's frustrated. He has little timing, feel, or confidence with all these new and unproven receivers.

July 27. A five-foot-by-eight-foot sign greeted the Dolphins in their locker room when they opened camp. THE ROAD TO THE SUPER BOWL STARTS HERE, it read.

Each game was listed in a little box, and the boxes rose, as if ascending a staircase, until reaching the plateau, the Super Bowl.

It is only July, only a scrimmage, but that goal seems very far away when the Dolphins fall, 12–6 to a Washington club coming off a 6–10 season. "That's the worst we've looked since training camp," Jimmy says after watching a deadly assortment of poor running, poor blocking, dropped passes, missed tackles, and a fumble on which the runner isn't even touched. Karim has the Dolphins' longest run, a nifty nine-yarder—and aggravates his sprained ankle and is done for the night.

Some starters, Jimmy warns, might not be starters much longer.

"Obviously, we're not the team to beat right now," he fumes. "We've got a long ways to go."

July 28. Maybe Johnny Mitchell got marriage advice from Liz Taylor. Maybe he got his heart from the Tin Woodman in *The Wizard of Oz*.

Eleven days after proclaiming his commitment to this beautiful marriage, Johnny retires. It isn't his back. It's his heart. Turns out those cynical New Yorkers were right. He doesn't have one.

Johnny drives to Davie on the players' day off and meets with Jimmy, tight end coach Pat Jones, and director of operations Bob Ackles for about fifteen minutes. Johnny says he's lost his desire to play.

"I was surprised because he was so enthusiastic about coming down here," Jimmy says. "I think after a few practices, he realized his heart wasn't in it. And if his heart isn't in it, I don't want him."

Johnny says he'll pay back his $500,000 signing bonus. He says he's set financially and doesn't need to play football for the money. Or does he?

"This guy's not going to medical school," agent Ralph Cindrich says. "When he stands in that unemployment line, he'll gain his desire."

Within weeks, he will.

July 29. Players return to practice and find Jimmy carried out his warning. Irving Spikes replaces Terry Kirby as the starting halfback and the late-arriving, often injured Karim Abdul-Jabbar is fifth string. Rookie Stanley Pritchett replaces Keith Byars at fullback. Rookie Shawn Wooden moves ahead of incumbent free safety Gene Atkins. Atkins is excused from practice with an ultimatum: Accept a pay cut by 3 P.M. or we'll release you. Atkins opts to slash his salary from $1.225 million to $700,000. And Kerry Cash replaces the retiring Mitchell.

Cash says he signed with the Dolphins because God told him to. "I called my mom and we both prayed about it," he says. "I could have gone somewhere for more money, but God put me here for a reason. I prayed to Him and He gave me the answer. No, it wasn't a thunderbolt. No, it wasn't the face of Jimmy Johnson—although around here, some people think he's God."

Cash grins, and his listeners laugh. But he is serious about his faith, and for a while, this will seem like divine intervention. He has dropped maybe one or two passes during training camp and drawn consistent praise from Jimmy. This afternoon, he will break open deep for a long gain, then slice outside for another. Cash is cashing in on his destiny. The Dolphins could, ahem, bank on Cash.

Or maybe not.

The job is his, and he drops it. He drops passes. He stops getting open. He doesn't block very well. And within a month, he is cut.

July 31. The preseason opener—Jimmy Johnson's first game as Dolphins coach—is three days away. You think he'll have butterflies? Think again.

"I won't have any anxious moments in a preseason game," Jimmy says. "I might have had some years ago, but not now."

Not until the games really count.

Oh, Jimmy used to think preseason wins and losses mattered. When he got to Dallas, he thought it important to establish a winning mentality and confidence. And so he won three of his four preseason games in 1989—and won but one of sixteen in the regular season. He went 6–11–1 his next four preseasons—but 50–22 in the regular season and postseason.

"Yeah, I'd like to win in preseason, but I'm not gonna sacrifice evaluating talent," Jimmy says. "I made that mistake my first year in Dallas. That doesn't mean I'm going to try to lose games, but my first priority is evaluating players and putting together the fifty-three men I want for New England. During the regular season, we'll spend six days preparing for the next opponent. This week, we probably won't spend but one practice, walking through a semi-game plan. By Minnesota [the third preseason game and the only one where Jimmy will play his regulars and try to win], we'll have two practices and four meetings on the actual game plan."

August 1. Football writers from some of the nation's biggest newspapers—*USA Today*, the New York *Daily News*, the *Chicago Tribune*, *The Dallas Morning News*—have trekked to Miami to write about Jimmy and his debut, and he clearly enjoys the attention. He spends extra time answering questions and even joking around.

"You're getting grayer every year," he tells Gary Myers, the *Daily News* writer who used to work with him at HBO.

"I'm not going to make a return comment," Gary says.

"Ah, you think I'm getting fatter every year?" Jimmy replied. "I know what you're thinking. I'm trying to lose weight."

Indeed, Jimmy is more than a little vain about his size. He held up production of the pocket schedules the Dolphins give to fans until he lost weight and his cheeks looked less chubby. He will lose twenty-five pounds on his diet before backsliding at the end of the year. And when *The Washington Post* suggests he stands on a little orange box to address the media because he's only 5'9", he says he's taller than that and the podium is for the media's benefit, not his.

Not far away, Bucs quarterback Trent Dilfer has finished a workout against the Dolphins and returns shots Jimmy took at him on Fox TV and in *Sports Illustrated*. Jimmy said he chose Miami over Tampa because he wanted to coach Marino, "not a guy I don't have faith in." Says Dilfer: "He didn't win those championships in Dallas, the team did. I just get sick and tired of hearing about how great he is. He is very good, but you get tired of hearing about it."

Jimmy just smiles and declines comment. He cares what his good players think of him; he does not worry about poor players, especially those on other teams. He says the return to coaching has "actually been easier than I thought. I'm at home. I'm talking to the same press I talked to at the University of Miami. I get in my car and know what street to go. The friends I had at the University of Miami and when I lived in the Keys are the same friends I have now."

He says he will not abandon the run. "At times, it's going to look ugly, but we're going to be persistent, keep working at it, and get it done. It won't be a situation where a team stops us—and some will—and we will just abandon it. No matter what, we're not going to say, 'To heck with it' and just go to our Hall of Fame player.

"You know you have a great player who can make big plays, but you also understand the dangers there. You've got to be able to run in critical situations and not have a candy-store effect with the run. You can't get frustrated and let him throw every down. You've got to be hardheaded and continue to run, and then at the end of the half and the end of the game when you've got a lead, you're able to hand the ball off and eat up the clock and let the game end with the ball in your hands, rather than giving it up on downs and letting the other team have an opportunity to win. Through five years in Dallas, with the running game we had, we only had one game where the field goal kicker had to win it at the end. I don't like those miracle comebacks. I don't like being in a two-minute offense trying to win the game every week.

"You look at the stats last year and opponents went for it on fourth down thirty-two times against us. That's almost twice what the rest of the league was. The reason they went for it on fourth down was they had good field position.

Rather than punting from their forty or fifty, they were down on the Miami thirty-five and going for it. Now, the running game will give you field position because you can pick up some first downs on third down rather than throw an incomplete pass and punt. You may not be able to take it all the way down the field and score, but you'll get field position, kick to them on their side of the fifty, and your defensive players aren't going to have their rear ends on the goal line every time.

"It'll help the offense, it'll help the defense, it'll help our field position. When we get in December and January, if it's a [bad] weather day where Dan may not be as sharp or for some reason we're unable to throw the ball, then you can depend on the run to win."

When it comes to a crucial game-turning sequence, Jimmy says he won't be so mule-headed that he will sacrifice victories by running. But the philosophy is so engrained, he will suffer but persist like Job.

August 2. The Dolphins struggled the previous afternoon against a Tampa club that had lost more than it had won for thirteen consecutive seasons. Usually this day-before-the-game workout will be light and loose. But this day, Jimmy tugs at his sleeves until they are up to his shoulders. He's like the air: He's everywhere. He applauds when fullback Robert Wilson catches a simple flat pass. He hurries downfield, watches the defensive backs catch passes, and claps again. When two balls go astray, he chases them down and tosses them back.

He watches his receivers go one-on-one with the Tampa defensive backs. He watches his defense go seven-on-seven with the Tampa offense. He does a little jog and skip, watches one play of his offense against the Bucs' defense, then skips back across the field, and corrects Gene Atkins about pinching down on the run. Back to the offense for thirty seconds, then a short conversation with Kevin O'Neill, then back to the defense, then the offense, then the defense. He is watching his safeties intently, and not liking what he is seeing. Instead of telling his players, he stomps over to the media.

"I've really got concerns about our team as far as how mentally strong we are," he storms. "I hope this practice wasn't an indication of how hard we're gonna play tomorrow night. I hope we're not feeling sorry for ourselves. We've got some who will lay it on the line day in and day out and some . . . lacking concentration.

"We have days like today, I realize we have a lot of work to do. I've had concerns from Day One. They got accelerated Saturday night [in the sloppy scrimmage with Washington]. We need more football players who are bound and determined to do whatever it takes to win. Do the little things. Do the extra things. Give extra time. Give extra effort.

"Every day I'm learning more about our team and players. I know this: When it gets to be crunch time right now, I have concerns."

Is he really angry? Maybe. Is he sending a message to his players? Absolutely. Jimmy realizes he cannot face the players with fire-and-brimstone speeches every week and expect them to work. He sure isn't going to waste one during preseason, but he can plant the message through the media, and all will deliver it for him.

7
THE PRESEASON

August 3. Miami. Jimmy said he wouldn't be nervous for the preseason opener, and ninety minutes beforehand, he sure does not look it. He's telling stories, arms flapping, grinning, enjoying himself, a far cry from his mood for the real games. "The days of butterflies for preseason games," he said, "are over."

But the urge to run and to win is not. He planned to play his first-team line the first and third quarters. No NFL coach plays his starters more than a half in the first preseason game. But, damnit, Jimmy wants to run, and how in the hell is he going to run when those bums on the second unit can't even pick up a first down? How is he going to show the first team unit he isn't happy with their first-half performance? By punishing them. How is he going to teach them to be mentally tough? By working them. How is he going to prove he's different from Don Shula? By playing his first-team line for three quarters. By running and running and running until it works. No matter that it's against Tampa Bay's second- and third-string units. He said he would be persistent even when it looked ugly, and tonight, he lives up to his word.

Shula, who had stormed the sideline for every Dolphin game since 1970, stands upstairs in his private box, alone with his family and his thoughts. You have to look hard to see him in the shadows, have to look hard to see any sign or semblance of Miami missing him. He might not even be here if his son Mike were not the Buccaneers' offensive coordinator.

The Dolphins trail 10–3 at the half, and Jimmy is not happy. Irving Spikes and Terry Kirby have averaged only two yards a carry. With his top four receivers injured or retired, Dan Marino has completed only four of nine passes, never knowing if his ragged receivers will turn the right way or catch the ball even if they do. And Jimmy's defense has been shelled for 216 yards by a bunch of nobodies.

Jimmy tells offensive coordinator Gary Stevens to focus on the run in the second half and to select plays knowing Jimmy will go for it on fourth down on any short-yardage or goal-line situation. And so, on their second series of the second half, the Dolphins pass on fourth and three from the Tampa nineteen, and Scott Miller takes a Bernie Kosar pass to the two. Kosar tries to pass on first down and finds nobody open. Same old Dolphins? Time for a statement. Jimmy sends Bernie Parmalee crashing into the middle of the line three straight plays, and finally, on fourth down, he gets the touchdown. It takes four plays to gain two yards, but damnit, they do it! It's 10–10 one play into the fourth quarter.

Time to see what the scrubs can do?

No. Jimmy approaches his linemen on the sideline. "Okay," he says, "we got the touchdown. Now I want to press it. I want to see if you can respond."

Jimmy believes in putting people in pressure situations and seeing how they respond. He wants to see who has the mental toughness to play through fatigue and pain. He wants to see how rookies respond against opponents' starters. He doesn't want to put people in pressure situations when he's sure they will fail, but only when they can succeed, because that will enable him to push even harder the next time.

Tampa punts and Jimmy barks, "First-team line! Get out there!"

Behind Richmond Webb, Keith Sims, Tim Ruddy, Chris Gray, and James Brown, the fastest Dolphin, Jerris McPhail, sprints for five first downs, and Jimmy coaxes fifteen plays and Joe Nedney's go-ahead field goal out of Jimmy's own stubbornness. When Michael Husted whiffs twice on tying field goals, the Dolphins win Jimmy's debut, 13–10.

"It was crucial to our team that the first offensive line got in there and crunched and ran the ball," Jimmy says. "I wanted them to be in there, in the heat of battle, to run the ball and not pass block. It was important for them to feel good about running the football down the field and scoring the winning points."

"We've taken a lot of criticism because we haven't been a grind-it-out team," Webb says. "I've taken criticism for that. This is one of the few times since I've been here that we stuck with the running game. That's what we've been asking for—and now we're getting that opportunity."

And yet even with the starters playing the second half, even with McPhail looking good, the Dolphins have run for only eighty-nine yards and a 2.8-yard average. Take away McPhail and they ran for forty-five yards and 1.8 yards a carry. The right side of their line is weak. Their top receivers are weaker: Miller is a 2,400-baud modem in a 28,800-baud world. Lamar Thomas is a castoff from the lowly Bucs, a veteran of all of one week as a Dolphin. They are not going to win playing like this.

Maybe that's why Jimmy hides his emotions at game's end, calmly sipping from a Gatorade cup and jogging off the field without pumping a fist into the sky or even grinning. Already, he is focusing on a blockbuster move.

August 4. The Dolphins know Jimmy does not believe in the old coaching axiom about treating everybody fairly. He tells them he treats all players differently, based on how hard they work and how well they produce. Michael Irvin, a good athlete who worked hard and played great, was benched for just a quarter when he missed a team plane. John Roper, a good athlete who did not work hard or play to his potential, was cut when he was late to two or three meetings and fell asleep in another.

"You're probably gonna want me to be fair," Jimmy explains. "Well, that's bullshit. This world is not fair, and it's not equal. I'm going to be *consistent*. I'm going to treat everyone different.

"Let me give you an example. John Roper was late for a bunch of meetings. He was a backup linebacker, a so-so player making about $400,000 a year. One day I'm running our special teams meeting, the projector's flickering, and I see his eyes are shut. John is nodding off sleeping. I decide I'm going to give him a little break, give him a few minutes. I look five minutes later and he's still sleeping. I said, 'John, evidently you're not getting enough sleep at home. We're gonna give you time to catch up on your sleep. You're cut.'"

Roper's wife had just given birth. The baby was awake most of the night, crying and fussing. Roper helped calm and feed the baby and gave his wife some rest. How could Jimmy be so cruel, so uncaring, to a guy who was just being nice to his family? Because Roper wouldn't help him reach the ultimate prize. Because John Roper didn't put his job first, and a lackadaisical attitude was cancerous.

"Had it been an isolated episode, I wouldn't have done that," Jimmy explains. "Had it been Dan Marino sleeping, I would have walked back there and said"— here he dropped his voice to a stage whisper—" 'Dan, wake up.' "

Everybody laughs. Everybody gets the point. Jimmy could be considerate, all right. He saw Dan work hard and gave him time off to play in a celebrity golf tournament. He saw Lamar Thomas, his former Hurricanes star, in a world of hurt and rescued him. LT had caught just twenty-five passes in three years in Tampa. He had been arrested and committed to a mental institution when police feared he would kill himself or harm others, and when he was arrested for aggravated battery on his pregnant fiancée, the Buccaneers waived him July 17. Jimmy signed him ten days later, but only after talking to everyone from the Dolphins' owner to a Woman In Distress counselor, only after LT promised to continue counseling, only after putting him on "probation." He signed LT because he might back up a weak position, but mostly to give a troubled soul a second chance at life.

And while Jimmy shared little time or money with charitable organizations, he gave gorgeous suits and ties to Father Leo Armbrust. He took all his coaches on vacation after every season, and one time when they were gambling, he gave one a $5,000 chip and told him to bet it or keep it or do whatever he wanted with it. Then there was that first year in Dallas with Dave Wannstedt.

"I had moved into a brand-new housing development, and it was so new they didn't even have cable TV," Wannstedt remembered. "We were sitting out back having a drink, and he walked inside, and my girls, who were about seven and ten at the time, were sitting in front of the TV. I had little aluminum-foil rabbit ears on the TV, and the picture looked like we were in the middle of a snowstorm in Chicago, and he asked the girls, 'What are you watching here?' I explained that was the best we could do without cable. He didn't say anything more about it and left.

"The next morning, my wife, Jan, called me about nine o'clock and said there was a big truck outside the house and they were delivering a satellite dish. Jimmy didn't want those girls watching TV like that, so he bought us a big satellite dish. It was about half the size of my house. That's a side of Jimmy that people don't hear about."

Tonight, the Dolphins see both sides of their coach.

Jimmy signed Jack Del Rio in June. Del Rio had been a quality player and person for him in Dallas, but thinking Jerry Jones shortchanged him financially, Del Rio signed with the Minnesota Vikings and made the Pro Bowl as a heady, hardworking middle linebacker. Injuries cost him the second half of the 1995 season, the Vikings chopped his big salary, and the Dolphins signed him for $275,000 in June.

Jack worked hard, got in shape, and went through every two-a-day without complaint. He was the starting middle linebacker and had made the defense's biggest play Saturday night, stuffing Tampa Bay on fourth and one. But when coaches reviewed the film, they saw Jack making three tackles and his backup, Zach Thomas, making eight. The coaches agreed Zach would deserve the starting job soon. The easy thing, the thing almost all coaches do, is to keep Jack around, let Zach learn from him, make sure they're right, and cut the veteran at the end of the month. But Jimmy does not play it safe. He cuts Jack, promotes Zach, and when the regular season began, Zach will have learned from his rookie mistakes.

The players don't have to return to work until tonight, but security boss Stu Weinstein locates Jack and asks him to meet Jimmy in his office early. Jimmy talks with individual players all the time, but to be called to his office is unusual and usually bad. Jack figures he's had a good game and camp and maybe Jimmy wants to know about something in the locker room.

"I'm thinking all kinds of great things." Until the first words spill from

Jimmy's mouth. Jimmy waves Jack into his office, and, still sitting at his desk, closes the door behind them with a wireless remote control. It's a little gizmo sure to impress, but it wasn't Jimmy's idea. It was a gift to Don Shula from Wayne Huizenga, who thought it unseemly that a living legend might actually have to open and close his own door. It's just one more way of showing the coach is in control, and yeah, it works.

"Jack," Jimmy begins, "this is a difficult time for me. I don't know that I've ever had to release someone that I felt as badly about. I brought you here, I had great hopes for you, and I wish every player on this team was a team player and did all the things you do off the field. You're smart, you say the right things, you work hard, you work through pain, you do all we ask, you're a great competitor, and you know how to win. But you know me, Jack: The bottom line is Zach Thomas is making more plays. It's not fair to the team or to Zach if I keep him behind you."

Zap! Jimmy is closing the door on Jack's career. Jack already has decided he will not be a nomad. He will retire if this does not work out. He is stunned, but he knows Jimmy's philosophy.

"Coach, I'm either a starter or I'm not on the team since I don't play special teams. I'm not gonna try to talk you out of it, because I know how you are when you've got your mind made up. But my legs . . . I'm going through two-a-days. I know I'll get my quickness back."

"I think you will," Jimmy replies, "but by the same token, Zach is going to get quicker, too. And in December and January, Zach will be quicker because he's younger."

Jack's eyes water up a little, and Jimmy is afraid his might, too. He hurriedly wishes Jack good luck and says, "I think it's best you go talk to Bob Ackles because Bob does the paperwork."

Jimmy is genuinely hurt. "Everybody on the staff knew how I felt about Jack," he says, zapping the door shut behind me. "He said the right things. He worked hard. He was hurting, but he never bitched or complained. He did everything you asked. It's not easy to go through double days when you've been doing it for eleven years. It's not easy to go through with a guy over you, screaming and cussing and hollering and doing everything in the world that I do. And so, especially in this first year, when I'm looking for 'my guys' who have been around me before, who know what to expect . . . I need those leaders in the locker room. And so I wasn't just releasing a player I had great respect for, but a player I *needed* in the locker room. So it was a decision I had to give a lot of thought to. But talking to the staff, we all agreed it was inevitable; it was just a matter of whether it happened today or a week or two from now.

"I could tell he was trying. He just didn't have the quickness. That wasn't a forte of his, anyway, and he's a step slower than he was. He's not as quick as I'd like, but we could have won games with him. Had Zach Thomas not come on strong, Jack would still be here, still starting."

At tonight's meeting, Jimmy does not tell the players Jack has been cut, and in fact when he tells Zach he's been promoted, Zach thinks the coach is just trying to motivate the veteran. But just before the rookie leaves for the night, the word filters among the players: Jack Del Rio has been cut. Wow! If one of Jimmy's all-time favorites can get axed this soon, who among them is safe?

They get Jimmy's answer via the media. Nobody. "A guy can be my best friend and if he's got someone behind him who I can't stand but performs better, I've got to make the change."

August 5. Zach Thomas isn't celebrating. He's working as hard as ever. "Coach Johnson is taking a chance on me, and I want to prove him right. What's good about his camp is you go all out. In most camps, the rookies don't get much of a chance, because they're going three-quarters speed, they've got shorts on, and they don't bang inside and go aggressively. He intimidates you. That gets the best out of you. You know he'll cut you in a second. Even when he's walking around in drills, you just feel, 'Oh, man, I better step it up. I don't want to make a mistake in front of Coach Johnson.' "

August 6. At the morning meeting, Jimmy senses the players are worn out by two-a-days and frightened by Del Rio's release. Jimmy tells them he understands, that he's down, too.

So he turns into an actor. He bounces around the field and gets in the middle of drills. He trails Scott Miller on a pass route. He grabs onto Jeff Kopp to show the linebackers how he wants them to tackle. He doesn't just use his helmet or forearm. He wraps his arms around Kopp and sinks his fingers into his jersey and flesh.

"Sometimes not only players but coaches, when they're not feeling real good, have to have a little false enthusiasm," he explains. "Sometimes that false enthusiasm turns into real enthusiasm. We coaches set the stage for the energy in practice, and if we've got some energy, they've got energy."

It works.

"He got everybody else bouncing around," O. J. McDuffie says. "Seeing him flying around and smiling just overflows. Coach Shula was excited, but Jimmy bounces around like a bundle of energy. It's fun to watch. He really does get you pumped. He'll let you know if you've done bad or good. That's important. Guys get down if they get dogged the whole time and don't get recognized for doing something good. Shula would give you both, but Jimmy's a lot more vocal.

"But the biggest difference is we've been hitting since Day One. This year, we hit! The 49ers are getting great results not beating each other up. They've got a veteran group that doesn't need to hit. We've got a lot of young guys. We can't go out there in hats and T-shirts and get a good workout because the knowledge won't be there. My friends in Buffalo let me know how nice their camps are, too."

Jealous?

"No!" O.J. says, quick as can be. "No other place I'd rather be. I've had the best. I came from Penn State and Paterno. I had Shula. Now I have Jimmy Johnson. And in South Florida! How's Buffalo going to be in December? Football's a contact sport. You gotta love it. You gotta be consumed by it."

August 7. Jimmy let Joe Nedney kick in the first preseason game, and the tall left-footer boomed both his field goal attempts, three if you count one called back. His leg was far stronger than Pete Stoyanovich's, but what would he do under pressure? Stoyo ranked fourth in NFL history in field goal accuracy, but Jimmy did not say the job was Stoyo's to lose. No, he says, "It's anybody's job to win."

If Stoyo didn't believe it, he did when he woke up this morning and saw the *Sun-Sentinel*. An unnamed NFL general manager said the Dolphins were shopping Stoyo among several teams. Stoyo had kicked two of the six longest field goals in NFL history, but his percentage had fallen from .828 in 1990, 1991, and 1992, to .773 the past three years, and he was leaving his kickoffs around the ten-yard line. His confidence—essential to a kicker—wavered after his forty-eight-yard miss cost the Dolphins a trip to the AFC championship game after the 1994 season, and the fans did not let him forget.

Shaken by the latest news, Stoyo hides in the players' lounge and does not return to the locker room until the media are ushered out. Then it gets worse. Nedney lines up on the practice field closest to the fans, and they cheer louder and louder as he booms kickoff after kickoff into the end zone. It is a competition Stoyo cannot win, so he does not even try. He walks around aimlessly, twirling a football, trying not to look. Nedney launches a kickoff from his thirty, over the goal line, over the end zone, and two yards beyond before its first bounce. Eighty-two yards!

And here's the thing: It isn't a fluke. Nedney airmailed a kickoff eighty-eight yards the previous year, when he was on the practice squad. He bashed another eighty-four yards this year and hit halfway up the upright from eighty yards. Oh my.

"Pete!" a fan screams, loud enough for everyone within a quarter mile to hear. "Pack your bags, baaaabeeee!" Stoyo doesn't want to pack. He just married a South Florida girl. He has roots here. He likes it here. But the Dolphins have been exploring a Stoyo trade for days now, and Kansas City is most interested. What's more, Miami is shopping Terry Kirby, and he's attracting a lot of attention, too. Scouts from the 49ers, Vikings, Jaguars, Redskins, Raiders, Jets, Lions, Panthers, Patriots, Steelers, and Seahawks will attend their next game.

"It's a new era around here," Stoyo says. "There have been a lot of changes, a lot of unexpected changes."

And more will come.

August 8. A few players celebrate the last session of two-a-days by pouring a huge vat of liquid refreshment over backfield coach Kippy Brown, and they get him good.

"I'm gonna punish all of 'em in time," Kippy rails. "I know what kind of cars they drive. I know where they live."

I ask Jimmy what he'd do if they gave him a Gatorade bath in August. "I would have a frown on my face," he says. "There's only one time I want to have Gatorade dumped on me."

Kippy is joking. Jimmy is not.

August 9. Today, for the first time, the Dolphins prepare for an opponent as if it were the regular season. A bunch of second- and third-string defenders on the scout team read Chicago's defense off a big card held up by an assistant coach, then mimic that look so the first-team offense can prepare. Backup offensive players likewise "service" the starting defense. The backups figure, "Hey, this isn't *our* scheme, so I can go through the motions," and go half-speed. That's how they did it before; various coaches called it "thud tempo" or simply "walk-throughs." Jimmy called it bullshit. He stops practice at 10:10 A.M. and tells them he expected full-speed, full-tackling drills this day and every day as long as the season lasts.

"If you want to run the ball, if you want to win, that's how you have to practice," he says. "When we were getting ready for Buffalo and our first Super Bowl, some of the newspaper writers said we'd gone through such hard practices, such a long, grueling season, we'd probably practice in sweats. When I read that, I started laughing and said, 'Bullshit! We didn't get here to take it easy. We came here to win it.' You don't get here and say, 'Oh, we're here. Hey, good job, we made it.' Nooo! We practiced just as physically for that game as what we do now. That's one reason we won, 52–17. Because we were prepared to play."

Then he sends everyone back to work. Publicly, he praises the hard work and progress. But privately, upstairs in his office, he frets, "Certain individuals are not pushing through pain. Certain individuals are getting tired, making mistakes, jumping offside. My deal is evaluating those players and eliminating as many as I can."

He could do without most of them. But what about Karim Abdul-Jabbar?

Jimmy thought Karim could be his feature back, a first-round talent stolen in the third round because he lacked breakaway speed. Jimmy had bragged about him on draft day and the first day of veterans camp, but then Karim sprained his ankle July 23, and when he wasn't back within three days, Jimmy bitched publicly.

"I'm probably more frustrated than him," Karim said, then reaggravated the ankle in the Redskins scrimmage. When the players returned two days later, Karim was fifth team, and when he finally practiced July 31, he did not go full speed, claiming both ankles were aching. Jimmy was so fed up, he said he didn't even bother asking about Karim's health anymore. Why was he less patient with Karim's injuries than Charles Jordan's?

"I saw what Jordan could do," he replies. "Jordan worked throughout the entire off-season. I saw things that make me believe he can be an outstanding receiver. We've had very little exposure with Jabbar except what he did in college. Plus, Jordan's ankle was pretty severe. Jabbar's, there's not a lot of swelling. I can't say when a guy's hurt or not. It's just frustrating."

Only Karim can feel the pain inside his ankles, but Jimmy figures since they're not that swollen, he should fight through the pain. But every time Karim tried, he made the ankle worse, and if they were not strong, he could not make the sharp cuts that made him special. Number thirty-three was in a catch–22.

"I try not to be a doctor. I try not to write him off completely just because I think his ankles are not that bad," Jimmy says, and waves his hands over his desk.

He prides himself on motivating players, yet nothing seems to be reaching Karim. "My suspicion," Jimmy confides, "is he's not really mentally strong. But I haven't come to a final conclusion yet. Especially when I've seen the talent there. If I didn't see talent, I would write him off. The talent's there, so I'm giving him the benefit of the doubt. The guy rushed for umpteen thousand yards at UCLA, so he had to be somewhat mentally strong."

In fact, Karim had a reputation for fighting through injuries at UCLA. So maybe he really is hurt. Or maybe big money is making him complacent. Or maybe he's just making the mistake of the young. "I think it's a rookie thing," Jimmy says. "He's not used to competing at this level. He's used to being *the* guy. He's not used to what we're doing."

So how will Jimmy push the right buttons? "You get to know individuals as well as you can," the coach says. "You see how they respond to praise, how they respond to criticism. You see what makes them go, what irritates them."

And what have you figured out with Karim?

"I haven't yet."

August 10. Three rookies started the opener against Tampa Bay. Three will start tomorrow in Chicago: Stanley Pritchett at fullback. Daryl Gardener at right tackle, and Zach Thomas at middle linebacker. Shawn Wooden and Karim will not start because of injuries but will play. Jerris McPhail will be the third-down back again.

Originally, Jimmy thought six to eight rookies would make the team. Now he's projecting nine, ten, or eleven, with about half of them starting before the year is very old. When the local writers ask if he can win this year with that many rookies, he replies, "We'll be a good football team." Pause. "In time."

But his players and fans will not see this book for a year, so Jimmy doesn't have to be so coy with me. Alone in his office, I ask if he truly believes his team is the one to beat this year or if he had just said that back in March to motivate his players.

"When I say something like that," he confesses, "I know I'm not talking to just a writer. I know I'm talking to other teams and coaches and my team. I like to do that on occasion to slowly build the confidence of our team and put pressure on our team and tell them up front what my expectations are. I don't mind planting some seeds of doubt in opponents' minds, even though it may backfire. There's a better chance that it'll plant that one seed of doubt in their minds, 'Hey, this guy's got credibility, he's done it before, he may be right.'

"Even originally, I knew it wasn't going to happen overnight. That's why I said, 'We're not the team to beat right now, but we will be.' If our players have it set in their minds that we're going to do this, and it doesn't happen on Day One, now all of a sudden, they lose faith. So I have to cushion it for them so they're totally confident it's going to happen even if it doesn't right away."

August 11. Chicago. Jimmy is coaching against his best coaching buddy, Dave Wannstedt. He's making his national TV debut as Dolphins coach. Two hours before the game, he's bouncing and wiggling. He's anxious for good reason. "Jimmy was very candid as he talked to us about the strengths and weaknesses of this team," Tom Hammond tells NBC viewers.

"He found a lot of weaknesses. He was hard-pressed to find positives," Paul Maguire adds.

"We had to get him on another subject," Bob Trumpy cracks.

Then the Bears kick off, and Miami is one big, long joke. A holding penalty wipes out a nice kick return. The blocking falls apart, and the Bears stuff the backs, then sack the quarterback. The Bears dink the ball down the field for a field goal, snuff Irving Spikes on fourth and one on his forty-four, and use the field position to kick another field goal. Pritchett drops a pass, guard Chris Gray is penalized, Kirby can't muscle for a first down, and Miami punts again.

On second and seventeen, third-team defensive tackle Norman Hand jumps before the snap, and Jimmy throws his hands up in despair. The next play, Chicago wide receiver Curtis Conway fakes outside and Miami cornerback J. B.

Brown bites on the fake. Conway cuts inside and runs a deep post. J.B. must cover the post, but cannot close on the 4.3 sprinter. Safety Gene Atkins should get over sooner, but does not. Touchdown. Eighty-three yards. The two-point try fails, but the Bears lead, 12–0.

Dolphins' ball. Two Kirby carries gain nothing. Keith Byars catches the ball over the middle but again a Dolphins back is too weak or slow to plow for that final yard. Chicago rookie Bobby Engram returns the punt forty-one yards. Seven plays later, Miami linebacker Dwight Hollier bites on a so-so play-action fake, and tight end Keith Jennings catches a four-yard touchdown pass to make it 19–0 and incredibly embarrassing.

"The Dolphins have a lot of problems to fill, and they don't have great players to do it with," Maguire says. "There are receivers on this team that Marino doesn't even know. He hasn't met them yet."

Problems? What problems? Dan Marino can erase a lot of problems. He re-acquaints himself with three incumbents. He hits O. J. McDuffie for ten yards, Kirby for thirteen, Randal Hill for fifteen. He looks left and throws right . . . right to Hill for thirty-four yards and a touchdown.

Says Trumpy: "Jimmy Johnson's got to be standing on the sideline thinking, What I want is a power running game, a power defense. But every time he sees Marino throw a pass like that, with that accuracy . . . he's got to be rethinking, Hey, wait a minute! There aren't three quarterbacks in the league who'd even try that pass—and Marino does it routinely."

"That candy store," Hammond says, "is looking better and better."

And better. Marino takes over with sixty seconds and sixty-three yards to go and finds the end zone again with ten seconds to spare. Donnell Woolford has Lamar Thomas covered, yet Marino's pass comes fast as a bullet and low to the sideline, where only LT can catch it. It is a nice catch—and a great, great throw. It is a pass very few quarterbacks can make and a route very few coordinators call if they do not have a Marino.

"That's not a normal route," Hill says later. "It's a route with a Dan Marino signature on it."

"An inexperienced quarterback gets intercepted there," LT says. "Dan's a great quarterback. He threw a dart. Most of his passes have a lot of stuff on them. He gets the ball out so quickly, you turn around it's there on top of you. I've got a few Wilson tattoos, a few Paul Tagliabues, on my arms."

The Dolphins have been totally dominated at the line of scrimmage on both sides of the ball, but when Terrell Buckley gets his second interception of the game and third in two games and Bernie Kosar follows with a touchdown pass, the Dolphins lead early in the fourth quarter. Still, a victory will unjustifiably mask the problems. Late in the fourth quarter, a rookie who's played guard for three days combines with a fourth-string quarterback to screw up a blocking assignment, and Karim's thrown for a safety to tie the score. The Bears backups then take the free kick and drive for the winning field goal as time expires.

"We made a dozen different dumb mistakes," a livid Jimmy huffs. "Any one of those plays could lose a game in and of itself in the regular season."

But if you think he will be tempted to visit the candy store to quench his sweet tooth, think again. "Everybody's gonna get caught up with the inability to run," he says. "Hey, it doesn't happen overnight. I've said it before and I'll say it a hundred times. This team hasn't run for I don't know how long. So I just don't all of a sudden come in one day, say we're gonna run the ball, and it happens. It's not easy, guys. We're gonna keep doing it and keep doing it until we *can* do it.

"If we're gonna be a good team in December and January, we have to be able to run. I don't want to start this season throwing fifty times a game. That's not going to get us where we want to go."

They believe. "I've never coached a Super Bowl team," Randal Hill says. "If Jimmy says it'll take a while, it'll take a while. He came to the locker room before the game, no smiling, no joking, straight face, and said I was going to make a big play, and then I catch a touchdown. He's like Nostradamus. He can predict the future."

But can he turn these stiffs into winners?

August 12. The day after every game, Jimmy and his assistants spend hours poring over every frame of video, analyzing what went right and what went wrong. The position coaches review the film with their players. Jimmy critiques special teams with the entire team because he wants everyone to know just how important the kicking game is to him.

The players and coaches gather tonight in the auditorium and Jimmy says he will use the first-team units most of the next game with Minnesota.

"That doesn't mean the lineup can't change," he cautions. "If you're not starting on offense or defense or special teams, you still have two weeks to make the team. You don't have it made unless *I* tell you."

He raises his voice. "Understand: Unless I tell you, you haven't made the team."

He points at Marino and says, "You're one."

Bernie Kosar laughs, leans toward Marino, and says, "Coach, you pointing at me?"

"No," Jimmy says, and everyone laughs.

Jimmy flicks on the video projector and shows Larry Izzo flying down the field on a kickoff, knocking one man down, getting up, and not just brushing another guy, but just burying him. When NFL coaches see such hell-bent effort, they wish they could transplant the scrub's heart in their prodigy's body. But they can't do that, and they don't keep the scrub, either. They keep the draft choice they risked their money and reputation on. They don't keep Larry Izzo.

Larry Izzo was barely 5'10"; 5'10" linebackers do not make it. Larry Izzo was from Rice; Rice grads run companies, not kickoffs. Larry Izzo went undrafted but has proven to be a lot like Zach Thomas, his new roommate. They are attracted to the ball as if it were a magnetic device. So far in camp he has outgraded everyone else on special teams by a two-to-one margin.

"You guys want to know what I want on special teams?" Jimmy asks his players. "Take a look at Larry Izzo!" He shows the kick return again. "Look at him coldcock that guy! I mean, *coldcock* him!"

He asks Izzo where he's from, though he full well knows the answer. "The Woodlands, Texas," Izzo says, sheepish, not knowing where this is leading.

"Near Houston?" Jimmy asks.

"Yes, sir," Izzo says, wanting to hide but needing to bark it out from the back of the room.

"You have family back in The Woodlands?" Jimmy asks.

"Yes, sir," Izzo says.

"Call your family tonight," Jimmy says. "You've made the team!"

Jimmy looks around the auditorium at all the players.

"Now we've got two. We're looking for fifty-one more."

Up front, Kosar nudges Marino. "Don't you know that motherfucker is peeing down his leg right now?"

August 13. When the defense lines up for the first time today, secondary coach Mel Phillips approaches Calvin Jackson and says, "Calvin, get in there with the first team."

That's how Jackson finds out he's been promoted to first-team right cornerback and J. B. Brown discovers he's been replaced.

Jackson jogs into the huddle, not even a smile on his face. "I don't think anyone has time to celebrate," he explains later. "The only job security around here is winning."

J.B. had made the Dolphins as a twelfth-round pick in 1989, had become a starter the following year, had been a fixture ever since. But he had not played well in 1995, and he had been burned deep twice in two preseason games. Jimmy said it wasn't just the games; Calvin had outplayed J.B. since minicamp. J.B. is contrite. "I'm mad at myself. It's Coach Johnson's decision, and for whatever reason, I hope it motivates me to get my act together and play better."

But it will not. Jimmy wants to see how he responds to the challenge. He will go into a funk, and flunk.

This is the stuff of dreams for Calvin. The Fort Lauderdale native signed with his hometown team as a free agent after two years at Auburn. He had been cut a few times, had worked his way through the practice squad and inactive list to start when J.B. was injured, and now, in his third season, he had arrived. He could have rejoiced, but he has seen too much go wrong to frolic now. "Can't take nothing for granted," he says. "You have to work harder than guys who were drafted. You have to make yourself noticeable."

Calvin and T-Buck are just 5'9". They'll face Minnesota's Cris Carter and Jake Reed, both 6'3", on *Monday Night Football*. T-Buck was drummed out of Green Bay because the Packers felt he couldn't cover big receivers.

"They're going to be facing tall guys all year long, but I'm confident they can make the plays," Jimmy says publicly. But in the off-season, he will make sure he doesn't have to play a pair of 5'9" corners again.

Yet this afternoon, Calvin Jackson shows he deserves the job. He drives on a Marino pass and knocks it away from O. J. McDuffie, who kicks the ball in frustration. "Way to break on it, Cal!" Jimmy shouts. Ten minutes later, Jackson jumps in front of rookie Brice Hunter and makes a diving interception. "Awwww riiiight, Calvin!" Jimmy says, and pats him on the butt when Jackson jogs by. Buckley breaks up another pass, and Jimmy hollers, "Awwww riiiight!" to T-Buck, too. Positive reinforcement, remember?

After practice, Jimmy tells the local writers the defense did a nice job. That's partly true. But it's also true that the passing offense has again looked ragged. Dallas coaches say Troy Aikman can go through a whole practice without a pass hitting the ground. But today, footballs hit the ground almost as often as players' feet. Marino has fretted all preseason about the lack of chemistry with his receivers. With O.J. slowed by a tender hamstring, Dan's top wideouts are Randal Hill, Lamar Thomas, Scott Miller, Kirby "Steak" Dar Dar, and Sir Mawn "On The Mount" Wilson, who combined for twenty-two catches and zero touchdowns the previous year.

Danny needs to know how fast the receiver will come out of his break and look back for the ball. He needs to know if the receiver will always cut exactly where he is supposed to or if he will turn a yard shorter or deeper, or round off his route. He needs to know how a receiver will react to the look of a defensive scheme, to a defensive back's position, to a blitz. He needs to know the receiver will get open fast. He needs to know the receiver will hold on to the ball. All this is part of the intricate chemistry that develops between passers and catchers over years, a chemistry where a simple nod or suggestion can lead to a touchdown, a chemistry that is sorely lacking here.

The quarterbacks and coaches take turns in frustration. A play breaks down and Marino flings the ball downfield in disgust. Kosar waits, waits, waits, waits, and finally aborts a pass when no wideout gets open. About the only completions this day are to running backs in the flat or across the middle. Kosar fakes an out pass to Miller, who breaks to and then up the sideline but lacks the separation speed to break away. The pass sails over his head. Larry Seiple, who saw a lot of great receivers in his first twenty years as a Dolphins player and coach, waves his arms angrily, thrusting his notes up and down, yelling to one receiver, "How many times do I have to tell you? Plant and come back to the fuckin' ball!"

Could it be that the Dolphins have lost so many good receivers and dedicated so much time to improving the running game that they will lose their greatest weapon, the one Jimmy thought would always be there?

The skies turn a dark gray. Thunder rumbles, lightning crackles, but the rains never come. Humidity hangs over the practice field like a sponge. Christians have seen hell, and the rumor is it's South Florida, in the dog-day afternoons of August.

August 15. With Eric Green and Johnny Mitchell gone and Kerry Cash fading fast, tight end is a problem. The coaches considered shifting Keith Byars there even before Stanley Pritchett beat him out at fullback. But Keith hadn't blocked anybody as a fullback, so why would he start now that he's been switched to tight end, where he'll often be asked to hit 300-pounders?

Publicly, Jimmy says the move has more to do with Pritchett's emergence than Cash's disappearance, that the routes won't be too much different and the blocking won't be that big a priority. But privately, he doubts Keith's evasiveness in the open field and his blocking with a defender in his face.

Publicly, Jimmy isn't talking about trading Terry Kirby, but privately, he has given San Francisco and Baltimore the right to talk to Kirby's agent, and Jimmy's eager to deal. Kirby is a superb receiver and a decent outside runner, but he runs upright and doesn't fit Jimmy's style. He doesn't have Karim Abdul-Jabbar's or Irving Spikes's toughness to run inside, he doesn't have Jerris McPhail's break-away ability as a third-down back, he doesn't have Bernie Parmalee's special-teams ability, and he sure isn't worth $783,000 as a fifth halfback. But he fits San Francisco's offense well, and the 49ers are desperate.

Jimmy has a strong rapport with 49ers president Carmen Policy, and they have talked about a deal for a while now. They talk extensively today and continue tonight as Jimmy drives from his weekly television show to his weekly night out with Rhonda and Nick.

Baltimore has balked at Jimmy's price, and Carmen has, too. "Some guys here only want to offer a sixth-round pick," Carmen says.

"Carmen," Jimmy replies, "last draft I came in with eight picks and came out with twelve. I tell my guys I can take a crap and get a sixth-round pick out of it. So don't offer me that."

Jimmy wants a third-round pick that will become a second-round pick if Kirby plays a lot. Carmen says he doesn't know how much Kirby can help, especially at this late date. Jimmy assures Carmen, "This guy will start. He will win games for you." They compromise on a fourth-round pick that can become a third-rounder if Kirby plays 65 percent of the 49ers' offensive snaps. Jimmy has a deal before he has his meal.

August 16. Jimmy hoped to find a special back by now. But Karim has been hurt. Spikes has performed better in practices than games. McPhail is more experienced as a receiver than runner. Parmalee is eight months removed from reconstructive knee surgery and doesn't have his quickness back. Jimmy says any can still win the job, but Karim's healthiest week of camp is confirming what the coach has suspected since draft day.

The running problem isn't just with the backs. Jimmy feels confident in left tackle Richmond Webb, left guard Keith Sims, and center Tim Ruddy. But Chris Gray and Andrew Greene are battling at right guard, James Brown and Billy Milner at right tackle, and all four have problems. Plus, even the Pro Bowl linemen are struggling with the new schemes and demands.

"It's almost like early childhood," Sims says. "We have to refine the nuances and techniques to make it perfect."

Shula used draws and sweeps and finesse, man-to-man blocking; Jimmy uses counters and counter-gaps and quick hits between the tackles, with more of the zone blocking popularized by Joe Bugel's Hogs in the early eighties.

"It's night and day," Sims says. "It's power zone blocking now. Every play, we're asked to drive them off the line. In the past, we were asked to do it some, but other times we weren't. Our running game was predicated on the draw, finessing and finagling and influencing people. Now, we're coming at you. Try to stop us. We want to develop five or six plays that we know are gonna get us five yards. We don't need a hundred plays that *may* work.

"We've had that reputation as the best pass-blocking line. We haven't had the repetitions to become that dominating run line like everyone thinks of Dallas. We've always wanted to run. Now, it's an opportunity to put our money where our mouth is. People have always labeled Richmond and I as finesse linemen. We feel we can drive people off the ball with the best of them. We're looking forward to the challenge."

August 19. Miami. Down on the field, Jimmy Johnson schmoozes with ABC's *Monday Night Football* announcers. Up in the press lounge, many reporters don't even bother turning around to listen when Don Shula makes himself available for interviews. His final year had been a cantankerous, contentious battle with the local media, but now, when media relations director Harvey Greene says Shula has only five or ten minutes, Shula jokes, "Hell, I've got all kinds of time. I don't have anything to do."

He talks about his golf game, and his sons coaching in Tampa and Cincinnati, and his new roles hawking DirecTV and studying NFL officiating. He talks about playing golf at historic St. Andrews in Scotland and watching Michael Johnson set records in the Olympics in Atlanta. He says he's at peace with his decisions to leave coaching and to reject Art Modell's offer to run Baltimore's front office, but he felt a tinge of emotion on draft day and won't rule out returning someday. And what does he think of Jimmy trying to establish the run?

"I think I said it one time," he says, joking. "You've got a dilemma when and if you take the ball out of Dan Marino's hands," he says, not joking.

The friction remains. Rationally, Don knows Jimmy must do it his way, but emotionally, every change is a jab to his ego, a repudiation of everything he's achieved. He walks onto the field at 7:28 P.M. and shakes Wayne Huizenga's hand. Jimmy spots them and instantly runs over and shakes both their hands. With six minicams and seven still photographers firing away, Jimmy and Don make conversation for less than two minutes, and then it's over. Don leaves. It isn't his field, his stage, any longer.

It is Jimmy's, and a half hour later, it's a mess. The rains come hard and long, and the fans run for cover and the players and coaches for their aqua raincoats. Minnesota's Warren Moon, who played his college ball in Seattle, acts as if he never played in rain before. He fumbles the ball away on the Vikings' first three series. But the Dolphins aren't doing any better. Punter/holder John Kidd is intercepted on a fake field goal, and Marino and Spikes get stripped of the ball.

On and on come the rains and the turnovers. Qadry Ismail drops the ball on fourth and one, but Pete Stoyanovich ricochets a forty-one-yard field goal off the right upright. The ball slips out of Moon's hand again when he tries to throw, and Trace Armstrong picks up the fumble and runs six yards for a touchdown. Jake Reed drops a touchdown pass for Minnesota and Lin Elliott's line-drive field goal from thirty-two yards is blocked. No wonder Minnesota was talking with Miami hours before the game about a Stoyo trade.

Nedney keeps booming his kickoffs, and when he nails a forty-eight-yard field goal, Stoyo might as well start packing. Minnesota loses yet another fumble, and Terrell Buckley, continuing his inspired preseason, high-steps fifty-one yards. Marino hits Charles Jordan in stride and he struts into the end zone for a twenty-five-yard touchdown and a 17–3 lead. T-Buck deflects a pass to Louis Oliver for the Dolphins' fifth takeaway, but J. B. Brown assures he will not win back his starting job when he interferes with Ismail and still gives up a touchdown catch. Lamar Thomas wins a job with a seventy-one-yard touchdown catch and 103-yard night, and the Dolphins win, 24–17.

"The true test of character is how you rise from the depths. When I was released by Tampa, a cloud lifted off my head," says LT, reborn as a Christian and a player when his old coach gave him a second chance in Miami. "Jimmy knows what type of person I am. Sometimes I have to pinch myself. It's like a dream come true."

August 20. The dream dies this morning for fifteen Dolphins, including third-round pick Dorian Brew and fourth-round picks Kirk Pointer and LaCurtis Jones. Brew, Jimmy's second selection as Dolphins coach, got injured early in camp, and neither he nor Pointer lived up to their promise as cover cornerbacks. By early August, they sensed they were on borrowed time and did little to change matters. Even on the practice field, they stood separate from their team-mates, minds drifting, and they did nothing on special teams to warrant sticking around. Jones worked hard but was inconsistent and outperformed by fellow newcomers Zach Thomas, Larry Izzo, Anthony Harris, and O. J. Brigance.

It's a busy morning. Jimmy, who typically arrives between five-thirty and six-thirty, gets in at six o'clock and goes over his list of cuts. Every couple of days since camp began, he worked and reworked his projected list of who would make this cutdown to sixty players, who would make the following week's cut to fifty-three, and who might be worth one of the five spots on the practice squad. He visited frequently with each position coach individually about who ranked where. He does not believe in staff meetings to decide such issues because he doesn't want to be swayed by the best debater. He puts a check mark next to each player he wants to see personally and gives copies of the list to Stu Weinstein and Bob Ackles so they can start calling the players to the office. Not all can be reached because they are off until 7 P.M., but the ones who can filter in quickly and most get the bad news straight from Jimmy.

If Jimmy doesn't think they can play in the pros, he tries to keep it short and tell them best of luck but not offer false hope. But he realizes it's a devastating day, and he tries to encourage most to stay in shape in case another team claims them or in case the Dolphins have injuries. For instance, today he tells Ethan Albright he'll re-sign him if long snapper Frank Wainright gets hurt.

He calls in wide receiver Kirby Dar Dar and his agent, Drew Rosenhaus, and tells them he wants to get one more look at draft pick Brice Hunter in the final preseason game, but he likes the way Dar Dar plays special teams and says there's a good chance he'll want Dar Dar back for the regular roster or at least the practice roster.

"If another club tries to sign you, make sure you let us know," Jimmy says, and they promise.

Dar Dar is convinced Jimmy isn't just being nice. "He doesn't look you in the face and shoot BS," Dar Dar says. "He's very honest."

Rosenhaus tells Jimmy that Eric Green wants to come back when his knee heals. Funny. At 8 A.M., Johnny Mitchell and his agent show up, unannounced, begging for another chance, too. Jimmy agrees to meet with Eric, and he does not rule out re-signing Johnny, either. He doesn't trust either tight end, but he doesn't have a lot of options, and he isn't going to burn himself just to make a point.

And Jimmy meets with J. B. Brown, too. J.B. had barely survived the cut, and while Jimmy doesn't say it, he hints that if J.B. plays that poorly in the final preseason game, he won't survive the final cut. He tells J.B. he thinks the veteran has a lot of talent, but hasn't responded to his demotion with any sense of urgency.

"I'll play a lot better," J.B. promises. "You won't see that performance again."

August 21. Joe Nedney spent a few weeks in Green Bay's training camp and another few weeks on Miami's practice squad in 1995. He was the kicking version of John Daly: He could kick a ball into the next ZIP code, but he never knew *which* ZIP code. He had to get rid of the natural hook in his kick. Special teams coach Mike Westhoff sent him home with some technique tips, and Nedney "must have kicked ten thousand footballs" in the off-season.

Throughout this camp, Nedney kicked long and straight, consistently airmailing his kicks four yards into the end zone, the ball hanging in the air 4.2 seconds, too deep, too long, for opponents to return. Westhoff says Nedney's leg is as strong "as anybody's"—even Morten Andersen's. By contrast, Pete Stoyanovich's kicks in 1995 traveled only to the six, with 3.8 seconds hang time, enough time for opponents to return the ball to the thirty. Stoyo's accuracy also had plunged—but his salary had skyrocketed. So even before camp started, Jimmy thought the kicking competition could be a real battle.

Jimmy does not put a big premium on accurate but expensive field goal kickers. Only once in five years in Dallas had a game come down to a last-minute kick, and he had gone through five cheap kickers without losing games. He wants a running game that will hold the ball at game's end and not rely on heroics by kickers and quarterbacks. He prefers a cheap youngster who can drive the ball into the end zone and force the opposing offense to start at the twenty. "With as young a defense as we're gonna have—only four guys who started here last year are with us now—it's critical that offenses start as far back as possible. I couldn't afford Pete's field position with our defense," he explains. "So my whole deal is, will Nedney be close to Pete on his field goal percentages?"

And will he respond to pressure? Jimmy simulates game situations every day in practice. He stands right behind his kickers and yells, "Five seconds left. Tie score. Field goal from forty-five yards!" and then watches who responds. The coaches chart every kick under pressure. Nedney hits forty-seven of fifty-three, Stoyo forty-four of fifty. Close enough. Jimmy will ax Stoyo at the final cut if he cannot trade him, but the Chiefs conclude nearly three weeks of casual conversation and three days of intense talks today when they offer the draft pick Jimmy wants.

The contact began in early August when Lynn Stiles, Kansas City's personnel director and a former special teams coach, called Ackles to feel him out about the kicking competition. They did not discuss the price then, but Stiles came away thinking the Dolphins would trade Stoyo if Nedney kept kicking well. And that's what he wanted to hear. The Chiefs weren't interested in Nedney; they had endured enough young, inconsistent kickers. They had a terrific veteran defense but an offense lacking firepower. Their defense could overcome poor field position after short kickoffs, but their offense lacked big-play people and relied heavily on field goals. They had wasted the league's best record when Lin Elliott missed from thirty-five, thirty-nine, and forty-two yards in a 10–7 playoff loss to the underdog Colts, and they did not want to go through that agony again.

Stiles reported back to general manager Carl Peterson, and Ackles briefed Jimmy. Minnestoa and Jacksonville expressed interest in Stoyo, too. Neither ever offered anything, but the Dolphins couldn't let the Chiefs know that. Jimmy and Ackles talked to Stiles and Peterson, trying to convince them others were making offers. "We fudged a little," Jimmy confessed later. "We had to create a little sense of urgency."

Stiles and Peterson debated whether they should wait and see if Stoyo and/or Oakland's Jeff Jaeger would be cut and they could get one of them without giving up a draft pick, but they feared Jimmy might trade Stoyo and Al Davis might hold on to both his kickers until after the Raiders played KC in Game Two. On August 20, Stiles called Westhoff, whom he respected and trusted, and got a glowing report on Stoyo. Westhoff said he would be very comfortable keeping Stoyo, but explained Miami's new philosophy: Shula's Dolphins took their chances with Marino throwing on third and five, and if the pass failed, they relied on Stoyo. But now if it's third and five inside the thirty, Jimmy will often use both downs, going for the first down rather than the field goal. KC pro personnel director Mark Hatley called and asked Westhoff a few more questions. And maybe this was the clincher: "If you had him last year," Westhoff said, "you would have won the AFC."

Peterson offered Jimmy a sixth-round pick that would become a fifth-rounder if Stoyo made the Pro Bowl.

"Hey, make it a five going to a four and we'll pull the trigger," Jimmy said.

Peterson balked. Then Stiles reminded Peterson what happened in the playoff loss. "A debacle," Stiles said. "Dumb, dumb, dumb. We're gonna play good defense and it's gonna be a low-scoring game and a lot of times it's going to come down to the kicker. We played three overtime games last year. If we weren't as close as we think we are, maybe we don't make this decision. But when there are just a few pieces missing and a kicker is one of them and you can get it resolved, it's a no-brainer."

So this afternoon, Peterson calls Ackles and agrees to pay Jimmy's price. Ackles gets off the phone, walks down the stairs, out the door, and right onto the practice field, where he tells Jimmy the news. Then Ackles tells Stoyo he's been traded, and Jimmy talks to both kickers.

Stoyo cleans out his locker, says quick good-byes to a few teammates, and with the cameras rolling, the kicker cries. "I just want to reiterate real quick . . . I'm a . . ." He stops, choked up. "How great things . . ." He swallows hard. "How great things have been." The words come haltingly between sobs. "And . . . it just . . . there'll always be a place in my heart for South Florida."

His voice cracks, and the tears stream down his day-old stubble, onto his gold chain and his gray T-shirt. "And I want to thank the Dolphins and Coach Shula and Joe Robbie, God rest his soul, and the entire Robbie family and Wayne Huizenga and everybody associated with my coming here. It's been a great, great thrill for me . . . and my family. I'll miss this place. I'll miss this place a lot. I've established a lot of roots here, met a lot of people, and they'll be missed. It's really not an easy thing to do."

"Pete and I talked," says punter John Kidd, his holder and friend. "He was very emotional. His wife's from South Florida. They just got married in June. He's leaving a lot sooner than he wanted to. He poured seven years of his life into here. You build attachments to your team, your friends, your community, and it's tough in five minutes to switch all that."

But Stoyo has a plane to catch. He walks to his car with one of those people he has touched, Scott Chait, the community relations assistant with cystic fibrosis, the disease that killed Stoyo's cousin at twenty-nine and will kill Chait in May 1997. Stoyo donated money to cystic fibrosis for every field goal he kicked. He founded a charity golf tournament and a fashion show to benefit the disease. He made speeches and called patients.

Chait says Stoyo will be missed by people with cystic fibrosis. And maybe by his coach, too. Westhoff had drafted Stoyo, had befriended him, had watched him become the fourth most accurate kicker in NFL history. Now he's relying on Nedney, who made just 56 percent in college and never has kicked in a regular-season game.

"I believe he's gonna do it," Westhoff says. "If he executes his techniques, he's got a heck of a chance. It's not some weird thing, where he kicks with some stupid style and I wonder if he'll make it. I'm more surprised when he misses. I'm not gonna stand there with rosary beads clutched in my hands."

Maybe he should.

August 23. Tampa. His young backs have Jimmy baffled. Irving Spikes looked good in practice, but he averaged less than two yards a carry in his first two games. Jimmy challenged him in front of everybody in a team meeting.

"You know, I'm a big fan of the fight game," he began. "There are two kinds of fighters: champions and club fighters. The club fighter has a five-day-a-week job and goes into the club on the weekend and gets beat up for a few dollars. But a champion works hard every day on making himself into a great fighter. He trains to go twelve three-minute rounds and goes out to win championships.

"You hear that, Irving Spikes? Are you a club fighter or a champion? I think you might be a club fighter."

"I'm a champion," Spikes replied.

"Then prove it to me, Spikes," Jimmy said.

Spikes averaged 4.5 yards a carry in his next game.

And then there is Karim. He isn't looking good in practice *or* games. He is missing practices and averaging just 2.3 yards a carry. Jimmy has big plans for his rookie. He does not want a running back by committee, as the Dolphins did for years. He does not want to go through an eighteenth consecutive year without a thousand-yard rusher, the worst string in the NFL. Considering what he wants this team to be, his feature back is every bit as important as his quarterback. Witness Jimmy's Dallas days: The Cowboys won five in a row without Troy Aikman in 1991 but started 0–2 without Emmitt Smith in 1993.

Jimmy wants to depend on one back but thinks his most talented back is utterly undependable. Karim is so serene. Is he California laid-back? Is it his Islamic faith? Is it the sudden riches? Jimmy keeps lobbing pebbles into this pool of tranquillity and causing not a ripple. Finally, he tosses a grenade—and gets an explosion.

During pregame warmups, Jimmy ambles over to Karim, down on the ground, stretching. Karim looks up, placidly. Jimmy looks down, imperially.

"This isn't UCLA. This is the NFL!" Jimmy growls. "You had a four-year scholarship there. Here, it's day to day. Your scholarship could be revoked tomorrow!"

Karim shoots a painkiller into his injured ankle. And then he goes out and averages 6.9 yards a carry. Spikes averages 6.1, Jerris McPhail 4.4, Bernie Parmalee 4.0. Hell, even Bernie Kosar, the guy who runs like a stork with arthritic knees, scrambles for a sixteen-yard gain. And, behind a line averaging 305 pounds, the Dolphins finally quit finagling and get physical, manhandling the Buccaneers for 228 yards rushing, or 5.4 yards a carry, en route to a very impressive 19–7 victory. The Dolphins gain 372 yards, the Bucs 134.

A Tampa Bay defensive line averaging 274 pounds isn't just outmuscled, it is outhustled. Chests heaving, mouths panting, the Bucs cannot catch their breath or the Dolphins' no-huddle offense.

Oh, how far the Dolphins have come in just one month. All those middle drills, all those conditioning drills, are starting to pay off.

"We were in better shape than they were," Keith Sims says. "We weren't nearly as tired as they were. You can tell. If you're out there, you can tell. Jimmy says we are going to be the best-conditioned team in the NFL. Are we? Who knows? But it was a factor tonight."

"We've come a long way," Jimmy says. "I'm never going to be totally satisfied, but considering the inexperience and the new faces, we've come as far as we can come with the people we have in there."

Jimmy pushed Calvin Jackson to drop ten pounds, pushed him into the starting lineup, and tonight Calvin returns an interception for a touchdown. "Aren't you glad you don't weigh 195 pounds anymore?" Jimmy asks Calvin as they leave the field, and Calvin nods in glee.

Another Jimmy project, Joe Nedney, kicks four short field goals, but misses a fifth, from just thirty-two yards. Two of Shula's linemen, Andrew Greene and Billy Milner, combine for three penalties. They will not last long. The Bucs would have been shut out if four guys didn't miss tackles and allow a ninety-one-yard punt return. That will change, too.

Inside the coaches' private dressing room, Jimmy sits on a wooden stool in the corner of the cramped, steamy room, chugging a Heineken and chatting with Bob Ackles, tight ends coach Pat Jones, and agent Nick Christin. Jimmy says he ran the no-huddle because it was part of the offense but also to give Bill Parcells something else to prepare for in the opener. He says Karim hasn't won the starting job from Spikes yet, that they will share carries, and he doesn't know what he will do the next morning when he met with Eric Green and Drew Rosenhaus.

"Drew's right out there," Ackles says, motioning out the door.

"On the phone?" Jimmy asks.

"No," Ackles says, "right outside the locker room."

"Bring him in here," Jimmy says, and Ackles goes outside and fetches the agent.

The game is barely half an hour old, but Jimmy is already thinking ahead. That broken punt coverage—partly because his "flyer" on the far left end didn't hear a fake punt called off and didn't get downfield quick enough—convinces him to re-sign Kirby Dar Dar, one of his best flyers. He tells Drew to get Kirby back in Davie in the morning to sign a new contract.

"I like Kirby," Jimmy says. "He's my kind of guy. I need more guys like that. I needed to look at other people tonight is all."

"I understand," Drew says. "I'll call him tonight. He had a couple of tryouts set up, but we'll cancel them. He'll be thrilled."

Jimmy isn't thrilled. "Don't screw with me on his contract," he warns Drew. He lowers and shakes his head. "Punt coverage," he hisses. "Fuuuuck!"

August 24. Kirby Dar Dar watched the game on television. When somebody named Nilo Silvan broke that long return, he sat straight up. He did not get excited and think he might get his old job back. He got depressed thinking he could have made a difference. He had a hard time getting to sleep.

When his phone rings at 3:30 A.M., it takes two rings to wake him and two more for him to reach his phone. He stumbles to his answering machine and hears Drew's message: The Dolphins want to sign him to the regular roster today.

Dar Dar is surprised; cutdown isn't until August 25, and already they're bringing him back? He calls his agent immediately and cannot fall back to sleep until six-thirty. At 2:30 P.M., he re-signs.

Dar Dar ran for 853 yards and ten touchdowns as a Syracuse senior. Fans made banners and T-shirts for the Kirby Dar Dar Fan Fan Club Club. He's fast and quick, but only 5'9" and 183 pounds, so the Dolphins are trying to make him a wide receiver. He spent 1995 on the practice squad and made his Dolphins debut in the last regular-season game. Whether he can be a great receiver is debatable—Dar Dar and family might be the only ones who believe it—but Jimmy always keeps two, three, sometimes four players just because they excel on special teams. The fans don't pay any attention to them, and on some teams, the players don't, either. They view it as hazardous grunt work, beneath them, worth very little glory or money. But Jimmy emphasizes special teams, and Dar Dar is one of those rare birds who loves covering punts and kicks.

"Being a flyer is a kamikaze job," he says, grinning. "Two defensive backs are lined up across from you, staring you down, trying to stop you. You've got to beat those two guys off the line. Then you have to get downfield. Sometimes there's another guy, sort of a safety valve, waiting for you. Even if you get by all of them, you've still got to tackle a great punt returner, a guy who's been making people miss for years.

"You still have defenders on your back, clipping you. You never get that call. I get clipped every game. I haven't got a call yet. The refs are more concerned with watching the trenches and making sure you're not hitting the punter or interfering with the fair catch. Of course, if you move too soon before the punt, they'll flag you, just like that. There's not a game that goes by that a flyer doesn't get clipped. Because once you beat them, they'll push you in the back to get you to stumble."

Geez, a flyer must really get beaten up.

"Depends on how good the flyer is," Dar Dar says, and grins. "I don't get beat up much. I make a move real fast at the line of scrimmage, get both defenders going one way or the other, and then I take off as fast as I can in the opposite direction. You set them up. Next time, maybe you give them the same move. So they start thinking you'll do it the third time, but that time, you give them a different move."

Even though Dar Dar will play more for the Dolphins this year than Eric Green, the media concentrate on the big name with the big butt.

Green arrives eight minutes early for the meeting with Jimmy. He had been surly with the media in his one year in Miami, talking twice a week, if at all. Today, begging for his old job back, he shakes hands and says, friendly as can be, "How are you, Steve?" He asks to speak to Edwin Pope and assure him he isn't a thug. Drew pats Eric's belly and says, "Look at this slim guy," and indeed, Big E looks slimmer of belly and butt than he has in years. And that is key because when Eric doesn't work, his thighs and butt get bigger than any lineman's and he loses quickness and stresses his shaky joints. He weighed 320–330 before, one reason his knees were shot and he couldn't practice. He looks to be about 280 now, a decent weight for him. But it's a mirage. The Dolphins weigh him on the exacting scale in their locker room. He is 297. He looks thinner because he's lost muscle definition. Eric claims he's been working out since his knee got healthy enough; Jimmy figures he hasn't "done anything."

But Jimmy, Bob Ackles, and Kevin O'Neill spend a full hour with Eric, Drew, and Drew's brother/shadow, Jason. Both sides are conciliatory. Eric says Jimmy misunderstood those thirty-nine missed practices. He says if he were lazy, he could have taken weeks off after knee surgery, but he rushed back within nine days and took painkilling shots and fluid-draining needles before almost every game because he wanted to play so badly. Playing hurt ruined his recovery. Drew says they will drop their $1.5 million grievance if Jimmy re-signs Eric.

"I want to work. I want to win," Eric tells Jimmy. "I want to keep my weight in check. I'm gonna be a practice player as well as a game-day player."

Jimmy encourages Eric to work hard to rehabilitate his knee and get in shape and maybe he will sign him. Secretly, Jimmy still figures it's less than fifty-fifty he'll sign Eric. Jimmy hates liars, and he doesn't want Eric's lax work ethic and party-hearty attitude poisoning his players' attitudes. But the big tight end might win him a game or two, and if the Dolphins can sign him for minimal salary and erase his grievance, maybe the master motivator can finally be the one to get him to work hard. But this is Jimmy's real motivation: The harder Eric works, the quicker he will sign, and the less the Dolphins will pay even if they lose the grievance, which they expect to win. Eric claims he'll be ready to play in three weeks. Drew says he'll keep working out and losing weight and will return in a few weeks for an update.

Drew says they are talking to other teams, but Eric says he wants to show Dolphins fans he's the player Don Shula thought was worth $12 million. "I think it's going to come together," Eric says, "and everybody's going to sit down and laugh and have a cup of tea over it and say, 'God, Jimmy Johnson sure is smart.' "

And then he drives away in his big white Mercedes S500, a cell phone and beeper by his side, a pink lei strung over his rearview mirror. Eric considers the lei a reminder of his trips to Hawaii and the Pro Bowl. Jimmy figures the lei means Eric likes to lay around in the sun.

August 25. Cutdown Day. The day that big, brave men turn into quivering cowards every time the phone rings. Teams do not call to say you've made it; they only call to say you should report to the office . . . with your playbook.

Once again, Jimmy arrives at 6 A.M. and gives his list of cuts to Bob Ackles and Stu Weinstein to call the axed players. He's gone over the cuts with not only the position coaches but also his salary and medical experts. Why? "You have to take into account how much money a guy is making and how much his signing bonus will be accelerated onto the salary cap," Jimmy explains. "And I always ask Kevin O'Neill, 'Is he an injury risk?' I don't want to keep a guy who's gonna go on injured reserve [IR] or get hurt a lot or continually complain about little injuries. Those are the things I consider besides performance. That and age. Is he a player who's leveled off? Or is he a young player who'll continually get better? Will he have fresh legs in December or be on IR in December?"

Fred Barnett has convinced his doctors and trainers that he can come back from knee surgery this year, and Jimmy listens to his plea and doesn't put him on injured reserve for the year. Jimmy also takes a chance by keeping just two quarterbacks, but he's hoping to add Craig Erickson soon.

Jimmy meets each of the seven waived players individually. Kerry Cash, who dropped another pass Friday night, loses out to Keith Byars and Brett Carolan, a slender tight end with sure hands and excellent quickness who was cut by San Francisco and hasn't even practiced yet. "We need to take a look at Carolan," Jimmy tells Cash. "Stay in shape and maybe we'll call you back in a few weeks." Cash will wind up with Jimmy's buddy Dave Wannstedt in Chicago.

Jeff Kopp, who made it the year before and will sign with Jacksonville, might be better now than the backup linebackers Jimmy is keeping, but Jimmy figures he's as good as he's going to get.

Mel Agee, Gene McGuire, and Garin Patrick are not surprising cuts, but Andrew Greene is. He was a 1995 second-round pick, started twice as a rookie, and came to camp battling Chris Gray at right guard. Now he's Shula's third straight second-round bust, joining Eddie Blake and Aubrey Beavers.

"Too many critical mistakes," Jimmy says. "Fourth and one, he lets his guy go. He gets a holding penalty, an offside penalty, and that's his track record. I can't allow that many mistakes."

Greene made his first mistake July 1, when he failed Jimmy's conditioning test. In fact, of the five guys who failed the conditioning test, the only survivor is Keith Sims. And the Pro Bowl guard had an excuse: He had surgery to repair turf toe barely three months earlier. Jimmy made him run the test again his first week in camp. Sims passed that time.

It's 10 A.M. All of the released players have shown up except Mike Buck. Jimmy pops out of his office and grabs Mike Westhoff in the hallway. This is how he works with his coaches on strategy and personnel decisions every day. He hates meetings. He gives his coordinators broad leeway to formulate game plans, but he bounds around the second floor like a guy on a caffeine craze—he likes his Diet Coke by day, his Heineken by night—offering his insights and input. He prefers not to demand changes—he'd rather frame it so the assistants think it was their idea—but the aides usually get the point.

Now that the roster is set, he pulls Westhoff aside to review who will start on the troublesome punt-cover team in the opener one week from today. Dar Dar and Sean Hill will be the flyers, Izzo the fullback, Shawn Wooden and O. J. Brigance the tackles.

"How about Bull in the line?" Jimmy asks, meaning Robert "Bull" Wilson, the second-string fullback.

"Yeah," Westhoff says, "we could do that. I was working him second team. We're on the same page."

At 10:38 A.M., Buck makes the longest walk of his life, through the Dolphins' lobby and up the long stairway to Jimmy's office. He had bombed Friday night in his shot to be the third quarterback. "We gave you a shot," Jimmy says. "We're only keeping two quarterbacks for now. Stay in shape, and if anyone gets nicked up, we could call you."

At 10:44 A.M., Buck is outside, looking in, looking bitter. He spent five years as a backup in New Orleans and Arizona, and now he's heading to his new home in the Florida Panhandle. "Jimmy gave me a lot of time to play in the game, but I haven't really practiced in four weeks, so I was rusty," he grumbles. "I knew his mind was made up the first day of minicamp."

Inside the locker room, a few more twenty-somethings have survived the Maalox months. Linebacker Anthony Harris, for example. He started and starred at Auburn and fully expected to be drafted, but the call never came that day.

"It was constantly ringing," he remembers, "but it was always from relatives or friends calling to say, 'Have you heard yet? Why haven't teams called you? We thought they'd call you.' I'd think, 'The next time it rings, it's gotta be a team calling to say they drafted me.' But they never called. The later it got, the more frustrated I got. I went off to a different room, all by myself. I'd hear it ring and if my dad said, 'Hold on, let me get him,' I knew it was from teams. Eight or ten called during the last two rounds to say they were interested in signing me as a free agent if I wasn't drafted. A lot more called after the draft was over. My agent and I agreed Miami was the place for me.

"When I got here, we had twelve linebackers. I never gave up hope. I'm a spiritual guy. I believed God sent me here for a reason. The way Jimmy gave everybody a shot, I figured I had a shot. After linebackers started getting released, I started thinking I had a shot.

"I pray each and every day," says Harris, son of a deacon in the Greater New Bethel Church in Fort Pierce, Florida. "Once you pray, you're not supposed to worry about anything. But being human, I'm still going to worry. Once I sat down and prayed last night, the tears got out of my body. After I dozed off, I was all right."

He woke up in his hotel room, and tried to watch TV, tried to will the phone not to ring. "It's the total opposite of the draft. On draft day, you want the phone to ring. On cutdown day, if they call and tell you to come in and bring your playbook, then you know it's over."

The phone rang.

"I was nervous. My heart was racing. It was my mom, calling with words of confidence before she went to church. She did the same thing the morning of the cutdown to sixty. I told her, 'Mom, I love you, I love to hear from you, *but don't call me this morning!*' " he says, shouting the last line.

"I got two other calls, and when I picked them up, nobody was there. They'd hung up. I didn't get a call from the team. I came to my locker, and my stuff was still here."

And that's when he knew he'd made it.

"My phone never rang," says Carolan, who arrived Thursday, thinking he'd just work out, and wound up playing the fourth quarter the next night. "I still wasn't sure when I came to the locker room. I didn't know if they'd get you over here and then tell you the news. Nobody told me anything, so eventually I figured I'd made it. It's a weird business, that's for sure."

Only now do Harris and Carolan dare to rent apartments; they had been staying in the team hotel. A first-round pick like Daryl Gardener, who already cashed a big signing bonus and is all but guaranteed a roster spot, can buy a lavish house. A fifth-round pick like Zach Thomas had rented an apartment back in June, but Zach was thrifty enough—and scared enough—that he shared the place with Larry Izzo. At least they have cars.

Joe Nedney hasn't rented a place or even a car yet, even after Stoyo was traded. He isn't taking any chances until every team makes its final cuts and the Dolphins don't change kickers. He will rent a car and apartment and furniture tomorrow. He won't buy silverware or sheets, let alone a car. He will rent everything on a month-to-month basis. To Joe Nedney, NFL is short for Not For Long.

Why, when his fiancée, Gina Urzi, wanted to buy an airline ticket to visit him for the opener, he told her to get a refundable ticket or wait until the last minute. She said she didn't want to wait and pay that exorbitant premium. She'd take her chances. She won. Joe will spring for her ticket with his first game check.

Larry Izzo is more generous. Last night he went to Circuit City and bought a forty-six-inch TV as his sister's wedding present. Tina Izzo is getting married in The Woodlands the day before Larry makes his regular-season debut in Miami.

"They set the wedding date a long time ago," Larry says. "When I signed to come here, I told them, 'I hope I don't make it to the wedding.' They said, 'Listen, we hope you don't, either.' "

It seemed a long shot until that night two weeks before, when all his teammates heard Jimmy query Larry.

"It felt like an outer-body experience, like I was outside my body watching the conversation. I was thinking, 'I'm sitting here talking to Jimmy Johnson in a team meeting?' I always thought I could make it, but the way he told me . . . whoa! I mean, me and Dan Marino? When I called home, my parents didn't believe me. One of my friends faxed a copy of *The Miami Herald* story to my dad's office. They liked the headline, MARINO AND LARRY IZZO. That's when they finally believed it. Maybe tonight they'll believe me."

8
GRAND OPENINGS

Keith Sims had called himself a Dolphin throughout the nineties. But when he walked through the locker room Monday morning, August 26, 1996, he could not name some of his teammates.

Twenty-four new faces. "The first thing you have to do," the gregarious guard said, "is ask some of them their names."

Ten rookie faces. J. B. Brown, a Dolphin longer than anyone save Dan Marino, didn't recognize everyone, either. "In two years," J. B. predicted, "I don't think there's going to be any faces in this locker room from when Shula was coach."

And if any thought they could celebrate surviving the cut and the camp, Jimmy quickly warned them, "It's business now. It's time to get down to work and get ready to play real games. This is the group of fifty-three that we'll go with, but there will be changes as time goes on. When I bring the practice squad members in, I will tell them to work as hard as they can and if they prove to me they're better than someone on the roster, they'll take his spot."

The players found the coach more serious than ever. They had prepared a little for the New England Patriots over the past two weeks, but now the cuts were done, the preseason was over, and the normal work week for the real season was kicking in.

"It's getting more tense," Sims said. "Preseason is for eliminating mistakes and getting better. The regular season is for getting the job done. This counts. You start working in early March for this, and now it's finally here. All the excitement, all the anticipation, builds up. All this talk about the playoffs and Super Bowl, now it's for real. You bust your butt during the week, and that makes Sunday easy. That's when it's really fun."

Sims ripped open three large boxes. One was crammed with linemen's athletic gloves. Two contained football shoes, size fifteen, in four styles to be worn depending on the playing surface: cleats for grass, cleats for artificial turf, cleats for wet turf, and seven-studded cleats for the absolute worst footing. Nine pairs. Enough for a lifetime, right?

"Half a year's worth," Sims said, checking inside each box and, when satisfied, storing them in the vacated locker next to his. "One thing about Nike, you ask them to send more shoes, they never ask why you need that many. They just send them."

Nike and Reebok were the NFL's official shoes; players could wear another manufacturer's shoes, but they would be fined if they did not mask any identifying logos with black marker or white tape. The first time they played on a different surface, a bulletin-board message would remind them to make sure they broke in the right cleats that week in practice. Equipment managers had been fired for packing the wrong shoes for a road trip. Shoes were serious business in the NFL. So were stadium names. A sports apparel firm paid Wayne Huizenga $20 million to name Joe Robbie Stadium as Pro Player Park for the next ten years. (A few weeks later it would go by its third name of the year, Pro Player Stadium.)

Jimmy signed a side deal with Pro Player Inc., too, but his business now was football. He had been as accommodating with the local media as any coach anywhere during the past eight months. But now he turned terse. He told the writers they weren't going to get as many one-on-one interviews. He told the TV cameramen they were only allowed to videotape a few minutes at the end of practice, and, when they did, they were allowed only close-up shots isolated on individuals, not wide-angle views that might tip off the competition about a play the Dolphins would run that week.

Paranoia? Maybe not. Jimmy was watching the sports on an Atlanta station the week the Cowboys were in Atlanta, preparing for Super Bowl XXVIII with the Bills, when he saw Jim Kelly warming up with Thurman Thomas before a practice. They were in sweats, didn't even have all the linemen in, but they were practicing a shovel pass, a play they hadn't run all season. Jimmy noted the formation and practiced against it. He told his defensive linemen if the Bills lined up in that set, they should not rush upfield after Kelly. They had to close inside, toward Thomas. "I think they ran it three or four times, and we stopped it every time," Jimmy said. "The first time the Bills tried it, Leon Lett stripped Thurman Thomas—and James Washington picked up the fumble and ran for a touchdown." The Bills were beating the Cowboys 13–6 before that shovel pass launched a Dallas run of twenty-four unanswered points.

The next day, Tuesday, was usually the players' off day and the coaches' game-plan day. But first they detoured to the Greater Miami Chamber of Commerce meet-the-Dolphins luncheon. A thousand guests gathered at the swank Hotel Inter-Continental down by the bay to dine on salmon and chicken and raspberry tarts. They cheered as each player was introduced, but they saved the loudest and longest applause not for Dan Marino but for Jimmy Johnson. And when Jimmy stood up to talk, he had them laughing and cheering and applauding wildly within two minutes.

"One thing I know about South Florida," he told the crowd, "you *love* a winning Dolphin team. You love winning, and that's what you expect. Well, let me promise you this: Your expectations are no higher than the expectations of this group of players and coaches. We know it's not going to be easy. We've got a lot of young faces. There's going to be times when we have some low moments. We know that.

"But this team's goal is to make continual progress and get better every single week. And I promise you this: With the new faces we do have, we *will* get better. And we'll be playing our best football in December and January. The way this team has worked—and they have worked harder in the off-season program, getting ready for the preseason and going through the physical practices than any team I've been around—we're gonna win games. There's no doubt in my mind!"

He was part TV preacher, part carnival huckster, part Anthony Robbins motivator. People clapped and hooted and hollered and screamed, "Allll riiiight!"

"How many people, whatever your career might be, can say they were the very, very best? The best sportscaster, the best priest, best husband, best wife. Let me say this: I'm not a big political fellow. But when the most powerful man in the world grabs your hand and says, 'Congratulations, Jimmy, you had the best team in the country,' it makes the hair on the back of your neck stand up. And the hair on my neck doesn't stand very far . . . because I've got it waxed down pretty good."

Everybody laughed. Jimmy's hair was famous. People talked so much about The Hair that sometimes they confused it with the man, made him a caricature, and Jimmy was a whole lot more complicated than that. The Hair masked the tough kid nicknamed Scar Head; the hair standing on end revealed why he was The Shark Among Dolphins.

"It's a special, special feeling," Jimmy said. "The first time I achieved that was when I was with the University of Miami and met President Reagan. Once you have it, you want it again. And you want it again! And you want it *again*! If you've never been there, you don't know what you've missed. That's the excitement of being with a group like this. I never want to go through life in the middle of the road. In some ways, the absolute misery of losing a key game, or the misery of training camp, the misery of working day and night, that makes you want to get to the top. That makes you want to have that feeling of being the best.

"Sometimes people say, 'Coach, you're too hard on the guys when they lose.' Hey, I *want* it to hurt. I *want* them to be *sick to their stomachs*! I want them to hate losing so bad that they won't ever want it to happen again."

The sermon was aimed more at his players than at fans. But Jimmy wasn't satisfied coaching the Dolphins. He wanted to coach Dolphins fans, too.

"Now," he said, "I've heard the story about Pro Player Park at times wasn't as loud and crazy as it was years ago in the Orange Bowl. Peeee-plll! When the opponent has the ball, when Drew Bledsoe is behind the center, spread the word: We want you to be loud! Let that place be rockin'! Let the crowd be screamin'!"

And the suits and pretty ladies screamed on cue as if they were Pavlov's dog hearing the dinner bell.

"I want you to be at the top of your lungs!" Jimmy said. "So when Drew Bledsoe makes an audible, Curtis Martin misses the audible and goes the wrong way!"

Everybody laughed.

"Spread the word! Tell your friends! If the media are here—and I know I saw a couple out there—you spread the word, too! Don't just be an observer! Be a participant in the game! *You* be a part of winning! Now, when we've got the ball . . ."

He paused and turned and looked at Marino. The quarterback motioned both hands down, and the coach copied him.

"Danny and I would both appreciate it if you hold it down," Jimmy said, and whispered, "Gooooo, Dolphins."

Voice normal again, he said, "And I'm serious about this. In fact, we talked about this before the Minnesota game. Because we do use a bunch of audibles and it will help us focus on what we have to do."

The Dolphins had played football for thirty years, and the coach and quarterback still felt compelled to explain when their fans should cheer. And they *were* serious. The Dolphins once enjoyed a big home-field advantage at the Orange Bowl. But ever since Joe Robbie financed his glitzy state-of-the-art stadium with expensive club seats and exorbitant luxury boxes in 1987, the lower half of the stadium was filled with upper-income people, and they did not go crazy over the Dolphins. They came for the entertainment, the event. They got passionate about stock options, not halfback options. So Jimmy had to motivate them, too. "I haven't said it yet," he told them, "and I bet ya I have had this request a thousand times. Well, we're starting off the season, and so I'll say it now:

"How 'bout them Dolphins!"

He was rewriting the tag line he'd made famous in Dallas. He shouted it just as loud as he could, and as a thousand people stood and applauded as hard as they could, The Shark and the Dolphins left the building. Twelve minutes, and he had converted even the staunchest Shula fan.

The next day, he launched an eighteen-minute private sermon, trying to convert the faithless. He would not win over veterans like J. B. Brown and Keith

Byars, but he had the most important Dolphin on his side. "We get along great," said Marino, happy to put aside the distraction of 1995's NFL records assault, "excited" about 1996. Maybe he could achieve what his rock 'n' roll buddies had wished for at their concert Tuesday night.

A Grammy for Hootie & the Blowfish.

A Super Bowl for Danny and the Dolphins.

"Sounds good to me," Danny said.

Another prediction did not sound so good to Jimmy's first-round pick, Daryl Gardener. He opened *Sports Illustrated*'s NFL preview issue Thursday and found this passage: "In an *SI* poll of NFL GMs, coaches, personnel directors, and scouts, Gardener was the overwhelming choice as the rookie most likely to be a bust, garnering fourteen votes. No other player received more than two. One NFL assistant says, 'You have to watch a lot of film to see this guy make a play. We were wondering who'd take a chance on him. We knew it wasn't going to be us.' Says one personnel director, 'In the Senior Bowl he'd have one good play and four bad ones, and he'd always have an excuse.' "

These were the same knocks expressed before the draft. But Jimmy gambled that he could motivate the gifted athlete, and pushed and prodded as never before, Gardener responded. He dropped thirty-one pounds and added immeasurable intensity. He enjoyed a strong preseason and glowing praise from Jimmy, but still hadn't convinced fourteen scouts.

"It tells me," Jimmy said, "that fourteen guys don't want to admit they made a mistake."

Gardener realized his mistake. In college, he thought he was playing hard, but here he learned the complaints were valid. Why, just last week, he had called Baylor coach Chuck Reedy to apologize.

"I apologized to my coach because I wasn't the dominating player that I could have been in college," Gardener said. "I'd make a big tackle, get all hyped up, and not make another one for four more plays. He said, 'It's a learning process. You're gonna be a hell of a player one day.' I said, 'I wish I could have done it then.' "

He'd been on a free ride then. College football was a game, and he was so much more gifted than most of the competition, he'd treated it as a lark. Now he had a seven-figure contract and expectations to match. The criticism would be quick and harsh if he did not live up to Jimmy's lavish praise.

"When you're a number one pick," he said, "there's a lot of pressure. You can't take any plays off. You're the center of attention. You will get embarrassed if your stuff is not right. Everything here is not promised to me. I've got to work for everything. I've got to work to change this image. In college, I could lay back and have fun. I didn't know what direction I wanted to go. Now, I have direction.

"I want a ring just like that." A new era begins with Jimmy Johnson shaking hands on a four-year deal as coach and general manager of Wayne Huizenga's Dolphins. *Photo by Dave Cross/The Miami Dolphins.*

The present doesn't always see eye-to-eye with the past. Jimmy and the newly retired Don Shula weather an awkward moment. *Photo by Dave Cross/The Miami Dolphins.*

Air Johnson. Jumpin' Jimmy tries to elevate his players' performance during training camp in July 1996. He was so excited, even his hair moved. *Photo by Dave Cross/The Miami Dolphins.*

Jimmy and his right-hand man, personnel expert Bob Ackles, work the phones on draft day and throughout the season, trying to improve the Dolphins' talent level. *Photo by Dave Cross/The Miami Dolphins.*

Dan Marino fights off Patriots blitz during Jimmy Johnson's Dolphin debut on September 1, 1996. Note the flak jacket on the aging Marino's ribs. Miami won, 24–10. *Photo by Dave Cross/The Miami Dolphins.*

Six weeks later, an injured Marino watches the action with Jimmy from the sidelines in Buffalo. It was one of the few games the Fish could win without their superstar. At Jimmy's left are coaches Pat Jones and Kippy Brown. *Photo by Dave Cross/The Miami Dolphins.*

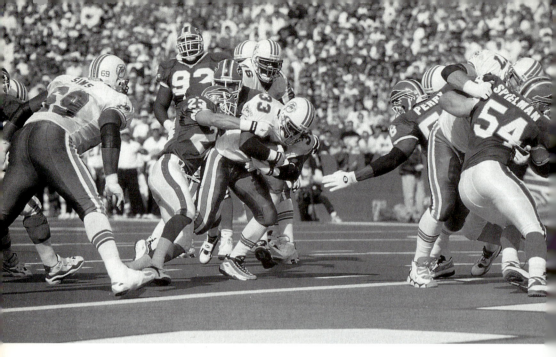

Rookie Karim Abdul-Jabbar, shown scoring against the Bills in Buffalo, became the first Dolphin in eighteen seasons to rush for 1,000 yards. *Photo by Dave Cross/The Miami Dolphins.*

Heineken time! A jubilant Jimmy does his victory boogie after the upset 21–7 win at Buffalo as punter John Kidd looks on. *Photo by Dave Cross/The Miami Dolphins.*

The hoopla comes to a head. Cowboys owner Jerry Jones (his back to the camera) pays a visit to Jimmy and Wayne Huizenga. The media has a field day, but Dallas wiped the smile off the face of its ex-coach, who second-guessed his approach to the game. *Photo by Dave Cross/The Miami Dolphins.*

Zach "Fred Flintstone" Thomas. *Photo by Dave Cross/The Miami Dolphins.*

Larry "Barney Rubble" Izzo. *Photo by Dave Cross/The Miami Dolphins.*

A pair of wide receivers in action. O. J. McDuffie breaks a tackle against Oakland (left), and Fred Barnett goes up for a pass against the Giants (below). Barnett made a miraculous recovery from knee surgery and provided inspirational leadership for a team that sorely needed it. *Photo by Dave Cross/The Miami Dolphins.*

David versus Goliath. Terrell Buckley, shown wrapping up the Giants' Howard Cross, overcame the rap on him and turned around his career with an excellent season. *Photo by Dave Cross/The Miami Dolphins.*

The inconsistent Joe Nedney boots one. *Photo by Dave Cross/The Miami Dolphins.*

Life is good. Sharing a laugh with co-host Tony Segreto on the set of "The Jimmy Johnson Show." *Photo by Dave Cross/The Miami Dolphins.*

Life is really *good.* Jimmy and girlfriend Rhonda Rookmaaker (far right) welcome Jimmy's sons Brent (left), Chad, and Chad's wife Belinda (right), aboard Jimmy's yacht, *Three Rings.* Only a fourth ring would make it better. *Photo by Dave Cross/The Miami Dolphins.*

I have a wife and a kid on the way. I have responsibilities. Jimmy is not asking me to do anything. He's demanding it."

He did not want to talk about being ripped in the nation's largest sports magazine. But he sure knew about it. He sat up, reached over his shoulder to a shelf in his locker, and pulled out his *Sports Illustrated*. He grimaced, held the magazine out, then flipped it back up on the shelf.

Jimmy didn't have to worry about this rookie being ready.

Turned out he didn't have to worry about any of them come Sunday, September 1. Gardener sacked Bledsoe and helped hold Martin to twenty-three yards. Zach Thomas collected a game-high thirteen tackles, a sack, and a forced fumble. Stanley Pritchett caught six balls for a game-high seventy-seven yards. Karim Abdul-Jabbar ran for a game-high 115 yards. And the Dolphins romped, 24–10, against an opponent that had played superbly in preseason.

Jimmy had questioned Karim's courage, probably the harshest indictment in the macho world of football. Karim suppressed any urge to swipe back. He said he really was hurt, and every time he tried to rush back to satisfy Jimmy, he'd aggravate his ankle sprains. But he said, "I knew where he was coming from. You have to learn to play hurt."

And now the coach knew where Karim was coming from. "I was beginning to wonder about the first month of training camp, but the guy responded," Jimmy said. "I don't know if his agent told him we have real physical practices and to hold back for a few weeks, say your ankles are hurt or what, but whatever he did, I'm thankful for it. Because once he hit the field, he hit it running.

"Jabbar is an intelligent guy, and obviously he's got great feet and is an outstanding back. And he showed toughness. I think the bottom line is, he had a couple of sprained ankles. Sometimes coaches are skeptical. That's just part of our nature . . . kinda like some reporters. There are times I'm wrong. I probably won't ever say I'm wrong," he said, and grinned.

But what did he make of Karim's beliefs? Praying five times a day toward Mecca? Fasting the entire month of Ramadan? Trying to heal himself by envisioning the blood flowing to the injured body part, by using Chinese herbs, acupuncture, and acupressure? Ever wonder what planet Karim came from?

"You never can tell," Jimmy said. "Jabbar could be smarter than all of us."

Everybody would know this kid's name for a long time.

And maybe they would learn how to pronounce Terrell Buckley's name. It's Ter-REL, not TIE-rel, as NBC's Mike Ditka pronounced it. And this year Ter-REL would prove he was no longer a "suspect cornerback," as Mark Malone, the failed quarterback turned commentator, said.

"A lot of guys on TV were talking about how terrible we were and how Bledsoe would be licking his chops," T-Buck said after knocking down two passes and stealing another. "They acted like Drew was a cat and we were fish, and he was just waiting to pluck us out. To insult us and downgrade us like that is not cool. Especially from an ex-player like Mark Malone. We'd love to have him out there quarterbacking. It's not like he was All-World. I'm hot, man! It blows my mind, some of the stuff they say without knowing.

"Ditka still can't even say my name. He could at least get my name right. It's been like that since I was in Green Bay and he was coaching Chicago. He thought I was soft. I told him, 'If you feel that way, throw every ball to my side and see what happens.' And he didn't like that."

Across the spacious locker room, the big men's exhausted but excited bodies streamed over their seats. They had met a less public but more important challenge. From their coach, in front of their peers.

"Initially," Sims said, "you're in shock that he calls you out. You realize, 'Hey, I'm on the hot seat.' He was talking to me about dominating a rookie, and that's something I would expect of myself anyway. But it's one thing to have your own expectations and another thing to have the whole team know what the coaching staff is expecting of you: 'We're watching you, each and every play, and we're running right behind you two. You are the guys who have to get the job done.' It was great. I've been looking for that for years."

For years, the Dolphins had looked to Marino and won only if he were great. In only twenty-three games in thirteen seasons had he failed to throw for a touchdown, and Miami had lost fifteen of those twenty-three. Today he had thrown for just 176 yards and no scores, and yet the Dolphins had won easily. From the January day Jimmy was named coach, he had told his quarterback and the world that the Dolphins would rely less upon him, and everybody kept asking how they'd coexist, and Danny kept telling them he didn't care about yards, just wins.

Today Danny talked for maybe five minutes before quickly dismissing the media horde he abhors. He waited for the cameras to depart and stuffed some chewing tobacco into his mouth. A nasty welt blotted his left arm—and this was a good day for his pass protection. Jim Mandich, the tight end turned radio analyst, lingered for a moment. "Wait till you see the fuckin' game Zach Thomas played," gloated Mandich, who sees another Nick Buoniconti or John Offerdahl.

At the dressing stall closet to the door, Zach held court. He was too new and too nice to boot the reporters, and they came at him in wave after wave for forty-five minutes. He had never heard of Nick Buoniconti, but he had heard skeptics say he himself was too short since he was in high school.

"Everybody doubts me. Even some of y'all have," Zach told the pack. "Everybody says, 'He's not the player we had in the past.' It's helping me."

He was the last player left in the locker room, and his parents, having flown in from Texas, were waiting for him. He grabbed his duffel bag. Inside was a copy of *Bad As I Wanna Be*, Dennis Rodman's autobiography. "I don't want to be like him," Zach said. "I don't want to be crazy. I'm not gonna wear a dress. But I try to read about how guys get to be the best."

They share a hunger. Dennis gets all the rebounds. Zach gets all the tackles. Thirteen all told, most for little or no gain. He collected his first sack, his first knockout, and should have been credited for causing a fumble, forcing a throwaway, and knocking down a pass. Not a bad NFL debut. Not a bad birthday.

"How 'bout that little munchkin?" Jimmy raved.

Upstairs, one Hall of Fame linebacker compared the munchkin to another Hall of Fame linebacker. Jack Ham said Zach was as heady as Jack "Splat" Lambert.

"His play on Shawn Jefferson's reverse is what really impressed me," said Ham, a millionaire businessman and radio analyst for Mutual Broadcasting's *Game of the Week*. "It was a great hit, but I'm even more impressed by the intelligence of the hit. Usually a rookie takes himself out of that play. I know *veterans* who take themselves out on that misdirection. But he's right there and knocks the guy out."

The first game was a knockout, all right.

So would the next be, albeit in a different way.

9
KNOCKOUT

Zach Thomas strutted. He high-stepped. He did a damn good imitation of the Deion Dance.

He wore nothing but a towel. His smile was bigger than his towel. It was a full day after the opening victory, and the Dolphins still hadn't come down. Zach said his birthday bash could have been better if he hadn't just missed an interception.

"I wanted a pick. I wanted to high-step. I can do the Deion Dance!" Zach said, and demonstrated across the locker room, to the hoots and hollers of on-lookers. "I'll do the Deion Dance against Dallas. That's my dream. I visualize plays like that: I get a pick against Aikman, Deion comes to stop me, I stiff-arm Deion, and do the Deion Dance."

Oh, the afterglow of victory.

The unpretentious good ol' boy from West Texas was dissing Deion and Troy and the 'Boys he grew up idolizing. The 'Boys would lose on prime-time TV tonight to Dave Wannstedt's Bears—worthy of a dual celebration for Jimmy. The Dolphins would announce today the signing of their quarterback of the future, Craig Erickson, and they would give up little more than baubles and beads for him. The Dolphins would appear this week on the covers of the nation's two big weekly sports magazines, *Sports Illustrated* and *The Sporting News*. They would be the lead story for the second straight week on ESPN's *Sports Reporters*, with panelist Bill Conlin comparing Jimmy to Julius Caesar.

Oh, life was good.

"What was important was not only that we won the first game, but how we won," Jimmy said. "We played defense with people everybody said would be run over ragged. Everybody looked at the names on the defensive team and said, 'This defense won't stop anybody.' But we played outstanding defense. We did it with a couple of rookies rushing the football and a rookie back getting 115 yards when everybody said they couldn't run. That will pay dividends down the road."

Did it validate all his changes and coaching? He dismissed the question with a wave of his hand. The hand that sparkled with championship diamonds.

"I've had validation for a long time," he said. "I needed to be validated when I went from Oklahoma State to the University of Miami. I don't need to be validated much anymore. But it's probably good with [convincing] the players. Everything I said was right on."

Don't think the players didn't notice. If they doubted Jimmy before, they didn't now.

"Here's a guy saying, 'This is how it should happen,' " defensive end Aaron Jones said. "Then everything he says comes true, and you build confidence because the coach knows what he's talking about. And you build confidence in yourself because you know when he tells you something about yourself, he's not shooting you a bunch of bull. It really builds confidence amongst everybody."

And Jimmy made them feel even better Wednesday. "If you take care of your business Sunday night," he told the players at the morning meeting, "I'll see you Wednesday. You don't take care of your business, we'll have our normal two o'clock meeting on Monday."

How much would the lure of Monday off, after an early-morning return flight, motivate them?

"If it's this much," Jimmy said later, holding his fingers a millimeter apart, "it's more than nothing. So any little bit of motivation I can use, whatever it is, if it helps us an ounce, that's enough."

Then the coaches went about correcting the one flaw in the opening victory: their "horseshit" kick coverage, special teams coach Mike Westhoff groused.

"I had Dave Meggett very frustrated on punt returns," Kirby Dar Dar said, "but his kick returns were killing us. There's a couple of us who know we have to make the tackles."

Like Dar Dar and Larry Izzo. "I didn't screw up—I blew up the wedge—but I give myself a minus for not making plays," Izzo said. "I take a lot of pride in special teams. That's what I'm here for. My performance, I'm disappointed."

And for that he missed his sister's wedding?

"I'm told I missed a good party Saturday," he said, smiling. But it turns out his family didn't miss *him*. Tina postponed her honeymoon and flew to Miami to watch her little brother's NFL debut, and big brother Len took a time-out from dodging bullets in Bosnia with the U.S. Army to attend the wedding and the debut.

Too bad the siblings couldn't go to Arizona because the Dolphins had some surprises planned for the Cardinals' punting game. Even though the teams hadn't met since 1990, the offense felt good about attacking the Cardinals' defense because it was the same scheme they faced twice a year when new Cardinals coach Vince Tobin coordinated the Indianapolis defense. And the defense was feeling pretty good about facing fading quarterback Boomer Esiason and his questionable running game.

The complaints and questions of camp were behind them. Confidence and cockiness replaced them.

The cornerbacks debated among themselves how tall they were. T-Buck got hot talking about the rap that he was too short to cover people and said he was 5'10", about the same size as the rest of the league's corners. Robert Bailey said he was 5'9", so no way T-Buck was 5'10". So Bailey measured him against the tape on the wall. For a true measure, T-Buck was supposed to stand on a wooden block, but Bailey convinced him to remove it—and then said T-Buck was 5'8½". The defensive backs roared.

And when practice ended Friday, the Southwest Conference alumni started bantering with each other about SWC cars and corruption. Then they turned to the equipment men, who were cleaning every helmet with paint thinner.

"Hey," Gardener said, "leave mine dirty so people know I'm hitting guys."

"You put scars on there," equipment manager Tony Egues replied, "and we can't get them out."

"See mine," Gardener said, and pointed to the crevice above his face mask. "My mama always told me to use my head."

Everybody laughed. The equipment guys peeled the Dolphins logo off the sides of each helmet, buffed it up, then attached new logos. Somebody stuck a logo on a writer's butt, and everybody snickered at him.

Heh, heh, heh.

Hey, it looks good on my file cabinet.

The frivolity ended the next day, when the Dolphins boarded their plane for Phoenix. The Dolphins had never played in Arizona. Yet there would be no time for sightseeing, no time for even seeing family.

Jimmy made sure everyone knew this was strictly a business trip. He required everyone to wear suits or sport coats, even though it was ninety degrees in Miami and 101 in Phoenix, even though the team left on a private charter from a private, guarded terminal at the Fort Lauderdale airport and arrived at a private terminal and received a police escort straight through the backdoors of the Airport Hilton.

He would relax the dress code on the way home or whenever the players pleased him, but he had imposed strict rules after his first University of Miami road trip.

"I had a guard they called Earthquake get on the plane with flip-flops and real short running shorts—these little old skimpy nylon kind, half vulgar," Jimmy recalled. "I saw that and said, 'What in the world is this?' I was astonished. Guys rode with popcorn and candy. I said, 'We have to be a little more structured than this. I want it to be a class business trip. I don't want it to be an excursion.'

"If I get on a plane and I look like a slob, that's going to be my demeanor the entire time I look like a slob. If I get on the plane and I'm the best-dressed guy there, I feel like I'm the best dressed. If I meet another head coach and he looks like a slob and I'm dressed to the T, he's nervous."

Jimmy had a vast collection of expensive suits, ties, and watches that he wore to and from games and for most televised media conferences. He wanted everyone to take football as seriously as he did. He planned every detail of every trip, right down to the meals. He scheduled extra meetings just to make sure players didn't have spare time. He rarely let them leave the hotel, even if they had family nearby. Family might be a distraction, and Jimmy disdained distractions. Quality time with loved ones? That's what the off-season was for. Security patrolled the Dolphins' hotel floor. No visitors allowed. No incoming phone calls allowed. No outgoing phone calls allowed after a certain hour. Curfew was strictly enforced. Jimmy even picked out the meals.

Ever leave anything to chance? "Not if I thought of it," Jimmy said. "Even if it's the slightest little detail, and 999 times it doesn't have any effect, why not do it if that one time it does? I don't like loose ends. Most guys are fine. But you have fifty-three guys, you're bound to have a couple of knuckleheads. So you need a strict itinerary . . . in my opinion. Not every coach does it this way. I know some of them are very loose. Some of them don't even go to the meetings the night before."

This was a dig at Barry Switzer, who skipped some Saturday meetings his first year with the Cowboys so he could attend his son's college games.

"Bryan Cox used to go to the racetrack," Jimmy said. "Talk about distractions. If they break curfew, they don't play for me. I've fined them five thousand dollars for breaking curfew the night before a game."

Everyone was given an itinerary and a seat assignment. Jimmy and Rhonda sat in 1A and 1B. The coaches, the front-office bosses, and the team doctors filled first class. The rest of the staff, the equipment men, a few TV and radio reporters (newspapers other than *Dolphin Digest* were excluded), a handful of sponsors, and the players occupied rows nine through thirty-six. Two players filled each three-seat section, but rank and seniority did carry special privileges. Marino had his own row. So did Richmond Webb and Keith Byars.

In each seat sat a bag of snacks that would serve six on a normal commercial flight. But that was just the start. It was followed by a gourmet meal: a choice of Cajun or rotisserie chicken served with a fresh salad, jumbo shrimp plate, and cherry pie. The flight attendants would come around with fresh fruit later. The four-and-a-half-hour flight featured two movies, *Heat* and *Broken Arrow*. Some players listened to the movies through headsets. Others slept, played cards, or chatted quietly—more quietly than a commercial trip filled with businessmen.

And still they did not satisfy their coach's demands.

He had heard players talking about the day's college scores, about the Mike Tyson–Bruce Seldon heavyweight fight that night. Just talking.

It was time for another lesson. "Guys," Jimmy began, in that little bit of a drawl that makes it more like "guuzzz."

"Somebody explain to me why normally teams have a better record at home than on the road. Hey, grass is grass, turf is turf, stadiums are stadiums. Whyyyy?"

He looked around the room and gazed at Richmond Webb, who suggested crowd noise.

"One of them could be crowd noise," Jimmy agreed. "But the noise out there tomorrow, puhhhh-lease! There'll be fifty-five thousand people there, and we'll have fifteen thousand, and there'll be however many not pulling for anybody and fifteen thousand pulling for Arizona. Crowd noise isn't going to be a factor.

"So why do teams have a better home record than road record? It's focus. That is why I keep things so regimented on the road. I don't want you to have a lot of idle time. I don't want you to be distracted with all these other things. If you have family coming in for the game, I don't want you seeing your family. You can see them after the year's over. You can see them a different time. I don't want you going down to the lobby. I don't want you going to another hotel. I don't want you doing other things. Everything we do is as a team.

"We need to stay focused! Teams lose their focus when they get in unfamiliar surroundings. They're sleeping in different beds, they're seeing different people, they're seeing different sights. I hear people talking about college ball games and Tyson and Seldon and all this stuff. Listen, I don't mind you *talking* about those things, but all the time, in the back of your mind, I want you to remember there's a reason we're here.

"How sick would you be tomorrow night if we walked out of here and you let one slip through your fingers that you should have had because you lost focus? If you let this one slip through your fingers, are you really gonna give a shit who won the Tyson–Seldon fight? Or who won Tennessee–UCLA? It's not going to matter to you, is it?

"So don't lose focus why we're here."

But then he not only let them watch Tyson-Seldon, he had it set up: The team boarded buses and watched the fight on closed-circuit TV at a local dog track. Jimmy didn't worry about this being a distraction. "It was monitored, all the coaches and players in a room together." He didn't do it to get them all charged up and ready to hit someone. "In fact, they were laughing at it," he said.

"The big thing I wanted to do is, I always like to have the team stay up late the night before a night game so they'll sleep in, especially going out on West Coast time. I didn't want them to go to bed at nine o'clock [Mountain Standard Time, but midnight Eastern Daylight Time on their body clocks] and toss and turn and wake up at five A.M. [eight on their body clocks] and toss and turn some more. I tried to occupy them. I knew the fight would be of interest to all the players and to myself as well. We stayed up a little later. That allowed them to sleep in, and that way they were fresh for the game."

Of course, it wasn't much of a fight. Seldon went down the first time after ducking a Tyson punch and having Tyson's tricep graze the top of his head. Seldon claimed it hit a nerve on the top of his head. He went down for good when Tyson caught him with a hook. Not much of a hook, really; Seldon had leaned back and it caught just part of his chin.

Even here, Jimmy found lessons to impart: "That fight is a perfect example of how a guy goes into a fight expecting to be knocked out and got knocked out without even being hit. It's what happens when the mind controls the body and you don't let the body control the mind. Even before, in warm-ups, you could tell the guy was scared to death. I've had talks with the team about the difference between champions and club fighters. The whole time this was going on, the players were hollering at Seldon, 'Club fighter! Club fighter!'

"And they were right."

Sunday, September 8, Tempe, Arizona. The Cardinals looked like club fighters, the Dolphins like champions. Miami's munchkins—Zach Thomas, Larry Izzo, and Terrell Buckley—looked like welterweights but hit like heavyweights.

Zach, all 5'11" of him, registered fifteen tackles and forced and recovered a fumble. T-Buck, all 5'9" of him, intercepted two passes, broke up two more, and forced a fumble. And the Wizard of Iz, all 5'10" of him, contributed the game's biggest play.

Westhoff had studied the Cardinals' punt protection and found holes. He spent all week practicing overloading to one side or the other and taught Izzo to use a "swim" technique to evade rookie snapper Aaron Graham and get to Pro Bowl punter Jeff Feagles. And on the Cardinals' first series, that's exactly what Izzo did. Westhoff's play was actually designed to get past another weak link, the right tackle, but Graham snapped high and Izzo swam by him and swatted the punt down with his left hand. The Dolphins recovered at the Arizona twenty-four, and, eight plays later, Karim made it 7–0. Arizona was forced to punt on its second series, and this time Robert Bailey crashed in from outside and nearly blocked another punt. Nine plays later, Karim made it 14–0.

Arizona was forced to punt a third straight time, and this time Feagles was totally spooked. He leaped for a snap that was fine, rushed his delivery, and hit the ball off his ankle, straight up into the air, and it came to a rest eleven yards away, at the Arizona twenty-seven. Two plays later, Marino looked right, fired left, and Lamar Thomas had a twenty-yard touchdown and the Dolphins a 21–0 lead.

Jimmy wasn't a play-it-safe coach. With twenty-six seconds left in the half, he went for the jugular. Marino launched the ball toward Charles Jordan— "Actually, I underthrew it or it would have been a touchdown," Danny complained later—and Jordan came back for the ball and made a spectacular leaping catch for a forty-three-yard gain. *Dolphin Digest* captured the catch on its cover and dubbed him Air Jordan. Not exactly. It would be Jordan's first and last big play of the year. But it set up Joe Nedney's field goal for a 24–0 halftime bulge.

"Hey, with the lead we have, we're gonna try to run and eat up the clock the second half," Jimmy told his team at the break. "This is why we did the middle drill all through training camp. The defense knows you're gonna run the ball. But you've got to put a hat on people and run hard and do it just like the middle drill."

And they did, en route to a 38–10 rout.

It was so easy that P.R. man Harvey Greene called down to the field and told trainer Kevin O'Neill that Keith Byars's consecutive-games-with-a-catch streak was in jeopardy. Kevin told Jimmy, who immediately asked for and got a pass to Byars. Nicolas Cage could call this one *Routing Arizona*.

It was so easy that Jimmy felt he could "sit back in a rocking chair and enjoy."

He had a lot to enjoy because his draft picks, his reclamation projects, his attitude adjustment were all shining through. This team was playing as a team, with the balance and the heart that was AWOL in 1995.

Imagine this: The home team was getting embarrassed, and the fans were cheering louder than ever. Dol-fans outnumbered Cardinals fans. Marino jerseys outnumbered those of all the Cardinals put together. Dol-fan signs were everywhere:

> ZACK ATTACK
>
> MARINO 4 PRESIDENT
>
> MARINO'S RING IS JOHNSON'S DESTINY
>
> JIMMY 'N DAN ARE SUPER BOWL BOUND

Imagine this: Izzo made a play bigger than any Marino made. Maybe the Wizard of Iz should have been the *first* guy to make the team.

Imagine this: Lamar Thomas, Jimmy's soul-saving project, caught a touchdown and called Marino Miami's "secret weapon."

Imagine this: The Cardinals stacked eight men at the line, daring Miami to pass, more scared of the run than the pass. When's the last time that happened to Miami? 1974?

"They're saying, 'We have to stop Karim. Karim's not going to run on us,'" said Karim, who ran for two touchdowns anyway. "Well, Dan Marino's thrown for forty-eight thousand yards. We don't have a problem throwing the ball."

Imagine this: A reporter asked Jimmy if the Dolphins were potentially as good as his Cowboys champions.

Jimmy laughed out loud. "Oh puhhhh-lease," he said. "We've got twenty-three or twenty-four new faces. We had a heck of a draft, obviously, but we've got too many young players to get too excited."

T-Buck was excited. He said he felt as if he were living a fairy tale. "This is how it was in college," he said, his megawatt smile shining brighter than his gold chain or his shaved head. "This is my fifth year in the league, and this is the first time I've felt this way as a pro. I didn't know what I was missing. I didn't know how good it would feel."

Zach felt good, too. He'd grown up watching NFL games on TV. Now he was starring in prime time. He was excited about being interviewed on TNT and getting a TNT T-shirt. "They didn't give it to me," he insisted. "I stole it!"

No, he earned it. "Zach was so far into the Cardinals' game plan, I thought he was standing in their huddle," said Jim Mandich, WIOD's color commentator. But Zach was more excited about his roommate's blocked punt.

"Oh, man!" Zach exclaimed. "That changed momentum. That got us pumped. Larry and I knew each other from the Southwest Conference. He was the whole team at Rice. We're a lot alike. We're both short. All our life we've been dealing with that. Everywhere we go, we hear that: 'You're too short. You're not gonna make it in the NFL.'"

Short in height, big in performance.

"We knew we needed to make an impact on special teams after last week," Izzo said. "It feels good to make plays. It worked just like Coach Westhoff drew it up."

The special teams had earned an F in the "report card" issued by the *Sun-Sentinel*'s Jason Cole the previous week. "I don't want to see any more Fs," Westhoff said, and nodded toward Cole. "Do I get an F tonight?"

"An A," Cole said.

This night, Westhoff had everything to be proud of, save his rookie kicker's two misses at the end of the game, when they didn't matter. "Those are kicks he'll make," he said. "I'm not worried." Later, he would be.

But for now, he could relish Nedney's long kickoffs and Izzo's block. Defensive coordinator George Hill, a big fight fan himself, could relish the knockout blow of five takeaways and 1.4 yards a carry. And offensive coordinator Gary Stevens could relish the career-high seventy-nine yards on just eleven carries by Irving Spikes, the guy who was supposed to start the opener before hurting his hamstring, the guy Jimmy asked if he were a club fighter or a champion.

Jimmy, the cutthroat who cut Curvin Richards for two fumbles in a single game, could encourage Karim after his two fumbles in this one.

"In a game, you always want to be extremely positive because you don't want to put a guy in a shell, thinking about mistakes," Jimmy explained later. "Now, if it were practice, I'd come down a little harder. In fact, I'd be the exact opposite extreme. But in a game, I never get on a player in a negative way unless it's a player I'm just so thoroughly upset with that I'm not gonna put him back in the game. And he's a player I don't see for the long-range future.

"Karim is going to be a good player for us for a long time. It's just like Jerris McPhail fumbling a couple of kickoffs against New England. We understand they're rookies and they'll make some mistakes and we'll have to live with those mistakes. Even when Nedney missed a couple of field goals, I was over there patting him on the rear end, saying, 'You're gonna be fine. You'll make those field goals when it counts.' "

Of course, positive reinforcement was easier amidst a romp. A loss could have made for a different Jimmy, an awfully long red-eye flight home, and a short morning sleep before reporting to work. But even when the plane departed nearly an hour later than planned, at 1:24 A.M. EDT, the only curses came from the movies: *Casino* and *Eraser*.

Some people can sleep on planes, and some cannot. A restless Marino got up at 4:30 A.M. and talked with receiver-turned-announcer Jimmy Cefalo for half an hour.

It was 5:40 A.M. when they landed, after 6 A.M. by the time most stumbled into bed. "I tried to sleep," Jimmy said. "I rolled over for about an hour and then said the hell with it."

Then it was back to the Davie complex, time to start all over again, breaking down film of the Sunday night game, grinding away to find if they could knock out the winless New York Jets.

Rich Kotite, the Jets' coach, had been the University of Miami's heavyweight boxing champion back in the sixties, had even sparred with Muhammad Ali.

But in the NFL in the nineties, he was Bruce Seldon.

And the Dolphins wouldn't have to be Mike or Muhammad to knock him out.

10

T-BUCK AND TROUBLE

Terell Buckley was saved. By Jesus. And by Jimmy. Jesus saved his soul. Jimmy rescued his career.

T-Buck came out of Florida State in 1992, the scouts divided on who was a better cornerback, the short guy with the big mouth and big plays of Seminoles predecessor Deion Sanders or the solid but unspectacular Wisconsin Badger, Troy Vincent. Green Bay took the Florida State kid fifth, and Miami took the Wisconsin kid seventh.

When T-Buck held out, the black kid from the Deep South did not appreciate the cold weather of Green Bay or the even colder welcome of the lily-white fans. If he had been a second-round pick in, say, Tampa, he might have been viewed as a refreshing rogue. But because of his money, mouth, and race, he was labeled a cocky, conceited, arrogant underachiever.

T-Buck stole three passes, scored twice, and averaged ten yards per punt return, but the rookie fumbled seven times. His second season, he intercepted two passes in the playoffs, but all anybody mentioned was Alvin Harper's short touchdown catch on a post pattern, even though it was a safety's fault.

His third season, he had two interceptions and hadn't allowed a touchdown entering the ninth game. "Even some guys who had been ragging on me were saying, 'Maybe he does have a shot at the Pro Bowl,' " he recalled. But then, in a game against the Detroit Lions, 6'3" Herman Moore beat the 5'9" Buckley for two touchdowns and a long bomb, and even though T-Buck forced and recovered a fumble and broke up a pass, "All of a sudden I can't cover a tall, physical receiver. They started saying, 'Buckley keeps coming up short.' Then we played the Jets. I played against Rob Moore, who's 6'3", and got a pick on him. Great game. Nothing was said. Played Dallas on Thanksgiving. Michael Irvin catches a post on me. I'm draped over him. Touchdown. They're back to: 'Oh, he can't cover tall receivers.' I got a pick in that game, made eight tackles, did my job. But the story was, 'Got beat, can't cover.'

"The next time, we play the Lions, we have another corner who's 6'1", and the coaches put him on Herman in pass situations. That game Herman Moore caught two touchdowns for 150 yards, and you know what they said about the other cornerback? He did a good job. Herman told me, 'I can't believe they took you off me. I had one good game against you.' "

The Packers beat the Lions in the playoffs, then were eliminated by the Cowboys again when Harper scored on another post pattern, this one a record ninety-four yards. Once again, a safety was responsible, but T-Buck got the blame.

"They're trying to hide him on all sides of the field," Jimmy said on Fox. "He's been burned all year long. I think the only place he can hide is over on the bench."

Green Bay general manager Ron Wolf left T-Buck available in the expansion draft, then traded him to Don Shula.

"I had put up good numbers: five picks, a career-high fifty-nine tackles," T-Buck said. "I got beat three times for touchdowns that year where it was really me, not somebody else blowing a coverage. I knew all they were talking about was not true."

Still, the skeptics scarred him. Short but stout, with a shaved head, expressive eyes, and often a wide smile, he remembers every catch, every criticism, in exacting detail. The fade, the lob, the slant, the throw, the coverage—everything is burned into his brain. I know this because he had listed them in vivid detail a month before, and now, as we dined at Applebee's, I asked how his new-found faith helped him, and fifteen minutes later, his lunch untouched, he had detailed his whole career and still not answered the question.

He had not enjoyed his sole Shula season, but it began his rebirth. As he rode around golf courses, swinging and talking with safety Michael Stewart, T-Buck marveled at Stewart's inner strength, and Stewart said he got it from God. T-Buck began to attend Friday-night Bible studies with Stewart, and though he had grown up in the church, for the first time the Bible's lessons seemed to speak to his life. In February 1996, he flew to San Antonio for the NBA All-Star game and a Champions for Christ convention.

The last night there, "Something just came over me," he said, and when they asked who wanted to be saved, T-Buck plunged into the pool and was baptized.

"It changed my life," T-Buck said.

So did his new coach. Jimmy asked him to give up minor-league baseball and concentrate on football, and he did. He asked T-Buck to take a pay cut, from $1.5 million to $700,000, and he did. Jimmy was still skeptical, saying at the March meetings that T-Buck could make plays, but too many were for the other team. "Before," T-Buck said, "I would have been insulted."

This time, he took the challenge . . . and led the league in interceptions with three in preseason and three in the first two games of the regular season.

Jimmy said he'd "jumped on the bandwagon" when he was at Fox and didn't know if the criticism had been justified, but "it was good TV at the time." Then T-Buck had another big game and the coach cracked, "I'm just happy I criticized him on Fox and Green Bay let him go. If I hadn't criticized him on Fox, I might not have him right now. So if y'all want to criticize players on other teams, maybe we'll get some."

Why was T-Buck so improved? Well, underneath his veneer of cockiness lay a little guy who needed reassurance. At Florida State, his coaches plastered a toma-hawk on his helmet for every big play. At Green Bay, he got scolded, not cod-dled, by Wolf, Coach Mike Holmgren, and defensive coordinator Ray Rhodes.

"I feel I failed as a coach," said Rhodes, the 1995 NFL Coach of the Year in Philadelphia. "He's one of the few guys I haven't been able to reach. You get frustrated and pissed off because here's a little guy who is cocky as all get-out and won't listen to anybody, always has all the answers, and it's really a sign of failure. I was mad at myself for not saving his career."

Jesus, Jimmy, and growing up saved his career.

"It's one thing to go in and watch five hours of videotape and you're sitting there nodding your head, half asleep," T-Buck said. "Now I've cut down on the time, but I'm going in there with a pencil, pad, taking notes.

"When Jimmy Johnson became coach, you had to prove yourself every day in training camp. You know how tough that is, mentally, physically, in that South Florida heat? The Lord got me through two-a-day practices in pads. I reminded myself the Lord was in the desert, and He didn't give up. He didn't say, 'Ah, just this one time.' Not only did I make it through, I competed every practice, every drill."

And earned Jimmy's constant compliments during the drills and press confer-ences. "I don't think you could ask any more than what Terrell Buckley has done," Jimmy said. "I'd match Terrell Buckley up against anybody in the league.

"Terrell is confident in his way, but he wanted somebody to believe in him. It helped that he had somebody—especially somebody who had bashed him in the past—show confidence in him. I like Terrell. He's a fun guy."

And he was having fun. He'd sulked in a hotel room his entire rookie year in Green Bay. He'd stood passively on the sideline as the Packers cavorted amid a playoff victory. "I had the money, the cars, the house—and I was still empty," he recalled. Now, he was making less and enjoying it more. He was a star again, and people fawned. The waitress giddily volunteered to play with his little girl while we talked, and she gave eighteen-month-old Sherrell Buckley balloons and crayons, and the manager picked up the check. Life was good again.

"I walk around with a smile on my face all day. I catch myself at the red light sometimes, smiling and waving to people I don't know, and they look at me like, 'Hey, what is he doing?' "

He had a contagious smile and a sweet disposition, and he was having fun because Jimmy wanted his defenders to attack—not a Blitzburgh or Buddy Ryan all-or-nothing attack, but an attack nonetheless. Tom Olivadotti had asked the cornerbacks to play soft, the safeties to line up deep and try to prevent the bomb.

"This defense allows you to do more, to play football the way football is meant to be played—aggressive, all out, all the time," said Louis Oliver, who had regained his starting safety job and collected two interceptions in two games.

"Before, you had to be lucky to get an interception at safety. That was mostly a zone, bend-but-don't-break defense. I didn't think it utilized the players' talents the way this defense does. This defense allows you to bend the offense and hopefully break it instead of the other way around. You need a defense that's aggressive, that's dictating to the offense. Because if you let offenses dictate what they're gonna do, when they're gonna do it, how they're gonna do it, you're in for a long day. Cautious was never my style."

T-Buck and Lou weren't alone.

"I think everybody likes it better," Calvin Jackson said. "It's totally different than last year. But look at the results. It's worked for us."

Sure had. Opposing passers had five interceptions, two touchdowns, and a passer rating of 50.5, about half that of the league leaders.

"It starts with the head man," T-Buck said. "You feed off what he wants. The scheme we were running last year was not bad, but as players, we couldn't make adjustments. We'd go to the sideline and say, 'This guy is doing this. I think I can do this and shut it down.' The coaches would say, 'Nah, we're gonna run our scheme.' This year we go to the sideline and say, 'Hey, coach, we can get one of these,' and they call it. We have to make the plays, of course, or they're not gonna do it anymore."

This week the pair of 5'9" corners would have to make plays against 6'3" Keyshawn Johnson, 6'2" Jeff Graham, and 6'1" Webster Slaughter of the Jets. They insisted height didn't matter. "I've been going against bigger receivers all my life," Jackson said, "and so has Terrell."

Jimmy's kids were 2–0 and dominating, and South Florida was giddy over the kids and the coach. It was humbling for the old coach, especially when his son the Bengals coach was 0–2 and his son the Tampa offensive coordinator hadn't produced a touchdown. For maybe the first time since he had cleaned out his office, Don Shula returned to it, chatted with his former secretary, and congratulated Jimmy. He played the peacemaker, and the next night at Shula's big tribute, Jimmy called him "the greatest of all time."

Shula said he'd tried to keep busy and didn't miss coaching that much until the regular season started without him. He spent the day alone at his Carolina retreat because, he said, "I didn't know how I'd react. It was very, very strange, but I got through it." He hugged and kissed people at the bash, and, every once in a while, the iron jaw quivered and the eyes watered. But he got through his farewell speech without breaking down, and then he kissed his wife and held her hand as he walked off the stage and hugged Wayne Huizenga. All around him, people stood and clapped and cheered and music serenaded him.

Sunday, September 15, Miami. Joe Nedney had missed his final two kicks in Arizona, but only by a little. Now, on another scorching Sunday, he was taking his warm-up kicks from the Florida Marlins' infield, and kicking off dirt was freaking him out. Bob Ackles and I stood at the back of the end zone, and we drifted left, five, ten yards wide of the goalpost, and Joe's field goals kept hooking at us. The more he kicked, the worse he got, and Jimmy thought about telling Mike Westhoff to move Joe back to the grass "because he was psyching himself out—and that's exactly what happened."

On the first play from scrimmage, Jerris McPhail lined up as a receiver, hoping to exploit hard-hitting but slow Jets safety Victor Green, and he did for fifty-two yards, but Nedney was wide left from thirty-seven. T-Buck intercepted Neil O'Donnell's second pass, but Jets cornerback Aaron Glenn went one hundred yards with an interception and Webster Slaughter beat a late-arriving safety for a thirty-yard score, and the Jets led, 14–0.

But these were still the Jets, and their psyches were daunted and haunted by history. And by bad management and coaching. Leon Hess, a tycoon in oil refinery and a buffoon in football hiring, fired bright young Pete Carroll because his first year as coach concluded with five straight losses—and replaced him with a coach who dropped seven straight. All because when Richie Kotite was a Jet assistant, he'd been nice to the old man. Kotite made disastrous personnel moves in Philly, and in New York he went back to the antiquated Joe Walton offense featuring one tight end with no heart and another with no hands. A Rich Kotite movie would be called *The Wizard of Oops*.

He traded his only quality wideout when the rest had only sixteen career catches combined, then was surprised to discover he needed wideouts, not tight ends, to make big plays. He went 3–13 that first year in New York, and now he had tried to buy a winner by spending $70 million on an average quarterback in O'Donnell, brittle and aging tackles Jumbo Elliott and David Williams, and a rookie receiver, Keyshawn Johnson, who grinned and laughed even as the Jets lost their first two games.

Player personnel director Dick Haley, perhaps the Jets' only competent front-office type—he guided the drafts that won Pittsburgh four Super Bowls in six years—stood upstairs and fretted. O'Donnell had played the equivalent of just one full game in preseason because Kotite was afraid to get him killed when his linemen were hurt and wanted to look at his backups. O'Donnell was a $25 million hope and Keyshawn the first pick in the draft, supposedly a franchise player, and they had never played together until the opener. No wonder the Jets weren't clicking.

"O'Donnell's not Marino," Haley said. "I know from my days in Pittsburgh, he needs the practice time."

By contrast, Jimmy had demoted his vets and played his rookies throughout preseason, and now they had eliminated most of their mistakes and were starring. Haley nodded and said, "You've got to have courage, confidence, a history of success—and a long-term contract."

Richie had lost twenty-two of his past twenty-five.

Jimmy had won twenty-two of his past twenty-six.

Richie coached scared.

Jimmy coached cocksure.

The Dolphins' scouting reports listed Jets linebacker Chad Cascadden as a 4.5 sprinter, but Jimmy figured he was a 4.8 slowpoke, and with the Jets using eight-man fronts and constant blitzes to try to stop the run, Jimmy wanted to isolate fast fullback Stanley Pritchett on the slow linebacker. On the first play after Slaughter's score, he got his matchup. Pritchett flew down the right sideline, a wide receiver blocked Cascadden's path, and Marino hit the rookie in stride for the first touchdown of his career. Pritchett went seventy-four yards—the longest reception ever by a Miami back—and the Dolphins' confidence soared and the Jets' sagged.

Next series, Lamar Thomas drew a key interference penalty on Jets rookie cornerback Ray Mickens, and on the next play, Karim crashed over from the five for a halftime tie. Then Marino hit backup tight ends Frank Wainright and Brett Carolan for the first touchdowns of their careers, and Lou Oliver got his third interception and Karim his fifth touchdown in three games, and the Dolphins had scored thirty-three unanswered points.

But just when it looked like a blowout, the secondary that had silenced the skeptics gave them reason to howl. Graham ran a little square-out to the sideline and T-Buck dove for his fifth interception. But he couldn't reach the ball. Graham grabbed it, Lou Oliver got splattered by Keyshawn, Gene Atkins and Robert Bailey took bad angles, and Graham had a seventy-eight-yard score. The Jets got the ball back when Irving Spikes fumbled, and, on fourth down from the twenty-nine, O'Donnell launched a Hail Mary, and Keyshawn, though surrounded by T-Buck, Lou, and Bailey, used his big body to bring it down. Suddenly it was 33–27.

But these were the new Dolphins. They hadn't given up on the running game even though it was shut down in the first half, and now Karim and Bernie Parmalee responded with sixty-three yards on seven straight carries, giving them 195 yards rushing and giving Nedney a twenty-nine-yard field goal to clinch it, 36–27.

"If you can make that many mistakes and still win, it says something about when you eliminate the mistakes," Jimmy said.

If you can eliminate the mistakes.

If you can play the Cardinals and Jets every week.

The mistakes could be glossed over in victory, but they were warning signs of trouble ahead. The slow safeties, Gene Atkins and Lou Oliver—plus T-Buck's gamble and Robert Bailey's stumble—were responsible for three touchdown passes. The secondary was singed for 325 yards. Nedney had missed three straight field goals in two weeks and even doinked an extra point. His hook was back, and hooks might be good for boxers, but not golfers or kickers. Nedney raised himself to his full 6'4" and said he didn't know what the flaw was, but he would find it. "If it takes kicking a lot more balls, if it takes staying out after practice, well, I'm not going anywhere."

And then there was Keith Byars, who watched both his backups catch touchdowns while his streak of consecutive games with a reception ended at 130, fifth longest in history. Keith had been stripped of the only pass aimed his way, but at the end Jimmy planned to put him at fullback and dish him a shovel pass until Keyshawn made it close and the Dolphins had to fight to run out the clock. As teammates celebrated and music blared, Keith glared. He slammed his helmet to the ground and sat alone on the sideline. His position coach and quarterback tried to comfort him, but he sat in the training room in full uniform and refused to talk. Finally, he grabbed his clothes, retreated back to the off-limit areas, showered, dressed alone, and left.

The next day, Keith went to Jimmy and tried to explain he was just disappointed, that he was willing to do whatever was asked of him. But his actions spoke louder than his words. He had pulled the same pout the previous year. Don Shula let him get away with it. Jimmy would not.

Jimmy did not scream at T-Buck the way Shula and his aides had; he told him to keep gambling but make sure he had a real shot at the interception. His best buddy, Dave Wannstedt, would fire his kicker after just three games, but Jimmy would not. When Matt Bahr's agent called and asked Ackles if the Dolphins would make a change, Ackles laughed and said, "You're the nineteenth guy to call me so far." Jimmy and his right-hand man told the agents, the media, and the kicker they were sticking with him.

It was the beginning of a wild ride for Terrell Buckley and Joe Nedney—and the beginning of the end for Keith Byars, Louis Oliver, and Gene Atkins.

11
DAN GOES DOWN

ESPN and NBC and *GQ* and *SI* and every alphabet intruder had trekked to South Florida to see if Dan Marino could transform from most prolific passer to most passive passer. Could he coexist with Jimmy Johnson?

Jimmy called him "a bonus." Lamar Thomas called him a "secret weapon." He threw no touchdowns in the first game and only forty-five passes in the first two, the fewest since he came off the bench his first two games as a pro. His game ball came not for throwing but for diving on a fumble at the goal line. "The fastest I've ever seen Dan Marino move," Jimmy said.

"How'd you like to have a team with Dan Marino as Plan B?" NBC's Cris Collinsworth asked. "I don't think any coach in the league convinces Dan Marino with that kind of plan other than Jimmy Johnson."

Dan told Jimmy he had all the records and all he wanted was a ring, and he'd be happy throwing ten times a game as long as the Dolphins won. And he gave similar answers every time the media asked. But no one seemed to believe it, and so they kept coming to Davie and pestering Danny Boy, and I . . . I was no different. Danny liked me because I was from Pittsburgh, and Danny knew this book wouldn't be out for a year, so Danny could confess what he really thought.

"Many times," he said, "I have thrown forty, fifty, sometimes sixty passes in a game—and got my ass kicked. It's a team game. It's about winning. Whatever that takes. If I don't throw a touchdown and we win, I have no problems with that."

And if it's like that all year?

"If it goes like that all year, it's fine." He grinned impishly. "It won't, I can tell you that," he said, and slapped me on the shoulder.

Danny knew. Jimmy knew. Sooner or later, the Dolphins would need Dan Marino to bail them out, just as he had so many times before.

Two days later, on September 15, his thirty-fifth birthday, he did it again.

Jets cornerback Aaron Glenn jumped in front of Randal Hill, stole Danny's pass at the goal line, and as Glenn brought it back one hundred yards for a score, New York defensive end Brent Williams mocked the legend. "Happy birthday!" he taunted.

"Get outta here!" Marino scolded, and shoved him in the chest.

The Jets blitzed him. Dan burned them for seventy-four yards.

The Jets stacked eight men at the line. Dan scorched them for fifty-two.

The Jets went up two touchdowns. Dan threw three—in just twenty-three at-tempts. He averaged 19.7 yards a completion. And when the Jets got close and the Dolphins needed to run out the clock, he led. "If we're going to be a good team," he told his huddled teammates, "this is what we've got to do."

They listened. They did it. They went home with a 36–27 win and a 3–0 record. And three more receivers went home with the first touchdown catches of their careers.

Stanley Pritchett was a rookie, so new he didn't save the memorable ball, so new he didn't have anyplace to display it anyway.

But Frank Wainright was in his sixth season, and with his third club, and, af-ter all that time, this was his first touchdown catch. The ball would find a place of honor in his den, alongside his framed jerseys and six or seven game balls. "Every little kid, from the time he starts playing ball, is thinking about the time he scores," he said. And now that score had come from Dan Marino. "It's some-thing I'll always remember. I'd like to think it was the route, but it wasn't. It was Dan's play action and his pass."

Brett Carolan was in his third year in the NFL. He was one of just two father-son duos with Super Bowl rings. The late Reg Carolan won his with the Chiefs; Brett won his with the 49ers. He'd caught his first NFL pass from Steve Young and his first touchdown pass from Dan Marino. "Pretty amazing, huh?" said Carolan, so gee-golly-gosh he asked Dan to sign the ball.

Dan was heading to a birthday dinner with his family. He already had gotten the only gift he had asked for. "Winning," he said, "is the best gift."

Dan's quarterback gifts were the best. Just don't ask him to explain them—or much of anything else, for that matter. When a TV reporter asked him his sweet-est birthday memories, he couldn't think of any. A few minutes later, she asked again. Danny didn't answer questions twice for most reporters, but she was cute, so he tried. "That's the second time you asked that question, so I know it's im-portant to you," he said.

"It is," she said. "It's key."

"What can I remember?" he said, and paused. "Oh, wow. Uhhh . . . let me think about it."

He thought for a few seconds. "I'm trying," he said, and stared at the ceiling. Seventeen seconds passed before he finally shrugged and shook his head.

He could not remember a single birthday in thirty-five years? Not one memory? Not one party? Not one little red wagon or some favorite gift? Not the two previous games he'd played on his birthday?

Dan had killed a few brain cells over the years. He was a deep passer, not a deep thinker. Peter Richmond, who knew him well, wrote in *GQ*: "The key to his brilliance as a quarterback has always been the absence of reflection—'The amount of time where he sees his target and then his mind tells him to throw it is a short span, you know what I mean?' says Jim Jensen, his old roommate. 'He sees it; it's gone. There's no thinking'—and this is probably also as good a way of describing him off the field as any."

When Danny departed the University of Pittsburgh, some scouts pointed to his interceptions and gave him a "dumb" rap, but Don Shula saw him check off a call and throw a touchdown in a postseason game, a complex task for most young quarterbacks, especially on an all-star team that's been thrown together for only a week. Shula made him the twenty-seventh choice in the 1983 draft and told him he was competing for the starting job from Day One and made him call the plays himself, so he'd learn them faster. Shula wanted Marino thinking, not robotically following orders and failing to understand the play's concept.

And from the start, Danny was brilliant at reading defenses, dissecting the scheme at the line of scrimmage or a couple of steps into his backpedal. Even if it took his receivers forever to get open—as it did this current crop—just as soon as they had the least little opening, that's just how soon he got rid of the ball and squeezed it through the little opening.

New England's Bucko Kilroy, who'd been playing or scouting football since the forties, said Marino had the fastest release in NFL history, and whenever he tutored new scouts on what to look for, he told them just to make Marino their prototype. Everybody knew it, but guys who watched football all their lives would watch him and still exclaim about how quickly Marino got rid of the ball. Whereas a Randall Cunningham stretched his arm fully behind him and flung the ball as if it were a whip or fishing reel, Marino held it close to his head and chest and zipped it as if it were a dart.

He'd learned it from his dad. Dan Sr. drove a truck for the *Pittsburgh Post-Gazette* in the early morning, then came home and spent afternoons with Danny, rapping grounders and playing catch with baseballs and footballs. Dad taught him to throw from the ear, not to wind up, not to waste any motion. A little kid can't throw very far that way, but Dan Sr. said if he practiced the right way, he'd throw better as he got bigger. Danny played quarterback from fourth grade on, in the Western Pennsylvania hills that produced Johnny Unitas, Joe Namath, Joe Montana, and Jim Kelly, and, by the time he got to Pitt, his mechanics were so good that coach Jackie Sherrill told him, "Whatever you do, don't ever let any coach tell you how to throw a football or change anything you're doing."

His dad honed not only mechanics but confidence. He left little inspirational notes:

If you win or lose, I love you.

You are the best. You are the most dominating player. Remember, nobody does it better.

Years later, his buddy and peer, Neil O'Donnell, said what impressed him most was not Dan's release but his supreme confidence, whether it was a last-minute comeback or drilling a pass through the tightest of coverage.

"He's arguably the best quarterback in NFL history. He ought to have confidence," Keith Sims said. "He's such a smart quarterback that the recognition is instantly there for him. He doesn't have to sit there and think, 'Where am I going to throw the ball?' He just knows it. When you have that kind of recognition, with that fantastic release, it's a deadly combination."

That rapid release meant the instant a receiver cut, he better spin his head around like Linda Blair in *The Exorcist.*

"If you're not Linda Blair, you'll get hit with it," O. J. McDuffie said.

"At my size, by the time I turn and look around the linemen, I see the ball coming out of nowhere," Randal Hill agreed. "I know I've got to adjust quickly. It's because of his quick release, not because the ball is moving fast. It's not a hard ball to catch."

At thirty-five, Marino's arm was still as deadly—and as live—as ever. Oh, he'd lost a couple of yards off his deep pass, but that mattered maybe once a year. The true test of a quarterback's arm came when the ball had to zing as if on a string, from the pocket to the sideline thirty yards away before a hard-charging cornerback could jump it, or down the middle between two defenders, and Danny delivered those balls like John Elway and very few others. His arm got a bit tired in two-a-days, but he never missed a practice, and now, he said, his arm felt "great."

"Do I feel thirty-five? Sometimes my legs hurt a little, but as far as playing the games and the enthusiasm and enjoying what I do, I want to do it for a long time."

Ah, but would those legs let him? Danny had endured five operations on his left knee, one on his right knee, one on his right ankle, and one on the Achilles' tendon he severed in 1993. The Achilles forced him to miss eleven games, and his right leg had never been quite the same. Even after the ankle surgery, even after months of rehab, the foot and calf were not as strong. If he had played before arthroscopic surgery, he would have been done by now, like Namath before him. As it was, he lumbered onto the field with little shuffle steps and the hunched-over look of a septuagenarian.

But Danny's body wasn't the problem so much as the bodies lining up as receivers. His best, Fred Barnett, was out after his second major knee surgery. O.J.

had sure hands and quick moves but not breakaway speed. Charles Jordan had the physical ability but was always hurt or in the doghouse. Scott Miller was supposed to have good hands but struggled to get open. LT and Randal had some big-play ability but total inconsistency. Keith Byars was a shadow of his former self, and Carolan and Wainright were career third-stringers for a reason.

Without a deep threat or productive tight end, Jimmy had resorted to gimmicks—exploiting the speed of rookie backs Jerris McPhail and Stanley Pritchett—and juggling. His wide receivers would start one week and be inactive the next. He was making them examples for all fifty-three players: Practice hard and you'll play; don't and you won't. He would spend all year auditioning wide receivers to see who could play, only to discover most could not. If it worked for the grand scheme, it backfired in the short term because the quarterback had little continuity or confidence in his receivers. Oh, he put up a front. He praised them publicly. Jimmy told his leader to be patient and not scar any youngster's confidence by screaming, and Marino yelled less than he had in the past.

The cameras had often caught him screaming at Mark Duper, Mark Clayton, Mark Ingram, and even Don Shula. But usually, those times came when he was yelling to be heard over the din of the crowd or when he was upset with himself. He'd be apologizing to a receiver, "That's on me. I fucked up," and TV made it seem as if he were cursing the receivers.

"There's been a misconception for a long time," Danny said. "The networks play it up. A lot of times I'm mad at me. If I'm not doing everything I want to do, I've always been very animated. People play it up more than it really is. This year, there's no doubt I have to be as patient as I can. We have so many young guys, sometimes they're gonna make mistakes. I'm gonna make mistakes, too."

A Hall of Fame quarterback accustomed to throwing to great receivers like Duper, Clayton, Nat Moore, Irving Fryar, and Keith Jackson now was throwing to semipros. Damn straight it frustrated him.

One day, Duper paid a rare visit to the locker room.

"Duuuuupppe!" Marino exclaimed, genuinely excited.

"What's up, baby?" Super Duper asked Super Dan.

"Man," Dan asked, "can you teach these guys how to beat the bump and run?"

Oh, that he could. Two days later, on fourth and goal at the Jets' two, Dan called upon Randal Hill to beat Aaron Glenn's bump-and-run coverage. But Randal did not fight off the little cornerback, did not juke him out, did not give him a little swim move like Michael Irvin would have done for an easy touchdown. He let Glenn outhustle and outmuscle him for the ball at the goal line, and what should have been a Dolphins touchdown turned into a Glenn interception and one-hundred-yard touchdown return. The fourteen-point swing capsulized Randal's career, why he would never emerge as a premier receiver and would merely tantalize—and torment—with his deep speed. Randal wore a Superman T-shirt under his jersey. He called himself Thrill Hill, even got Thrill legally added as his middle name. Ran-doll was more like it.

A Duper, a Clayton, an Irvin—why, any good receiver—fights for that ball and scores a touchdown. Size was no excuse; Duper, Clayton, and Glenn were an inch shorter than Randal. But Ran-doll just didn't get it. He didn't blame himself. He sulked over the coaches and quarterback showing so little confidence in him. Ran-doll would not be active for the next game.

This next game would be the Dolphins' first true test of 1996. They had not played a good team playing good yet. On *Monday Night Football*, inside Indianapolis's loud and hostile dome, they would find one.

The Colts were a Failed Mary away from the Super Bowl in January. Now it was September and they were 3–0, coming back from a 21–3 deficit to shock the champion Cowboys in Dallas, 25–24, when Chris Boniol's desperation field goal bounded off the crossbar as time expired. "How 'bout them Colts?" Harbaugh shouted, stealing a game from Barry Switzer's Cowboys, stealing a line from Jimmy Johnson's Cowboys heyday.

"When I came here in 1994," Harbaugh said, "a lot of my friends didn't know a lot about football, and a couple said, 'The Indianapolis Colts? What league is that?' I had to tell them, 'It's the NFL.' A lot of teams saw the Indianapolis Colts on the schedule and looked forward to a win. Now the Colts have an identity."

A week before the game, the hype was already building, and Jimmy didn't want to tone it down. "Why?" he asked the media on Monday. "Hey, that's why we're in this business. I'd much rather have two 3–0s than two 0–3s."

And he told his players Wednesday, "Listen, guys, in my little sabbatical away from coaching, I sat at home and I didn't miss the games where we beat somebody by twenty points. You know what made the hair on the back of my neck stand up? You know what excited me? I missed getting ready for the *big game*. Just like this game! You look forward to two undefeated teams playing on *Monday Night Football*. I don't want you to be afraid about it. I want you to be excited about the challenge. This is about showing the country what we can do!"

Thursday morning, he taped his weekly radio show with WQAM's Hank Goldberg, and Thursday night, he zoomed to downtown Miami to film his TV shows at Channel 6. The shows ran on the local NBC affiliate and the SportsChannel cable network; they were almost identical except for different openings and closings.

Jimmy arrived early and spent a good half hour chatting with girlfriend Rhonda Rookmaaker, agent Nick Christin, and hosts Tony Segreto and Joe Rose before taping began at 7 P.M. Resplendent in a navy-blue suit, a patterned tie, a gold watch, and diamond-and-gold studded Super Bowl ring, Jimmy sipped a

Diet Coke as twenty-six people scurried about, one adjusting his microphone, another his makeup.

Don Shula's show always ran on the ABC affiliate, just before the Monday-night game. Jimmy worked Monday nights on the game plan with his coaches, but by Thursday nights, the long hours were over, and, after filming the shows, Jimmy, Rhonda, and Nick would hop in their Corvettes and head to Miami Beach for dinner and drinks. This night the tapings dragged beyond nine o'clock because Dave Calabro from Indianapolis's WTHR-TV was in town to do a piece and because they were having audio problems connecting with Harbaugh's TV show back in Indianapolis.

The people who saw Jimmy only as a dictator would have expected a blowup—and been surprised. He grimaced at the delays—and went back to joking around. Calabro said people told him he had Jimmy Johnson hair.

"You don't have enough spray on," Jimmy said. "I want lots of spray. I don't like hair in my face during practice."

When Nick stood stone-faced in the back of the room, Jimmy prompted Segreto to ask if Nick had any tattoos.

"No, no, no," Nick said. "Rhonda does."

"I'll find out tonight," Jimmy said.

"Oh," Rhonda said, "promise me!"

She was a slim, attractive brunette who believed in irreverence and informality; even at black-tie events, she wore pantsuits. They had met in 1984, when Jimmy was coaching the Hurricanes and looking for someone to cut that soon-to-be famous hair and she was a thirty-year-old single mom. When Jimmy moved to Dallas and divorced his wife in 1989, Rhonda got a job and an apartment in Dallas. When they returned to Florida, they were almost inseparable until Jimmy reverted to coaching. Jimmy didn't tell her he loved her, but his actions made it obvious.

Finally, the glitches were fixed and the coach turned to the quarterback and said, "I hope that new baby is keeping you up at night and you're tired at practice."

Jimmy Johnson didn't remember his family's birthdays or anniversaries or even Christmas, but he knew Jim Harbaugh just had a baby? Why?

"That's why he is who he is," P.R. man Harvey Greene said.

Why? Because it might give him an edge on Monday night.

Monday, September 23, Indianapolis. As much as he loved Monday nights, Jimmy hated sitting around the hotel all day waiting. So instead of the normal morning or early afternoon walk-through Sunday, he held it Sunday night in the RCA Dome, followed by a late dinner and late curfew, hoping the players could sleep in a little Monday before launching into meetings.

Jimmy's kids hadn't visited a city stewing for a big game like this one was. It was Indianapolis's first Monday night game in three years, and the locals went nuts. Two pep rallies were held downtown. The mayor declared it Colts Loud and Proud Day and urged everyone to wear Colts colors. Scalpers got $100 for $25 upper-deck seats. It was the biggest crowd—and, the Colts' fan club president said, the biggest game—since the Colts had arrived in Indianapolis.

It wasn't just ABC and prime-time TV. *The New York Times*, the *Los Angeles Times*, *The Washington Post*, the *Chicago Tribune*, and *USA Today* were there. The commissioner and governor were there. A cheerleader rode a white horse onto the field before the game and after every Colts score. Fireworks went off during the national anthem, and the smoke hung inside the dome for minutes. Fans waved white rally towels and screamed so loud, it sounded as if you had chain saws attached to your ears.

Amid the bedlam, the Dolphins drove sharply down the field in their first series and had a first down at the Indy seven when O.J. made a superb catch for thirty-four yards. Never has such a good play turned so bad for the Dolphins. Marino wasn't even hit, but his right foot—the one with all the previous problems—rolled over after the throw, and the pain was intense. He limped down the field, and, though he stayed for three more plays, he could barely get off two passes before he was crunched, and Joe Nedney came on to give the Dolphins a 3–0 lead.

Dan was done. And so were the Dolphins.

Bernie Kosar replaced him, and Bernie wasn't sharp because backup quarterbacks get about 10 percent of the repetitions once the regular season begins and because the Colts weren't afraid of the dinker beating them deep. The Colts bombarded him with blitzes and stunts. The fans screamed so loudly that even the tackles, let alone the tight ends and wideouts, could not hear Bernie call plays. On first and second down, the guards had to shout Bernie's calls so the tackles next to them could hear the count, but on third down in shotgun formation, nobody could hear Bernie. So the ball was snapped on a silent count and the linemen could not anticipate; they had to watch the ball move before they moved. Might not sound like much to the average fan, but the difference in attitude and in that split second is the difference between success and failure.

"Knowing the snap count is an advantage for the offense because you get a chance to drive into your guy and react to what he's doing instead of trying to look at the ball and the guy you're trying to block at the same time. Most of the time, he beats your reaction time," Richmond Webb explained.

"It's probably as loud a place as I've ever been in," Jimmy said. "It's hard for the guards and tackles to communicate with one another. It's hard for the quarterback to point out the blitz. It's hard, almost impossible, for the quarterback to change the play when he reads it's a blitz. If you're in a bad play for a blitz, it's hard to get out of the bad play; you just have to live with it."

Bernie ran even slower and more awkwardly than Marino—picture an arthritic stork—and he could not slide around the pocket and evade pressure the way Marino could. If Marino had the league's finest delivery, Bernie had the worst. He wound up, threw sidearm, threw every which way. He had been deadly accurate his first few years in Cleveland but was never the same after hurting his elbow. The years had ravaged his body, and all he had left was smarts and leadership, and they could not overcome a pass rush as frenzied as Dobermans in a butcher shop.

Bernie lost nearly as many yards on sacks (twenty-seven) as his ball carriers gained (twenty-eight). The Dolphins totaled seventy yards in their first ten plays— and 120 in their final forty. They got three points their first series and three more the rest of the night.

"We were discombobulated by different stunts," line coach Larry Beightol said. "They'd never done it before, and they caught us with our pants down. Shame on me!"

The boss didn't blame him. "That's a line coach's mentality," Jimmy said. "They're a little bit masochistic."

The Dolphins trailed just 7–6 at the half, after the Colts drove ninety-seven yards, helped greatly by a debatable roughing penalty on Daniel Stubbs and Lou Oliver getting fooled on the touchdown toss. And they had a chance to lead, but Webb's holding penalty wiped out a first down and Nedney was short from fifty-three yards. Indy had a first down at the Miami one, but the defense held the Colts to a field goal and a 10–6 lead.

Then came controversy. Colts fullback Clif Groce fumbled, and Dolphins linebacker Chris Singleton pounced on the ball at the Indy thirty-nine. Several officials called, "White ball," and the Dolphins celebrated. And then, after a long delay and a lot of pushing and shoving, referee Dick Hantak ruled the Colts had retained the ball because Singleton and Harbaugh had recovered it simultaneously.

Singleton was enraged: "They said, 'White ball! White ball! White ball! Okay, Chris, you can get up and let go, it's white ball.' I had it under my chest. There was no indication it would be a tie or the blue team would get the ball. And then somebody came out of nowhere and said, 'Blue ball.' I've never seen a play like that. Next time, I'm not getting up. They'll have to bring a crowbar to get it away. We'd still be out there now, wrestling for the ball. It was definitely a momentum changer. You think you're getting off the field and your offense is going in to score. That let the whole defense down. Totally unfair!"

Under the pile, Harbaugh saw it differently: "I heard 'em say, 'White ball!' I don't know why he was saying that. I had half the ball the whole time. I was wrestling for five minutes straight."

The Colts had to punt, but the Dolphins got it at their fourteen, not the Colts' thirty-nine, and went nowhere. They got it back just once more, at their three, and went nowhere. The Colts ran for 171 yards on the league's top-rated run defense, using delayed draws to exploit Zach Thomas's aggressiveness.

First place belonged to the Colts.

Distress belonged to the Dolphins.

Marino leaned on his crutches, head down, and whispered they'd have to see what an MRI revealed the next day. But they already had seen the crack on the X rays.

In emergency-room terms, he'd suffered an acute, nondisplaced fracture of the medial malelleous. In English, that's a small break in the area where the ankle meets the big bone in the lower leg. Marino had to choose between a cast and a screw. The cast would take longer to heal. He chose the screw.

Were the Dolphins screwed?

Photos of a grimacing Marino topped the front pages of *The Herald* and *Sun-Sentinel*, playing above John F. Kennedy Jr.'s marriage and Russian president Boris Yeltsin's proposed heart surgery.

"The Dolphins losing Marino," Edwin Pope wrote in *The Herald*, "is the Yankees losing Babe Ruth."

Doctors figured he'd miss four to six weeks.

Would time run out on Danny and the Dolphins?

Would the season be shot without him?

"The Miami Dolphins haven't been in the real world for however long Danny has been here," Jimmy said. "This is the real world."

12
ERRORS AND
HEIRS APPARENT

This is the type of leader Dan Marino is. "I went in after the Colts game, and I was feeling bad for Dan. He's thirty-five years old, his career is winding down, he doesn't have much time left," Jimmy recalled. "He looked at me and said, 'Coach, I'm sorry I let you down.' *He let me down? How? He fractured his ankle!* That's the type of player you want leading your team."

But this is the type of leader the Dolphins had. Two and a half months later, when the players would elect Pro Bowl teams, Jimmy would ask them also to vote for their best leader, their most inspirational teammate. Fred Barnett and Dan would get the most votes, Zach Thomas would be close behind, and very few veterans would get more than a stray vote or two. A rookie would outpoll all but two veterans, which said a lot about the rookie but even more about the veterans Jimmy had inherited and why this team had not been mentally strong the past few years.

"I don't think there was a lot of leadership," Jimmy would say in December. "There might have been guys who were vocal, guys who did some talking, but nobody who really laid it on the line. Most of our leaders now are either brand-new like Fred Barnett or rookies like Zach and Larry Izzo. That's good for the future, but it's not good for when we're going through this tough stretch.

"The example set by some veterans was not very good. In fact, the example set was negative. I've had veterans tell guys they shouldn't come back from injury so quick because they risked permanent damage—when there was nothing to it! They're getting some bad advice. They may outwardly show the right things, but back behind the scenes, they weren't doing the job.

"You want to have somebody they respect, they can count on, and there's not many of them playing. You need some guys they can look to who are tough sons of a gun who work their ass off, who they can believe in and say, 'If we're in a crunch, they're gonna help us win.' They need a Michael Irvin."

They needed a Dan Marino, and now they didn't have him. They had lost seven in a row when Marino had not started. Now they had managed just three points in three and a half quarters without him and faced the prospect of falling out of the playoff race. When Jimmy met them Wednesday, he knew they were down, and he did not want to risk upsetting their fragile psyches by dwelling on Monday night's mistakes. He wanted to give them a pep talk about being 3–1.

"A losing team looks at excuses," he told them. "A championship team looks at solutions. We can gripe about injuries, we can groan about officiating, we can groan about being on the road and crowd noise. A championship team overcomes all those things. We've got to be good enough and have individual players ready to step up and be first-teamers and perform and win.

"Let's look at the last ten Super Bowl winners. Not the Super Bowl participants, but the winners. Only three opened 4–0. One went 2–2. Six of the ten went 3–1 their first four games. The same record we've got! It's not a sprint. It's a marathon. It's who's got the strongest will and who's got the strongest mind. We knew we'd have a little adversity. So now we deal with it."

Bernie Kosar probably had the Dolphins' sharpest mind. He was a leader and the ultimate team guy. But with his slingshot arm and quicksand feet, he just could not make the tough throws or escape the rush anymore.

Jimmy had signed Craig Erickson to spend a year learning the offense, then become the backup, and eventually Air Marino's heir. Craig had spent some extra time learning the offense, but he hadn't taken a single snap with the Miami offense in practice, simply running the scout (or service) team to give the Dolphins' defense a look at the opposing offense. But here it was, three weeks later, and the future was now.

Luckily, the Dolphins had a bye week before they played Seattle, so the coaches gave Craig a crash course in the offense. He needed it.

"Today we ran a check," Karim Abdul-Jabbar said the second day of practice, "and they were screaming at him, and he said, 'I don't know it!' I don't think it's that tough an offense to learn, but it's harder for him. He got here late, and a quarterback has to know *everything*. I have to know a lot to perform, but not everything."

Craig had looked like such a promising young starter for the Tampa Bay Buccaneers—he threw for thirty-four touchdowns and nearly six thousand yards in two years as a starter—that Indianapolis gave up first- and fourth-round picks for him. He opened 1995 as the Colts' starter, but Jim Harbaugh played so well he won the job, and, at the end of the 1996 preseason, the Colts asked Craig to accept a pay cut to $500,000 a year. Thinking he'd find better play and pay elsewhere, he declined the offer and was waived. But lineups and payrolls were set, and nobody overwhelmed him with an offer, so Craig took Jimmy's lowball offer—even suggested they make it two years instead of one—but only after talking it over with Bernie and even Bernie's dad. He was thrilled to learn from Bernie, one of his best friends in football, and Danny, the legend he grew up emulating in West Palm Beach, an hour north of the Dolphins' Davie complex.

"I was no different than anybody else in South Florida," Craig said. "I was one of the kids on the block wearing number thirteen jerseys."

And so when Jimmy named him the starter the following Monday, six days before the Seattle game, Craig fulfilled a dream.

Danny met the media leaning on crutches, his right leg wrapped from knee to toe. Four local TV stations carried it live. The president didn't get this coverage, but, then, what's more important: politics or playoffs? Danny said he was frustrated, but he didn't think his string of injuries meant he was suddenly frail and would be forced to retire anytime soon.

"Anytime you get injured, you always think about the long-term future. But I believe that I can play and I can play for a long time. The unfortunate thing is lately I've had a few things where I've been out a couple of weeks. But I can come back."

He'd better. The season depended upon it.

Eric Green never returned to work out for the Dolphins. Jimmy wouldn't sign him until he was totally healthy, but the Baltimore Ravens would, which said a lot about why they went 4–12. Eric's $425,000 salary said a lot about his true worth, and Jimmy was thrilled because the signing reduced the Dolphins' potential for losses in a grievance and chopped the money they had to reserve against the cap from $750,000 to a little more than $300,000. That freed up money for him to re-sign Johnny Mitchell if he couldn't work out a trade he'd been discussing with the Rams for Troy Drayton, he confided as we hustled out of his office, down the stairs, and out to practice September 27. He didn't expect Mitchell to be a savior, but he knew his current tight ends weren't the answers.

That led to one of the wildest weeks of the season: After taking the weekend off, the players returned Monday, September 30, and practiced so sloppily that Jimmy exploded. He promoted Erickson over Kosar, Carolan over Byars, and Randal Hill over Lamar Thomas. "We're going to have to practice much better Wednesday," he warned, "or else I'm going to make more changes."

Someone asked if a week off contributed to the sloppy practice.

"I think weak minds had a lot to do with them not practicing the way I want. *Weeaak miiiinds,*" he said, drawling out the words angrily.

This echoed one of his favorite maxims: Let the mind control the body and not the body control the mind.

Tuesday, October 1, he struck again. He released Byars and former starting guard Bert Weidner. With the new salary-cap room, he extended contracts of center Tim Ruddy and safety–special teams star Sean Hill. And he traded Billy Milner, who'd lost the right tackle job to James Brown, for Drayton, a big tight end he had coveted since the '93 draft. Jimmy targeted Drayton as his second-round pick, but the Rams grabbed Troy first, and Jimmy settled for Kevin Williams, an explosive return specialist who's yet to come through as a true receiving threat for the Cowboys.

Wednesday, the players responded. Zach Thomas hit Karim Abdul-Jabbar so fiercely, Karim could not move his legs, hands, or head and feared he was paralyzed until the "stinger" went away in a few seconds.

And Byars responded by ripping Jimmy.

He said fullback "wasn't a fair competition at all," that Jimmy "had made up his mind after the draft" and "there was nothing I could do. I can play any position on the football field," Byars continued. "I can play fullback. I can play tight end. The only position I'm not too good at playing is obscurity. That's what the Dolphins had me playing at this year. I'm one of the best option runners in the NFL, but I haven't run one option route all season long. There was no sense of urgency to get me the football. The majority of plays I was in, I was just blocking, and the pass routes I ran, I was like the third or fourth read.

"The new Miami Dolphins, Jimmy is the leader, he's the general. You need understudies. You need people who can lead as well. But Jimmy doesn't want that. He just wants a lot of followers. I've never been a follower in anything I've done. I know how to follow a chain of command, but I'm a leader. Maybe Jimmy was somewhat intimidated by my leadership skills."

Byars suggested Jimmy "didn't have the endurance to go the long haul" and wasn't sure if Jimmy could succeed "in the new world order of the NFL with the salary cap there. He has to prove he can win in that era."

But here were Keith's two biggest beauties: "When they told me I was released, the first thing that came to my mind was the Martin Luther King speech: 'Free at last, free at last, thank God Almighty I'm free at last.' " And the end of his 130 games streak of catching a pass? "That was a bunch of crock: 'We were gonna throw you a shovel pass at the end of the game.' I'm not looking for one pass; I'm looking for a lot of passes. I'm still saddened by the streak ending. It was like Pete Rose trying to get that consecutive hits record."

These were jaw-dropping accusations. They were also a "bunch of crock." There is the real world, and then there is Keith's world, and, apparently, never the twain shall meet.

Unfair competition? Byars opened camp as the starting fullback, but he played poorly in the Redskins scrimmage. Rookie Stanely Pritchett blocked so well and made so many big catches he earned the job. Veteran Robert Wilson said camp was very competitive, but Byars's blocking wasn't suited to an offense where the fullback and tight end must be blockers first and receivers second. Byars was switched to tight end and almost instantly promoted ahead of Kerry Cash, who had started several years in the league and for the first month of camp. But Byars had just four catches for thirty-nine yards in preseason. On third and ten against Chicago, he caught a nine-yard pass and couldn't push for the extra yard, forcing a punt. In his first start at tight end, he was shut out as a receiver, dropping one pass as he got hit and incurring two penalties. In his next start, he had his best game, with three catches for thirty yards, but he also dropped a simple flare pass.

In the regular-season opener, he had his best play, a sixteen-yard catch and run, but also a drop. He had two more catches against Arizona, but none against the Jets, when one catch was stripped from him. Against the Colts, he had one catch for five yards.

Keith no longer had sure hands, and he displayed absolutely no power, speed, or elusiveness once he caught the ball. Blocking? I took notes on every play—and never wrote down Byars's number for a good block. Privately, Jimmy said Byars graded "terrible" as a blocker. Publicly, he held this exchange on the Fabulous Sports Babe's nationally syndicated radio show:

THE BABE: Maybe I could play tight end for you.
JIMMY: You could block better than our guys have.
THE BABE: The thing is, every time I block, I say, "Ow!"
JIMMY: That's what ours have been doing lately.

Leadership? Jimmy, one of the world's most confident people, wasn't intimidated by Byars's leadership—he was incensed by Byars's lack of leadership. How could this alleged team leader sulk so long, so openly after the win over the Jets? What kind of message was that?

To compare the "burden" of a $300,000 salary and a Boca Raton mansion to the incredible injustices that Martin Luther King died for was a blasphemous insult to every person who suffered through hundreds of years of slavery and racist discrimination. To compare his catch streak to Pete Rose's forty-four-game hitting streak, second only to Joe DiMaggio's fifty-six games, was a joke. Getting one hit in three or four at-bats is infinitely harder than a fullback catching one swing pass a game. It wasn't even a matter of durability; the NFL didn't count games for which players didn't suit up.

So it was an incredibly overrated stat, yet Keith took incredible pride in it, foolish pride, really. Like many star athletes who had been coddled since childhood, Keith had an inflated opinion of his value, an opinion stoked ever since he had been hailed as the second coming of Archie Griffin at Ohio State.

Jimmy addressed Byars's charges in a team meeting. He knew cutting Keith provoked fear in his players, and that wasn't necessarily bad.

"Fear can be a motivator for everybody," Louis Oliver said. "I'm motivated because I fear failing."

Sunday, October 6, Miami. The Seahawks hadn't had a winning record since 1990, and now they were 1–4 and looking awful. Golden Boy Rick Mirer had been horrendous, and, as Seattle tried furiously to trade him for Jeff George, career backup John Friesz got his first Seattle start against the Dolphins. Chris Warren, a four-time thousand-yard runner, had run tentatively and heartlessly behind a papier-mâché line. If they kept losing and lost voter approval for a new stadium, the players and coaches might be hauled out of town. Seattle was last in the league in run defense and minus ten in turnover differential. Miami was plus eight in turnovers and favored by eight in Vegas.

Even with a quarterback making his first start less than a month after joining the team, there was no way the Dolphins should lose this one at home. But they did.

Craig Erickson would be a good quarterback some day. But on this Bob Dylan day—a hard rain was gonna fall all weekend—he turned simple snaps into adventures. Five times in the first two and a half quarters he and center Tim Ruddy botched snaps. One was a bad shotgun snap; the rest were simple exchanges. None led to Seattle points, but all thwarted Dolphin drives, the first on the Seattle one. He was tentative and took sacks, causing fans to chant for Bernie, and on the last, desperate drive, O. J. McDuffie cut outside as designed, but Erickson read the coverage and threw inside, and Seattle intercepted to clinch a 22–15 victory.

And yet for all the struggles of Erickson and his Pro Bowl left tackle, Richmond Webb, Miami would have won if it were not for any of three monstrous touchdown tosses given up by its suddenly scorched secondary.

First, Joey Galloway flew down the sideline for sixty-five yards against Calvin Jackson. If Jackson had looked back and played the ball, or if he had timed his jump better, he would have knocked it down. Instead, Galloway caught it, and Jackson flailed, failed, and fell. A free safety with any instincts would have gotten over and shoved Galloway out of bounds. Gene Atkins did not.

Then Galloway ran a post deep over the middle for fifty-one yards, and the defensive backs' failure to communicate cost them a touchdown for the second game in a row. Oliver called for a three-deep coverage in the huddle, but as the Seahawks lined up, the call was changed to a four-across. Terrell Buckley, hustling out to line up across from his receiver, never heard the safeties change the call. So Buckley stayed outside when Galloway cut inside, expecting a safety to be there. Atkins arrived late. Oliver took the wrong angle to cut off Galloway and looked like an eighteen-wheeler trying to turn around and accelerate.

And yet behind a rallying Erickson, the Dolphins were clinging to a 15–14 lead, and the Seahawks were eighty yards and one play away from extinction with little more than two minutes left when Deep Friesz gave Miami Friesz-er burn. Jackson started slipping on the wet field, so all he could do was try to dive at Brian Blades. But he missed, and, again, the free safety failed to anticipate or make the routine play on a crossing route. Atkins took a bad angle, and Blades, who's not nearly as fast as Galloway, blew by them for the eighty-yard winning touchdown, a triumphant homecoming to a hometown where a jury convicted him of shooting his cousin but a judge overturned the verdict and set him free.

The pass rush had put no pressure on Friesz, and he threw for 299 yards in his first start, 196 on just three passes.

And the Dolphins had lost a game they should have won, would have won if not for Atkins's dreadful performance.

Atkins was a hard-hitting safety, and Jimmy had hoped to keep him in the lineup for run support against Buffalo, Philadelphia, and Dallas. But his lack of communication, speed, and instincts could not be overlooked a minute longer. He was a sour soul. Within the past year, he had endured his half brother's suicide, had knocked down Jason Cole of the *Sun-Sentinel*, had feuded with and fought Oliver during practice, had screamed at and nearly come to blows with coaches and teammates. His cantankerousness contributed to three defensive backs moving to the other side of the locker room. He had walked out of a team meeting when he refused to take blame for a blown coverage the year before, and now he wouldn't admit his mistake, either. Jimmy wanted people to acknowledge their mistakes.

Shawn Wooden had beaten out Atkins in preseason before injuring his neck. Atkins had played well enough that Jimmy had canceled his fine after the New England game and even added a $50,000 incentive to his contract. But now Atkins was killing the Dolphins on the field and in the locker room. Jimmy wanted to replace him with Wooden, and since Atkins didn't play special teams, Jimmy didn't want him on the team, period. After the game, Jimmy met with Bob Ackles for a long time. They'd have to take salary-cap hits of $915,000 in '96 and $1.295 million in '97 if they cut Atkins.

The next day, when the players gathered in the auditorium for their 2 P.M. team meeting, Jimmy was late, and Jimmy was never late. They surveyed the room and started whispering among themselves. Atkins wasn't there, either.

Gene was in Jimmy's office. Did Jimmy get across that Gene was partly responsible for all three touchdowns? "I didn't get it across," Jimmy said. "I released him."

And he promoted Wooden, his fifth rookie starter. And he named Drayton, a Dolphin for just six days, as the starter ahead of Carolan. And two days later, he promoted Shane Burton, his sixth rookie and tenth newcomer, as a starter ahead of team sack leader Daniel Stubbs. And he challenged the offensive linemen to quit playing soft or they'd be next.

A reporter showed Jimmy a photo splashed almost eight inches across *The Herald*'s back page. Lamar Thomas was walking off the field, an arm around his old coach Dennis Erickson, a big smile on his face. When Jimmy had seen Cowboys cornerback Everson Walls smiling with the enemy after a big loss, he'd come down on him hard. But when he saw this, Jimmy told the local media he had no reaction. Then his eyes darted around the room. Was he looking for the next question? Or looking to avoid the truth?

Lamar Thomas was not active for the next three games.

13

REDEMPTION IN BUFFALO

Jimmy's 3–0 start had disintegrated just as Don Shula's 4–0 start had the year before, and if Jimmy's kids didn't handle adversity a whole lot better than Don's vets, 1996 could turn into a disaster.

Losing in Indy was one thing. But losing to a bad team playing bad . . . why, that could be the difference between playoffs and layoffs. Instead of 4–1, the Dolphins were 3–2, losers of two in a row, potentially losers of five in a row with Buffalo, Philadelphia, and Dallas next. And it didn't get much easier after that: four more playoff–caliber foes in New England, Indianapolis, Houston, and Pittsburgh.

"We lost one we felt we should win, and now we've got to win one that people think we should lose," Jimmy said.

"He always tells us, 'You don't want to lose a game you should win and then have that sick-to-the-stomach feeling,' " Larry Izzo said. "That's exactly what this game was."

If losing games didn't make the Dolphins uneasy enough, losing jobs sure did. Jimmy had let go thirty-one players who finished 1995 on the Dolphins' roster. Offensive coordinator Gary Stevens said the biggest thing Jimmy brought to Miami was "fear motivation." And fear, says Dan Reeves, who's gone to eight Super Bowls as a player or coach, is "probably the greatest motivator that I know of." Even the new starters worked their butts off because they knew they wouldn't last long if they didn't.

Shawn Wooden said he'd lost his starting job after getting hurt in preseason, so he didn't take this promotion for granted. "When I was in college," Wooden said, "my teammates who made the pros would come back and say the NFL stands for Not For Long. I thought they were joking. Now I know they weren't joking."

The Dolphins had lost eight in a row without Dan Marino, and now they had to play without him in Buffalo. Their last visit there, they were humiliated in the 1995 playoffs, the last game for Shula and Coach Uh-O.

"When we rushed for 341 yards," Buffalo's Jim Kelly cracked, "we said the only thing bad about it is we got rid of Tom Olivadotti."

Kelly wasn't as insulting as the extra game film that Trace Armstrong and Tim Bowens watched. "It was ugly as ugly could be," Trace said. "If that doesn't get you excited, nothing will."

And if Rich Stadium didn't get them excited, nothing would.

Buffalo was a little house of horrors for the Dolphins, and not just because they had lost ten of twelve there but also because of the fans. These were not your normal NFL fans. These were loud and proud—and often drunk and obnoxious. They had hurled not only racial epithets but batteries at Bryan Cox, who gave them both his middle fingers in 1993, then got in a fight in 1995 and spat his way to the locker room as trash—including full beer cans—rained on the Dolphins.

Ah, but what about the guy in the cuddly Santa Claus costume handing out mints? Bills fans hurled thousands of the candies—plus batteries, rocks, and oranges—at the Dolphins' bench. Buffalo security threw out just one fan, a guy who threw a Snickers bar. Another Santa threw an egg at the Dolphins' bus. Even *The Buffalo News* admitted Bills fans were over the edge:

"Other cities have pro football teams, right? Other cities have fans who go to games, cheer their teams on, buy goofy souvenirs and otherwise enjoy themselves, don't they? Then the games end and the people get on with their lives . . . Here football is our drug of choice, our municipal religion. Why? In a single sentence, one expert offered the perfect explanation: Cities that don't have much going for them tend to overemphasize sports."

Dolphins rookies thought they'd been in some tough college towns. Shane Burton remembered when Florida fans threw ice and hot dogs on Tennessee players. Zach Thomas remembered when Baylor fans threw peanuts on him. And Wooden remembered when Boston College fans spit on Notre Dame's priest. Yes, spit on a priest. And BC is a Jesuit school.

Dolphins veterans warned the rookies about Buffalo. They told them how the team buses had been stoned and snowballed and rocked . . . and mooned. Players told Zach a whole line of male fans had mooned the bus on the way to the stadium.

"They said, 'Look at the guy on the end.' The guy stood up—and he had a badge on!" Zach shook his head. "Man, even the cops are crazy!"

Loud crowds forced the Dolphins to avoid audibles and use a silent count in shotgun formation, and that disadvantage had crippled their pass protection in Indy. Jimmy second-guessed himself for throwing so much that game and vowed not to repeat the mistake. So as the coaches prepared for the Bills, he decided they were going to keep running even if they gained little or no yardage because one or two yards was better than having the Bills' defense—one of the league's best with 1995 Defensive Player of the Year Bryce Paup and soon-to-be-successor Bruce Smith—sack or intercept still learning Craig Erickson. Jimmy had beaten the Bills twice in the Super Bowl by taking advantage of their turnover tendencies, and that's what he planned to do again.

Jimmy even prepared for the Buffalo wind; he talked to punter John Kidd about it three or four times during the week. Kidd had played for the Bills and knew all about the wild winds, so Jimmy asked him to keep checking on the forecasts for Sunday. Kidd had talked to assistants about the wind before. "But it's unusual for the head coach," he said. "I haven't found anything that gets by him yet. He's got everything covered."

Jimmy challenged the pride of his linemen and all his players. But he also reminded them: "As down as we may be, we also have to understand we're 3–2, Buffalo is 4–1, and a win at Buffalo really puts us right back where we want to be. Yes, we can win without Dan Marino. If we can't, we're in trouble!"

Vegas said they were in trouble by five and a half points, and the spread would have been more if Kelly were not questionable with a pulled hamstring.

"Nobody," Zach said, "will expect us to go up to Buffalo and beat Buffalo. That's good. I like being the underdog."

Most coaches would have been afraid to start newcomers like Craig Erickson and Troy Drayton when they joined the team after camp and didn't know the offense. But Jimmy was willing to sacrifice knowledge for big-play potential. Most coaches would have waited to see them earn their jobs on game-day performance. Jimmy was willing to project.

Most coaches would not work their players as hard during the regular season as Jimmy was doing. In fact, Ronnie Lott, the hard-hitting former defensive back who took Jimmy's place at Fox Sports, said Jimmy ruined their legs with all those tough practices, and dead legs caused them to lose to Seattle.

Jimmy's response? "Puhhhh-lease."

But while Buffalo's Marv Levy wouldn't say Jimmy was wrong and he was right, he did not believe in physical practices for his vets.

"I'm not looking for our players to prove every day how tough they are," Levy said. "I know how tough Bryce Paup and Bruce Smith are. If there are two coaches that I studied and admired—and there's more than two—they were Paul Brown and Bud Wilkinson. And they did not do a tremendous amount of endless scrimmaging and hard hitting in their practices. And I believe your team is much fresher if you don't."

"We get more hitting work for our rookies, but I'll tell you something: We don't want to put them to the test 'You're under the gun every minute.' We want them to feel good about playing football, and if a guy isn't tough enough, I don't make a big deal and a big speech about it. I just don't keep him. I don't have to get in his face every second and grab him by the lapels."

Sunday, October 13, Buffalo, New York. The Bills fans screamed at the Dolphins and soon as they deplaned Saturday, and as the team buses drove by a gas station, a guy stopped pumping gas and gave them the finger.

On game day Jimmy made his rookies take the first bus to the stadium at 9:30 A.M. Veterans had the option of 9:30 or 10:30 departures. "Smart move on his part," Louis Oliver said. "He didn't want the young guys to get caught up in all the hoopla, the hostile and crazy fans."

Because by ten-thirty—or two and a half hours before kickoff—the parking lots were full of tailgaters cooking Buffalo wings and drinking brew, the traffic was jammed for miles, and fans lined the streets and screamed their fool heads off.

And then the game began, and Zach intercepted Kelly's first pass. And the next series, Kelly had the ball stripped by Bowens and recovered by Armstrong—the two guys who'd watched extra film. The Dolphins got nothing from those turnovers because Joe Nedney hooked a thirty-three-yarder and Jimmy had so little confidence in his shaky kicker that he faked a forty-one-yard attempt.

But after some big plays by Jerris McPhail, Craig Erickson, and Karim Abdul-Jabbar, the Dolphins made it 7–0 on Karim's three-yard run in the second quarter, and 14–0 after Randal Hill's sixty-one-yard catch and Irving Spikes's one-yard dive late in the third quarter. Kelly silenced the boo-birds momentarily when he directed a drive capped by Thurman Thomas's nineteen-yard run, but when Armstrong and Daniel Stubbs collected sacks six and seven and Calvin Jackson collected Kelly's third turnover, things were looking good for the Dolphins defense.

And then they reverted to Seattle Slew form.

Andre Reed made a catch twenty-one yards downfield at the Miami thirty—and Wooden missed the tackle, and Reed was running free toward the end zone, and it was unfuckingbelievable that their free safety could blow a game two weeks in a row. "I can't believe I missed the tackle. It was just a simple tackle. All I had to do was push him out of bounds!" Wooden said later. "T-Buck saved me. I mean, he saved *us*."

Because Terrell Buckley did not give up hope. He chased and chased and finally dragged down Reed after forty-nine yards. The Bills had 115 seconds and four downs to traverse two yards.

And they couldn't do it.

"Four plays to go!" the Dolphins defenders told each other. Defensive coordinator George Hill called for a blitz, with the defensive ends covering the tight ends, Stubbs on Lonnie Johnson, Armstrong on Tony Cline. Kelly looked toward both and found them blanketed. Bowens chased Kelly and was about to sack him when Kelly heaved the ball away. Referee Bernie Kukar made the gutsy but correct call: grounding.

"Three plays to go!" the Dolphins shouted. The Bills had twelve yards to go and no time-outs. George and Jimmy figured the Bills would have to pass three straight times and they set their defense accordingly. Kelly found his receivers blanketed again and threw out of bounds.

"Two plays to go!" the Dolphins shouted. Kelly tried to fool the Dolphins, but Burton, the rookie making his first start, stopped Thurman Thomas, the guy who'd killed the Dolphins so many times, after two yards.

"This," T-Buck shouted, "is for the season!" He was convinced Kelly was coming at him, looking for Reed, since they had "hooked up for about a thousand touchdowns" the last eleven years. Sure enough, Kelly aimed toward Reed along the right sideline. T-Buck broke for the ball, could see it coming as if in slow motion, could see the rotation on the ball, and he knew it was his. And then he bobbled it . . . but held on . . . and pranced down the sideline, all the way to the end zone, for ninety-one yards and a 21–7 victory. Somewhere between ten and twenty Dolphins chased him all the way and mobbed him in the end zone.

And a stadium that had roared a moment before was silent.

"I can't hear you!" Oliver screamed, dancing at the ten.

What a wild swing of emotions it had been: Dolphins win! No, Dolphins blow it! No, Dolphins win it!

"They should have a counselor in the locker room after this game for all the emotional highs and lows you go through," fullback Robert Wilson said. "To go through all that in three hours, that's more emotions than most people go through in a damn year!"

Kelly had collided with Oliver for the winning quarterback sneak as time expired in 1989, and the Bills danced while Oliver lay unconscious in the end zone. Kelly had exposed Oliver and the Dolphins with three deep touchdown passes in a wild 44–34 playoff victory in 1991. Kelly had embarrassed them in the playoffs in 1995.

And so now, finally, Louis Oliver could torment his tormentors, and, boy, did he love it. He ran toward the tunnel leading to the Dolphins' locker room and stopped. And for a full minute, he wiggled his hips. He danced. He strutted. He pounded his chest. He woofed. The fans stabbed their arms at him, screamed obscenities at him. And he taunted right back, though he knew they could hit him.

"I had a helmet on," he explained half an hour later, still deliriously giddy. "I think that fan is looking for me with a sniper about now. I was talking so much, I don't even know what *he* said. I said everything you can imagine, from A to Z. Oh man! I was killing that guy. I was calling him motherfucker and everything you can imagine! He doesn't want to see me no more!"

Wilson saw three fans give him the finger. He stopped. He smiled. He pounded his chest and screamed, "Next time we play, y'all ain't gonna be here! We're gonna be in Miami!"

Jimmy jogged through the tunnel, and the fans poured beer on him, and they screamed, "Fuck you, Johnson!" and Jimmy just pumped his fists over his head. He ran in the locker room, hugged coaches, hugged players, screamed out their names as they approached, and no lottery winner ever looked more jubilant. Oliver came up to Jimmy and hollered, "I can't hear nothing out there! I think there's Dolphins fans out there now!"

And a few players yelled, "How 'bout them Dolphins?" And several more repeated, "How 'bout them Dolphins!"

"First things first," jolly Jimmy said. "Let's take a knee, grab a hand," and everybody knelt, bowed their heads, and recited, "Our father who art in heaven . . ."

And when they finished the Lord's Prayer, Jimmy jumped up and shouted, "Heeeeyyyy! Yes! Yes! Hey! Hey! We're gonna have so many game balls, we may not have enough players for all the game balls we're gonna give. Let's see! Where all do we start? The first game ball, and we're gonna give the rest of 'em tomorrow—yeah, we *need* it tomorrow—first one to Terrell Buckley!"

And T-Buck's teammates hooted and hollered and called out his name, and no man on Earth could have felt better at that moment than T-Buck.

Except maybe Jimmy. "Hey, listen!" the coach hollered. "Everybody was saying, 'Those poor Dolphins, they got all those people hurt, they're starting six rookies, how can they compete? I don't know how they can compete!' "

Lamar Thomas leaned close, cupped his hand to his ear, and said, "Is that what they were saying?" He danced and shouted, "What they gonna say now?"

"Whooooo, whoooo, whoooo!" the players hooted.

"On three," Jimmy said, "we're gonna say Doolllppphinnnns! One, two, three . . ." He bent over, then flung his body back and his arms skyward as everyone screamed, "DOOLLLPPPHINNNNSSSSSSSSSSSSSSSSSSSSS!"

They were so loud the Bills could hear them through one concrete-block wall, across maybe a twenty-foot hall, and through another cinder-block wall.

When the media asked what he said, he couldn't recall. "I was in a state of euphoria," Jimmy said. "There's no telling what I said. We've been a-working and we've been a-hurting here the last couple of weeks. After as low a feeling as we had last Sunday, to come back and win at Buffalo—I mean, if there's one game that you want to win, you circle this one. And our guys did it with such adversity facing them! With all the injuries, with Dan not being in there, with all the young fellows starting up here in Buffalo, our guys made a commitment after last week's game that somehow, some way, they'd take it on themselves not to rely on somebody else.

"When Dan went out the very first series against Indianapolis, I thought the confidence and production and intensity went down. I've been around when we've lost great players and you expect the rest of the team to respond in a positive way. But Dan is not just an average great player. He is such a great and dominating player that it was hard for our guys to really believe we could win without him. This is a big step for them to understand we *can* win without Dan. I can talk about it until my face is blue, but they've got to *do* it. New England was a big, big win to start the year. But this is by far the biggest this year."

Because they had come up that tunnel with very different emotions most of their trips to Buffalo. "Disappointed, embarrassed, you name it, we've been it," Louis Oliver said. "Only a few times have we come through that tunnel elated, and today was one of those days. I was just hyped up, clowning. It just feels great! This gives us a whole lot of belief in ourselves that no matter who we play, where we play, we've got a chance if we put our minds and hearts into playing well.

"We know we'll see them again. I know that one particular fan will be gunning for me. He's probably gonna have a sniper waiting on me. I think it is hunting season. As a matter of fact, I brought my hat!"

And he turned, pulled a hat out of his travel bag, and put it on. It was a tan safari hat.

LIVE HARD, the hat read.

"We're gonna have a blast on this bus heading home," Oliver said.

The buses parted a sea of fans an hour or so after the game. Why, a full 160 minutes after the game, fifty-two campers and hundreds of fans remained in the parking lots, the children playing catch on broken asphalt, the men and women drowning their sorrows and cursing Jim Kelly. And in the sky above them, a delirious coach announced that every single Dolphin had just earned a game ball.

14

FRED AND FRYAR
AND FRIED

The headline was taped to Fred Barnett's locker for inspiration:

BARNETT HAS TORN LIGAMENT

RECEIVER'S CAREER MAY BE IN DOUBT

The Herald story—in fact, all the South Florida stories—said Fred's career was in jeopardy. For the second time, he had torn his right knee's most vital ligament—the anterior cruciate ligament, which controls the lateral moves vital to anyone, but especially to a wide receiver. He did not know of any NFL player who'd come back after two ACL tears on the same knee.

He left Philadelphia for Miami in March with the promise of becoming the Dolphins' playmaking receiver. And yet in July, a week into practice, no one touched him and his ACL tore in two. He was financially but not emotionally stable.

"In the back of my mind, I was thinking, 'Okay, what if this is it? No one's ever done this before.' I had to be stronger," Fred said.

He turned to a stronger body part: his brain.

"I just sat down and decided I was brought here to make plays. I felt time wasn't up for me. It wasn't time for me to be hurt again. I didn't try to use scapegoats, didn't use excuses. Even when there was pain, I knew if I continued to work hard, I'd be where I wanted to be."

He was so confident he pleaded with Jimmy not to put him on injured reserve for the season. Not many people can change Jimmy's mind. Fred did.

ACL comebacks often took eight to twelve months, but Bernie Parmalee had come back in six months, Rod Woodson in five months, and Fred set his goal for four months, then three months. On October 14, just eleven weeks after the reconstructive surgery, he was cleared to resume full practice, and on October 20, he would make his return in Philadelphia, against the same Eagles who had been his bosses and peers for six years.

In his 1993 surgery, doctors replaced Fred's ACL with the middle third of the patella tendon from his good knee. That meant both knees had to heal, and he had to wait for the tendon to die and then regenerate. This part alone took two to four months. This time, Fred chose a faster option by replacing his ACL with a cadaver's ACL. This was a less common option because it cost more, because few doctors had enough experience and aggressiveness to excel at the new technique, and because some people didn't want part of a dead man inside them.

Fred got hurt on a routine move in practice July 25. When Dr. John Uribe went inside the next day and discovered the damage was too much to repair arthroscopically, he delayed full surgery until August 5. The pause allowed the swelling to subside, assuring Fred could do exercises to increase strength and flexibility.

The same night as his surgery, Fred began his rehab by moving and lifting his leg. The next day, he began working with Ryan Vermillion, the Dolphins' rehab director and associate trainer, putting his full weight on his leg while using crutches. Ten years before, his whole leg would have been in a cast and his muscles would have atrophied and he would have had to learn to walk again. But with a more proactive approach than most teams used, Fred discarded his crutches within days and jogged within a month.

Most people prolong knee rehab because they stop when they feel pain. They're afraid they'll rip their new knee apart. But they need to rip through some adhesions, fight through the pain, and because Fred and the Dolphins' doctors and trainers had gone through this before, they knew what to expect. It helped that Jimmy had retained Vermillion and brought in Dr. Uribe and trainer Kevin O'Neill. All three were superb talents. And it helped that Fred was supremely motivated, staring at that headline and then spending six hours a day, seven days a week, riding a stationary bike, lifting weights, contracting and flexing his muscles and ligaments, fighting through pain most of us will never feel.

"I have an unbelievable amount of pride in Fred and what he's done," Vermillion said. "This is unbelievably fast."

Dr. Uribe told Fred he couldn't explain why he had healed so fast, and Fred credited his rapid recovery to *The Herald*'s headline and to God's blessings, which might be the only time you see God and journalists in the same sentence. Jimmy said the doctors told him Fred's recovery was so "unheard of" that they did not want to be the ones to say whether or not he could play. So Jimmy watched him closely in practice all week and decided Fred was sharp enough to play if he wanted, which he surely did against his former team.

Dan Marino practiced a little that week, too, but Jimmy would not play him in Philadelphia except in an emergency. Danny felt pain every time he put weight on his ankle, and the risk was just too high, especially on Philadelphia's artificial turf, which is despised around the league for its dangers. Jimmy was reluctant to risk either star in Philly, but Fred said he felt no pain or soreness, so Fred suited up against his old teammates.

Fred Barnett had not flourished in Philadelphia in 1995 when the Eagles brought in coach Ray Rhodes and a 49ers-style short-pass offense. There were even whispers he wasn't tough enough to go over the middle.

Fred had something to prove to the Eagles, and so did Daniel Stubbs. Stubbs sat out the 1994 season but had an impressive comeback in 1995, and he was thankful for Rhodes and a chance to play in his hometown area. But Eagles management gambled Stubbs wouldn't re-sign with Jimmy, who'd once cut him, and Stubbs called their lowball bluff. Rhodes was not happy to lose either one.

Meanwhile, Jimmy had lost two prominent Dolphins to the Eagles. He decided he could not afford to match Troy Vincent's $16.5 million salary and that he'd rather invest in Fred and young Charles Jordan than Irving Fryar, who had dropped a lot of passes in 1995 and didn't figure to get better at age thirty-four.

Philly signed Fryar, and Rhodes said he saw no evidence that Fryar had slowed down, that he had the body of a youngster, the mind of a leader, and the heart of a champion. He came back from injuries two or three times the previous game to make spectacular catches and show the kids how to play through pain— just the opposite of Jordan, who had done nothing in Miami all year because of minor ankle and knee injuries.

Which side would get the better of the deals?

Which side would earn vengeance?

It all made for good soap opera.

Then you had the matchup of the two coaches who took losing harder than anyone. Losses had sent Jimmy into unbelievable rages. Losses sent Rhodes into such funks, he actually compared them to having his wife and children raped.

"The thing I admire about Jimmy is he came in and got rid of a lot of players, brought in new players, got everybody playing with a sense of urgency," Rhodes said. "You see players moving around like they're trying to put a fire out."

Troy Vincent wished he had seen that fire in the 1995 Dolphins. "Even when we were 4–0, there was still turmoil in the locker room," he said. "It carried on the whole year. Now, guys are playing the way I've never seen them play. They're showing a lot of heart."

He said Jimmy already had eliminated 90 percent of the selfish players. "There's probably still a few there. They can't hide from him. He's finding his workers. Which is great. If we'd have had that a few seasons, we might have had a couple of titles under my belt. Instead of having a wedding band, I might have me a [championship] ring or two on my finger."

"My role as coach," Jimmy agreed, "is not only to bring in the right people but to eliminate the wrong people. You don't win with wrong people. Some of the 10 percent he might be thinking about may have converted over. The majority stay the same, but there are some fence-sitters occasionally who will come to your side. You can live with what some people might consider a wrong person—if you have fifty-two right people."

Sunday, October 20, Philadelphia. Dressed in their Sunday best, the Dolphins filtered past the throng of fans gathered in the lobby of the Philadelphia Airport Marriott, climbed onto the nine-thirty or ten-thirty buses, and rode into the grimy underbelly of the city, past the sewage plant, past the oil refineries belching smoke and fire, past the swampland, past the navy shipyard, into South Philadelphia, home of race crimes and Mafia hits. They were facing a tough team, a tough town, tough fans.

"I've driven up in the parking lot and literally seen people just beat to hell," Vincent said, remembering some fans who made the mistake of wearing Cowboys jerseys. "They're getting pounded. Two hours before kickoff. You see people running after guys with bloody heads. This is Philly. It's a different breed. A different breed."

Tougher, even, than Buffalo fans.

"Buffalo was a hostile crowd; this is a hostile but feisty one," Vincent said. "You can get hit or beat up. I don't care how old or young you are. With your children or your wife, it doesn't matter. Family day? It doesn't matter. You're not cheering for the Birds, you're liable to get hurt."

They booed Santa Claus. They dragged the Redskins mascot into the stands and broke his leg. They pelted Jimmy and his 'Boys with snowballs and trash.

In 1992, seven hours before a big Monday night game with Jimmy's Cowboys, Philadelphia defensive tackle Mike Golic was driving on I–55 in South Jersey when he saw an eighteen-wheeler clip the back end of a car. The car flipped off the road, went airborne into the median, crashed down on one side, then rolled three times before stopping. Golic pulled over, jumped out of his car, and ran toward the wreck. He found the windows blown out and the driver bleeding and slumped over the steering wheel.

"Man, you all right?" Golic asked.

The driver came to, looked up . . . and grinned.

"Hey! You're Mike Golic! I'm going to the game tonight!" he said, and tried to get out of his car.

"No, no, no," Golic pleaded. "Sit still!"

"Man, how do you think you guys are gonna do tonight?"

The guy went to the emergency room. And the game. And wasn't worried about his bloodied body or wrecked car because, hey, the Eagles won . . . and he met Mike Golic. That's how crazy Philly fans are.

And then there were fans in Miami, where Jimmy had to go to chamber of commerce luncheons and explain when they were supposed to cheer. And still they did not get it.

"I still, to this day, do not understand it," Danny said. "Our crowd is not as smart as they should be. They should be quiet when we have the ball and sometimes they're yelling and screaming."

And when they should scream, they were not nearly as loud as the fans were in these road games in Indy, Buffalo, and Philly. When the Dolphins left the Orange Bowl for Joe Robbie Stadium or Pro Player Park or Pro Player Stadium or whatever they were calling it this week, the volume had been turned down. Not just because the Dolphins lost more. Not just because South Florida's population was transient and felt fewer allegiances to the Dolphins. But mostly because many rabid fans had been replaced by the corporate types who could afford the luxury boxes and club seats that financed the stadium's construction.

They didn't wear as many Marino jerseys as the fans in Arizona had. They didn't draw their identity from whether the Dolphins won or lost, and, often, they didn't stick around long enough even to see who did win or lose. They showed up long enough to be entertained and to be seen, but God forbid the rich would sweat or get wet.

I watched one particular club-seat couple with amusement all year. He, probably in his fifties, thinning hair. She, in her twenties, killer blonde. They cheered a little, kissed and cuddled a little, chatted a lot—and left anywhere between halftime and the middle of the fourth quarter. The real fans filtered down from the affordable seats and took their good seats, and the sugar daddy and his trophy went home and . . . well, you decide who had their priorities in order.

"Miami is more richy-richy, upper-middle class," Troy Vincent said. "Just sitting there. They'll come and they'll get a little tipsy and boo, yeah. But it's a more mellow crowd. Here in Philly, it's not that way. They're very intense all the time."

Same as in Buffalo. "The Buffalo fans have a hate for the Dolphins they can't control," Robert Wilson said. "Our fans don't treat people like that."

And maybe that's why the other guys really did have a home-field advantage and the 1996 Dolphins' home and road records would prove identical.

"I love Buffalo fans, to tell you the truth," Louis Oliver said. "They're always behind their team, no matter what. I just wish the fans were like that all the time in Miami."

The Dolphins came into Philadelphia focusing on stopping the run and short passing game. Made sense. Ricky Watters was a Pro Bowl runner and Ty Detmer was a weak-armed backup with one start and one touchdown pass in five years in the pros. The Eagles had thrown only three touchdowns all year, none in the past thirteen quarters, but they were 27–0–1 when a runner topped the century mark.

The Eagles wanted more than one hundred. Their linemen watched the Dolphins film and felt confident. "All week they were saying to me, 'one-fifty, one fifty,' " said Watters. "They must've known something."

They did. The Eagles ran for a season-high 196 yards, and Watters ran for a career-high 173. And when the Dolphins tried to stop the run with their base 4–3 defense, the Eagles would often use three receivers because they knew if they lined up Fryar in the slot, the Dolphins usually tried to defend him with a safety—just as the Cowboys did under Jimmy and then Barry Switzer. And whether the safety were the slowpoke Louis Oliver or the second-start-of-his-life Shawn Wooden, it was a colossal mismatch.

Fryar abused four defensive backs for four touchdowns in the first two and a half quarters. His four scoring receptions—the most in the NFL in three years—tied Eagles and Dolphins records.

"We saw some things we could exploit against them, and we were able to do that," Rhodes said. "They play a lot of the same coverages as the Cowboys, without all of the pressure. I knew Fryar wanted to have a good game against his former team. To have this kind of game against them is every player's dream."

Fryar, an ordained minister, claimed vengeance was not his. "If it had been any other team, it still would feel good to score four touchdowns," he told the media.

But his teammates knew better. They said Fryar had talked about proving Jimmy screwed up ever since he joined the Eagles.

"That's something he's talked about since minicamp, about the bad taste in his mouth about the way he left Miami," receiver Chris T. Jones said. "I guess he had something to prove to them, that he still had some youth in him."

And oh yeah, he was thinking about it. At game's end, Fryar turned to Rhodes and offered a warning. "If you ever cut me," he said, "I'm going to come back and haunt you the same way."

The haunting began early. The Dolphins had been allowing just seventy-seven yards rushing a game, and Watters had that midway through the first quarter. Fryar capped the Eagles' first series with a thirty-eight-yard touchdown and their second with a two-yard score, and the Dolphins "didn't seem like we came out ready to play," Wooden said.

At least on defense. But Craig Erickson, playing his best game, guided a field goal drive, then threw for a touchdown and a two-point conversion, and the Dolphins were within 14–11 with 1:55 left in the half. And then they blew it, with more than a little help from the officials. First, Stubbs was flagged for a debatable roughing-the-passer penalty that gave the Eagles a first down at the Miami thirteen. Then Stubbs beat left tackle Barrett Brooks and was about to sack Ty Detmer when Brooks simply tackled him. An offensive lineman cannot grab a defender's jersey, let alone tackle him, but somehow the officials didn't see it. Fryar put on a move that sent T-Buck flying outside and Fryar flying inside, and Detmer, given the extra time, hit him for a killer 21–11 lead at the half.

Fryar beat Wooden for a thirty-six-yard score. But the Dolphins came back with Erickson's second touchdown toss and Joe Nedney's second field goal and were within 28–21 with 3:45 left. But the Miami offense got shoved back to its four, and the first play after John Kidd's punt, Watters went forty-nine yards around end for the clinching score.

The trap play didn't fool rookies Shane Burton, Daryl Gardener, Zach Thomas, and Shawn Wooden. It fooled seven-year pro Chris Singleton. The hole was huge. The game was history.

"We're back in the game and we let him bust it fifty yards?" Oliver railed. "Shit! How you gonna win playing like that?"

Jimmy was livid. At his defense. At referee Ed Hochuli. "Hochuli officiated about the way we played defense," he stormed. "I know we can tackle better. I know we can cover better. I know we can play defense better. We'll have to be better if we're going to be any good the rest of the season."

A week after sacking Jim Kelly seven times, the defense sacked Detmer once. And as they had with John Friesz, they made a backup look like a star. Detmer completed eighteen of twenty-four for 226 yards and four scores.

Irving Fryar caught eight passes for 116 yards. Barnett caught two for twenty-seven yards. Jordan didn't even suit up. Stubbs had one sack and should have had two. Vincent broke up two passes.

"Last week," Wooden said, "we took a step forward. Today we took a couple of steps back."

And a long plane ride back to Fort Lauderdale. The players watched *Get Shorty* and *Pulp Fiction*. A few played cards and drank smuggled-on liquor. They talked about their hometown NBA teams and, by night's end, mournful silence had turned a tad noisy.

Up front, Jimmy stewed. He had hoped he could get revenge over his former club the way Irving Fryar had against his. Jimmy wanted to show Jerry Jones, Dallas, and the country just why the Cowboys had won those Super Bowls. He wanted it almost as much as life itself. But his dream was turning into a nightmare. He'd tried everything he could, and lack of talent betrayed him.

If the Dolphins couldn't stop a backup quarterback and an ancient wide receiver, how the hell were they gonna stop Troy Aikman and Michael Irvin?

It was gonna be a long night and an even longer week.

15

BRASS BALLS AND FAMILY FEUDS

Once upon a time, Jimmy Johnson played for Barry Switzer, coached with Barry Switzer, vacationed with Barry Switzer, even dressed in drag with Barry Switzer. Jimmy was the chesty one. Jimmy and Barry and Larry Lacewell were, uh, bosom buddies.

And then Barry had an affair with Larry's wife in 1978. Larry left Oklahoma in a rage, and Jimmy might have been just as furious. "Larry was his best friend all his life," Jimmy said, eyes narrow, nearly two decades later. "That's when my relationship with Barry was over, in my mind. And it will always be strained."

It got more strained in 1979, when Jimmy returned to the state and Barry was coaching a national champion and Jimmy was coaching a foot-wipe stuck on probation. Barry's Oklahoma Sooners massacred Jimmy's Oklahoma State Cowboys 38–7 that first year and 63–14 the next. And if that weren't humiliating enough, Barry didn't even stick around for the ending. Jimmy went to shake his hand . . . and Barry wasn't there to offer it. Barry's assistant head coach mumbled some lame apology about Barry needing to leave early.

"We were such a bad team or they were such a good team, Barry didn't want to waste his time," remembered Dave Wannstedt, then Jimmy's defensive line coach and good friend. "Barry had more important things to do."

Fours years in a row, Barry drubbed Jimmy by a combined 155–33, and when Oklahoma State finally kept it close the fifth and final year, it blew a 20–3 half-time lead and lost, 21–20. Jimmy went to the University of Miami and beat Barry three straight games, once for the national championship. At an Orange Bowl media conference, the cameras caught Jimmy jokingly choking Barry. At least people thought he was joking. That photo is blown up, bigger than life, in Jimmy's restaurant.

When Jerry Jones bought the Dallas Cowboys and hired Jimmy, Switzer said,

"I wish I had a roommate rich enough to buy a team and name me coach." Jimmy fumed. Not long afterward, Switzer was ousted at Oklahoma and turned up at Cowboys practices, and Jimmy was asked if he'd hire Barry. Jimmy's reply was stern and succinct. "That's not ever going to happen."

Fast-forward four years. Before Jimmy played the Dolphins, he invited *The Herald*'s Edwin Pope home to his living room, and just about all Jimmy could talk about was getting back to South Florida, planting a seed for Wayne Huizenga to read. And then he told ESPN he'd be interested in coaching the new Jacksonville franchise. How could he say that amidst a playoff run? How could he say that when Jerry kept saying they were together for the long haul? Now it was Jerry who was furious.

The tension between the JJs was fast becoming unbearable. Little things that once didn't matter began to add up. Jimmy and Jerry had to be pulled apart more than once when Jerry escorted celebrities to the sideline for games and practices. Jerry demanded more control, and Jimmy balked. Jerry wanted more credit, and Jimmy's ego couldn't allow it. Jimmy sniped. Jerry seethed.

Jimmy craved the power, the credit or blame, and when he didn't get it, he had a history of alienating bosses, from Frank Broyles at Arkansas to Jackie Sherrill at Pitt to Sam Jankovich and Tad Foote at the University of Miami. Yes, Jerry was more involved than most NFL owners, but most others had enormous egos, too. Insiders said Jimmy couldn't last five minutes coddling the late Jack Kent Cooke in Washington the way Norv Turner and Joe Gibbs had. And could you imagine if he were with the Rams when Georgia Frontiere kept everyone waiting an hour and a half for the team photo and two hours for the team charter?

Win, Jimmy preached to his Cowboys, and there will be enough glory for everyone. But that's what brought Jimmy and Jerry down.

All that glory, and it still wasn't enough. All that winning, and it still wasn't enough.

The Cowboys had to be perfect, or their driven coach drove himself over the edge, his assistants and players afraid to smile or even talk on flights home after a loss lest he go berserk. He fretted over the most insignificant of details. Not even in his sleep could he forget; his dreams were of football. Not even in his off-season could he forget; he would vacation for no more than a few days, would come to the office (three blocks away) for a weekend workout only to waste hours on trivial things like complimentary cars and tickets.

You can violate the laws of nature only so long. Corvettes go fast but run out of gas. Rubber stretches only so taut before it snaps. Even the most spectacular of fireworks flame out. Bodies and brains are no different. Joe Gibbs got headaches that wouldn't go away. Dick Vermeil was wracked by hepatitis, neck and back spasms, and blackouts.

And now, at the end of his second Super Bowl season, Jimmy was burned out, bored, looking for an excuse to leave. And then, in the famed family feud at the March 1994 NFL meetings, he got it.

In Orlando, ABC Sports rented Disney World's Pleasure Island for a private NFL party, and while some of us strolled around, playing games and drinking free booze, Jimmy and Rhonda were sitting at a big round table near the entrance with Wannstedt and his wife, Turner and his wife, Bob Ackles and his wife, and Brenda Bushell. Jerry had fired Bushell, whom Jimmy had brought in from Miami to handle TV deals, and Ackles, who had helped scout all those great draft picks and free agents. Ackles had wanted Jerry to give the hardworking scouts playoff bonuses, and Jerry refused. Jerry was jealous of Bob's relationship with Jimmy at the same time Jerry's relationship with Jimmy was deteriorating. And so Jerry replaced Bob with his twenty-seven-year-old son, Stephen.

Larry Lacewell had pleaded often with Jimmy to hire him as a defensive coach, but Jimmy found his defensive staff was "a hundred percent against it" and said no. Jimmy had "reservations because Larry's personality can get under people's skin," but recommended him for college scouting director.

"I told Larry our relationship would be different than what he remembered, and it was from Day One. By 1994, it wasn't a strained relationship. It just wasn't a relationship. I told him, 'There's tension between Jerry and me. You're going to be here for the long haul. You better get close to Jerry rather than me.' "

Larry and Jerry became one. And so now maybe you can understand the emotions when Larry and Jerry, feeling no pain, approached the table, where Jimmy was telling Jerry stories and everybody was partaking liberally from the free bar just a few feet away. Jerry proposed a toast to the people who had helped the Cowboys win another Super Bowl. Jerry probably didn't notice Bob and Brenda, but it sure seemed like an insult to those who did, and nobody toasted or made room for Jerry, who attempted another toast, got another awkward response, cursed the goddamn people and their goddamn party, and stormed away. The people at the table shrugged and kept partying.

Ackles, one of football's most genial gentlemen, says the game has been too good for him to be bitter about Jerry firing him, and, personally, he and his wife took the toast as an acknowledgment, not an insult. He says Jerry and Stephen Jones later recommended him to the Seahawks, who wondered why Bob had been fired. "Because his name wasn't Jones and mine was," Stephen replied. And when Stephen told Bob the story, they had a good laugh over it.

But Jerry Jones wasn't laughing that night. What should have been dismissed as drunken foolishness devolved into a nasty divorce of the JJs.

Several hours and drinks later, Jerry approached a group of writers leaving the bar at the league headquarters, the Hyatt Grand Cypress, and warned them not to go to bed and miss "the story of the year." Jerry told Ed Werder and Rick

Gosselin of *The Dallas Morning News* he was thinking of firing Jimmy and hiring Barry Switzer. Then came his infamous remarks:

"There are five hundred coaches who would love to coach the Dallas Cowboys."

Five hundred who would love to or five hundred who could?

"I think there are five hundred who could have coached this team to the Super Bowl. I really believe that."

When the writers relayed the news to Jimmy, he was furious, and when the stories hit the newsstands, Jerry tried to backpedal. That day, I was talking with Tom Donahoe of the Steelers when Wannstedt walked over and said mentioning Barry was the worst insult Jerry could pay Jimmy. He told about Barry snubbing Jimmy back in the OU–OSU days. Still, he had no idea a divorce was imminent even when he saw Jimmy packing his Corvette and leaving for South Florida.

"I knew Jimmy was uneasy about a lot of things, but not to that extreme," Wannstedt says now. "I really didn't see it coming. I know how tough it is to win in this league. God, when you have a great team and you're winning Super Bowls, it's just tough to comprehend that you can't make things work."

Over beers out on Jimmy's boat, Wannstedt discovered the Disney diss was simply an inevitable last straw. "If it weren't that night, it would have been the next day or the next meeting or something in Dallas."

On March 28, 1994, Jerry called Barry and asked if he wanted to coach again. Barry said he did, and Jerry told him to sit tight. The next day, Jerry and Jimmy met one last time and quickly quashed any hopes of reconciliation. Jimmy says he wanted to quit and got what he wanted. Jerry says he fired Jimmy, or he wouldn't have given him $2 million as a contract settlement. That night, Jerry and Barry agreed on a contract, and the next day, Barry was introduced as coach. He'd be working with Larry Lacewell, the best friend he'd betrayed. Larry had forgiven him.

Jimmy had not. Jimmy sniped at Barry on Fox and HBO and in his syndicated newspaper column. He ripped into him for skipping some Saturday team meetings, for lax discipline, for his infamous fourth-and-one failure in Philly. Barry suspected Troy Aikman was sharing secrets and Jimmy was backstabbing and undermining Barry in their frequent phone calls, then using the insider information to sabotage Barry publicly. When Huizenga made Jimmy the league's highest-paid coach, Barry said he couldn't understand how a coach was worth that much money. And Barry said if the Cowboys won the Super Bowl, maybe he'd buy a boat and name it *Four Rings*, a dig at Jimmy's yacht and restaurant named *Three Rings*.

Barry and Jerry had been ridiculed since the day Jerry said good-bye to Jimmy and hello to Barry. Everyone ripped Jerry's egotism for not making it work with Jimmy, and Barry was constantly and unfavorably compared to Jimmy. Barry was a nice, easygoing guy, but he could not win over the media and fans who loved Jimmy. Every loss and off-field problem was blamed on Barry and Jerry. They thought Super Bowl XXX validated and vindicated them, but then an off-season soap opera tainted the image of America's Team and revived questions about Dallas's discipline and arrogance.

In *Hell-Bent*, Skip Bayless dismissed many of Jimmy's personnel decisions as luck, gave him virtually no credit for building the Cowboys, and headlined a chapter on the JJ breakup "Super Ego." He quoted Jerry as saying, "You have gangrene in the finger, you cut it out." And: "If I had known what I know now, I wouldn't have hired Jimmy in '89. The key word is undermine."

Jimmy was "an actor . . . trying to show everybody how tough he was," Lacewell said in the book. "Most coaches are actors to some degree—you almost have to be. But Jimmy was the master. It was almost silly how he was always trying to show everybody how tough he was."

This was no act: Jimmy would never forgive Jerry. Several ad agencies had proposed Jimmy-Jerry commercials, and Jimmy rejected them instantly. It didn't matter how many thousands or even millions were involved. "There isn't a number that exists. That's nonnegotiable," said Nick Christin, Jimmy's buddy and attorney.

Jimmy said his relationship with Jerry in Dallas wasn't as stormy as people think: "I was hurt and disappointed in his remarks after he had too much to drink in Orlando, but I was ready to leave the Cowboys, ready to move to South Florida, so really, I got what I wanted. I wasn't as bitter at Jerry then as I was afterward, when I saw how he tried to take away the five years of work I did. That's when I became bitter at Jerry Jones. On a continual basis, he tried to diminish my contribution. He continued to tear down my contribution . . . not only in public comments but one-on-one to writers and friends of mine. As time went on, I became more and more bitter. And then probably the bitterness came on Jerry's part because of my reactions to his comments."

And Jimmy's reply to Lacewell? "I don't want to respond to that BS."

Jimmy said he had had virtually no contact with Larry since leaving Dallas.

Weren't you the best man at Larry's wedding?

"I was the best man available," he said. "Everybody else was tied up."

But is acting part of coaching? Did you exaggerate your tirades after losses to motivate your players?

"I wanted them to be upset," Jimmy replied. "I didn't want them to say, 'We lost, it's fine.' But I'm not gonna fake emotion. I'm gonna be upset if we lose. Someone else might let it eat 'em up inside. I'm not afraid to show it to the players. It's not acting. It's showing your emotions. How other people read it is their business. People can question my intentions, my methods, my motives, but just like I tell the players, it really doesn't make any difference if it's raining and they drop the ball or they're hurt and not able to do it because the only thing people care about is the end result. And the end result was we won back-to-back Super Bowls. And that's all I care about."

And Bayless? Aikman asked his lawyer what it would cost to punch out Bayless and was told it would probably be $1 million to $5 million. Aikman said a million was worth it, but he wasn't sure about $5 million. Jimmy would have pitched in. Publicly, he called Bayless "really a sick person." Bayless wrote a column for a Dallas fax newsletter, wrote books, and served as an ESPN commentator. Jimmy had talked to ABC and ESPN executive Steve Bornstein about firing Bayless, and Aikman refused to talk to ESPN because of Bayless. Even one of ESPN's NFL analysts said privately that he was sickened by what he felt were rumors and innuendo and thought retaining Bayless diminished the network's credibility.

Jimmy warned the media that he did not want to discuss these feuds, especially before the Dallas game, but consented to a brief interview with a favored paper, *The Dallas Morning News*, nine days before the game. With every question from reporter Kevin Sherrington, Jimmy's eyes grew colder, his answers shorter. Desperate, Sherrington thought he'd loosen up Jimmy. Barry had told Sherrington he'd gotten a couple of letters from Jimmy's ex-wife mentioning how people in Helsinki, Finland, where she now lived, mistook her for the former Mrs. Switzer. Barry had said he'd shared this news with Jimmy and they had laughed about it.

Jimmy did not laugh. He walked out of the interview, out of the lobby, and up the stairs to his office. A few minutes later, he came back downstairs, motioned Sherrington into the hall, stuck a finger near his face, and said he didn't appreciate Sherrington implying Barry was having an affair with Linda Kay, and everybody knew Barry's history with other coaches' wives. Sherrington was dumbfounded. He tried to explain that Barry never suggested an affair and had passed it off as funny. Jimmy stormed back upstairs, yelling as he went, Sherrington pleading his case, Jimmy saying he had seen his wife once since the divorce and never talked to Barry and what the hell was Sherrington doing smirking when he asked those questions?

Jimmy told media relations coordinator Mike Hanson to expel the reporter from the complex, and he called the *Morning News* executive sports editor and one of its football writers, complained vehemently, and said if Sherrington appeared at one of his press conferences, he wouldn't talk to anyone until Sherrington left the room.

Dallas week hadn't even begun and this was what lay in store? Hundreds of reporters were going to swarm into South Florida and ask Jimmy to respond to every allegation, every insult, every painful moment he had tried so hard to forget?

And that was just *off* the field.

On the field could be even more painful.

Jimmy Johnson is an aggressor, a gambler. That's not just his philosophy of coaching. It's the fiber of his life. He likes to gamble in the Bahamas, in Vegas, and in the NFL.

When his Cowboys were underdogs, he asked them, How do you beat a gorilla? Jimmy screamed his answer: You bop him right across the nose! Pop him in the mouth when he's not looking! You shock and stun him! That meant surprising a stronger opponent, getting him thinking, breaking his momentum. Against the unbeaten Redskins, he used an onside kick, fake punts, a Hail Mary, went for it on fourth down. He ran a fake punt from his own twenty-eight in the playoffs against Green Bay.

He ignored football coaching convention and turned toward his boxing brethren and predicted the Cowboys would beat San Francisco for the 1993 NFC title. It wasn't just an idle little "Yeah, I think we'll win if we play our best." No, Jimmy was listening to Randy Galloway, Dallas's most influential sports voice as a columnist and talk-show host when he was driving with Rhonda for some Italian food. He got on his car phone and called the show and said, "You can put it in three-inch headline: We *will* win the ball game."

That made headlines coast to coast.

George Seifert, the 49ers' coach, said Jimmy had a lot of balls, but he didn't know if they were brass or papier-mâché.

Jimmy implored his Cowboys to back him up, and, fired up, they did. The next week, they repeated as Super Bowl champions.

Jimmy said they were brass balls. And if you go to his restaurant today, you will find inside the trophy case a wooden box with a brass plate stamped with these words: IT TAKES A PAIR OF THESE TO BE A WINNER. Two brass balls, a reminder from attorney friend Joe Ficarrotta, rest inside the box.

But this week, when he prepared for the Cowboys, the man with brass balls opted for papier-mâché. He went against his philosophy and personality. He played it ultrasafe.

If John Friesz and Ty Detmer could rip his secondary, how badly would Troy Aikman, the most accurate passer he'd ever seen, tear it apart? His safeties and corners were much too small and slow to cover Michael Irvin and Deion Sanders, his linebackers too poky to corral Emmitt Smith, his ends too small to take on "the NFL's biggest, most talented offensive line." And so he asked his defenders to drop into deep zones, to play soft on the receivers, give up catches in front of them so long as they came up hard and made the sure tackle.

He saw his offense overmatched, too. Troy Drayton was hurt and Dan Marino and Fred Barnett were just coming back from injuries. He worried that his line couldn't block the Cowboys: Leon Lett was football's best defensive tackle, Tony Tolbert was having his best year, and Charles Haley hated Jimmy and would be fired up to show him up. He worried his receivers would be blanketed by Kevin Smith and Deion Sanders, who between them had allowed just one touchdown pass and one pass of twenty-plus yards.

Dallas had allowed seven touchdowns in seven games. Miami had allowed five last week alone and a whopping ten of twenty-nine yards or more. So Jimmy asked his coaches to concentrate on conservative game plans to keep the score close. He was coaching not to lose rather than to win. He figured Dallas had the emotional and physical edge. The Cowboys were defending champions who would be fired up to play their old coach, and the Dolphins were young kids who'd be in awe, with no special motivation. And while the Cowboys had a bunch of All-Pros, all he had were "some guys who went to some All-Star games in college . . . Sometimes against an outstanding team that's very talented, we're exposed."

He hated reliving the past almost as much as he hated going against personality, but the Dallas days and the JJ feud were all the media focused on this week, and the media were everywhere. Jimmy carefully avoided swipes except for a locker room cartoon. It depicted a Cowboy talking to a radio guy after a game and saying, "I think we overcame an insurmountable obstacle, unbelievable adversity, and a tremendous liability . . . but enough about Barry Switzer."

Wednesday morning, he again warned his players about the hype: "Before we get started on the preparations for Dallas, let me make a couple of points," he told them in the big auditorium. "Obviously, there will be a lot of media attention. There's gonna be a lot of extra people from out of town. I know Harvey Greene said he's issued something like 750 media credentials for the ball game. Now, everybody's going to be looking for information, they're gonna dig around, they're gonna be looking for quotes, on and on. The only thing I want you to understand: What we say in here, what we say as far as technically about Dallas, that stays in here.

"Now, to me, there's no doubt you guys will be pumped up. The game's going to be all hyped up. The entire country is going to be watching. We're going to have a packed house. There's going to be a lot of emotion. You're going to be going up against a team that's arrogant, that's cocky, that has been very good, and they're going to be all into it. Get ready for it: They're gonna celebrate after every play. After every tackle, they celebrate. After every catch, they celebrate. After every first down, they're marking first down. Dooonnn't let that intimidate you. Because that's their whole style. They're gonna wanna try to intimidate you. Coming into *your* place and trying to intimidate *you*!

"The only thing that matters, and the key word, is focus. If you focus today, Thursday, and Friday, if you prepare the way you did for Buffalo . . . we've got to have that same intensity. We've got to make sure ev-er-y-bod-y is involved."

Jimmy nodded toward his assistants.

"Now," he continued, "the coaches have been working their *asses* off. We've had coaches in here past two o'clock this morning getting together a hell of a game plan. We've got a hell of a package that will really give us a big break offensively, will prevent the big play as far as our defense against them, plus we've got an advantage in the kicking game. So we've got a bunch of information. But it really doesn't make any difference what kind of plan we have. The only thing that makes any difference is how you prepare today, Thursday, and Friday. And everybody's got to do it."

His voice bore little passion. He doubted Miami could win, and he couldn't fake it. He just wanted this week over with. Instead of emotional challenges, he turned toward technicalities.

"Not only do the defensive backs have to understand the Cowboys' passing game, but our receivers have got to understand it so they can simulate it. For instance, everything in their passing game is rigid. Aikman's going to throw the ball to a spot. When they're gonna run an out, that receiver is going to be three yards outside the numbers. When they're gonna run a curl or an inside breaking route, their receiver is going to be two yards outside the numbers. When they're gonna run a skinny post or what they call an eight route, he's going to be over the numbers. Everything is so rhythmic, that's where the ball's going to be. They changed against Atlanta last week, tried to run an out from the numbers, and the timing was completely screwed up. The ball was short and outside, and Irvin couldn't get it.

"So if you're the back side and they flood away from you defensive backs, you've got Irvin one-on-one, and they flood away from you, and he's three yards outside the numbers, what's he gonna run? He's gonna run an out. If he doesn't run an out, they're going strong side. If you are effective, that's where you'll line up. If he's right there on the numbers and you're in three deep, you know right now. Terrell, what's he's going to run? He's going to run the eight route, the skinny post. You see what I'm saying? Not only does Terrell need to know that, but, Charles [Jordan], you have to know that, too. And so everybody has to be on the same page. *Everybody.*"

Jimmy's voice got a little louder: "Now, understand: This is not the same Dallas team of three years ago. We're both 4–3. I don't give a shit about comparative scores, but it is interesting. We've played four of the same teams. We both go up to Buffalo and play at Buffalo within a two-week period of time, they lose, we win. We both go to Philadelphia, they win, we lose. We both play Indianapolis. They were in Dallas, we were in Indianapolis on a Monday night. We both lost tight games. We both played Arizona. They had 'em at home. We beat the shit out of Arizona; they had to score a late touchdown to win 17–3.

"Understand who we're going against. Chicago's won two games—but the Bears kicked Dallas's ass on Monday night. We're halfway through the season and Atlanta's not won a single game and they've got Dallas by 28–25 with a minute to go. *Doooonn't* let the hype and the bullshit and what you saw three years ago affect the way you play.

"*Know* that if you prepare, and if you practice the way you did against Buffalo, you'll kick their ass on Sunday. But don't wait until Sunday to do it! Do it today! Don't take things for granted! There's a hell of a lot of people working their ass off to make sure you're totally prepared, but it doesn't do any good unless you go in yourself and enter that film room and study that tape yourself.

"And let me tell you what, guys: I'm staying away from personal things. It really doesn't mean a shit. The only personal thing for me is for us to win the fucking AFC East. Let's win our division, get the fucking home-field advantage, get a bye. That's what's important. To hell with my feelings on anybody else. It's your feelings. You're the ones who are going to benefit with a win. All of us. If we take care of our business, you think about how good you'll feel Sunday night.

"Listen to your coaches. Pay attention to what they're saying. We don't have to have knock-down, drag-out practices the next three days, but be focused. Every time we run a play, let it be precise. Let's make sure every time we run a play, either side of the ball, you paint a picture, you're into it, and we don't have to repeat a bunch of things. We've got a few new things offensively, but it's cut down pretty good, and the things we have can get us the big, big play. It's gonna happen. Just get ready for it and prepare yourself for it, and let's have that good feeling."

And then he announced the captains for the Dallas game and dismissed his players in less than ten minutes. When they finished their position-group meetings, they found their locker room overrun by cameras, microphones, and media. Nine TV cameramen and scores of reporters surrounded Marino. The players were not exactly enraptured by all the extra attention.

"Bandwagon motherfuckers," one grumbled.

Even T-Buck, perhaps the most amenable and quotable Dolphin, put a towel over his head and took a nap. Many others, as had become their custom every day during the media's forty-five-minute locker-room access, squirreled themselves away.

The Dolphins were not accustomed to this much hype, and it would help rattle youngsters like Zach Thomas come Sunday. By contrast, the Cowboys were used to the circus coming to town. Even normally laid back TV reporters went crazy over the Cowboys. When Jimmy and Kevin O'Neill went for their Friday run, one Dallas camera crew jogged alongside, asking questions, sticking a mike in Jimmy's face, and shooting video until the backpedaling cameraman stumbled and fell hard.

"Hey, that's worker's comp!" Kevin joked. "I saw it. I'll testify."

Jimmy laughed and waved good-bye.

"That happened a lot in Dallas," Kevin said later. "Both the TV cameramen and the photographers shooting stills would get ahead of us and shoot us going by. The TV announcers would run a few steps with us, just like those guys did. For those [Dolphins] people who haven't gone through this media scrutiny, it's intense, but this is just like a normal big-deal week in Dallas, certainly not as much as the NFC championship game or the Super Bowl. Every newspaper and every station in the state, from San Antonio to Houston to Austin to El Paso, send people to the Cowboys. Everyone wants a piece of you."

WQAM got a piece of Jimmy Thursday morning for his radio show that would air that afternoon. Channel 6 got another piece Thursday night for his TV show that would air Sunday morning. Troy Aikman was Jimmy's special TV guest, and, before they went on the air, they bantered via satellite with Rhonda. Troy asked how Rhonda liked being back in Miami, and she said, "I like it. I've got water." She and Jimmy lived in a luxury condo on exclusive Williams Island during the season and slipped away to their channel-front home in the Keys occasionally in the off-season.

"Troy," Jimmy said, "she thinks she's a queen now. She's got a maid, a tennis pro, a trainer. Wonder what they'll be trying to do."

"It's done already, babe," Rhonda replied.

Rhonda traded earthy insults and drank beer just like one of the guys, which was probably why Jimmy liked her so. She was a funny, saucy diversion from his high-pressure world, and she helped keep his personal life sane.

Rhonda turned to Channel 6's celebrity gossip reporter and said all her friends were jealous because she'd been to Troy's house and sat on his bed while checking out his aquariums. Jimmy and Troy had bonded, strangely enough, when Troy became interested in Jimmy's aquarium passion.

On the air, Troy promised not to share any embarrassing Jimmy stories, and Jimmy laughed. Jimmy asked Troy about Dallas's injured left tackle, and Troy laughed. Typical Jimmy. Always digging for information. The show moved quickly, with no technical glitches, and they were done in less than an hour. Off the air, Jimmy drank a Heineken with hosts Tony Segreto and Joe Rose and talked about what a great job his medical staff had done getting Marino and Fred Barnett healthy—and how he loathed Skip Bayless and this week's hype about the Jimmy and Jerry and Barry and Larry feuds.

Sunday. October 27, Miami. The game attracted a bigger media horde than Jimmy's first game with the Dolphins, a bigger contingent than all but conference title games and Super Bowls, a pack so big that the electronic media were shunted to the baseball press box and even an in-stadium restaurant.

Sports Illustrated and *The Sporting News* were there. Reporters from Toronto and London were there. Reporters from four New York papers and two Chicago papers were there. Reporters from Washington, Los Angeles, Cleveland, Kansas City, Atlanta, Philadelphia, Phoenix, Baltimore, San Francisco, and *USA Today* were there. Houston, Austin, San Antonio, and Oklahoma City each sent two writers. Plano and Port Arthur and Weatherford sent one apiece. Orlando and Tampa and St. Petersburg and Fort Myers and Daytona Beach and Cocoa Beach and Sarasota and Naples and, hell, Hallandale, were there. ESPN and CNN and TNT and Fox were there. Even an on-line service was there.

The Dolphins didn't gain a yard on their first play. The Cowboys got thirty-six. T-Buck held Irvin, and "The Playmaker" pulled away for a big gain anyway, then jumped up, danced around, and stabbed his arms into the sky. Emmitt juked out Chris Singleton on third and two, and Chris Boniol kicked a field goal. The next series, Emmitt abused the other outside linebacker, Dwight Hollier, and Irvin beat T-Buck again, Boniol connected again, and Jimmy's nightmares were coming true.

But Charles Jordan's diving thirty-six-yard catch set up Marino's sixteen-yard touchdown to Stanley Pritchett, and Randal Hill's diving forty-six-yard catch set up a field goal. Dallas flew downfield against that soft Dolphins defense, and when Shawn Wooden dropped an interception, Boniol closed the gap to 10–9 Dolphins at the half. It should have been 13–7 Dallas because the officials mistakenly ruled a Dallas touchdown return of a Marino fumble was just an incomplete pass, and Joe Nedney kicked a field goal on the next play. And it could have been worse if the Cowboys had converted a trio of first-and-goal opportunities into more than just three field goals.

But then the Cowboys adjusted to Jimmy's soft strategy, and the fourth time they were inside the Miami ten, they finally got a touchdown, Aikman throwing for the go-ahead score. Dallas quickly got the ball back, and, on third and seventeen, Aikman found Irvin all alone deep down the right sideline, no Dolphin within twenty yards of him, and Irvin went sixty-one yards before Wooden hauled him down at the three.

The Cowboys came out in a spread formation against the Dolphins' two-deep zone. The corners jumped the outside routes, and when Aikman faked inside toward Kelvin Martin working on Calvin Jackson, Louis Oliver jumped the short post route, abandoning his deep responsibility and leaving Irvin all alone.

"It was a hell of a call," T-Buck said.

And it took all of the heart out of the Dolphins.

Two plays later, Aikman found Irvin open for a four-yard score, and Irvin held his arms spread wide, strutted slowly, and threw the ball to the sideline for a keepsake. Deion forced a Bernie Parmalee fumble, and Kevin Smith wrestled an interception away from Fred Barnett. Five plays later, Emmitt drove through Zach Thomas for a 29–10 lead.

It was all over except the gloating.

The Cowboys didn't just beat their old coach. They humiliated him. They flaunted their superiority. With three minutes left, they had a first down at the Miami forty, and Irvin, who had converted from a Jimmy fan to a Barry fan, lined up near the Dolphins' sideline. And then he went down on one knee and never moved as the play was run. He just knelt there, smirking, staring at the Dolphins. They could not believe he was trying to embarrass them so.

"What the fuck you doing?" Stubbs screamed, as loud as he could. Alongside him, Tim Bowens yelled and gestured angrily.

And to make it worse, even with Irvin kneeling down on the play, Sherman Williams still busted twenty-seven yards up the middle. Then he carried to the seven.

Two minutes left. Chance to run it up against an enemy known as Run It Up Jimmy during his college days. Jerry flailed his arms, motioning to go for the score. "I bet Jimmy would grab the ball and go for it!" he shouted.

Barry said there was nothing to prove, and told his quarterback to take the knee three straight plays to let the clock run out.

"You're too fuckin' classy for me," a laughing Jerry shouted to Barry, making sure he was loud enough for reporters to hear. Jerry and Barry and the 'Boys had a good laugh about that one. They were toying with their tormentor.

Was Troy taking a knee a gesture of contempt? "That's sportsmanship," Stubbs said, still angry twenty minutes later in the locker room. "But when Michael takes a knee and we don't do anything, everybody in the league sees that."

"What did you think of it?" a TV reporter asked.

"Never mind," Stubbs said. "The whole team knows. It's private. We sat there and took it. We need to find some heart and courage."

He slammed his chair, the sound reverberating around the room. "I'm fucking mad!" he said. "It's going to eat me up for two days."

After the TV lights and reporters left, I approached Stubbs again. He had played with Irvin at UM and Dallas. What did he really think of Irvin's mocking? Stubbs dodged the question, asked what I'd do. He started to leave, trying to hide his real emotions. I followed. "No," I said, "you tell me: How do you respond when someone does something classless like that?"

Stubbs slammed his fist into the door. "You bust him in his fuckin' mouth," he thundered, the disgust trailing him to the trainer's room.

The talent gap had never before seemed so glaring. At game's end, a depressed Jimmy did the obligatory handshake with Barry, but it didn't last more than a second before Jimmy sprinted to the locker room. He told his players to take two days off, forget this one, and get ready for the next two division games. No need to ruin a young team's confidence; Dallas had already done a pretty good job of that. Then he walked into a side room where twenty-two cameras and more than a hundred reporters waited to record his every word. They didn't get many. He talked for a minute and forty-five seconds and bolted.

Down the hallway, Irvin, dressed in a gangster suit—black with white stripes probably an inch and a half wide—plus a thick gold necklace with a massive diamond in the center, claimed he took the knee because he was cramping up. Yeah, right. Jimmy said Irvin "disappointed" him and so annoyed Aikman that Troy told him to "show a little class."

Probably forty minutes after the game, Jerry stood in a bedroom-sized room crammed with reporters, still talking non-stop. He smiled wide even as the sweat dripped off his forehead and the hair at the back of his head glistened. His loquacious guard, Nate Newton, had showered and dressed and talked to the media and packed his bag and was headed out the door when he shouted, "Mr. Jones!"

Jerry peered around the pack and saw Nate.

"The game's over, man! C'mon!" Nate said, and motioned toward the door, toward the bus, toward Dallas, and away from Jimmy.

But how could Jerry stop? They have met men they didn't like—now including each other—but Jerry and Jimmy never met a camera they didn't like. This was Jerry's time to gloat, and though hoarse from screaming during the game, on and on and on he talked, never castigating Jimmy, but always reminding everyone he's gotten along just fine without the supposedly irreplaceable coach, that Jimmy didn't deserve all the credit when he was there. That he was lucky to get the first pick and Troy Aikman and all those extra picks in the Herschel Walker trade.

Jerry claimed his desire to go for it at the end was tongue in cheek, and if he'd really wanted a score, he would have demanded it. He said he respected Jimmy and didn't want to waste time being his enemy or dwelling on bitterness. He said he didn't want to gloat, but the victory gave him closure and validation, just as winning Super Bowl XXX had. That was the one ring he wore, and it was the biggest, "like a class ring on steroids," Jerry said.

"I said earlier, there's no way we will get the credit for having won the game that Jimmy would have gotten if he had won the game. There's no way. That's unacceptable to everybody [among the media and fans]. Not to me. What I think it should do is reinforce the fact the game is played out there by those players. I'm really proud for Barry. He's really a lot more productive and a lot more effective than anybody gives him credit for. He's always measured against Jimmy and Jimmy's style. This game helped, maybe, when you're measured. Add one more to it. Add the fact that Barry's coached a Super Bowl team and Barry's played Jimmy heads up and had his share of wins."

Less gracious was Charles Haley, the explosive personality and pass rusher, still angry because Jimmy goaded him in Dallas and then took credit when Haley responded with a big game. Haley called Jimmy a "coward." He said he had "a lot of hate in my heart" and Jimmy was "at the top of the list."

Haley predicted Jimmy would "flop here because guys are not going to listen to his bullshit that he tries to bring down . . . Barry is the best thing that ever happened to the Cowboys because he's not a tyrant. He's not jumping in people's face and belittling them all the time. If he didn't come, we wouldn't win at all. Because half the guys would have said the hell with it and be gone."

Jimmy's reply? He pointed to Haley's stat line versus the Dolphins: zero tackles, zero sacks, zero pressures.

The loss crushed Jimmy not only personally but professionally. Newspaper writers and talk-show hosts such as former Dolphins linebacker Kim Bokamper questioned his decision to play soft coverages, and he questioned it, too. Yet on one of the few downs the Dolphins played more aggressively, Oliver didn't protect the deep pass and Irvin made the big play Jimmy had tried to prevent. And when they played soft, Aikman threw darts in front of them. Aikman's thirty-three completions were a career high, his 363 yards ranked second, his .805 percentage third. Irvin, a Fort Lauderdale native playing his first pro game back home, had a monster twelve catches and 186 yards.

Jimmy was still in a sour mood the next day. He said the big plays allowed in the past few games, plus the big-play potential of Michael and Deion, caused him to play it safe even though it went against his nature. Pressed, he got up and walked out of his press conference. This would bother him for a long time. He apologized to his players for being overly cautious. Nearly three weeks later, alone in his office, I asked if he second-guessed any decisions he'd made this season. He said he rarely dwelled on the past, but Dallas bothered him.

"Because I had such great respect for their talent, I was *much* too conservative defensively," Jimmy confessed. "I was remembering their talent when they were at their very best. I didn't allow for us to have an opportunity *if* they were not at their best. I wish we would have challenged them more. The result might have been the same because there's an obvious mismatch in talent. In fact, they could have put us out of the game in the first ten minutes rather than us having the lead at halftime. They could have hit some long touchdown passes if we'd challenged them and had us 21–0 in the second quarter. As it was, we were ahead at the half. But at least we would have forced them to make it happen. That's the only thing I second-guess.

"I told the team, 'I'll take the blame for that.' I didn't allow our guys to win it. Our play was almost like my attitude all week long—just sticking my head in the sand and saying, 'Let's get this week over.' "

"That goes against the way you coach ninety-five percent of the time," I suggested.

"Right," Jimmy said. "And that's why I second-guess myself. That's not my style. It was such a horrible week for me. I spent the entire week dodging questions and walking the tightrope, walking the fence. My personality and style is to fire back all week long and challenge them and then be aggressive on game day.

"But I knew how talented they are, and it was one of the few games I went into I really didn't feel like we had a chance. I just did a poor job all week long. I psyched myself out. Because there's always a chance, I don't care how good the opponent is. The result probably would have been the same [if he had challenged], but I would have felt better because that's my style."

He sought solace from his buddy Dave Wannstedt, who had blitzed and upset Dallas in the opener. The difference was, Wannstedt had a good cover corner, Donnell Woolford, and Dallas didn't have the suspended Michael Irvin.

Yet three months after Dallas, Jimmy still was bothered. While scouting potential draftees at the Senior Bowl, he told Dallas offensive coordinator Ernie Zampese about his "mistake."

"Ernie said even though I second-guessed myself about it, he thought I made the right decision. He knew and I knew we didn't have anyone who could handle Michael one-on-one. Had we challenged him, Michael would have had a big game deep instead of just short. They thought we'd challenge him because that's my style. Looking back, we were ahead at halftime and they played as good as they played all year to beat us, but I still second-guessed myself."

Because he didn't punch the gorilla in the mouth.

"I kept tapping and tapping. I didn't hit him as hard as I could."

16

THE TUNA FRIES
THE FISH

When Jimmy was getting belittled that first awful 1–15 season in Dallas, Bill Parcells predicted Jimmy would become a force in the NFL, and people snickered at the Giants' coach. When Jimmy was 3–1 in 1992 and Parcells came to Dallas as an NBC announcer, Jimmy grilled the two-time Super Bowl champion for four hours for details on Super Bowl logistics, and that information helped the Cowboys prepare for two straight Super Bowl victories. Then Jimmy asked Parcells to write the foreword to his autobiography, and The Tuna did.

Theirs was a relationship based more on respect than friendship. Parcells, who won just three games his first year with the Giants and nearly got fired, saw similarities: determination, fearlessness, hard work, sound philosophy. So did Aaron Jones, who played for Parcells in New England and now Jimmy in Miami.

"They're both rah-rah, but they let you know they're business right off the bat," the journeyman defensive end said. "I remember Parcells told one guy to dress out. The trainer told the guy he couldn't practice, so the guy came to practice in street clothes. Parcells said, 'When I tell you to do something, do it!' He cut him on the spot.

"Jimmy's the same way. He'll tell us, 'I want guys hustling in practice. If you're not, I don't want you on my team, because you'll sell us short in the crunch.' You may be mentally tired, but then you think of what he said, and you hustle more."

Parcells's Patriots had turned it around since losing their first two games to the Dolphins and Bills. They'd won five of six while averaging 30.3 points a game. Since Drew Bledsoe threw three interceptions and had two more dropped against the Dolphins, he had thrown just two in seven games. And now, instead of throwing to somebody named Will Moore, he was throwing to first-round pick Terry Glenn, who was en route to setting the NFL rookie receptions record.

Throw in Pro Bowl tight end Ben Coates and Pro Bowl runner Curtis Martin, and the Patriots were going to test a defense that had just been plundered by two previously struggling offenses.

Sunday, November 3, Foxboro, Massachusetts. This game began as a repeat of the opener.

The Dolphins reverted to pounding the Patriots' soft defense, and Karim Abdul-Jabbar scored twice. Bledsoe reverted to throwing off his back foot, and T-Buck made his career-high sixth interception. And the Patriots' catchers reverted to fumbling, and the Dolphins had the ball at the Patriot thirty-three with 2:34 left and a chance to go up 21–7 at the half.

But on third and two, the Patriots overpowered the Dolphins' line and knocked Karim for a two-yard loss—and then Joe Nedney, continuing his season-long struggles, kicked wide left from forty-five yards.

Bledsoe took the Patriots sixty-five yards in fifty-nine seconds, aided considerably by soft coverage and three penalties, including a debatable call against Louis Oliver, and instead of 21–7, it was 14–14 at the half. But when the Dolphins turned a Bledsoe fumble into three points and Shawn Wooden intercepted Bledsoe, the Dolphins were thirty-six yards from a 24–14 lead.

And then came the terrible call that turned the game. Karim rumbled to the Patriot twenty-eight and was down, on his back. The play was over—or should have been—but referee Bob McElwee's crew called it a fumble and gave New England the ball.

"Pretty bogus," Karim said.

Earlier, the officials said the Patriots' Martin scored when, in fact, he fumbled before crossing the goal line. Months later, when the NFL debated whether to bring back instant replay, ESPN pointed to this as one of five NFL games that could have had different winners if incorrect calls had been reversed by replay.

"That was a crucial time," Jimmy said. "We had a chance to take control. But after that, it just went downhill."

Like an avalanche.

Martin took a screen forty-one yards, and Bledsoe threw to Coates for a 21–17 lead. A Dan Marino overthrow forced a punt, an underthrow into double coverage caused an interception, two drops forced another punt, and then a penalty and a poor route forced another.

Still, the Dolphins had the Patriots pinned at their own three, and when Chris Singleton stripped a catch from Keith Byars, the Dolphins thought they had the ball at the New England sixteen. This time, the officials ruled the ball carrier was down. The next play, Bledsoe aimed toward Coates. The linebackers blitzed but didn't get to Bledsoe. Wooden missed the tackle. Calvin Jackson got screened and slowed by field judge Ken Baker. Byars, cut by Jimmy because he couldn't block, knocked down Oliver. And Coates went eighty-four yards, and it was 28–17.

"Demoralizing," Jackson said.

Quit, many Dolphins decided.

Willie McGinest flew around Richmond Webb, forced Marino to fumble, and Bledsoe threw his third touchdown. McGinest sacked Marino on fourth down, and Martin ran for his career-high third touchdown. Bledsoe finished with 419 yards, and Glenn and Coates gave the Patriots a pair of hundred-yard games when they hadn't had one all year. The Dolphins surrendered 468 yards, dropped six passes, committed a record-tying fourteen penalties, got just three points out of four takeaways, and lost discipline and heart.

The Fish got fried, 42–23.

Jerris McPhail, the big-play nickel back, walked up the exit ramp with a broken wrist in a sling. Tim Bowens walked up there with his middle finger in a salute. Jimmy buried his chin into his neck as the New England fans mocked him. "Jiiiimm-meeee, Jiiiimm-meeeee," they chanted. "You suck!" another screamed. The Patriots' taunts lingered longer. Byars talked about how elated he was to make a big block, about how he didn't say a word to Jimmy because "I only talk to coaches I respect." And McGinest, who dominated Webb with eight tackles, two sacks, and a forced fumble, said he'd heard how Jimmy had challenged Webb to dominate "a 250-pound kid."

"I wonder what Johnson's saying now," McGinest crowed. "Like I said before when I heard what he said, it's not about the size of the player, but how much guts you got. I fed off that. I read those newspaper stories about what Johnson said about me after our first game down there and I saw those newspaper reports that said they ran the ball down our throats."

Bill Parcells made sure McGinest saw them, made sure to expose the Dolphins' defense. The Tuna melted the Dolphins into mahimahi meal and said, "We have some more fish to fry."

The Patriots would keep frying until Super Sunday. But Parcells and the Patriots were the past. What really troubled Jimmy was the future. Would his players quit on the season, as they seemed to do in the fourth quarter of the past three losses, as they had done on Don Shula after good starts in the past? Would they lose faith in their teammates and coach? The Dolphins had many problems, and they were big ones. They had no pass rush, no pass defense, no pass catchers. They had an old quarterback making young mistakes. They had too much temper and too little heart. They had an erratic running game and kicker. They had sporadic playoff hopes.

They had lost five of six, the promise of that 3–0 start long forgotten. They were 4–5, and they hadn't been under .500 since 1991, hadn't endured a losing season but twice in Don Shula's twenty-six years. They were buried in fourth place in the AFC East, two games behind New England and Buffalo, one behind Indianapolis, which would arrive Sunday at Pro Player Stadium to meet a team in trouble.

"Suddenly this season teeters," the *Sun-Sentinel*'s Dave Hyde wrote, "because it isn't just talent the Dolphins lack. It's composure. It's fight. It's little things, from discipline to determination, that had seemed the foundation of this young and ambitious team."

The Herald's Armando Salguero wrote: "After the game, some players privately questioned other players' abilities and the manner in which they were being used by the coaches. It's the same blueprint for a team's collapse that was seen last season."

WQAM's Jody Jackson quit signing off on her reports as "Jody Jackson, on the road to the Super Bowl."

Jimmy's honeymoon with the fans was fading; the *Sun-Sentinel* received its first batch of bash-Jimmy letters to the editor. But even Barry Switzer thought those jabs were off target. "There's not a player on their team, including Dan Marino, who could start for us," Barry said.

And you know what? The way Marino had played his first two games back, Barry might have been right. Oh, Troy Drayton and Fred Barnett could have started for the Cowboys if they were healthy, but they were not. Zach Thomas and Tim Bowens might have started, but they were about it.

It was easier to score on Miami than with Madonna. In three straight defeats, the Dolphins allowed 35.3 points and 456.3 yards a game. Opponents completed 76.4 percent of 106 passes for 1,008 yards, ten touchdowns, and only three interceptions and three sacks. That's a passer rating of 126.9—almost fifty points better than the league average.

Marino's rating the past two games was 60.7. The Dolphins' sole superstar appeared brittle, rusty, forcing passes into double coverage to make up for his receivers' inadequacies. He threw at least one touchdown in 163 of 186 regular-season starts entering the JJ Era but in only half of his six starts in 1996. He completed less than half his passes in back-to-back games for only the third time in his career.

In short, the Dolphins had many reasons to be depressed.

"When you've lost five of six," Richmond Webb said, "it's tough to convince yourself you can turn it around."

How would they cope mentally? Emotionally? Lamar Thomas and Craig Erickson had played on Tampa teams that never turned around losses. Other Dolphins, like O. J. McDuffie and Terrell Buckley, had never dealt with losing like this.

"My freshman year at Penn State, we were 5–6, Joe Paterno's only losing season," O.J. said. "Other than that, I haven't been below .500 ever. In high school, we were 10–0, 12–1 every year. Ninth grade, we were 9–0, eighth grade, 7–1. We even won the championship in my midget league two years in a row.

"I was trying to tell LT how hard it was. He said, 'Man, don't start.' LT was talking about how all the Tampa players had their cars packed at the last game of the season, everybody trying to get out of town. He said they just dealt with it, which I don't understand how you can. Really, the frustration just stays there. It festers."

"You come home on the plane," T-Buck said, "you're emotionally drained, you don't feel like eating, you don't feel like talking. It takes a couple of hours to get the life back in your body."

So how would Jimmy, author of *Turning the Thing Around*, turn them around? He decided they were young and learning and trying, and if he lashed out, he could send them into a deep funk.

No, it was time to accentuate the positive. He told his defenders they had played well until the final eight minutes. He told his quarterback he realized how much the wind affected his passes in New England. He applauded his corner-backs, running backs, and defensive linemen. He told them they could have won if not for lost-poise penalties and officials' mistakes. He told them to expect nothing from the officials, who'd screwed them twice in three weeks.

He told them about history. A veteran 1995 Miami team was 6–6 before it won three of four and made the playoffs. If this young and improving Miami team won Sunday, it would be 5–5 and able to make the playoffs. After all, at least one 9–7 team had qualified for the playoffs every year since 1988. And how about the 1988 San Francisco 49ers? They were 6–5 and won the Super Bowl. He told them don't be cowards and point poisonous, anonymous fingers to the media.

"Everybody in the world is going to try to pull you down," Jimmy told them. "Just stick together. Just hang together. You've got to believe good things will happen."

It was time to test Jimmy's motivational magic.

17
FINDING THE FAITH

The Dolphins faced a crisis of confidence. It was time for crisis intervention. But how?

In the Monday mourning after the Patriot pounding, Jimmy and trainer/confidante Kevin O'Neill jogged their bodies and brains. When they mentioned "feeling sorry for ourselves," the words reminded them of people who had overcome far worse adversity, and it made them think of the John Foppe video that Father Leo Armbrust had given Jimmy in the preseason.

John Foppe couldn't point fingers at anyone else because he didn't have fingers. He was born without arms—and yet he didn't let it stop him from driving a car, shopping for groceries, cooking meals, earning a degree, and succeeding in life.

By the next day, they had formulated their plan: Jimmy would skip his normal Wednesday Xs and Os and motivational talk and let Father Leo show the John Foppe tape and deliver a motivational message. They would reinforce the message by shouting it at the end of each practice that week, and they would custom-order T-shirts emblazoned with the message.

But first Jimmy had to put out another brushfire. WIOD's Jim Mandich, the former Dolphins player turned Dolphins rooter, said Dan Marino was showing signs of diminishing skills for the first time. And fans began calling the talk shows and suggesting Marino would be finished by the time this team was any good and Jimmy might as well trade him for Herschel Walker–like booty so Jimmy could jump-start the Dolphins as he had the Cowboys.

A trade was far-fetched on several fronts. First, the trade deadline had passed four weeks before, so the Dolphins couldn't deal Dan until 1997. Second, Dan's contract allowed him to veto trades to any of seven teams, which he could name annually. Third, Dan's contract had a cap value of $5.6 million in 1997, and the few teams who could fit him in under their cap were so many years away from winning that they needed every draft pick they could get, not a thirty-five-old quarterback. Fourth, having seen the Herschel heist and the caponomics value of youngsters, only a fool would give Jimmy seven draft picks for Danny.

Most important, Danny was signed for three years, Jimmy for four, and Jimmy's clock was ticking just as fast as Danny's. He envisioned vying for AFC contention in 1997 and Super Bowl contention in 1998, when the season concluded in Pro Player Stadium. And Jimmy didn't say it, but he could probably see both quarterback (at age thirty-seven) and coach (at fifty-five) walking away, into the South Florida sunset, Super Bowl rings glistening.

Jimmy read the papers every morning to see what the writers and players were saying. He listened to Joe Rose's show on WQAM when he drove to work in the morning to feel the public pulse. If they weren't talking about football, or if somebody was obnoxious, he'd flip on Mariah Carey, Boyz II Men, or Celine Dion. But usually about once a week he'd call the show to spin public opinion another way or just to earn points with Rose, who was co-host of his TV show and one of South Florida's most influential voices.

Jimmy always tried to get the key opinion makers in his back pocket. He bribed them with exclusive interviews and extra time and insights, and though they tried to be objective journalists, they also knew they wanted to hold on to the extra goodies they were getting. And so they usually gave him the benefit of the doubt when anything went wrong, as it often did in these initial rebuilding years. They did not question his decisions or his losses as much, did not let angry agents or released players vent as much as they would have for other coaches. So Jimmy's extra efforts stoked not only his vanity but kept the press, public, and players positive.

Jimmy had given extras to Edwin Pope and *The Miami Herald* when he coached the Hurricanes and Dolphins. He did it with Randy Galloway, a Dallas talk-show host and columnist, and *The Dallas Morning News*. He did it with *Morning News* beat writer Rick Gosselin. He hated golf, but he stroked golf balls and the ego of Dave Smith, *The Morning News* executive sports editor and power broker.

He hated giving the media behind-the-scenes access, but he gave it to *Sports Illustrated*, and Peter King and Ed Hinton built his legend, and Hinton spun his autobiography. (And yes, he granted extra access for this book, albeit a bit reluctantly, figuring it would favor him more than if he didn't cooperate. Actually, this book probably would not have been written without his cooperation.)

When he was about to interview with the Dolphins, he talked to *The Morning News* and *Herald* but didn't return calls from the *Sun-Sentinel*'s Jason Cole. Jimmy and his agent/attorney Nick Christin didn't see the *Sun-Sentinel* or *Palm Beach Post* and figured they weren't that important. But Peter King told Jimmy the papers competed feverishly against one another, that most of the Dolphins' players and staff lived in the *Sun-Sentinel*'s circulation area, and suggested it wasn't wise to alienate its reporters and columnists.

"Peter put in a good word, but that wasn't all of it," Cole said. "I knew Nick, and I told Nick I wanted a level field. Nick got defensive and said, 'What are you going to do about it?' I said, 'I'm not going to take potshots, but I'm also not going to be happy.' Nick called Jimmy and said, 'Call this guy.' "

So Jimmy called Cole and gave him information, including his home phone number—a rarity among NFL coaches today. Jimmy occasionally called reporters at home if he didn't like their story or thought they had a fact wrong, but he rarely was confrontational or held it against them for long.

"Jimmy studies us, just like players," Cole said. "He knows how to push each of our buttons. I know I'm being used." But Cole didn't mind because he used Jimmy to deliver better stories to his bosses and readers. And Jimmy was a welcome contrast to Don Shula, who seethed when the media carped on his drafts, free agent moves, and failure to win a Super Bowl in two decades. He could have found ways to answer their questions and win them over, but Shula had a hard time admitting when he was wrong, and he was so accustomed to bossing around players and assistants, he wouldn't do the dance. He pared his Christmas card list to a handful of media members and made sure some media critics did not get invitations to his farewell bash. By the end, Shula would not answer Jason Cole's questions, made Joe Rose feel unwelcome if he appeared at practice, and snapped at even longtime allies such as Edwin Pope.

Shula shunned the talk shows as "attack radio." Jimmy used them as another platform. And so when he heard fans moaning about Marino, he called WQAM at 6:45 A.M. Wednesday from his car phone. "Anybody who's calling in saying we should trade Dan Marino, you're wasting your breath. You're wasting your time. Save your dime," Jimmy told listeners. "I'm not gonna do it. Dan Marino's been a great quarterback for the Dolphins, and he's a great quarterback now. He'll finish his career with the Dolphins winning games. Hey, forget about it."

"It's nice that Coach Johnson says that, but, personally, I don't think I need that kind of support," Danny said. "I'm very confident in my abilities."

But not so confident in his receivers. O. J. McDuffie, a good possession receiver, had thirty-seven catches. The other five wide receivers had thirty-six—combined. The coaches kept rotating receivers, hoping one would emerge, but "Nobody said, 'I want the damn job and I'm going to take it,' " receivers coach Larry Seiple said, admitting Randal Hill had made some "stupid" plays and Lamar Thomas some "bonehead" plays. Charles Jordan had frustrated the coaches with his failure to play through injuries, and Marino had yelled at him for a poor route in New England.

O.J. wasn't happy because he didn't play as much as he wanted in the first half, and Fred Barnett wasn't happy because he was inactive in New England. Jimmy thought he had "heavy legs" from working too hard to come back so soon.

Prodded by Danny, Jimmy made a key decision: He'd stick with O.J. and Fred and get Troy Drayton more involved. It made sense to rotate defensive linemen and keep them fresh. It made no sense to rotate receivers and lose the timing with quarterbacks that is so essential to a good passing game.

The coaches made three more adjustments. They decided to run more to the right, behind Drayton, but also occasionally to use a new formation with full-back Stanley Pritchett lined up as a tight end on the left, so the Colts, who had shut down the Dolphins' runners in Indianapolis, could not stack up on their strong side. They also decided that with Colts halfback Marshall Faulk slowed by a dislocated big toe, they would focus on pass defense by removing line-backer Dwight Hollier and adding cornerback J. B. Brown whenever Indy used three wide receivers. J.B. had not responded well to his benching, playing soft when he did play, but all week, Jimmy would tell him he would make great plays and earn a game ball.

And in a few days, J.B. would make a big interception and come to the side-line clutching it and saying that was his game ball. And the Dolphins would fool Jim Harbaugh by using that formation on twenty-five plays after using it just five times all year.

But first it was time for an attitude adjustment. Jimmy launched the 9:30 A.M. Wednesday team meeting by talking for less than a minute. He introduced Father Leo, whom most players already knew. Father Leo had been the University of Miami's team chaplain for a dozen years. He'd talked to the Cowboys before at least one game a year, including both Super Bowls. He'd led the Dolphins' chapel services all year. He'd even had private talks with players Jimmy was try-ing to motivate, like Charles Jordan.

Father Leo didn't think many NFL coaches would hand over a Wednesday meeting to a chaplain or priest, but Jimmy had enlisted his priest, ex-players and assistant coaches with ties to an opponent, and professional motivational speakers such as Zig Ziglar and Dave Rover. And now he turned to John Foppe and Father Leo.

"Instead of talking about how we'd beat Indianapolis, I thought it was more important for self-inspection," Jimmy explained later. "I've got such respect for Father Leo and his intelligence and how he can communicate, he was a good one to introduce this. When you have someone as inspirational as Father Leo, you turn it completely over to him."

Father Leo spent a couple of minutes introducing the video. "All of you guys, at one time or another, have faced genuine obstacles," he told the players. "I'm going to show you a video now of a young man who has overcome a lot of obstacles. I want you to listen to the narration because you'll be so caught up in what you see, you'll fail to hear what he has to say."

And for the next twenty-two and a half minutes they watched *Armed with Hope: The Inspirational Story of John Foppe*. Foppe said he had been born twenty-two years ago without arms and had relied on the help of his parents and siblings until his mother gathered his seven brothers and told them only tough love would teach John to become self-sufficient. John was ten and still needed help getting dressed.

"Let him run around this house naked. He won't go to school," his mother said. "If John needs help getting that plate down from the cabinet, let him do it himself. If he breaks every plate in the house, fine."

And so he learned to balance on one leg and use the toes of his other foot with almost as much dexterity as the rest of us have in our fingers. The video showed him frying bacon, breaking eggs, eating a hamburger, typing on a computer, turning the pages of a book, using an ATM, playing cards, sipping a cup of water, and signing autographs with his feet. He opened doors and pushed grocery carts with his chin, grabbed groceries with his feet and neck, put on a tie with Velcro strips, horsed around in the family pool and on the trampoline.

He steered a car with his feet—and accentuated the positive. "When I was sixteen, I was on top of the world. I was the only kid in a six-state radius who could drive a car with his feet. I mean, this was cool!"

He said he learned to like himself and stop "thinking everyone owed me everything because of my handicap." He said physical handicaps were not as paralyzing as mental and emotional handicaps.

"What do I mean by mental and emotional handicaps?" Foppe asked. "I mean things like fear, anger, guilt, doubt, pity, resentment . . . anything that gives us an excuse to sit on the sidelines of life and not go out there and make it happen."

So if this kid with no arms and a scrawny chest could do all that, then these big, strong football players ought to be able to overcome a losing streak, right?

"See, there's one thing you don't want to do: You don't want to tell John he can't do something. It's just not a good thing," Foppe said. "God does not roll out the red-carpet treatment in advance of our coming. But He promises us He'll walk down our path in life with us. And what more could we want? As I stand in front of my path, and I say, 'I think I can, I think I can, I think I can,' the answer is this: 'Beginning today, I *willlllll*.' "

The room went still and quiet. The macho players hid any tears or emotions, but Father Leo knew he did not need to say much more. He talked for just three or four minutes about learning to overcome adversity. "So often, we complain about obstacles and feel defeated," he said. "Survivors in life find an inner strength they didn't know they possessed. I want you all to spend some quiet times alone and look into yourself and find out how you can be more personally responsible and individually accountable. Find a way!" And that was it.

"Let's go!" Jimmy said. "Offensive and defensive meetings."

After meetings, they walked back into the locker room and found the message scrawled on the bulletin board:

> PERSONALLY RESPONSIBLE
> INDIVIDUALLY ACCOUNTABLE
> FIND . . . A . . . WAY

They closed each practice by shouting "Find a way," and by week's end, Jimmy saw the effect.

"Friday was the best Friday practice we've had all year long," he said later. "I think our guys took on an attitude, hey, things aren't so bad, and we *can* do this and we *are* going to make things happen."

Sunday, November 10, Miami. When players arrived this morning at Pro Player Stadium, they discovered T-shirts in every locker.

On the sleeves were Father Leo's message: PERSONALLY RESPONSIBLE on the right sleeve, INDIVIDUALLY ACCOUNTABLE on the left sleeve.

On the front, over the heart, were Jimmy's buzzwords: FIND A WAY.

That morning, Father Leo addressed the players again. "Every one of you guys wants to do something for your children that you didn't have when you were growing up. You have to really examine whether in some way you're harming them. By that, I mean the most important things you can give them are here . . ." He pointed to his head. "And here." He pointed to his heart.

"I don't know any material object that was ever given to me that helped me as much as the lessons I learned in life about being accountable and responsible. So all you guys who want to give your kids some *things* to make up for your absence, think about ways you can give them something that will last much longer."

And then Father Leo addressed the whole stadium for the invocation. Unlike a partisan preacher who had offended the Cowboys, Father Leo's only partisan remark was one only the Dolphins would recognize. "Help us find a way," he concluded. "Amen."

And then the Dolphins won because of God . . . and their god.

The Dolphins gained just two yards on their first three series, and they were down 3–0 when Larry Izzo got his hands on a punt for the third time in ten games. The big play energized Miami. Eight plays later, Danny hit O.J. for a touchdown, and the Dolphins led for good. On the next series, O.J. made two nice catches and Karim Abdul-Jabbar charged in for a 14–3 lead. Marino became the first quarterback to throw for fifty thousand yards on a gorgeous thirty-six-yard pass to O.J., the first to complete four thousand passes on an eight-yarder to Fred Barnett, and then the first to throw a touchdown to Fred in fifty-one weeks.

Danny scrambled left, sidestepped a pass rusher, and displayed that famed quick release and rifle arm with a bullet to a leaping Barnett for a twelve-yard score, and it was like watching Michael Jordan play basketball. How could anyone want to miss this? It was 21–3, and Danny got a standing ovation.

Daniel Stubbs forced Jim Harbaugh into a safety and J.B. picked off Harbaugh to set up Karim's tenth touchdown in ten games, and it was 37–6 before Indy managed its only touchdown with five minutes left.

Marino's numbers were spectacularly efficient: seventeen of twenty-three for 204 yards, three touchdowns, and no interceptions. He hit 73 percent, and that was after two drops, a miscommunication, and a throwaway. Just as spectacular was the leap Barnett made with a dead man's knee ligament.

Fred had two TDs thanks to MDs. He gave one keepsake ball to Dr. John Uribe. He gave credit to God and the Dolphins' god. "I have a God who performs miracles," Fred said. "It's the type of comeback you can't explain, I can't explain, and the doctors can't explain, so it has to be a superior source."

Fred's mom was a devout Jehovah's Witness so disturbed by the violence and worship of football that she did not let him play the sport until he was a high school senior. He had strayed from his faith until he tore up his knee in 1993.

"That made me look at my life and realize some things. I wondered what if all I had gained was now gone. It brought me close to God. I came back the next year and had a career year in catches, yards, everything. God used trials to strengthen me. That's the way it should be: You see how adversity can build a person's character."

Such as Dan Marino.

"It's great to play with a quarterback who'll probably go to the Hall of Fame even before he stops playing," Fred said.

"I can't even spell fifty thousand, let alone comprehend someone getting that much yardage," Colts coach Lindy Infante said. "I still marvel at what he does."

Joe Rose, the tight end turned radio and TV star, thought the talk show traders were crazy but had inspired Danny. "I don't care what he says publicly; he was jacked up. He's got big *cojones*. When he's told he can't do it, he loves to do it. I remember one game we played in the snow. All the guys were bitching, 'Let's make this a three-hour game and get out of here.' He said, 'Are you kidding me? This is a four-touchdown day.' He got Duper and Clayton jacked up and threw for four hundred yards."

This was like the 1994 opener. The ruptured Achilles' tendon had led to inflammation in his ankle, atrophy in his calf, and a pronounced limp in his walk. And when rain turned Joe Robbie Stadium into a muddy mess, the media and even Don Shula wondered if Marino should start. But Shula had never seen him so intense in practice. And in the game he scolded receivers for poor routes, yelled at linemen for missed blocks, snapped at coaches for sending in plays too slowly—and defiantly waddled upfield for ten yards, diving into the mud head-first for a first down.

And he threw for 473 yards and five touchdowns, the last a picture-perfect thirty-five-yarder on fourth down in the fourth quarter, for a pulsating 39–35 shoot-out victory over Drew Bledsoe and the Patriots.

"I wasn't sure I was ready myself," Danny said, smiling at that memory. "I just put it in my mind to go out and turn it loose and see what happened."

Okay, Danny. Come on, tell the truth: Didn't the critics motivate you?

"You know it, you realize it, but, with or without it, because of the importance of the Colts game and the fact I didn't play as well against New England, I would have been excited," he said. "I get excited and put pressure on myself to play well regardless of outside situations. The motivation for me is the pressure of playing quarterback."

"I don't ever worry about Dan's motivation," Jimmy said. "He's always going to be gunned up. Anything I say to him motivationally is wasting my breath. But the guy who went to college last year and is in awe of the NFL, sometimes I've got to get him on the right track." Which is why he leaned on Father Leo and John Foppe. And why Father Leo got the only game ball.

"We were going through a tough time and getting very close to the time when players start pointing fingers and start saying 'It's not my fault' and a time when people start feeling sorry for themselves. A young team could have unraveled if you let them," Jimmy said.

"Every coach and every player enters the season with high expectations, and realism was setting in that we weren't quite as good as we wanted to be. I'm no different than the players. I had high expectations, too, even though I may be a little more realistic because I anticipated some problems. Without question, the victory helped pick me back up; because had we gone further under .500, the realism would have been, there wouldn't be a light at the end of the tunnel this year. I know there's gonna be a light at the end of the tunnel, but it's not this year. I knew that even prior to the season. Optimistically, I wanted to be in the play-offs this year. And at least the win kept the hope alive."

At least for another few weeks.

18
YABBA DABBA DOO!

Chris Singleton's toothy grin earned him the nickname Roger Rabbit. But he didn't appreciate his alias, and so when Zach Thomas repeated it, Singleton decided to retaliate. But how? He was searching for a comeback when Buffalo's replay screen kept flashing Flintstones scenes, and it dawned on him: Why, Zach was a dead ringer for Fred Flintstone, and since he and his roommate were almost inseparable, that meant Larry Izzo must be Barney Rubble.

The nicknames stuck. Not only teammates but television picked them up. NBC flashed their mugs alongside their cartoon counterparts, and Zach, with Fred's hair and a sawed-off neck as wide as his head, and Larry, with his square face and shock of blond hair, actually did resemble their namesakes.

"I'd rather be Barney than Fred," Larry said. "Barney's got Betty, and she's better looking than Wilma."

"I like Wilma myself," Chris said.

"I'm no yabba-dabba-doo guy," Zach said. "I'm a Scooby-Doo fan."

Most everyone in South Florida was a fan of Zach and Larry, the little guys with the big hearts, the underpaid, overexuberant rookies who were the antitheses of the overpaid, underperforming veterans that led to Don's demise and Jimmy's rise. They were the heart and soul of the new Dolphins.

Everybody loved the sweet, unaffected kids, from the fans who streamed to autograph shows to meet them, to the coach who called them his "little munchkins," to the Dolphins program that dubbed Larry "The Wizard of Iz," to the countless former and current players who compared Zach to his heroes: short stars.

Zach had vaulted into the headlines August 4, when Jimmy promoted him and released one of his favorite veterans, Jack Del Rio. Zach confessed he's maybe 5'10³/₄", that he cheated and raised his heels just enough so the scouts wouldn't notice but would list him as 5'11". He swore he would be 6'2" if his neck were normal length. He weighed 233 pounds, but did not look it, because his shoulders were thick but not wide. The Dolphins' 6'4" kicker and 6'3" punter looked a lot more like pro football players than Zach did.

And maybe that's why he played so well. They said he was too small to play at a big high school. He made All-State. They said he was too small to play at Texas Tech. He twice made All-American and Southwest Conference Defensive Player of the Year. They said he was too small for the pros. He made NFL Defensive Rookie of the Month in October and was fifth in the league in tackles. They mistook him for a high school player at a barbershop and a parking-lot valet or agent at nightclubs. Everybody was always doubting Thomas.

He wanted to prove the naysayers wrong and Jimmy right. "I wouldn't want to be 6'2", he said. "I wouldn't be as motivated, probably wouldn't be as good. I wouldn't work as hard. I'm ready to prove my family right, Coach Johnson right. It's all about making plays. If you can make plays, it doesn't matter what size you are, and it doesn't matter what speed you have. You've got to know the game and not make mistakes."

Zach knew the game. He'd been playing middle linebacker since third grade, back on the Mean Machine, back when he was faster and bigger than everybody else and just "killing people." He stopped growing and stopping playing basketball in eighth grade, but he didn't stop working, didn't stop watching every game, every linebacker he could. He had an autographed poster of Junior Seau, who had the prototype size, strength, and speed that he would never have. He had posters of John Offerdahl, the smart ex-Dolphin, and Deion Sanders, the cocky cornerback. He worshipped the pro linebackers who were supposed to be too short: Jessie Tuggle, Sam Mills, and especially Mike Singletary. He listened to a series of Singletary's inspirational talks twice on the drive from Texas to South Florida.

He was a tough kid before he ever played football. At two and a half, he was playing near a pickup truck when a family friend didn't see him, backed over his head, felt the bump, panicked, put it in drive, and ran over him again. That's one reason why, even after surgery to repair his face, broken arm, and hearing, Zach has that Flintstone face. To compete with his 6'2" father Steve and 6'2" brother Bart, both more athletic, both Texas Tech football players, Zach had to try harder. Why, he even took his weights on vacation.

He learned his work ethic from his dad, who grew up dirt poor but turned an engineering degree into millions in Texas oil. Dad made Zach drive a 1976 Monte Carlo until a wheel fell off, then didn't let him have a new car until he saved half the money himself. Dad Steve and Mom Bobby Thomas taught everyone within twenty miles about their faith; they erected a steel cross that's nineteen stories high, weighs 2.5 million pounds, and cost nearly half a million dollars.

Zach played so hard in college he broke his face mask three times, and they wrote a song about him called "The Mad Dog Blues." He hit so hard in the pros, Iron Mike Ditka was using him as the exemplar of hard hitting after two games. He knocked Shawn Jefferson so cold, Shawn woke up asking for his *high school* coach. He hit Karim Abdul-Jabbar so hard in practice, Karim's limbs went numb and he feared he was paralyzed and prayed to Allah.

Yet for all his achievements and intangibles, the pro scouts looked at his height, his 28.5-inch vertical jump, and his 4.7 speed in the forty, and dismissed Zach Thomas.

"All those four years of hard work and making plays didn't matter come draft day," Zach said. "They throw you back and you start over again. They were measuring my height."

They should have measured his heart. The Dolphins did. Six Miami scouts and coaches saw Zach before the draft, and all loved him. But Jimmy knew few other teams did and waited until the fifth round and 154th pick to take him. Most pros wanted bulky linebackers who could take on linemen. But Jimmy asked his defensive linemen to occupy the linemen and let his linebackers run free, and in such a scheme, Zach, with his incredible instincts, was perfect.

Jimmy envisioned "an outstanding special-teams player and probably a real solid backup. I didn't expect him to jump in from Day One and play this well. But you can talk to Bob Ackles. After the first minicamp, I identified the guys who would make our team. I said, 'Hey, let's make sure we get a long contract on this guy.' He was one of the first guys who jumped out at me."

By August, Jimmy decided Zach was better than Robert Jones, his first-round pick who'd helped him win a Super Bowl as a rookie middle linebacker. By September, Jimmy thought he could be better than Ken Norton, Jr., the perennial Pro Bowler. By October, Jimmy said Zach was "as fine a linebacker as I've been around, and that's just being a rookie." And by November, Jimmy decided he "wouldn't trade him for any other linebacker in the league."

Players, coaches, and scouts compared Zach to Singletary, Offerdahl, Seau, Mills, Tuggle, Nick Buoniconti, Jack Lambert, and Chris Spielman. Barry Switzer called him "a rolling ball of butcher knives." ESPN's Tom Jackson, another small linebacker, pointed out that holes don't open vertically, they open horizontally. And Jimmy said some guys run a 4.7 and play at 5.0 speed, but Zach studied so much film and was so instinctive, he played like he ran a 4.5.

"He's so refreshing to coach," Jimmy said. "He plays hard and practices hard. It's really contagious to the other players. Every time I see Zach off the field, it puts a smile on my face.

"And Larry Izzo has really been a pleasure to work with since Day One. He loves to play. He gives great effort, and he makes plays. He's got a knack for making plays on special teams. He's our highest-rated special-teams player."

At 5'10", 220, Larry was even smaller, his odds even longer.

Like Zach, Larry came from Texas, where high school football is considered a religion and a book about Permian High football, *Friday Night Lights*, is called "the Bible." Back in suburban Houston, Larry's defensive coordinator, Doug Orebaugh, ate a bumblebee—his lips stung and swollen before swallowing—to show McCullough High how badly he wanted to beat the Huntsville Hornets. Larry loved it. His coach, Weldon Willig, called him the toughest player he'd ever seen. Larry played so hard, he needed IV fluids at the halftime of six games as a Rice senior. He was all-conference, the team MVP, and permanent captain, made 301 tackles and started three years, and yet when the scouts came through they looked at another linebacker, and Larry had to beg them just for a workout. A Washington scout told him he should get on with his life because he could get hurt trying out for the pros.

Larry didn't listen. He worked out for NFL, CFL, and even Arena League teams. Suzanne Sutton, one of his parents' friends, had gone to high school with Mike Westhoff, the Dolphins' special-teams coach, and already written him one letter about Larry. She offered to write again and send his highlight video. What were the odds? Why bother? Larry debated for a while, then drove home and got a tape he'd put together of some big plays.

Westhoff had spent time on longer shots than this. "Some are ridiculous, from guys loading trucks at night, but, then, Bernie Parmalee was loading trucks, so you never know. I think I've worked out more kickers in my life than anybody—guys from Australia, Germany, Saudi Arabia. The first play on the tape, Larry blitzed and knocked [Texas A&M] star Leeland McElroy for a loss, and that caught my eye."

So Westhoff called Izzo, and, all serious sounding, asked, "Who the hell made this tape? This is the worst-quality film I've ever seen."

Izzo was afraid Westhoff was mad about wasting his time. But then Westhoff said, "I like what I saw," and asked, "Can you be a special-teams player like Bill Bates?"

Izzo said yes, of course, and told Westhoff he was working out that afternoon for the BLESTO and Dolphins scout Bobby Williams. Westhoff told him to have Williams call him after the workout. All three of Izzo's forty-yard dashes were in the 4.6s, and a few days later the Dolphins called and asked where he'd be on draft day. They didn't draft him, but when they offered a free agent contract, Izzo signed quickly. He knew Jimmy had a history of keeping small linebackers and undersized playmakers. Still, Izzo wondered:

"Throughout the minicamps, I had some doubts. I just wasn't moving up the ladder, and I thought, 'I'm just here to be a body.' But then in training camp, Coach Westhoff gave me a chance to be on some special teams so I could get in the games. I wasn't just a practice dummy. Then, once I got a chance, I made a few plays."

He knew he needed to make a quick impression, and he did. When the Dolphins were still in shorts and supposed to just tap running backs, he tackled Terry Kirby, and Kirby screamed at him. When they practiced against the Redskins, they weren't supposed to tackle, either, but Izzo hustled twenty yards downfield and crunched Washington star Terry Allen.

"You must be a stupid motherfucker!" Allen screamed.

"And I got offended by that," Izzo said. "Just the way he said it sounded so condescending, demeaning, like 'You stupid free agent, trying to make the team, motherfucker.' He threw the ball at me, and I caught it. I had respect for the guy because I'd watched him play, had had him on my fantasy football team. So I thought, I'm not getting into a fight with Terry Allen.' I couldn't imagine doing it.

"But Ed Simmons, their 6'6", 320-pound lineman, came up right next to me, and he's MFing me, too. So I threw the ball at him instead of Terry. He grabbed my face mask, I grabbed his face mask, and it just turned into a big brawl. I mean, this was a huge brawl. And we're rolling around and I've got five Redskins on top of me and then my teammates come to the rescue. It was crazy. After I got up, it was still going on, twenty yards down the field. It was great!

"Then the next day, I got into another scrap with the Redskins. I got some scars from that one. The beginning of practice, the first thing we did was special teams, and we were working on our punt return against their punt team and they were running downfield to try to cover the punt. I tried to get a block, and it was a borderline clip. That, topped along with the fact the whistle had supposedly blown, but I didn't hear the whistle, pissed him off. I knocked him on his butt, so he got up and started swinging. We started wrestling, and Brian Mitchell came in and started fighting. I got a couple of cuts. They probably got the better end of that one."

But Larry and Zach would do anything to avoid getting cut. They shared an apartment and their fears. "Zach and I would always talk: 'Man, I just don't wanna go home. I don't wanna go back to school. Everybody's gonna be asking, "What happened? Oh, you didn't make it?"' The fear of failure was the biggest motivation for getting through camp. I was trying to get a big hit to get some notice."

He got it, all right. Got it so much that when Jimmy said Dan Marino and Larry Izzo had won the first two roster spots, *The Herald* put a story and photo across the top of its first sports page, and Rice coach Ken Hatfield plastered them on the door to the football offices. They stuck all year, and Hatfield cited

Izzo as an example so often that even his best friend, Aaron Stanley, got sick of it. "Making him out to be a god," Stanley said, shaking his head and laughing. "But actually, it's really cool to see one of your good friends succeed through hard work."

Izzo had blocked a punt against Arizona and tipped ones against Seattle and Indianapolis, all three setting up touchdowns and swinging momentum, twice for victories.

Westhoff thought Izzo was playing well enough to deserve the AFC special-teams spot in the Pro Bowl. He figured Izzo's biggest competition would be Houston's John Henry Mills—and here they were, going to Houston this week-end, staying at a hotel just off the Rice campus, a few minutes from Izzo's home, and facing Mills and one of the best kick returners in NFL history, Mel Gray.

"This will be the biggest test we've had for our special teams," Jimmy said. "I feel real good about what our guys have done. I feel every week when we go into a game, we've got an advantage in the kicking game, and I'd be willing to bet we'll win the kicking game in a dozen [of the sixteen] games, maybe even more."

John Kidd was second in the league in gross and net punting and tied for the lead in inside-the-twenty punts. Joe Nedney, despite his field goal struggles, was leading the league in touchbacks on his kickoffs. The coverage and protection units, led by Izzo, Kirby Dar Dar, Bernie Parmalee, Sean Hill, and Tim Jacobs were terrific. The Dolphins weren't getting a lot from O. J. McDuffie's punt re-turns, but Irving Spikes was among the AFC kick return leaders.

Every coach talked about the importance of special teams, but Jimmy deliv-ered. He gave Westhoff time for a long meeting with the players each morning and again the night before games, and he gave Westhoff as much as half an hour at the start of each practice. Jimmy personally helped Westhoff review the kick-ing game with every player and coach present in the Monday film review. He wanted everyone—from Dan Marino to every starter to every guy who might think he was just a scrub running down on kickoffs—to realize how important the kicking game was.

"If the special team has its own little group and 'star' players are doing some-thing different, well, it's truly not special," Jimmy explained. "That's why I want Dan Marino and Bernie Kosar and Craig Erickson and Gary Stevens in there when we do special teams. I want them to know how important it is.

"There's nothing more rewarding for a player than for the rest of his team-mates to know he's actually done something. A lot of teams, a lot of their players don't even watch special-teams film. So if Larry Izzo makes a great block, half the team doesn't know he made a great block because they don't watch the tapes. If the head coach is up there bragging about a player or chastising a player, it has a little more impact than if an assistant coach does it. We're one of the few teams in the league that have more than half a dozen players on the roster just for special teams.

"I've always emphasized special teams. It goes back to Oklahoma State when we had a bad team. Our only chance to stay in games against better talent was to run fake punts, fake field goals, onside kicks. We did it at UM and Dallas. Some coaches with dominant teams would rather play it closer to the vest. I think those plays just add to your team. I use them as momentum breakers."

Jimmy would need Larry Izzo and Zach Thomas to swing the momentum if this Texas trip were to succeed.

Sunday, November 17, Houston. The Oilers were favored by three and a half points, so just to remind the Dolphins that underdogs can win, Jimmy had the players watch a video of Evander Holyfield upsetting Mike Tyson on Saturday's charter to Houston.

Then he named a whopping six honorary captains, all with Texas ties: Zach and Larry, O. J. Brigance, Robert Wilson, Daryl Gardener, and Richmond Webb. O.J.'s high school band was playing at halftime. Larry had seventy-five friends and family attending, including his grandmother from Norway and his brother from Germany. Jimmy knew how much the game meant to them; he got about forty tickets for his parents, C.W. and Allene, brother Wayne, sister Lynda Hodges, sons Chad and Brent, and assorted family.

And, in one last little motivational ploy, a grease board in the locker room showing the schedule for warm-ups concluded with the kickoff time and this message: KICK THEIR ASSES!!!

But for most of the first half, the Dolphins got their behinds booted. Chris Chandler fired a pair of touchdown passes, and Louis Oliver, continuing his decline after a fast start, was responsible for one and part of the other. Houston led, 121–0 in yards and 14–0 in points. Finally, the offense moved—and Nedney missed his eighth field goal in thirteen tries from thirty yards or more.

"Keep your heads up," Jimmy told Joe. "We'll need you." False bravado? Or premonition?

The Dolphins were lifeless—until the special teams swung the momentum. Westhoff knew Reggie Roby took his time punting the ball because Roby played for Westhoff for years. And, watching film, he noticed long snapper James McKeehan lifted his head the instant before he snapped. So he lined up Spikes and Dar Dar over the Oilers' outside flyer and told his rushers to go as soon as they saw McKeehan's head bob. You remember Dar Dar—the special-teams star Jimmy decided to re-sign as soon as Tampa scored a preseason touchdown? Dar Dar flew in, untouched, from the far right and bam!—you could hear the sound throughout the Astrodome—Miami had a blocked punt and the ball at the Houston thirty-one.

Five plays later, on third and one from the ten, the coaches anticipated Houston would cover Spikes with a linebacker, and called a play put in special that week. Bam! Marino found Spikes beating Micheal Barrow in the left side of the end zone, and it was 14–7.

Nedney drove the kickoff a yard deep, Dar Dar snuffed Mel Gray at the fifteen, and, given bad field position, the Oilers promptly punted. The Dolphins had enough time to drive for a Nedney field goal just before the half. After the teams traded second-half field goals, the Oilers led 17–13 early in the fourth quarter when Jimmy made his boldest call of the season.

It was fourth and nine at the Miami thirty-two.

Between five and ten times this year, Jimmy had signaled for Izzo to run Shark—their code name for a run off a fake punt—if the opposition lined up in the proper formation. But it hadn't happened yet. Early in this game, Westhoff had suggested it, but Jimmy wasn't sure. This time, he looked over at his boss, and Jimmy hesitated, then nodded: "Run Shark."

It was a hell of a gamble. And it worked. Izzo got the formation he wanted, found a hole "the size of the Grand Canyon" at the line, leaped over two fallen Dolphins, and didn't go down until twenty-six yards later. Houston's special-teams star, John Henry Mills, missed the block on Dar Dar and missed a tackle on Izzo. (And still would make the Pro Bowl ahead of Izzo anyway. Go figure.)

The Dolphins were just about to convert Izzo's big run into the go-ahead score when Karim was stripped at the Houston one, and the ball rolled out of the end zone for a heartbreaking, maybe backbreaking, touchback.

But on the very next play, Trace Armstrong, who practiced all week despite bruised ribs after Jimmy announced Shane Burton would replace him as a starter, got in Chandler's face. Chandler didn't see Dwight Hollier delay intended receiver Frank Wycheck. He didn't see Zach Thomas step in front of Wycheck, steal the pass, and streak twenty-six yards into the end zone for the go-ahead score.

Izzo's run had put the Oilers deep into their own territory. What's more, it kept the Houston defenders on the field, and they started to wear out. Four Oilers went down in a five-play span. "The fake punt took everything out of them," Kevin O'Neill said. "They had about five guys cramp up after that. They were on the field too long."

Still, when O. J. McDuffie fumbled and the Oilers got away with a blatant hold to spring a big gain, Houston tied it at 20–20 with just 3:20 left.

For the first time all year, Marino launched the fourth-quarter comeback for which he had become famous. He beat one blitz for twenty yards to O.J. and another for fifty-one yards to Troy Drayton, Drayton's biggest play as a Dolphin. O.J., making up for his fumble, sprung his old Penn State teammate with a block that sent two Oilers flying. The Oilers pulled down Drayton at the five, and after Spikes was stuffed, Jimmy put his confidence in his shaky rookie kicker. He ordered Marino to kneel down twice, then waved in Nedney for a twenty-nine-yard try with two seconds left.

Nedney had been so erratic, not even this was a gimme.

The Dolphins inhaled and prayed.

Nedney hadn't had a chance to win or lose a game in the final seconds in four years. He could feel the nerves rumbling in his belly, the adrenaline pumping through his body, but he tried to wipe away negative memories of past misses. He thought of Jimmy's confidence in him. He thought of the ball being in the middle of the field, inside the thirty, a no-brainer.

"Not once did I think, 'I'm going to be stepping on my lower lip.' That's when you kill yourself. When I lined up, I thought to myself, 'In three seconds, the game is going to be over.' I pictured the ball splitting the uprights like an extra point—and that's exactly what happened."

It was Miami 23, Houston 20, and Miami was 6–5 and back in the playoff hunt. Jimmy and Joe embraced for a very long time. "I don't think there's any two happier people in Houston, Texas," Joe said. Jimmy had risked his reputation by trading Pete Stoyanovich and keeping Nedney, and now the risk had paid off.

And the risky fake punt had paid off, too.

Larry Izzo ran to the stands and high-fived friends and family. A Rice teammate, Brynton Goynes, waved a hand-painted sign: GOTTA RESPECT DA IZZO.

Zach Thomas stood at midfield, surrounded by two cameras and ten reporters, did a network interview, and high-fived fans as he ran to the locker room.

Inside, army first lieutenant Lenny Izzo hugged his little brother and fought back tears. He flew eighteen hours round-trip from Baumholder, Germany, for this. Was it worth it? "Are you kidding me?" Lenny asked. "Coming home to beat Houston like this, you couldn't ask for a better script."

"To do it in the Astrodome, in the House of Pain, where I watched the Oilers play for so many years," Larry said, "was a dream come true. This is the dream of every little kid growing up. I'm living a dream."

Could he have imagined this back when the scouts ignored him?

"No!" he shouted. "This is pretty crazy." He turned and pointed to his roommate. "Along with the blocked punt by Kirby Dar Dar, Zach's interception won the game. He's not playing like a rookie. He's playing like an All-Pro. The legend continues to grow!"

The legend left the locker room, and in the tunnel leading to the buses were the Dolphins' supporters. Twenty-five friends and family, including his sister, brother, brother-in-law, and assorted cousins, had trekked from El Paso and the

Texas Panhandle to be here. Zach hugged some beautiful blondes, signed autographs for little girls and grown men, posed for a picture with his cousin, talked
with his brother.

Larry went up and down the line, high-fiving friends and signing autographs.
Lenny grinned and said he'd faced land mines and snipers in Bosnia, but little
brother had the tougher job because "I don't have 275-pounders piling on me."

Heroes were everywhere, none bigger than the littlest Dolphins, Fred Flintstone and Barney Rubble.

This wasn't Houston.

This was Bedrock. This was a Flintstone family reunion. This was a yabba-
dabba-doo time.

"Right after a game when you've won and played well, that's the best time
you have as a player," Zach said. "That's the best thing about football, the best
feeling in the world."

Hundreds more fans, restrained by temporary fences and guards, screamed
outside near the team buses. They even wanted Mike Westhoff's autograph.
Even an old vet like Trace Armstrong loved it. He came into the game with a
torn muscle in his rib cage, twisted his ankle during the game—and still came
up with a sack and the pressure that forced Zach's interception for a touchdown.
"This is one time I'm glad I didn't get the sack," Trace said, and twirled a fat sto-
gie. "Hey," he said, grinning, "I don't drink. I gotta do something!"

For Dan Marino, author of thirty-two comeback victories, it was just another
day at the office. Surrounded by three guards, he strode quickly past the adoring
fans and onto the bus. Then Zach stopped and signed and signed some more.

One straggler remained: the one that outsiders portrayed as coldhearted.
Jimmy Johnson had slipped out of the locker room to a little room across the
hall, where about forty of the Johnson clan ate and drank and talked and hugged
for the next twenty minutes.

Mother and Daddy had made the ninety-minute trek from Port Author despite
failing health, and the victory and visit salved their souls. C.W. was seventy-
eight and coming off two surgeries in six weeks that removed sixteen inches of
cancerous colon. He postponed a sixth chemotherapy treatment to attend. Allene
was seventy-six, and her kidneys were failing her. She had needles stuck in her
arms three days a week, four hours each time, for the dialysis to pump the fluids
from her body. This left her weak and nauseous, but she willed herself to come.
She was stubborn, like her son, and she didn't want anyone seeing her in this
wheelchair, so when it was time to go and the guards offered to drive her away in
a golf cart, Jimmy grinned and said, "You don't have to be Ironside!"

"How you feeling now?" someone asked.

"Great!" Allene said.

"Great!" everyone else chimed in.

What crazy coach runs a rookie linebacker on fourth and nine? "It's not like Dave Meggett was back there," Marino said.

What crazy coach gambles on a fake punt from his own thirty-two? "A coach who's won two Super Bowls and a national championship and has a lot of confidence in his players and system," Larry Izzo said.

What crazy coach does it in the fourth quarter of a four-point game? A coach with brass balls. "He's got 'em!" Kevin O'Neill said.

"Given the field position," Ed Fowler wrote in the *Houston Chronicle*, "the fake was a play no NFL coach but Johnson would have called and none would have even suspected. It goes against every coaching dictum and that's why it achieved such a spectacular result. Focused on percentages and in dread of the second guess, football coaches call a game framed in little boxes from which they never stray. Sunrise is less predictable. Jimmy Johnson cashed a victory on the road against a more talented team because he dared. There should be a lesson in that."

How much of a risk was it? "A lot of risk," Jimmy said. "We don't make it, I'm skewered. I'm an idiot. I've lost my mystique." Pause. "But the mystique is back!"

Big grin.

19

CROSSED OUT

Beat the Pittsburgh Steelers on *Monday Night Football* and the Dolphins would be 7–5 and tied for the AFC's final playoff spot. But trouble was lurking. Pro Bowl guard Keith Sims was out for at least a week with a sprained knee and the other guard, Chris Gray, was out for the year with a broken leg. That meant the Dolphins would be stuck with a waiver-wire pickup, Everett McIver, and a seventh-round pick, Jeff Buckey, to pick up the frenetic, confusing Blitzburgh zone blitzes.

Worse, Jimmy was furious with fast but flighty young wide receiver Charles Jordan. He fretted about the continuing slide of safety Louis Oliver. And he had multiple problems on his defensive line. Veterans thought first-round pick Daryl Gardener was so soft, they called him "Pudding" behind his back. Jimmy thought Gardener was playing well for a rookie. He was more concerned about the lack of consistency from one veteran defensive end, Trace Armstrong, and the lack of effort from another, Jeff Cross.

Cross had led the Dolphins in sacks five of his eight seasons and ranked fourth on Miami's all-time sack list. But he had complained about back pain in May, had gone to a specialist in July, then gone on his honeymoon, and, when he returned, he couldn't even get through the first day of camp. He had surgery for a degenerative disk July 23 and was expected to miss two months. But he told writers he might retire if he were not healthy, and he wanted to take it slow so he wouldn't reinjure his back. That told Jimmy that Cross might be milking this injury to collect his full salary. Cross did not even practice for three months, and when he returned, he spent three weeks easing into practice. That left the Dolphins facing a deadline on whether to activate him or lose him for the entire season.

Jimmy met twice with Cross's agent, Drew Rosenhaus, the day after the

Houston win and decided to activate Cross even though Rosenhaus cautioned he wouldn't be ready for Pittsburgh and might not be ready all season. Jimmy was not happy. Charles Haley had come back from back operations in three or four weeks. Cross wasn't back after nearly four months.

This wasn't the first time a coach had questioned Cross's courage. Don Shula and Tom Olivadotti were disgusted when he didn't play through an ankle injury in 1994 and re-signed him reluctantly only after seeing how little else was available in free agency.

Then, in Thursday's videotape session with his defensive linemen, position coach Cary Godette shouted at Cross. Godette was a screamer who tended to tick off his defensive linemen, and Cross angrily replied that he was a nine-year vet and Godette didn't have to yell at him. Both men got hot. Godette ordered Cross out of the room, and Cross wouldn't budge.

Now, if Cross had come to Jimmy and said he didn't respond well to yelling, Jimmy might have tried to patch things up. "But if a player challenges one of my coaches, I will never waver," he explained over Heinekens one night. "I will always back my guy. The players have to know that."

Jimmy would not tolerate even the hint of insubordination. The next day, he called Cross into his office and fired him—even though it would cost money against the cap in 1996 and 1997, even though he knew Rosenhaus would file a grievance claiming Cross wasn't healthy and deserved the rest of his 1996 salary. The Washington Redskins claimed Cross, but he told the team doctor his back wasn't healthy, so the Redskins said he flunked their physical. Was Redskins coach Norv Turner trying to help out his buddy Jimmy? Both said no, that the decisions belonged to the Redskins' personnel and medical staffs.

Upstairs, alone in his office, Jimmy explained: "There were a lot of conversations before the season started that he'd be one of the salary casualties. I couldn't even consider that because Jeff came in and said he had a bad back. There were strong suspicions Jeff truly didn't want to play. All our people felt Jeff was stringing this thing out and could have been healthy a lot sooner than he eventually was. He wasn't truly, in my opinion, a team guy.

"The bottom line is, Cross did not fit into our plans. I'm extremely excited about Tim Bowens, Daryl Gardener, and Shane Burton inside, and Danny Stubbs really has been productive for us. Outside of that, decisions still have got to be made. That [Gardener soft reputation] comes from jealous players who are not starters. Daryl Gardener is the second-leading tackler on the defensive line. To give you an idea, I'll show you right here."

He pulled a chart off his desk listing the defensive linemen's number of plays and tackles. "Stubbs has 609 plays, Bowens 605, Armstrong 532, Burton 464, Gardener 463," Jimmy explained. "Here are the tackles: Bowens is the highest at sixty-three. Gardener is second at forty-two. Even though he's fifth as far as number of plays, he's got the second-highest tackles. Gardener and Bowens are really playing good. Now, by the same token, one of the guys bitching, the self-appointed attorney, has 532 plays. He's sixth in tackles. He's only got twenty-four tackles. But one guy's supposed to be a hell of a player, and the other guy is a rookie making a lot of money. It's jealousy."

Jimmy blamed Trace Armstrong for the Gardener complaints, but they came from another source. He also blamed Trace, the union president, for the union protest over his physical minicamps, but the complaint actually came after a union lawyer saw the workouts on a routine visit. Trace had had his run-ins with Jimmy's buddy Dave Wannstedt in Chicago, where a few writers called Trace "Moth" because he was attracted to the camera lights. Jimmy didn't mind a guy talking the talk if he walked the walk, but he thought Trace and Jeff were too media friendly. And Jimmy was not at all happy that Trace spent the off-season at his Gainesville home, steadfastly refusing to move to South Florida to work out and to rehabilitate from two operations.

He had torn ligaments in his right ankle reconstructed, had a screw inserted in his right wrist, and wore a cast from his knuckles to his armpit until April. The injuries caused him to miss minicamps, and he couldn't lift until May or run until June. Without lifting to keep the muscle on, he lost so much weight that he tried to conceal it by wearing layers of T-shirts and baggy pants.

A weak 255, he had zero tackles after three games and four after five games until he responded with 2.5 sacks at Buffalo. "Trace needed to have a game like that," said Jimmy, who, though frustrated, decided to keep him because his salary was high and defensive linemen were scarce.

"I pretty much had one foot in the grave," Trace said. "I had some doubts as to whether I'd be able to play again. I came to training camp not really knowing if I could make it through it. I was still at the point where I might run well for two days and then have a hard time walking for the next couple of days. Jimmy and a lot of people don't realize what I went through in the off-season. It's not like you have just one, just the wrist, and you can run and work on your legs. I couldn't do anything. When you go six or seven months without being able to do anything, it takes its toll physically."

But he packed the muscle back on until he was up to 270 and overcame a torn muscle to play his best game in Houston, until he collected 6.5 sacks in the final three games and wound up with a career-high twelve. Only then would Jimmy decide to keep him and not ask him to take a big pay cut.

He already had decided he'd cut Jordan in the off-season if the wide receiver didn't accept a slashed salary. Jimmy had taken a real chance on Jordan when he could have kept Irving Fryar. Jordan was a great athlete, a leaper with 4.3 speed, but he had little football experience and a troubled past.

Jordan grew up in a gang-infested Los Angeles neighborhood and joined his first gang at eleven. In 1990, Jordan and two Bloods were arrested for murdering one of the rival Crips. The cops figured he knew who killed the Crip, but Jordan wouldn't rat on the Bloods for fear of what they would do to him. He spent several months in jail before a judge dismissed the case for lack of evidence. He also was arrested but never convicted of armed robbery, drug dealing, driving a stolen vehicle, and carrying a concealed weapon. Jimmy said the NFL and the Dolphins checked Jordan's background and found no problems.

Jordan was the star of minicamp, when there was no real hitting. But he severely sprained his ankle the first day of camp and aggravated it again in late July and early August. "Jimmy wants you to play through injuries," Jordan said. "I felt it really wasn't ready to play on, but I didn't want to get in his doghouse. I tried to practice. It was the wrong decision."

Jordan finally showed what he could do with a dazzling, leaping forty-three-yard catch at Arizona—only to hurt his knee when he came down. Five days later, he complained of light-headedness and Jimmy, exasperated, banished him to the locker room. Ten days later, Jordan sprained his ankle at Indy, and since Jimmy had made the mistake of activating only four wide receivers for the game, the Dolphins had to scrap their normal four-receiver set on passing downs and go with a three-receiver, two-back set they rarely used.

Jimmy wouldn't play Jordan because he wasn't practicing or preparing mentally to practice, and Jordan didn't prepare because he wasn't playing. It became a nobody-wins cycle. Jordan was late to meetings, and Jimmy seethed and fined him. Jordan paid his fines and sulked. Jimmy tried everything to get through to him and talked to him two or three times a week. Trainer Kevin O'Neill talked to him even more. Father Leo talked to him a few times. The Dolphins even set up an appointment with a psychologist, thinking he could help Jordan find more determination and confidence. Jordan skipped the session. He eventually went twice, but felt insulted.

"He asked me what my problem was, and I said there wasn't no problem. I've got no mind problems. I'm not a psycho. When you're stressing a lot, it tends to tighten your muscles up. He taught me some relaxation techniques that were pretty good. He wanted me to continue to see him, but I decided not to. My problems lie here with the Dolphins. My problems don't lie off the field. My stress and problems were coming from not getting a legitimate chance to play."

Unhappy about being inactive for the Indy game and worried about the pregnancy of his wife, Kymberly, Jordan was late for several meetings before the Houston game. Their first child had been born seven weeks early, with premature lungs. Now Kymberly was seven months pregnant, having contractions, and getting sewn up to help prevent another premature delivery. Jimmy berated and fined Charles.

Didn't Jimmy have any compassion? "I'll take time out of my schedule to talk to him because I've got compassion, but it has no effect on whether I play him or not," he responded. "If a guy drops a pass because he's sick, what am I gonna say? 'Well, Miami fans, I'm sorry, he was sick.' I don't want to sound cold-hearted, but I've got to make decisions on who's gonna win games."

He would have shown more mercy if Jordan's play had earned it. "There would be some slack as far as fines and practice, but no slack as far as production. If a player is not being productive on the practice field or the game field, then there is no slack. It'd be easy to say, 'Well, his wife's having a difficult pregnancy, and that's the reason,' but his track record suggests otherwise. He's been late to meetings, not totally focused, not totally prepared."

Jimmy's most disappointing player? "Yeah," the coach replied, "he's a disappointment because we expected him to contribute more. The disappointment is not in the talent. The disappointment is in his mental approach and his focus. We're trying to do everything we can. At some point, we say, 'We've covered all the bases, and he's just too set in his ways.' If he'd had a long history in college ball or pro ball, we would have been able to foresee this. And since there's not been a long history, that's why I haven't given up on him. I don't know that he can salvage this season, but I'm still going to give him a shot next season. Now, if he continues like this next season, I'll say, 'That's it. We tried, but it didn't work,' and go on."

Still, Jimmy defended his decision to choose Jordan over Fryar, pointing out Jordan's 1996 base salary was half that of Fryar's and his three-year contract cost $2.6 million compared to Fryar's $4.5 million with the Eagles. Fryar, however, would have signed for maybe $2 million for two years to stay in Miami. Jimmy figured Barnett and McDuffie were starters, and he preferred a young Jordan to an aging Fryar as his third receiver. And even though Fryar was having a career year in Philly while Barnett and Jordan were limping, Jimmy said, "The jury's still out on Fryar. How is he going to produce in 1998? The jury's out on Jordan, but he's got a long way to climb."

Monday, November 25, Miami. On top of all these problems came the Steelers, the AFC's defending champions and winners of eight of their past ten. The Dolphins jumped to a 14–3 lead, but Kordell "Slash" Stewart relieved a dreadful Mike Tomczak briefly and sparked a Pittsburgh touchdown. Richmond Webb was whistled for a false start. Scott Miller, playing in the four-wide offense instead of Jordan, dropped a pass for what should have been a first down. And Joe Nedney, pushed back to fifty-six yards, was just wide right, and it was 14–10 Steelers at the half.

Don Shula was inducted into the Dolphins' Ring of Honor at halftime. Forty-two former players lauded him. A sold-out stadium stood and applauded him.

He talked for several minutes, then did a victory lap perched above the back seat of a black Ford convertible, seemingly oblivious to his delay of game penalty. He made no mention of his successor, but in pregame remarks to the media he was less than magnanimous. "Well, he's 6–5," Shula said. "He'll be judged at the end of the year, just like I was judged."

And then Jimmy was second-guessed just like Don was.

With the score 17–17 in the final minutes, and Pittsburgh's offense facing third and eight at the Miami twenty, the Dolphins coaches warned their players to expect Tomczak to run a bootleg and throw deep over the middle to a receiver on a crossing route. And that's exactly what happened. But like so many times before, Miami's pass rush didn't get near the quarterback and a safety screwed up. Louis Oliver busted his coverage, abandoned his zone—and ran into his own man, Terrell Buckley. The collision left Ernie Mills wide open for the go-ahead score with 2:10 left.

"It's as elementary as you have," Jimmy seethed. "In three-deep coverage, the safety has to stay in the middle of the field. Louis should know better. It's frustrating because it's happened on more than one occasion. You can accept a young player who hasn't seen it before making some mistakes. The frustration comes when you have a veteran player do it. If we held them to a field goal there, now we've got a shot to go down and win it."

They still had a shot to win it when Marino launched a perfect forty-five-yard bomb to Randal Hill to the Pittsburgh sixteen, then hit Miller for eight. The Dolphins had seventy-five seconds and eight yards left to force overtime.

Second and two: O.J. was wide open for a first down. "He could even make a move and score a touchdown. But we don't make the throw [accurately]," Jimmy said. Incomplete.

Third and two: Marino threw short to his back. Jerris McPhail was so quick he would have gotten the first down and maybe the touchdown. But he was injured, and replacement Bernie Parmalee was never all that quick to begin with, and, less than one year after major knee surgery, he was stopped a yard short by cornerback Deon Figures.

Fourth and one at the seven: With thirty-one seconds and no time-outs left, the coaches chose to pass. "We run and fail and we're dead," offensive coordinator Gary Stevens reasoned. They called a play where Marino could throw to O.J. in the left flat for the first down or Miller in the left slot for the touchdown. Hill's slant route cleared open the flat for O.J., and Karim was wide open in the opposite flat, but Danny never looked that way. He stared left and fired for Miller. The pass was high and hard, but the average NFL receiver makes the touchdown catch. Miller is not very athletic. He jumped only high enough for the ball to graze off his fingers. And the Dolphins lost, 24–17.

"Goddamnit!" Randal said, and flung his helmet to the turf. In the locker room, Danny slammed down his knee brace, Jimmy was hoarse, and frustration was everywhere.

"The ball was a little high, and we don't come down with the ball," said Jimmy, who acknowledged O.J. and Karim were wide open. "But we took a shot in the end zone. That's our style. That's the thing that's made Dan Marino great. He's going to take a shot in the end zone."

But this was an aging, injured Dan Marino. He wasn't perfect anymore. And his receivers came up short. Again. But Charles Jordan was buried so deep in Jimmy's doghouse, he would not replace the journeyman Miller the rest of the season. Lamar Thomas would.

Jimmy would also replace Oliver, moving Shawn Wooden from free safety to strong safety and inserting Sean Hill at free safety. Just as he had replaced Gene Atkins with Wooden, he benched an aging safety who was better against the run for a smaller, younger, converted cornerback. The next game would be his thirteenth different lineup in thirteen games.

"Louis gave up a few big plays early, but I stayed with him because he made some big plays," Jimmy said. "But he was guessing and gambling so much, it hurt more than helped. Sometimes it's not who makes great plays, it's who makes the fewest bad plays."

Jimmy reminded his players the 1995 Dolphins also were 6–6 but won three of their final four to make the playoffs, and that was all these younger, hungrier Dolphins had to do. The players huddled and vowed not to lose even one of the four. But to keep their vow, they would have to win in Oakland, where no Dolphins team had ever won, and they would have to sweep Buffalo, which no Dolphins team had done in a decade. They would have to win four in a row when they hadn't won more than three straight all year, and that was back in September, when Jimmy was still a genius and Marino was still magical.

When the players returned to work, the "ROAD TO THE SUPER BOWL" bulletin board had been dismantled. The boxes signifying the first dozen games, which climbed a metaphoric ladder toward the Vince Lombardi Trophy, had been removed. Just the four boxes for the final four games remained, with a new message:

CAN YOU WIN FOUR?
THREE OUT OF FOUR
AND YOU ARE
IN THE PLAYOFFS

20
MARINO IS HUMAN, AND MIAMI IS SUNK

Sunday, December 1, Oakland, California. His was a legend born of reality, not hyperbole. So many Sundays, so many years, Dan Marino completed passes that no other quarterback dared, let alone did. Watching him was like watching Michael Jordan. Even fellow pros gaped in open-mouthed awe. They sought to shake his hand and get his autograph. And so even after Marino's most miserable game, even after Miami's meltdown, Oakland's Jeff Gossett, a guy who'd spent fifteen years in the National Football League, a guy not easily impressed, slipped into the Dolphins' locker room and asked for Dan to sign some photographs. Danny obliged, but the immortal felt decidedly mortal, like Joe Montana in his twilight. Yes, he could still summon up the greatness. But greatness no longer answered 99 percent of the time anymore.

Once he had started 155 consecutive games. But he had missed eleven games with a torn Achilles in 1993, two full games (and parts of three others) in 1995, and most of four games with the broken foot this year. His body was wearing out. His right foot and ankle ached, his right calf was withered, his left knee just about devoid of cartilage, his entire body tenderized by jet-propelled helmets and massive blobs of beef. He was thirty-five years old, and the aches he used to shake off by Tuesday lingered until Thursday or Friday now.

Ah, what a pain it is to grow old. All of us, from the greatest to the weekend warrior, endure it. The greats might postpone the inevitable, but they cannot cancel it.

Dan Marino limped when he walked. He ran with shoulders and upper torso hunched over like a seventy-year-old, with feet shuffling like an arthritic sixty-year-old. And yet that golden arm could still produce lasers. Despite his injuries, despite his receivers, he arrived in Oakland leading the league in passer rating—but left in seventh place. This day even his magical arm betrayed him. The rifle turned blunderbuss, scattering shot all over the Coliseum. How does an immortal cope with being a mortal?

Minutes after the devastating 17–7 defeat, Marino peeled off his jersey and shoulder pads. He kicked off both shoes, including the one with the special heel insert and ankle brace. He discarded the twelve-ounce brace from his left knee and the metal lateral stabilizer from his right knee. He wore a corsetlike brace around hips that had been so badly bruised in 1995 that blood and fluid were drained for ten days. His arm had fifty thousand yards on it, but his legs must have had fifty thousand miles. "Maybe a hundred thousand," O. J. McDuffie said.

"He has a big heart for the game," Fred Barnett said. "Just to see the guy limp out to the field, you know he has to suck it up every play. I mean, his heel, his knee, his ankle, his finger—everything's aching on him. He has a pad on *everything*. There's nothing exposed except his shins. He's like the bionic man."

But all the protective armor in the world could not stop the ravages of time. Dan Marino sat on his stool silently for a long time, staring into space, wondering about his own mortality and his team's failings. He leaned forward, elbows resting on his knees, hands holding his chin up, thinking about another game gone wrong, another season shot to hell.

The Dolphins were 6–7 with three games to play, and even if they won them all, they might not make the playoffs. And the way they were playing, the way he had played the past two games, how could they think they could win three in a row?

Like an old man, he struggled to bend over far enough to yank off his socks. Then he leaned over and chopped off the protective tape around his ankles with a tape cutter. His gray 2X Dolphins T-shirt, the sleeves cut off, was soaked in sweat from his belly up. His hair was matted down. His eyes were weary. He did not look like the matinee idol the women all covet, like the corporate spokesman in the thousand-dollar suit and million-dollar smile, with the multimillion-dollar endorsement deals.

He looked like a beat-up shell of the man. The previously ageless arm sprayed footballs that wobbled like some of Jim Plunkett's old ducks, Raiders defensive end Aundray Bruce said. One flew so far behind Stanley Pritchett, I asked Dan if it had slipped.

"I wish I could tell you it slipped," he said.

He threw three interceptions and saw three more INTs dropped. The first theft? "I tried to force it in there." The next? "Which one was next?" That's how bad it was. The great Dan Marino had so many turnovers, he couldn't remember them all. Maybe he didn't want to remember. Who could blame him?

He could. "I haven't played this bad," he said, "in a long time."

The last time he threw more interceptions was 1988. Only once in 196 games had he thrown five interceptions. Only twice had he chucked four. Now he had thrown three picks and coughed up the fumble that cost the Dolphins their last chance to get back in the game.

Danny threw for 290 yards, but one hundred came in the final five minutes, when Oakland was up 17–0 and playing prevent defense, and only a touchdown toss with 2:34 left averted Miami's first shutout since 1987. Danny talked to the media for 135 seconds—or eighty-seven seconds longer than Jimmy had—and cut off the questions. When a writer who hadn't been there, or hadn't been near enough to hear his whispered answers—Marino's postgame comments arrive in a voice softer than Marlon Brando playing Don Corleone—he snapped, "I already did my thing, man," and walked off, seemingly lost. He started into the trainer's room, came out momentarily, and then back in.

Early in the year, Jimmy had called Danny "a bonus." Lamar Thomas had called him "our secret weapon." But the quarterback was a lot more than that because the Dolphins still couldn't depend on anyone else. In the first three games, against inferior foes, Karim Abdul-Jabbar had averaged 93.3 yards a game and 4.3 yards a carry. They had won with the running game. But now they were playing better teams, and the running game was just as soft and ineffective as it had ever been under Don Shula. Karim had averaged only 51.2 yards per game and 3.0 per carry the past ten games, seven of them losses.

The longest run in those ten games? Just twenty-six yards. By Larry Izzo. On a fake punt. Only once in those ten games did a Dolphins running back bust loose for even a twenty-yard gain.

Their best run in that span came when Jimmy sprinted off the field, dodging hordes of photographers, after the Dallas debacle. On this Sunday, the Dolphins had run for a pitiful thirty-four yards on twenty carries, an average of 1.7 yards per carry. Four carries had lost yardage, and fourteen had gained two yards or less. Karim had not cut well, and nobody had blocked well.

Jimmy wanted a big, physical line like he had in Dallas, but he was getting too many blown assignments and too little aggressiveness. The line was pushed around by an Oakland defensive line that was good but not great. The Dolphins tried and failed to get outside even though tackles Richmond Webb, with a fifty-eight-pound advantage, and James Brown, with a seventy-nine-pound advantage, should have been able to mash the defensive ends, Pat Swilling, a converted linebacker, and Lance Johnstone, a rookie from Temple, of all places.

Keith Sims, trying to come back after just one game off his bad knee, tried to lead one sweep, and all he could do was stand in the way. He seemed lost, unsure whether he should move or try to hit somebody, and Karim was creamed after a one-yard gain. Not long afterward, Sims benched himself.

"I tried, but I just couldn't do the things I need to do," he said later, grimacing as he pulled tape off his throbbing knee. "It was painful from the get-go. I had a devastating time trying to pull. I couldn't pull, couldn't get to my man on power plays. I felt like I was carrying a piano on my back. The offensive line did not have a great game. Dan can't overcome everything."

It wasn't just the O line or, in this game, the NO line. The receivers could not shake free from the Raiders' outstanding man-to-man cover men. Nor, Jimmy said, did they block the Raiders' safeties on running plays. He had only two competent wideouts, O. J. McDuffie and Fred Barnett, and with Fred coming off knee surgery, neither was a game-breaker. Don Shula had chosen Mark Ingram over Tony Martin, and now Ingram was trying to hang on in Philly and Martin was emerging in San Diego as "the best receiver in the NFL, bar none," according to ESPN's Sterling Sharpe. Shula had paid big bucks for Eric Green, and now he was in Baltimore, and the local Sports Authority couldn't sell his Dolphins jersey for half price. Troy Drayton had finally ended the tight end shuffle, but not until the morning after this debacle did Jimmy decide to use the dangerous tight end on third down. The Dolphins still needed their All-Pro to play like an All-Pro. And when Danny didn't, they were done.

This was how bad it got: Barnett felt the need to approach Marino on the sideline and say, "I'm with you regardless of what happens." And when Danny moaned, "Coach, I was awful," Jimmy felt the need to console and encourage him.

This was how bad it got: Another defense dared Dan to throw. Defenses had taken to stacking eight men near the line of scrimmage, snuffing the run, leaving the receivers in man-to-man coverage, daring the receivers to beat them. When was the last time defenses preferred Marino to throw than to hand off?

This was how bad it got: Swilling could have blasted Marino on an interception return, but barely laid a hand on him. Aundray Bruce said the Raiders preferred to keep Marino in the game rather than face his substitute. Bruce called Marino "semiawful." An *Oakland Tribune* columnist called him "the Big Awful." Even *Dolphin Digest* called him "awful."

Marino showered and pulled on a black T-shirt, a purple windbreaker, white socks, brown dock shoes, and light-blue jeans. A fading legend in fading jeans walked off, not into a glorious sunset, but up the stairs of an ugly stadium, out into the toxic fumes of the buses, into an ugly industrial neighborhood, in a town no more exciting than when Gertrude Stein described Oakland decades ago: "There is no there there." He climbed on one of the four buses that hurried the Dolphins to the plane. Marino threw down his bag in his aisle near the back of the plane, dug out his toothbrush, and went to the rest room to wash away the bad taste in his mouth. It was going to be a long, quiet ride home.

Some players immediately curled up with blankets and tried to sleep. Others talked quietly. Others watched the two junky, violent movies offered, *Fear* and *Escape from LA*. A few milled in the aisle. Jimmy sat in 1A, sulking next to Rhonda as he watched a replay of NBC's broadcast of a very bad loss, to a team that was getting its coach fired, to a team that was beatable, to a team the Dolphins almost had to beat if they were going to make the playoffs. Now they had to sweep their final three against New York State—the Giants, Bills, and Jets—and then pray for losses by the five other clubs that were 7–6 or 6–7 and vying for that final playoff spot.

When the Dolphins landed in Fort Lauderdale at 2 A.M., the plane emptied within ten minutes, save for Keith Sims, squeezing his wide frame and stiff leg down the aisle, hobbling badly. Five hours in a plane is no way to treat a bad knee. He would need off-season surgery not only to repair this damage but to remove a thick bone chip that had floated above the knee and left him in pain every day since May. He winced with every step. And as he neared the door, he realized he'd need to put even more weight on that bad knee. "Oh, great," he said, sarcastically. "Stairs. This is going to be fun."

The mourning after would be even worse for Keith and crew. Because Jimmy's mood was even worse than Keith's knee.

21

SO MUCH FOR RIOT ACTS

At six-thirty Wednesday morning, Jimmy called WQAM and forecast a victory over the Giants. "Hey, everybody's gonna have smiles on their faces after Sunday," he vowed. "You can count on it."

But he was acting. He was still in a bad mood. He had done everything he could think of to motivate Charles Jordan—and the flighty flier still missed the team flight on the way back from Oakland and didn't bother to talk to Jimmy until Wednesday, lamely saying he was hanging with his old teammates and the buses left early. Uh-huh. "We must have honked the horn forty times before we left," security boss Stu Weinstein said. Jordan's latest bungle earned him the fifth of seven consecutive games on the inactive list.

Jimmy abhorred turnovers and penalties, but the 'Fins had four turnovers and eleven penalties in Oakland and forty-five penalties in the past five games. Jimmy believed turnovers were football's most telling statistic, and penalties weren't far behind because they cost more than downs and yards. They wiped out points and possessions; Jimmy could detail single games when penalties had cost seventeen points.

Some old-fashioned coaches thought discipline meant avoiding showboating and celebrating. Jimmy thought it meant avoiding turnovers and penalties. Michael Irvin, his flamboyant ex-receiver, explained it well: "Discipline isn't saying, 'Don't throw your hands up in the air when you score a touchdown.' Discipline is when it's 110 degrees in the Orange Bowl, no breeze, fourth quarter, a minute left to play, fourth and three for the other team, you are dead tired, they come to the line and that opposing quarterback gives you a hard count: 'Hut, *hut!*' and you don't jump offside. Because you're disciplined mentally and physically. That's Jimmy's discipline."

And Jimmy no longer saw the discipline and all-out effort of summer and early fall. His players were not working as hard during the week, and were going out the night before games, returning to their hotel rooms just minutes instead of hours before curfew. He wasn't seeing the same pain over defeats. He saw Dolphins posing for photos with Raiders and laughing with their families and friends after the bad loss. Rookies who had never played this many games in a season were weary. Veterans who had lost starting jobs such as Louis Oliver, J. B. Brown (who lost not only his starting job but now his nickel back job), and Chris Singleton (who was getting benched for rookie free agent Anthony Harris) were just putting in time, and, Jimmy feared, leading his youngsters astray.

And so when his players returned to work Wednesday, Jimmy opened the nine-thirty meeting by saying they still had a shot at the playoffs if they won the final three games. But then he ripped into them. He told his rookies they could no longer use youth as an excuse and they should quit looking up to the veterans and step up as leaders themselves: "We have vets who are not even active having rookies go get them breakfast or sandwiches. If a veteran tells you to go get him breakfast, tell him to go fuck himself! Get his own breakfast! You young guys are the ones who have to take a leadership role, and you're not going to take a leadership role if you're going and getting breakfast for guys who are not even playing."

Jimmy lashed into everybody's attitude but used his linemen as an example. They had failed to sustain blocks the way they had learned in all those middle drills in training camp, the way their old right tackle used to do before bad knees forced him to retire before the 1996 season. "I never coached Ron Heller, but I watched him play, and he was a tough SOB. Our offensive line, we've got to get that attitude—and right now we don't have it," Jimmy railed. "I want to see that nasty attitude, that win-at-all-costs effort come back. When you block [Giants linebacker] Jessie Armstead this week, knock him down! And if he gets back up, knock him down again! Don't block your guy and let him come off the block and make the tackle after a two-yard gain! That's an 'assignment' attitude. I want a nasty attitude!

"I don't see the same focus that I saw a couple of months ago. Sometimes guys get into a rut of just putting in time. Everybody gives great effort on Sunday. But hey, you ask yourself as individuals: Are you giving the same effort on Wednesday, Thursday, Friday, and Saturday and the same focus on the game and focus prior to the game that you gave a couple of months ago? Don't let yourself say a couple of months from now, 'Oh shit, we could have beaten so and so if . . .' The opportunity was a couple of weeks ago, a week ago. Pittsburgh didn't beat you. Neither did Oakland. We beat ourselves. It wasn't because of effort Monday night or Sunday. It was because everybody is not totally into it."

He told them he realized all these changes were difficult. But he pointed out that when he came to the University of Miami, the Hurricanes went 8–5 the first year—and 44–4 the next four. And Dallas was 1–15 his first year—but won back-to-back Super Bowls in years four and five.

"People will say, 'What's Jimmy going to do? Well, Jimmy makes changes.' But I'm not going to make all these changes next year," Jimmy promised. "Understand this: I'm not going through this shit again. We'll study these tapes, and we'll do what we have to do. When we go to training camp next year, we'll have a group that *is* going to be sick to their stomachs when they come up short. Everybody hurts for a few minutes when they lose. But if you're truly sick to your stomach after a loss, you can't put on a happy face. You can't laugh and cut up with your friends. How many of you are truly sick to your stomachs when we come up short? We'll find those guys, and that's who we'll go to war with next year." Leaving the auditorium, he turned back and said, "I hate not being able to be more positive, but I want you to feel as sick as I do when we lose."

And then he walked upstairs to his office, and we talked about his self-proclaimed "riot act." When he was hired, he said he chose the Fish over the Bucs because they didn't need a major overhaul. But now he said that while he always overhauled in his first season, he hadn't expected this year to be such a struggle or the talent to be this weak.

"I thought we had a better group of veterans," Jimmy allowed. "Unfortunately, the better group of vets left through free agency. We lost some strong leadership and character on this team. Ron Heller was a tough son of a gun. From what I understand, Marco Coleman had strong character and worked hard and played hard. Forget how good a player he was. Bryan Cox, obviously some people may say he did it in a distorted way, but he did give them fire and spark. Forget about how good a player he is.

"Now, we've got so many young guys, they're looking for leadership. And hey, some of these guys *will* be leaders. But it's hard to be a leader when you're just learning what to do. So the original estimate of the talent is looking at what it was when I arrived, not what we went to camp with.

"I didn't know Marino would be out for three losses. I didn't know we'd have to have seven rookies starting and two other rookies starting at one time or another. My estimate was that many would make the team and maybe we'd have three or four guys starting by the end of the season. Puhhhh-lease! We've had five or six start the majority of the season. So yeah, I did a little bit of overestimating what we had. But being realistic and not optimistic, we're not more than a game or two off of what a realistic prediction should have been. At this stage it would have been unrealistic to be much more than 7–6; 8–5 would have been a stretch."

He gazed at a fish floating languidly in his ninety-gallon aquarium. Jimmy established his home and his condo by the seas that calmed him, but the Dolphins' Davie offices offered no such views, so this child of the sea installed his favorite tranquilizer smack-dab in front of his desk. Jimmy could melt away his troubles by staring at the real coral undulating—none of those fake painted rocks for him—or the fish swimming in his many aquariums, but this fish was barely moving. Jimmy walked around his desk and tapped on the glass to see if the fish would move.

"I don't know if this guy is dying or just resting." He climbed on a chair, stuck his arm in the tank to prod the fish, and it finally swam away. "Guess you were just resting," Jimmy said. The metaphor was hard to miss. Jimmy was goading lethargic fish . . . and Fish.

He wanted his porpoise to play with a purpose. He did not want to be a gentle dolphin. He thought of himself as a lionfish. "It's got poisonous spines," he explained, "and people are afraid of it."

He wanted his gentle tackle, Richmond Webb, to become more poisonous, but he wanted his halfback, Karim Abdul-Jabbar, to run smarter than he had in Oakland.

Son Brent called, and they chatted for maybe two minutes. Even Jimmy's weekly calls with Mother and Daddy didn't last much more than three or four minutes; he only talked longer to friends like Nick Christin, Dave Wannstedt, Norv Turner, and Al Davis about business or football matters. Then it was time for the weekly conference call with the media covering that week's opponent.

Jimmy rocked back in his chair and rested a sneaker on a big desk. His credenza and desk drawers were crammed with pertinent papers, but nary a one rested on the neatnik's desk. The office decorations were almost as sparse. Along the bookshelf were photos of his boat, of Jimmy shaking hands with Wayne Huizenga the day he was hired, of Jimmy at the White House giving Bill Clinton Cowboys jersey number one. Three game balls, one enclosed in glass. Baseball caps from Fox, ESPN, and NBC. A UM Sports Hall of Fame plaque. An honorary doctor of philosophy degree from Yentz Western University Graduate School of Humanities. A *Sports Illustrated* cover of Jimmy and Danny dubbed "The Sunshine Boys." Three plants, two Dolphins hats, and a tiny Christmas tree.

"Hey," Jimmy told the New York writers, "first years are tough. My style is, I want to make a mark on my team, and sometimes I'm a little more aggressive putting young players into the lineup than other people. With as many changes as I usually have my first year, we're not as consistent. But if we do it the first year, I know we're gonna have a lot more pleasant days the second and third year.

"I don't want to keep the players on this much of an edge. But when I'm in a new place the first year, everybody's thinking, 'Am I going to be here next year?' It's hard for a player to play his best if he's playing scared. I know that. But it's something I can't avoid because I want to get our guys in the lineup. My whole focus is to make sure I eliminate the wrong people and make sure I get the right people. But you can't do that, in my way of thinking, on a gradual basis.

"I want to do it now."

Jimmy told South Florida writers his radio "smile" forecast wasn't a victory guarantee, like that NFC championship game against San Francisco, just a prediction the Dolphins would "play well." And he said they had responded with maybe the best Wednesday-Thursday practices all year.

But the outcasts rebelled after Jimmy ripped them. "I'm out of here after this season," one unnamed veteran told the *Sun-Sentinel*'s Jason Cole. "They can take my locker and clean it out as far as I'm concerned. I'm done. I'm not coming back."

Jimmy stormed back: "Some of them, I would cut them today, but it would accelerate their bonuses, and we can't do that. If they don't like it, then quit. Save me some money on the cap. But they don't mind taking that check. If they want out of here so bad, fine. They're not playing anyway. They're drawing a paycheck for doing nothing."

Sunday, December 8, Miami. Virtually no Dolphin earned his paycheck. Against a second straight opponent playing out the string with a coach about to be fired, Miami was outmuscled and beaten by its own mistakes.

The week before, the Giants produced 131 yards and no points. A week later, they managed 138 yards and three points against a New Orleans team that had lost seven in a row. But they took the Dolphins' opening kick eighty yards, capped by Rodney Hampton's first touchdown run of the year.

Dan Marino's sixty-six-yarder to Fred Barnett set up a short tying touchdown pass to Robert Wilson, but Jimmy passed up a forty-yard field goal attempt by the struggling Joe Nedney to run on fourth and two at the twenty-three, and Stanley Pritchett, given a rare carry, didn't convert. Jimmy bitched at his linemen that if they wanted him to go for it, they better get it.

They never got it.

The Giants' Howard Cross caught his first touchdown in two years. Then Marino, less than brilliant for the third consecutive week, made a bad decision and gave Conrad Hamilton, a nobody from Eastern New Mexico, his first career interception, and the Giants turned it into a field goal.

Another Webb holding penalty cost the Dolphins a first down. A holding call on Michael Stewart, one of the soon-to-depart veterans, cost them thirty yards on a repunt. And then Marino threw behind Karim, and the rookie tipped the ball to the Giants' Corey Widmer for an interception. The Giants dropped a third INT, but Chad Bratzke, he of three sacks in three seasons, went around Webb to nab Marino, and New York won 17–7.

The Dolphins scored one offensive touchdown for the fourth straight game. They let the league's lowest-ranked offense control the ball for 36.5 minutes.

They let Dave Brown, the league's lowest-rated starter, complete 75 percent. They let a simplistic offense without a single playmaker control the tempo.

A frustrated Irving Spikes fought with Jesse Campbell, and the Giant simply backed off and pointed to the scoreboard. The only smiles belonged to New Yorkers and South Floridians who were observing Hanukkah or shopping for Christmas.

So much for Jimmy's prophecy. "I was trying to give our guys a little spark," he said, "and obviously it had no effect." Except on the Giants.

"Him saying they'd smile on Sunday certainly motivated us," Dave Brown said. "I didn't want to see him back in that locker room saying, 'How 'bout them Dolphins!' "

No, this is what he said 'bout them Dolphins: "We're not a very good team."

Jimmy had asked them to sustain their blocks, and they had not. He had stressed winning the short-yardage plays, and they had not. He had preached about avoiding penalties and turnovers, and they had not. He had talked all year about playing their best ball in November and December, and they had not. They had whipped New England in September, but now they were slumping and New England was soaring. Now, they were playing the worst ball in the state—worse than Jacksonville, Tampa Bay, Florida State, Florida, even UM.

He said they had not quit. Which might have been the scariest part. "We're just not good enough," Jimmy repeated. He walked out of his press conference and muttered under his breath, "Oh boy, this fucking season is over."

Actually, the Dolphins still had one chance in 113 of making the playoffs, but that chance was likely to disappear even before they played the Bills Monday night.

"A whole year of work is now down the drain," Danny said.

"A couple of weeks ago," T-Buck said, "we were on cloud nine. We beat Houston, and we partied and had a good time on the way back. Now, it's a horrible feeling. All you want to do is go home and lay in bed and hope it's a bad dream. But it's not."

Jimmy Johnson and his coaches would spend a sleepless night trying to figure out why.

22
HE'S NOT SHULA

After every game in Texas Stadium, Cowboys coaches and closest friends and families mingled over munchies and drinks in a large room, and those last few years, it was one big party, the hottest ticket in Texas. Jimmy kept the tradition alive in Pro Player Stadium, albeit forced into two adjoining rooms—and more postmortems. No matter how miserable they felt, he encouraged the coaches to stop by and unburden their troubles in a relaxed setting "before it festers."

And after this Giant defeat, they had plenty of problems to purge. The coaches huddled deep into the night, and then again most of the morning, trying to answer one basic question:

What the hell happened to our offense?

Jimmy was drawn and dejected when he met the media twenty-three hours after the Giant debacle. He said the coaches concluded the offensive failures stemmed from three problems. First, turnovers. The Dolphins had thrown just six interceptions the first twelve games but five the past two. Second, penalties. They had fallen from the fifth-least-penalized team at midseason to seventeenth after drawing twenty-seven whistles in three weeks. Third, busted assignments.

All three problems, but especially the latter two, were more mental than physical mistakes. Jimmy had retained most of Don Shula's playbook and offensive players because they had ranked in the top ten each of the past five years. But when newcomers hadn't played to their potential because they were befuddled by the offense and when even veterans like Richmond Webb were making mental mistakes, Jimmy decided the playbook was too complex and thick. He told his assistants the offense had to be simple enough that newcomers like Troy Drayton wouldn't be standing next to him on key downs and a smart veteran like Fred Barnett wouldn't be missing "hot reads."

"The problem is our style of offense, as much offense as we have, really requires experienced veteran people," Jimmy said. "That day is gone. The salary cap really forces every team to play young players. With free agency, you're going to have movement every year. And it's very difficult to have a very complicated scheme and have new players on a yearly basis.

"If you pay a ton of money for a free agent and he can't contribute the first year because your system is too complicated, then you made a mistake. You wasted a lot of money. You have to have a system they can easily grasp. You don't want to handcuff a great quarterback. But if the quarterback understands the system and the receivers don't, then you haven't accomplished anything.

"We're not a very aggressive running team. So much of our offense is predicated on calling plays at the line of scrimmage, I think it takes aggressiveness away from the linemen when they are at the line not knowing who to block."

Dan Marino had so mastered calling audibles that there were times in the eighties when he'd *fake* changing to a play to beat a blitz, and the defensive captain would call off the blitz, expecting the Dolphins to be stuck with the new call—except the audible had never really been called.

Depending on the game, Marino might change 10, 20, even 30 percent of the calls at the line. "Instead of getting focused on what you're doing with the snap count, you're listening to the play call," Keith Sims said. "In the audible system, you only have a split-second to react: 'Okay, that's the new play. What calls do I have to make to my other linemen? Who do I have to block?' Boom, the ball's off."

But Jimmy would limit one of Marino's fortes because his receivers didn't always respond correctly and because his linemen weren't as physical when they were at the line still figuring out who they should block when the ball was snapped.

Charles Jordan said the state-of-the-art West Coast offense actually employed more basic plays, but the receivers didn't have to adjust their routes if the defense blitzed. By contrast, a Dolphins receiver must choose between two or three "hot read" options, depending on how he reads the defense and where the blitz comes from. So he must know the original call, must hear and adjust to any changes Marino makes at the line, and must read the blitz the same way the quarterback does, or he goes one way and the ball goes the other. With a playbook crammed with hundreds of plays, with loud crowds, with different wideouts playing every week, with wideouts focusing on what move they should use to beat their defenders, was it any wonder Marino and his receivers weren't in sync?

Drayton, who'd had four offensive coordinators in four pro seasons, said on a scale of one to ten, ten being the most complex, Penn State was a one, the Rams a three, the Dolphins a ten. "I can't say I know this system because I don't,"

Drayton said. "You have a lot of memorization, and either you know it or you don't. Because if you half know it, that's going to take away from your aggressiveness. Sometimes I'll look at O.J. and say, 'Juice, what was that one?' The volume of plays is just endless."

The Rams' game plan might include twenty-five plays each week. Dolphins offensive coordinator Gary Stevens said he used about a hundred. There were so many, they couldn't practice every play in that week's plan and simply walked through or reviewed some. And there were so many plays with such long names, by the time they were relayed from Stevens upstairs to Kippy Brown on the sideline to Marino on the field, they were often late or mixed up. Jimmy decided to shorten the numbers, names, and process in the off-season.

Stevens said he had pared the number of plays in each package by 30 percent already this year and for the final two games would cut the number of plays in his weekly game plan another 25 percent and might eliminate some groupings, such as the four-wide formation. They'd pare further in the off-season. "It'll be the same offense," Stevens said, "just cut down."

The local media exaggerated the changes, suggesting Jimmy was scrapping Shula's playbook, may it rest in peace, and Shula was offended by the swipes. "That playbook won a lot of football games for a lot of people," he angrily told ESPN. "It won a lot of games with the Colts and Dolphins. Howard Schnellenberger took that playbook to the University of Miami and did pretty well with it. Chuck Noll, one of my assistants, took that playbook to Pittsburgh and did pretty well, got four Super Bowl rings that I see."

Jimmy did take one low blow by comparing Miami's offensive problems to Dallas's struggles with David Shula's offense. But he wasn't discarding Shula's thick playbook, which was like a pack rat's house after twenty-six years: It just needed pruning.

"I don't see why he'd take offense," Jimmy said in April 1997. "Puhhhh-lease! A new coach will run a new offense and new defense. I'm *keeping* his playbook. We're just cleaning up some duplication. A lot of it won't even be done until training camp. So much was made out of it, like we're going to a totally new playbook, which isn't true. Very little of the structure and philosophy will change."

Their egos would not allow the two great coaches to repair the relationship. They had seen each other only a handful of times in the past year, and their conversations had been stiff, cocktail-party-type small talk. "Nothing has changed," Jimmy said.

Shula's feelings weren't the only ones pricked. After *The Herald*'s Armando Salguero wrote that J. B. Brown would be waived and Chris Singleton, Charles Jordan, Randal Hill, Lamar Thomas, Louis Oliver, Steve Emtman, and Bernie Parmalee would have to accept minimal 1997 salaries or get cut, Jimmy tried to quell any mutiny with a team meeting.

But J.B. knew he was gone, and Singleton did, too, because he said he would not accept a pay cut. Jordan was more conciliatory. He met with Jimmy before practice Saturday morning, apologized for sulking when he didn't play, and said he'd take a pay cut and do whatever it took to be a Dolphin in 1997. That afternoon, both sounded excited. But when we spoke five days later, Jordan wasn't exactly a new man. He admitted he had taken the wrong approach, had gotten so angry and depressed he'd felt like retiring or asking the Dolphins to release him, and now he understood Jimmy wanted him to be more mentally tough, to fight through defenders to get the ball, and fight through injuries to practice.

But . . . "I'm not saying Charles Jordan is the best receiver they have, but I think Charles Jordan should have been playing and he wasn't," Charles Jordan said. "I started to see they're not gonna play me no more this year and then they're gonna try to ask me to take a pay cut because *they* didn't play *me*. It wasn't my choice not to play the whole season. For the last nine games, y'all just sat me for no apparent reason, in my eyes. How can you say I haven't been productive when you haven't put me on the field?"

Jimmy's reply: Jordan didn't get on the game field because he didn't earn it by practicing and preparing. Jimmy wanted him to work like Zach Thomas, not cruise like the outta-here vets. "Zach will grab a lot of young guys and go in and watch extra tape," Jimmy said. "But even Zach is hesitant to grab some of the older guys. A year from now, he'll be an older guy. He won't be hesitant."

"I'm a rookie," Zach agreed. "I can't really tell guys, 'Let's get going.' I've got to lead by example now. After the season, I'll go back to the way I was in college and get everybody going."

Their leader was miffed by three weeks of losses and questions about whether the offense and the quarterback were obsolete.

Phil Latzman of WINZ Radio: "Do you think your skills have diminished? Sorry to ask it, but you know . . ."

Marino: "Then why do you ask?"

Latzman: "Well, because I wanted to know the answer. Seriously . . ."

Marino: "No. Okay? How's that for an answer?"

And a bit later: "If you want to say that I personally am in a slump, that's fine. But I think as an offense we're not playing well as a group. Me being the quarterback, I guess you could say I'm somewhat responsible for that, and that's okay. It's not acceptable to me, but that's the way it is."

Doctors have a technical term for the affliction the Dolphins were suffering: tight asses.

Marino snapped at the media, and Jimmy snarled at the media, coaches, players, and even P.R. people. Secondary coach Mel Phillips called *Dolphin Digest* to complain about the grades given his players. Line coach Larry Beightol railed about the grades in *Dolphin Digest* and the *Sun-Sentinel*. Most of the players went into hiding, and the rest went on the defensive. Only one Dolphin made the Pro Bowl, the smallest number since 1980, and a lot of people thought Richmond Webb again made it on reputation. He topped the list of least-deserving Pro Bowlers according to a *Pro Football Weekly* poll of pro scouts, who rated him as only the eighth-best AFC tackle. Webb had committed eight penalties, had another three declined, and, after a strong start, had given up several sacks. Miami actually had run better to its no-name right side than behind the Pro Bowl left side of Webb and Keith Sims.

"Richmond has not had a great year, but he really didn't have a very good year last year, either," Jimmy confided. And though Sims would need major off-season surgery to correct his knee, Jimmy seemed to dismiss that as an excuse for his second-half falloff. He said both linemen had been sporadic and had to perform better.

Both had soft bellies. The new right guard and tackle also topped three hundred pounds, but none played as physically as their size implied. Everett McIver and James Brown had played for Beightol with the Jets, Webb and Sims had regressed in Beightol's first year with the Dolphins, and all were drawing too many false start and motion whistles, which Beightol called "dumb penalties." Webb and Sims had gotten all the criticism when the Dolphins failed on consecutive short-yardage plays against the Jets, but actually they were not to blame; a linebacker came untouched from the back side and made the tackle both times.

I asked what had happened. Simple question, right? Beightol stuck his nose about an inch from mine. He said the local media made too much of two plays, and "They don't know their ass from first base." So why not explain it? Jimmy answered such questions matter-of-factly, but Beightol was afraid to sound too critical of his players. I told him I was just looking for a one-sentence explanation for this book.

"I don't care," Beightol replied, voice rising. "Write it any damn way you want, okay? Because you don't know. You gonna bring me the book and let me criticize the book and let me put it in the newspaper and say, 'You've got a goddamn comma splice over here. You've got a preposition out of place over here'? You want me to do that and say this son of a bitch can't write? That's about what it's like, am I right? I'm attacking your ass now. I'm telling you that you're trying to make a point that you don't know anything about, and you don't. Jason Cole doesn't know, none of the other guys do, and if they say they do, they don't. They're full of shit."

Me: "So educate us."

Beightol: "I don't have time. Was there another goddamn snap in the game? The game's for sixty minutes. Write about it! If the momentum left them, write about it. But don't write these two poor sons of bitches . . . Unless you come in here, sit down, and I tell you exactly what the play is, what it's designed, and where the breakdown was, you don't know. And you're giving out fuckin' false information."

By now, Beightol was yelling, and a few of the local media inched toward us.

Pat McManamon of *The Palm Beach Post*: "I'm getting the impression this was not Keith's and Richmond's fault."

Beightol: "I'm not gonna say nothin'. You're not gonna bait my ass into that."

Tight asses.

Jimmy knew how to work the media better. He spent an hour with WQAM's Hank Goldberg, even though his Thursday radio show's interview actually took just half an hour. Before they went on the air, he talked quietly, almost conspiratorially, giving Hank behind-the-scenes stuff about the offense's problems and lack of leaders so Hank could go on the air and look like a brilliant insider. Like Edwin Pope and Joe Rose, Hank was one of South Florida's most influential voices. He let Nick Christin know Shula was quitting, and he and Edwin were the two media members Nick called when Jimmy accepted the job. Plus, Hank had a national audience with ESPN, and Jimmy wanted the network announcers on his side.

Jimmy normally met with the network crew in person the day before the game, but because this was ABC's fourth Dolphins broadcast of the year, because ABC had just been here three weeks ago, and because the announcers would rather watch Sunday's games at their fancy digs near the water than waste time coming over to Davie for a 6–8 club, they just talked via conference call.

Jimmy gave the ABC announcers two more reasons for simplifying the offense: because audibles weren't as effective against complicated zone blitzes and because they could run better and rely less on the quarterback when he had a bad day. He said the Dolphins had been in a funk since the Monday night Pittsburgh game and he wouldn't experiment in the final two games because he didn't want to finish in a funk.

Flipping between NFL games on the office satellite dish, Jimmy said Jordan was "a little knucklehead" but he still liked him, and he said he wished he had turned to Harris a month ago because "Singleton wasn't making any tackles at all." And he said he'd drop the troublesome four-receiver set and use two backs with three wideouts or two wideouts and Drayton. Then he yukked it up for a few seconds and left for the night.

Monday night, December 16, Miami. Jimmy's gang looked down on him from their end-zone luxury Suite 226A. Rhonda sat in front with a girlfriend, and Nick leaned nearby. Rhonda sent out invitations to select guests for each game.

Jimmy's sons, Brent and Chad, sat in director's chairs in back. They'd flown in Friday and Saturday, and Jimmy hadn't even seen them yet. Dad didn't have time for the sons? Nah, Jimmy said, the sons sought sun, not him. "See," Chad said, pinching pink cheeks. He has the same beefy cheeks and thick, lustrous hair as his dad. He's a first vice president for investments at PaineWebber in Dallas. Brent, with the angular face of a model, is a Dallas lawyer who's dabbled in modeling and writing.

Their workaholic dad wasn't around much when they grew up, but once they got in their twenties, Brent and Chad were more buddies than sons. This was their fourth game in Miami, and even when they didn't come to town, they talked to Jimmy at least a couple of minutes every week. They'd sometimes flown on the team plane when he'd coached the Cowboys.

Chad played poker in the back with Rhonda—until she enjoyed herself too much after a Dallas loss. Now, she said, she sits in the first row next to Jimmy and just goes "Uh-huh, uh-huh" when he gets in one of his zones. Like his players and coaches, she has learned not to chatter, to take every loss as if it were a death in the family. Betray Jimmy or his rules and you won't be part of his family. The man who doesn't believe in Christmas just gave her a diamond bracelet and earrings and the lifestyle of a princess. She does not want to go on waivers; she'll swap sarcastic jokes with Jimmy when he's feeling good and shut up when he's feeling bad.

"This is pretty boring," she said, as the Dolphins and Bills slogged through the first quarter. Buffalo's offense was struggling, too. Jim Kelly was thirty-six, and, like Marino, unable to avoid the pass rush or the killer interception. (I can personally attest that his problem was not velocity but accuracy; when I looked away during pregame warm-ups, Kelly's errant sideline pass hit me flush in the groin, and it was a half hour before I could walk without breathing funny.) The Bills had lost two in a row and needed to win to tie New England for the AFC East lead.

"C'mon, guys," Rhonda yelled toward the field. "Let's do something!"

And they did. Joe Nedney kicked three field goals, Marino hit O. J. McDuffie for a 16–7 lead, and the defense pressured Kelly to misfire on fourth and two midway through the fourth quarter. But when Miami faced fourth and one at the Buffalo thirty-nine, Jimmy's aggressiveness backfired. Instead of punting and pushing the Bills near their goal line with a nine-point deficit and six minutes left, the Dolphins sent Karim around left tackle—around Webb—and didn't get it. Kelly quickly pulled the Bills within 16–14 with a sixteen-yard touchdown to Eric Moulds, and Terrell Buckley pounded the ground in frustration.

But Marino played keepaway until twenty-six seconds remained, Kelly was forced into a consecutive sack and fumble, and Miami's three-game losing streak was over.

The Dolphins still committed eight penalties, wasted three time-outs in the first eleven minutes of the third quarter, scored just one touchdown for the fifth straight game, and could have lost if Steve Christie hadn't missed a twenty-yard field goal after a high snap.

But the defense shut down Dolphin-killer Thurman Thomas again and handled Buffalo except for a sixty-seven yard touchdown pass. The offense held the ball for nearly forty-two minutes. A running game limited to 2.2 yards a carry in the first half broke out for 103 in the second half, Drayton finally got involved with five catches, and Marino was Marino again.

Fred Barnett, emerging as the go-to receiver and most exuberant leader, said they won because of guilty consciences, and rookie safety Shawn Wooden, reducing his mistakes and increasing his big plays with every game, agreed.

"We feel bad we did it to ourselves," Wooden said. "It's definitely frustrating. When we play good football, we wonder, 'Why couldn't we play like this against the Raiders? Why couldn't we come up with these drives against Pittsburgh? Why couldn't we stop Pittsburgh? Why couldn't we beat the Seahawks? The Giants?' I mean, if we'd played this kind of football for fifteen games, we'd be up there with Denver in won-lost record. Next year, it's going to be there."

"We all have to shake our heads at what could have been," Sims agreed. "But you can't do that. It's over. All we can do is try to beat the Jets next Sunday and try to get ready for next year."

The Bills were playing for the playoffs. The Dolphins were playing for their jobs. "I don't understand when people say we don't have anything to play for," Trace Armstrong said. "Those questions are silly. This is my *life*. This is what I do for my living. You're known by your work. And nobody wants to go out 6–10. The two most miserable days in football are Monday and Tuesday after a loss. They are torture. Winning this one will make tomorrow a little better."

Jimmy certainly felt better. Past midnight, bearing down on 1 A.M. in the inner sanctum, he shook hands, posed for photos, introduced friends ranging from his accountant to his diet doctor, and gathered a few around to tell a story.

"Before we go on the air for these *Monday Night Football* games, Lynn Swann always says, 'What do you want to talk about?' I said, 'We could talk about how we've got a young team, the youngest twenty-two starters in the league. Or I could say what I really feel like: Fuck! How can I get this week over with so I can get on the boat and drink Heineken?'

"And Lynn said, 'I don't think you can say *that* on national TV.' "

Everybody broke up laughing. It was good to win again, especially against these Bills. Marv Levy had gone 17–4 against Don Shula the previous nine years. But now Marv was 1–4 against Jimmy Johnson, and the Dolphins had swept the Bills for the first time since 1986.

"Ten years!" Kevin O'Neill yelled. "How about that sweep!"

Jimmy hoisted a Heineken. The pain was gone.

23

WRAPPING UP
THE SEASON

Maybe twenty minutes after the Buffalo game, someone handed Keith Sims a set of game statistics. The big guard quickly surveyed the only stats that mattered to him and called them out to tackle James Brown: The Dolphins had run for 145 yards and a 3.6-yard average.

He tossed the stats on the stool next to him and said if the Dolphins couldn't make the playoffs, the linemen at least wanted to get Karim Abdul-Jabbar his thousand yards.

"Let's see," I said. "He needed 112 or so going into tonight . . ."

"He had seventy-six today," Sims interrupted. "He needs thirty-six. I already did the math."

"Ah," I said, "that's a no-brainer against the Jets."

"There was a game or two we couldn't get him thirty-six," Sims said. "Nothing's a no-brainer around here. But that's something we want to do, I can tell you that."

Karim promised his linemen steak dinners if they got it. Richer backs had sprung for Rolexes.

"He isn't making big-enough bucks to give us watches," Keith said. "Of course, it's not a season you want to celebrate too much anyway. But that's the goal. We haven't had a thousand-yard rusher around here, we all know, since 1978, since Delvin Williams, and it's about darn time we got one. Longest streak without a thousand-yard rusher—that's one record we don't enjoy holding."

Why, an average of ten NFL backs a year had topped a thousand yards in the past seventeen years. To get a thousand in sixteen games, you didn't need to be a superstar (see Sammy Winder, John Settle, Barry Word, Gaston Green, and Ron Moore) or on a super team (see the Buccaneers' six thousand-yard seasons).

You only had to average 62.5 yards a game. But the last time the Dolphins had a thousand-yard rusher, the 49ers hadn't won a Super Bowl, Ronald Reagan hadn't become president, and Karim hadn't entered kindergarten.

A thousand yards was more Miami's millstone than milestone. Jimmy's goal was not a thousand-yard back but a consistent running game, and he admitted it wasn't there yet. Still, the Dolphins were running better at the goal line and game's end, and getting a thousand would mean they had begun the desired transformation, that they could rely more upon the run and hold on to the ball.

Dan Marino's miles always impressed people in his heyday with Shula and helped the 'Fins finish at or near the top of the league in total yards every year, but they didn't produce proportional points or championships, and, every year since 1984, Miami had more giveaways than takeaways. But the 1996 Dolphins would finish with a turnover differential of plus-twelve, second in the AFC and tied for fourth in the league, and Jimmy thought turnover ratio was the key to winning.

So when the Dolphins got the ball at their twenty with 1:43 left in the first half against Buffalo, Jimmy employed the same let-the-Bills-beat-themselves philosophy as in Super Bowl XXVII, when Buffalo had nine turnovers and lost, 52–17. In two meetings in 1996, the Bills committed six turnovers, the Dolphins none. Jimmy wouldn't try to go eighty yards with no time-outs when the Bills relied almost solely upon a great defense and pass rush, when the Miami offense had scored just five touchdowns in five games, when Marino threw five interceptions in two games, when Marino didn't have a supporting cast like the Magic Marks anymore.

In different circumstances, opponents, or players, Jimmy could be as aggressive as any coach. But he played percentages to win, not to showcase Marino, not to look flashy. "Our fans were booing at the half," Jimmy pointed out, "but they were cheering at the end because we won."

Don't think coaching philosophies make a difference? Contrast the first year of Jimmy's rebuilding to the second year of Rich Kotite's Jets disaster. The biggest problem in a season full of them, Kotite said, was turnover ratio. New York would finish last in the league at minus-twenty and last in victories at 1–15. "I've always asked, 'Did they do it to us or did we do it to ourselves?' I'd have to say we did it to ourselves," Kotite said.

And it wasn't because the Jets were talentless; they probably had more good players than the Dolphins. No, they were just clueless. James Lofton had played for Kotite and said, "It was utter chaos, guys wandering out late . . . no organization and no continuity." Seconded Boomer Esiason: "The guys didn't know what they were doing. There were schemes that had no rhyme or reason."

Why, after Miami beat New York back in September, Jimmy started rattling off the list of good players and said, "Hey, they're gonna be good. I wouldn't be surprised if they win soon when . . ." He looked at a couple of writers and stopped himself. "Well, I'm not telling you what I was thinking."

You mean when they get a real coach? Jimmy just smirked and walked away.

Two days before this season finale, Kotite said he'd walk away afterward— walk before he was shoved. He was 4–28 with the Jets, 4–35 counting his final seven games with the Eagles in 1994. Richie Kotite was Red Klotz in disguise.

What New York needed, ex-Jet Joe Klecko said, was a tough coach like Mike Ditka or Jimmy Johnson. "Professional football is a bunch of prima donnas, and I was one of them. Jimmy Johnson works through fear. But he wins with it. You can't be their friend."

Sunday, December 22, East Rutherford, New Jersey. Richie's Jets jumped to 14–0 leads both games against the Dolphins . . . and blew both. They would have shut out the Dolphins in the first half if not for a dumb interference penalty in the final seconds by Jets cornerback Ray Mickens.

"Mickens knows better than that," Jets personnel director Dick Haley, a former defensive back himself, said at halftime. He shook his head. "We're gonna find a way to lose this game, too." He was right. For the fifth time in 1996, the Jets would blow a double-digit lead.

Marino threw two touchdowns and Karim ran for another to make it 21–21. Karim's carries set up the go-ahead field goal late in the third quarter. Marino rifled a fifty-yard score for a ten-point bulge, and the Dolphins won, 31–28.

The Dolphins wanted to get Karim thirty-six yards for a thousand, and they got him 152 for 1,116. They wanted to run when it counted, and Karim ran out the final 3:33 to assure victory. They only beat the Jets, only finished 8–8, but it was a start. Winter solstice—the year's shortest day and longest night—had come the day before. From this day forward, each day would look a little brighter.

Players walked off the field and down the tunnel together, arms around each other, wishing each other well, sharing reverie and relief, some Jets still loitering near the Dolphins' locker room when Jimmy was ready for his last speech of a long, exhausting season. It was three days before Christmas, ten days before the new year, 252 days until the 1997 opener, and he was already impatient for 1997.

"You damn Jets guys!" he hollered. "If you want to be with the fucking Jets so bad, get your ass in the locker room after the damn ball game!"

The locker-room doors were slammed shut, and the psychologist turned to face his players for the last time in 1996. He did not wish them Merry Christmas or Happy New Year or Happy Holidays or, as he would say, "any of that bull."

His players gathered around him near the door. For some, it was an exit. For most, it was an opening. "Now," Jimmy began, "everybody remember one thing: All you had to do . . ." Pause. "Is win one game." Pause. "You win one game, and we'd still be playing. Think back, every one of you. Just take a second and think back over this season." Pause. "In any one of those games we lost, think about what *you* could have done . . . what *we* could have done." Pause. "I mean, we're damn close, guys. But we let some games slip through our damn hands when we shouldn't have let them slip through.

"Now, we made a lot of changes. We had a lot of guys on edge. I understand all that. Hey, there's gonna be a lot of off-season conversation. They're gonna be talking about free agents coming in. They're gonna be talking about guys that we draft. But let me explain one thing: If we don't win next year, it's because of the guys in this locker room. It won't be the new guys. We've got the nucleus of our team *right now*. So this is the group that will win. This group will win because it starts March third with our off-season program. We'll have continuity. We'll have a little help with a few new guys. But more than anything else, this bunch will be so much better. We're on the right track.

"Hey, let's have a hell of an off-season. Let's make up our minds that we're gonna go out there and play every week like we're capable of playing. If we do that, we'll have a hell of a football team. Ninety-seven on three, guys. Ninety-seven on three. One . . . two . . . three . . ."

And they shouted as loud as they could: "Ninety-seven!"

A few minutes later, Keith Sims limped out of the locker room. He had a date with a surgeon's scalpel in eleven days.

"As Coach Johnson said, one more win and we'd be in the playoffs now," Keith said. "That's what's most disappointing. We know we still have a ways to go. But we made progress. We wanted to get Karim his thousand yards. We focused on it all week. To eclipse the eleven-hundred-yard mark is something really special for Karim and this organization."

"It was satisfying," Karim said, "but I also broke the record for most carries."

Karim wanted to get stronger legs and surer hands. Zach Thomas wanted to gain a few pounds and flexibility. Shawn Wooden wanted to gain weight and strength to complete the switch from cornerback to safety.

Zach, Shawn, and Daryl Gardener made *USA Today*'s All-Rookie team. Zach, Daryl, Karim, and Larry Izzo made the *Pro Football Weekly*/Pro Football Writers of America All-Rookie team. Jimmy thought they achieved more than any of his Cowboys had as rookies and said nine or even all ten *could* become Pro Bowl players within three or four years. Zach and Larry were second alternates to the Pro Bowl and Karim a third alternate already. Eight rookies started at least once, more than any team in the league. Seven rookies started the last game. Six started regularly.

The boxed chart shows how the Dolphins' lineup changed from Jimmy Johnson's 1996 opener to the 1996 finale. Rookies are listed in italics.

POSITION	1996 OPENER	1996 FINALE
WR	Scott Miller	Fred Barnett
LT	Richmond Webb	Webb
LG	Keith Sims	Sims
C	Tim Ruddy	Ruddy
RG	Chris Gray	Everett McIver
RT	James Brown	Brown
TE	Keith Byars	Troy Drayton
WR	O. J. McDuffie	McDuffie
QB	Dan Marino	Marino
RB	*Karim Abdul-Jabbar*	*Abdul-Jabbar*
FB	*Stanley Pritchett*	*Pritchett*
LE	Trace Armstrong	*Shane Burton*
DT	*Daryl Gardener*	*Gardener*
DT	Tim Bowens	Bowens
RE	Daniel Stubbs	Stubbs
LLB	Dwight Hollier	Hollier
MLB	*Zach Thomas*	*Thomas*
RLB	Chris Singleton	*Anthony Harris*
LCB	Terrell Buckley	Buckley
RCB	Calvin Jackson	Jackson
SS	Louis Oliver	*Shawn Wooden*
FS	Gene Atkins	Sean Hill

Zach was runner-up as NFL Defensive Rookie of the Year and runner-up in single-season Miami tackles. Only four NFL players made more tackles than Miami's munchkin. Karim didn't have the tackle-breaking thighs of Emmitt Smith, but Jimmy thought he was close to Emmitt's ability to find the crease and hit it quickly. He scored eleven times, tied for the NFL rookie lead, and ran for 1,116 yards, second among NFL rookies and third in Dolphins history, 142 yards behind Delvin Williams and only one yard behind Hall of Famer Larry Csonka. Of course, Barry Sanders had the same number of carries but 437 more yards, and Napoleon Kaufman averaged 5.8 yards a carry to Karim's 3.6.

Wooden didn't start until the sixth game but still wound up second in tackles and stopped the big-play bleeding. Gardener didn't make many big plays, but Jimmy constantly praised his consistency and thought he played very well for a rookie defensive tackle. Izzo blocked a punt, tipped two more, ran twenty-six yards on a fake punt, and finished just one behind Kirby Dar Dar in special-teams tackles. Another rookie free agent, Anthony Harris, started the final three games at weakside linebacker and instantly produced more than millionaire slowpoke Chris Singleton.

Stanley Pritchett started all year and was a far better blocker and more elusive receiver than Keith Byars. Jerris McPhail was more of a big-play third-down back than Byars or Terry Kirby, and Jimmy thought he "could be a special player." Shane Burton started half the year and proved he could help the defensive line rotation, and the coaches thought Jeff Buckey could start at guard or tackle in 1997.

Of course, not every player who looks good as a rookie progresses, and some regress. "The ones who normally don't get better are the ones that aren't real sharp mentally. And our guys are sharp mentally, and so I think they are going to continue to get better," Jimmy said. "People may say, 'I don't know how much better they're going to get.' Well, in some cases, I don't know how much better they've *got* to get."

Fred Barnett made a miraculous recovery from major knee surgery, and if his pace over the final seven games were projected over a full year, he would make seventy-seven catches for 1,223 yards. But Jimmy expected him to be faster, better acquainted with the offense, and even more of a leader in 1997.

O. J. McDuffie had a career year as a solid possession receiver, but a big-play receiver still topped Gary Stevens's wish list. "If you had a Michael Irvin or Isaac Bruce . . ." he said dreamily in December, never realizing he'd get a first round pick with that potential, if not production.

He already planned to design more of the offense around Troy Drayton, the tight end obtained October 1 and signed December 23 to a four-year contract. "This may go down as one of the best trades Jimmy Johnson ever made: Drayton for Billy What's His Name [Milner]," Stevens gushed. Fourteen tight ends had come and gone in 1996 before Jimmy found a keeper in Drayton, who showed he could catch the ball deep (he burned Houston for fifty-one yards) and knock people down (he put a Buffalo linebacker flat on his back). Jimmy raved that Troy had "just scratched the surface" because of his late arrival, and Troy said he loved everybody here and vowed to prove the Rams wrong for trading him for Milner, who couldn't even start for a pathetic St. Louis line.

Craig Erickson showed he could win games while learning the offense in just six weeks. If Marino were hurt or ineffective again—and with Danny's age and mounting injuries, Jimmy fully expected that—then Craig would be a lot more effective as the backup the next three years and the likely successor whenever Marino retired after that.

Jimmy said Danny still would be a Hall of Fame quarterback more games than not, but because of age would have more clunkers and come back from injuries more slowly and less sharply. Still, forget about any trade rumors.

"Dan gives us the chance to achieve what I want, and that's to win it all," Jimmy said. "Even if he's not healthy for every game, he gives us an edge in a lot of those other games he is healthy. I'm not expecting to ride Dan Marino to the Super Bowl, but I feel he can help us win some close games on our way. So trading him would defeat my purpose. By trading him, I'd be grooming someone else for another coach. When we traded Herschel Walker, that was for four, five, six, seven years down the road. That's when those draft picks paid dividends. I'm not looking at the fourth, fifth, sixth, seventh year here. I'm looking at the second and the third.

"Dan was inconsistent at times, but that had more to do with his supporting cast than him. If he's not able to be a hundred percent, I've got a quarterback behind him who can win for us now. Craig will be an outstanding quarterback. I can't say how many, but I would anticipate that next year he will be the guy in some games. Craig is a hell of a player."

And they got Air Marino's heir apparent for minimal cost, just as they got nine sacks from Daniel Stubbs for his $325,000 base salary, while his predecessor, Marco Coleman, was giving the Chargers four sacks in return for their three-year, $9.6 million deal. Zach gave the Dolphins 180 tackles for $131,000, while Bryan Cox gave the Bears ninety-nine tackles and a career-threatening injury for their four-year, $13.2 million deal. And Terrell Buckley gave the Dolphins six steals for his $700,000 salary, while Troy Vincent gave the Eagles three interceptions for their five-year, $16.5 million deal.

Oh, Jimmy had a trio of third- or fourth-round picks who didn't make it in Miami, and he signed some cheap free agents who proved no bargain. But the only personnel decision that really hurt was choosing Charles Jordan (seven catches) over Irving Fryar (career-high eighty-eight catches and eleven touchdowns).

T-Buck, dismissed as a bust at the year's start, responded to Jimmy's positive, more aggressive style by making so many plays that opponents quit throwing at him. Trace Armstrong, a bust at season's start, responded to Jimmy's goading and scolding with a career-high twelve sacks.

The Dolphins did not have Dallas's stars. They would not have the salary-cap room to add free agent stars until 1998, which meant any improvement in 1997 would come mostly from the draft, a couple of mid-priced free agents, and the current nucleus. But at least they had thrown the mutineers overboard, and the flotsam would be gone before the '97 season started. As tumultuous as '96 had been, it was better than Jimmy's first year at the University of Miami, when he was the Oklahoma hayseed, or his first year in Dallas, when he was the college coach trashing America's Team.

"If anything, this group of players has been more positive and second-guessed less than I would have expected," Jimmy said. He admitted his overhaul probably cost the Dolphins a playoff spot, that he had lied when he was hired and announced they didn't need an overhaul.

"I didn't want to send the message to the players that we'd sacrifice this year," he said. "So I did fudge that. I knew we weren't gonna sell out just to win games this year. I knew I wouldn't keep aging veterans just to win this year.

"I could have maybe used Jack Del Rio at weakside linebacker and won another game. Singleton wasn't very good. But then we would have had to change in 1997. The bottom line is, I didn't want players in the last year or two of their contract. That doesn't help me in two or three years. The only exception would be Danny. I'd rather throw rookies in the lineup now and give them experience rather than try to replace veterans piecemeal.

"We lost some games because I was just learning who the players were, seeing who would make plays, who would not. But if we did something this year that caused us to lose one or two games, but it helps us win one or two or three or four more games next year, we did the right thing.

"It's the difference between being as good as you can be the year after next or being in the middle of the pack every year. I don't want to be pretty good two or three years in a row. I want to be *real good*. We're not just trying to make the playoffs. We're trying to be the best team in the NFL. And so some of the moves we've made have not been for the short term. We're not trying to do a Band-Aid effect. We're trying to contend for a championship."

That was the difference between Jimmy and almost every other NFL coach. Icons like Don Shula and Tom Landry and Chuck Noll had too much pride to tear down and start over, and so after their Super Bowl days, they still made the playoffs more often than not, but never won it all again. Lesser coaches had too little job security to start from scratch. Look what happened to the Rams' Rich Brooks: He developed Isaac Bruce, Eddie Kennison, Lawrence Phillips, and Tony Banks—but someone else will reap the rewards of his patience.

Wayne Huizenga said when he hired Jimmy, he realized the Dolphins might regress before they progressed. But now the honeymoon is over, and Huizenga expects what Jimmy publicly promised: The Dolphins will win the AFC East and some playoff games in '97, then make a run at Super Bowl XXXIII when it comes to Pro Player Stadium.

Don's 1995 Dolphins went 9–8 with vets and were embarrassed in the first round of the playoffs. Jimmy's 1996 Dolphins went 8–8 with the league's youngest starting lineup, and were eliminated from the playoffs earlier than any Miami club since 1988. But Jimmy told team president Eddie Jones he thought winning the last two games might leave the players with a better feeling than making the playoffs "and getting your ears pinned back."

Jimmy promised his club would be the team to beat, but it was Don Shula who went to the Super Bowl, where he was elected to the Pro Football Hall of Fame. Jimmy promised his club would play its best ball in November and December, but it was Bill Parcells who turned a humbled club into the AFC champion and joined Shula as the only men to take two franchises to the Super Bowl.

Don Shula and Bill Parcells went to the Super Bowl, and Jimmy Johnson did not.

Keith Byars went to the Super Bowl, and Jimmy Johnson did not.

Vinny Testaverde went to the Pro Bowl, and Dan Marino did not.

Jacksonville went to the playoffs, and Miami did not.

And maybe some people even believed Byars's boasts about proving Jimmy wrong. Puhhhh-lease. You wanna bet against a card shark, a Shark Among Dolphins?

Show me the money.

24
MOTIVATING PEOPLE

Jimmy Johnson believes people from players to press to presidents need motivating. Psychology—the study of the mind and human behavior—isn't just a college degree on his shelf, it's a lifelong fascination. He planned to coach corporations before he planned to coach football players, and, to this day, he teaches more than just players.

Throughout these pages, you have seen examples of how Jimmy tried to mold players and press to his way of thinking. But he also motivated the Dolphins' computer programmer just by saying hello in the hallway and his secretary by explaining his expectations on even the slightest detail (example: don't let a single caller ever get stuck with voice mail).

He challenged scouting assistant Anthony Hunt to top his predecessor on what could have been seen as a thankless job: plastering the locker-room bulletin board with items about the opponent. Hunt relished the challenge. He searched newspapers and magazines and the Internet for headlines and foes' quotes that might inspire the Dolphins. He photocopied million-dollar bills with Drew Bledsoe's face on them. He crawled under a bench and duct-taped a tape recorder to it, and it took the players half an hour before they found the annoying tape of jet sounds during Jets week. He put up cactus for Arizona week, dummies of cowboys with rifles and pistols during Dallas week. And when Jimmy publicly praised Hunt as his all-time best, Anthony got his name in the local papers, got interviewed on local TV, carried himself a little taller, and added seven to ten hours to his workweek just on the off chance that something he did might tweak a player for a play or two.

Jimmy coached his coaches, too. If one came to him about a problem player, Jimmy wouldn't flat-out tell him what to do. He'd say, "Well, you know him better than I do. What do you think works? Whatever you want to do, it's your call."

And he'd let the assistant verbalize a solution, and if it didn't sound right, he might say, "Hmmmm. That could work. Or maybe you could try X. I don't know. What do you think?" and he'd slyly coax his coach so he never grumbled, "I don't want to do Jimmy's fucking idea." If he liked his aide's answer, his eyes would light up and he'd nod his head as if the coach were soooo smart and say, "Hey, you may have hit on it right there," and the coach would go away thinking it was his idea all along.

Though his blowups drew more attention, Jimmy believed more in positive than negative reinforcement. He motivated some people because they feared him, others because they liked him, but most because they respected him and believed he would win again. He dared. He encouraged. He pulled out a priest and a no-armed man. He flashed a Super Bowl ring. He cited examples of players who failed or flourished. He drew analogies from his favorite book, *Flow*.

"The point it makes is about the mountain climber who's hanging on by his fingernails," Jimmy said. "He's focused. His focus is to stay alive and get to the top of the mountain. It's not what happened yesterday. It's not what's gonna happen tomorrow. It's not any other people. I mean, when it's a life-and-death situation, you have focus. And so when a player says he's focused for a game, he's focused to a degree. A lot of people say they're focused, but in reality, distractions cause them to lose focus. I want my players focused."

Their minds were muscles to be worked harder than their biceps. "Let the mind control the body, not the body control the mind," he liked to say.

And because of his reputation for winning and motivating, corporations made him one of the country's highest-paid motivational speakers. Jimmy demanded and got $30,000 for local speeches, $40,000 and sometimes even $50,000 if he had to waste a day out of town. He did ten to fifteen talks each of the two years he wasn't coaching. He planned six to eight in the 1997 off-season.

Could a half-hour speech really be worth all that money? What did businessmen get from one?

Here, for your mere $25, is a peek at what some people pay $50,000 to get. Now, this isn't every word, and it doesn't convey every emotion, but imagine you were at the swank PGA National Resort, listening in with about eighty of the top sales and operations managers of Hostess Frito-Lay in February 1997.

"We talk about what Hostess Frito-Lay has to do is build the best team," HFL president Chris O'Leary began. "There's no one better at building a team than Jimmy Johnson. He's one of the most successful coaches in football, and coaches, period. We've talked about the characteristics of great teams: great leaders, great players, teamwork, drive, spirit, and uncompromising standards. So, ladies and gentlemen, please welcome Jimmy Johnson."

They applauded furiously, laughed loudly at the punch line of Jimmy's opening, and listened intently as he talked about "being the best."

"Now, as I understand it, Frito-Lay made a turnaround in '94 and had outstanding years in '95 and '96 and this relates well to what we did with the Cowboys," Jimmy said. "We had a turnaround and we won the Super Bowl. People asked me after the first one, 'What do you do now?' I said, 'There's only one way: Never compromise.' And we didn't, and we came back and won again.

"Then I left Dallas and did TV. Terry Bradshaw told me on the air, 'If you had stayed, you would have had an older team that knew how to do it. You obviously would have pulled back and been easier on them.' I said, 'Terry, knowing human nature, I would have been a tougher SOB than ever.' Human nature is such that with success—like this company has had—it's easy to pull back and get complacent. It would have been easy for me to say, 'Emmitt Smith will be ready on game day. Michael Irvin knows what to do. I'll pull back, and they'll be okay.' In psychology, they have studied companies and countries and teams, and with success came complacency. Every individual feels, 'I'm not getting my fair share of accolades. I'm not making enough money.' And they start pointing fingers. As you have success, jealousies creep in. That's why I would have been a tougher SOB if I had stayed.

"What relates to your company? There are three things you have to handle: How you deal with people, how you deal with yourself, and how you deal with a team."

He told the snack salesmen he judged each employee individually; the ones who work harder and produce more get more rewards and leeway. He recounted how he fired unproductive John Roper for sleeping in a meeting but would have whispered for Dan Marino to wake up.

"If you have a top salesman, are you gonna fine him if he's ten minutes late? No! But if you have someone who's not productive and is late for meetings, what are you gonna do? Like I tell my guys, 'I don't fine you. When you're late for a meeting, you fine yourself. You're costing yourself money. Don't think because you're my friend that I'll be easy on you. Personalities mean nothing. If you're not productive and you don't work, you won't be here.'

"There's a saying here, and it's important: Treat a person as he is and he will remain as he is. Treat him as he could be and should be, and he will become what he could be and should be. Psychology is self-fulfilling prophecy. Psychology is the Pygmalion effect.

"Dr. King did a study with unskilled laborers. He told a welding instructor, 'We've done tests, and we know who will do the best in your class. Chris will do well, and Doug won't.' Dr. King hadn't done any studies, but the instructor didn't know that. He'd say, 'Chris, that's good, you're gonna do good.' Because of positive expectations, Chris got worked with. Doug didn't get worked with because the manager didn't expect him to be good.

"So if you expect your secretary to be efficient, treat her that way. Reward the things she does right. The things she does wrong, say something like, 'I'd like this to be done better, but I know you can do it. I know you're good.' If you expect her to be better, she will be. If you expect someone to buy from you and you know when they walk in the door they're gonna buy, then some way, somehow, you're gonna make them buy. Your expectations—controlling your mind—will control your results.

"I've told my players, 'You can't control how tall you're gonna be, but you can control your attitude and effort, and there's a direct correlation between attitude and effort and performance.' If you say, 'Today I'm gonna do it the right way, I'm gonna go in an hour early and stay an hour late,' that's motivation. But it's got to become a habit. If you do it today and tomorrow and the next day, it becomes a habit. That's when performance comes.

"You can say to me, 'Hey, you got a Super Bowl ring. You were lucky.' Lucky is the used car salesman. He thinks he's an unlucky guy. At four o'clock, he decides no one is coming in and he goes home, tells his wife, 'No one came in. I'm so unlucky. Get me a beer.' The lucky salesman stays until five o'clock, and a guy comes in and says, 'I want to buy a fleet of cars from you.'

"You can say we got lucky drafting Daryl Johnston or Zach Thomas. We were lucky because we did our homework. We took forty-five people to Indianapolis for the scouting combine a few weeks ago. We didn't measure just their height and weight and speed and strength. We did a psychology test and an IQ test. We took our security man, Stu Weinstein, to check on them with the FBI, the local police, the college police. I took our priest, Father Leo Armbrust. One day he interviewed fifty-one players. Why? Father Leo is a smart guy. When we get ready to draft, I want everybody to feed me information on what type of person the player is."

What type of person does he want? One like Dan Marino, who's so committed he apologizes for getting hurt. Not ones like the five veterans who didn't attend the 1996 off-season conditioning program; only one survived training camp. Not ones like the rookies who were out of shape and cramped up when they arrived in Miami; he told them if they cramped in camp, they'd be gone. Cut one slack and everyone will want it, and so no one gets it.

He told about giving the Cowboys a night off before their second Super Bowl and how Erik Williams got so drunk and hung over that he missed a media session the next morning and was fined $10,000. That night, Jimmy reminded everyone they shouldn't cheat themselves or their teammates out of a lifetime dream for "a few hours of hee-hee haw-haw."

"I don't know if that talk had anything to do with us winning again, but I know this: If people are not committed to the common cause, it's hard to win," Jimmy said.

"There's only one way to win: Discipline. Attitude. Working hard. And working together. There's no magic formula. You can't read a piece of paper and find the secret. If you work hard every day and treat people right, then positive things happen.

"Some coaches would just get up here and tell you, 'We're gonna kick ass,' and they can't tell you much more. I believe there's a way to succeed, a way to win. I tell my players, 'Maybe Rhonda and I had a fight. Maybe I'm sick. Maybe I'm depressed. Maybe my family has health problems and they're on my mind. But if I'm so weak-minded that outside distractions affect how I treat you, then I'm cheating you. I have to be strong-minded enough to be demanding of you and expect the best of you.' You have to control your own mind. How good do you want to be? You have to wake up every day and say, 'I'm gonna do it today.' "

And when he was through, they stood as one and gave him a standing ovation. Hostess Frito-Lay was based in Toronto, yet these Canadians admired Jimmy Johnson so well that they hired him to follow Norman Schwarzkopf (1995) and Colin Powell (1996) as their annual keynote speaker.

"Colin Powell really impressed me. Jimmy Johnson did, too," said Gerry Bouffard, a bilingual Montreal manager. "I will remember that one saying—'Treat people like they could be and should be, and they will become what they could be and should be'—for a long time. All the people here are responsible for people, so we're like coaches, too. Jimmy Johnson is a role model for us."

And the boss said Jimmy was well worth the money.

"I thought he did a great job," O'Leary said. "He understands what business is all about, and he can freely communicate. You look for a person known for winning—someone who knows how to build a team, assess what's going on, and motivate people. That's part of our success, and Jimmy is perfect to talk about those things. There's a huge correlation between business and sports. Organizations are organizations. Teamwork is teamwork. Managing people is managing people, whether in snacks or football."

25
PICKING PEOPLE

Bob Ackles laughed about the incongruity with his buddy the Harvard Business School dean: Fortune 500 companies swooped into Harvard every spring and, with scant investigation, threw handsome salaries at anybody with a Harvard MBA. Each NFL team invested thousands of hours and hundreds of thousands of dollars just to draft, let alone sign, a handful of prospects. They did physical, psychological, intelligence, medical, and security checks. They examined everything about prospects from their driver's license number to their sleeve length.

And nobody picked people better than Jimmy Johnson. He drafted more stars in Dallas than any two teams had, and his first Dolphins draft class was the league's finest. The Associated Press wrote he was the NFL's premier draftsman, "probably a better personnel man than he is a coach."

But Jimmy was a full-time coach and part-time personnel man, and personnel was a year-round collaboration. Ackles oversaw Jimmy's scouts in Dallas and Miami, filled whole rooms with black binders crammed with exhaustive research on every prospect, suspect, and reject. The Dolphins began preparing for the 1997 draft class two or three weeks after the 1996 draft, when college scouting director Tom Braatz went to the BLESTO scouting combine meetings to discuss the upcoming college seniors. Then Braatz and his scouts fanned out across the country, spending endless hours traveling, working out players, studying game tapes, interviewing coaches and trainers, and grading players before Jimmy and his coaches ever got involved.

The coaches watched college games when they weren't traveling or working, even studied some game tapes, but their first real look at the draft prospects came January 13 through 16, 1997, at the Senior Bowl.

Scouting assistant Anthony Hunt flew into Mobile, Alabama, to check on arrangements Sunday, January 12. The rest of the scouts and coaches flew in Monday morning on Wayne Huizenga's private plane, arriving in time to attend both of the day's practices. They huddled for three hours that night over beer and finger food, the scouts giving capsule summaries of every prospect on the North and South rosters. The scouts did not go into great detail or give precise grades because they wanted the coaches to keep open minds on players; these synopses merely helped the coaches target players. Then Jimmy drank some more with his old coordinator, Norv Turner, who reviewed every player on the North team Norv was coaching. Norv liked his huge quarterback, Jim Druckenmiller.

These drinking nights could be productive. Tuesday, Jimmy imbibed not only with the Dolphins but with 49ers personnel director Vinny Cerrato, who clued him in on the coming coaching storm in San Francisco, and John Hendrickson, one of his former players and now a Mississippi State assistant who offered a good scouting report on defensive lineman Terry Day. And each noon he traded insights as he jogged with buddy Dave Wannstedt.

NFL teams always sent at least a few scouts to the Hula, Blue-Gray, East-West, and small-college all-star games, but almost every employed coach and scout—and just about as many who were looking for work—came to the Senior Bowl. This had evolved into the unofficial coaching convention. Why? Because all coaches save the two Super Bowl staffs had finished playing. Because head coaches had been fired and hired and people were interviewing for jobs and swapping information. Because the Senior Bowl was coached by pro staffs that put the prospects through physical practices and drills the pros wanted to see. "If the players want a vacation All-Star game, they go to the other games," Jimmy said. "They know if they come here, they'll have physical practices."

And that's what Jimmy wanted to see. He first saw Daryl Gardener at the 1996 Senior Bowl. Now, after talking with his scouts, he already had targeted some players he thought were special. He carried a depth chart with stars and circles around promising players, little notes scratched beside them. But Jimmy didn't need to refer to his notes often; he had a phenomenal memory, and when he met Clemson cornerback Dexter McCleon, he rattled off his exact height, weight, forty speed, and Wonderlic intelligence score. McCleon intrigued Jimmy, and he liked the confidence the corner showed when he looked the coach in the eye as they chatted for a couple of minutes. Jimmy would order his secondary coaches to study a lot of game film, go to Clemson, and investigate McCleon further.

As hundreds of scouts and coaches circled the various position drills Wednesday, Jimmy crowded close to the defensive linemen, watching Terry Day, the lineman John Hendrickson recommended; Pratt Lyons, the big guy from little Troy State; and Jason Taylor, a quick but undersized pass rusher from little Akron. Some teams virtually refused to take players from small schools. Jimmy would take the chance because he'd hit on prospects like Central State's Erik

Williams, now one of the game's premier tackles. He checked out a big-college star, Florida State's Reinard Wilson. He loved Reinard's work ethic—he could bench press five hundred pounds—but if he were already a weight-room fanatic and yet only 6'2", 250, how much bigger could he get, and would he be pushed around in the pros?

He checked out three other priority positions—receivers, linebackers, and defensive backs. He loved Texas cornerback Bryant Westbrook, but figured he'd have to move from the draft's fifteenth pick to about the fifth to get him. He watched the feet and hips of Alabama's Ralph Staten, trying to project whether he could switch from college linebacker to pro safety, the way Darren Woodson had with the Cowboys. He watched Maryland's Chad Scott, wondering if he would be quick enough to play cornerback or would have to move to safety.

Mark Duffner, the deposed Maryland coach, sidled up beside Jimmy and recommended Scott. Jimmy peppered him with questions: "You think he can play safety? Smart kid? Work hard? Hit hard?"

Duffner kept replying affirmatively, and concluded, "He'll knock the shit out of people. You'd love to have him."

"I kinda like him, more as a safety," Jimmy said.

Duffner nodded and said, "If you ever need a defensive assistant, I hope you'll keep me in mind."

"I sure will," Jimmy said.

He talked a bit with ex-aide Ernie Zampese and TV insider/oddsmaker Danny Sheridan, then sprinted over to Ralph Cindrich, who represented Craig Erickson. Once, Cindrich and a drunken Jimmy were pulled apart before they got into a fistfight, but Cindrich earned Jimmy's respect, and even though Erickson was signed for 1997, Jimmy told Ralph he wanted to start talking extension in the fall because Craig "can be The Guy" if Marino is injured and ineffective and not worth re-signing after the 1999 season.

Practice over, Jimmy asked McCleon, Wilson, and Staten questions for a few minutes, and shook hands with KC general manager Carl Peterson, who'd given him a fifth-round pick for Pete Stoyanovich. "What is it with me and you and kickers?" Peterson asked. "Every time I get one from you, he ain't worth shit the next year."

Jimmy nodded sympathetically, but on the car ride back to the hotel, he couldn't help but gloat as he recounted the conversation to Ackles and Pro personnel director Tom Heckert. He said he wasn't sure if Staten could play safety, but he could be a good special-teams player and a linebacker with ten more pounds. Ackles said the scouts' grades weren't that good; they would study him some more. Jimmy said McCleon wanted to play for the Dolphins and his agents promised he wouldn't hold out.

"The guys I target now, we might pull back on when we find out more,"

Jimmy explained to me as Heckert drove. "You start with one group, and some drop out and others catch your eye. We'll go to Indianapolis [where the top 320 prospects would converge for running, jumping, and medical tests plus one-on-one interviews at the annual February scouting combine] and then have our coaches and scouts watch more films and go to colleges for workouts. We won't really target who we'll draft until the last few weeks before the draft. That's when Tom [Braatz], Tom [Heckert], Bob, and myself will meet with each scout one at a time and go over each player. Then we'll meet with each coach individually.

"Kevin O'Neill will brief us with reports from the Dolphins' doctors and his interviews with college trainers. I rely on Kevin a lot. He's smart, very efficient, knows what I'm looking for, and really works at it. He's in a position to find out stuff other people cannot. The college trainer may bullshit a coach, but not a trainer. Just like the strength coaches. You don't bullshit your peers. John Gamble and Brad Roll will report back on their interviews with the college strength coaches. The NFL furnishes us with [security] background checks, but they're not quite as in depth as what Stu Weinstein gives us. He'll have every altercation with the law, right down to speeding tickets. He spends extra time investigating the players we target. We'll hash and rehash those players a minimum of three or four times, then start our final rankings."

Each player would be ranked on two big boards: a master list of all players and then position-by-position lists.

This was the same personnel process Jimmy used in Dallas, with one addition. He retained the thirty-minute psychology test the Dolphins gave to most top prospects. From a list of 360 adjectives, players chose which words others would use to describe them and then which ones the players would use. This was the third year the Dolphins had used the test. The Dolphins used three psychologists in 1996 to develop personality profiles, measuring such traits as aggressiveness, coachability, work habits, and self-confidence, then chose the one they felt was most accurate, Dr. Dave Michiels. Certain traits are more important for certain positions; the Dolphins want cornerbacks and quarterbacks to be confident, defensive linemen to be aggressive and physical.

A bad psychological profile might red flag a player, but was only one part of evaluating character, less important than the interviews with the player, his coaches, and trainers. Even Father Leo got involved, interviewing 162 players in Indianapolis for about eight to ten minutes, trying to gauge motivation and intelligence. Jimmy thought both traits were huge, but he judged intelligence less on the twenty-minute Wonderlic test and more on whether a kid played smart. He had analyzed his mistakes and decided the biggest came when he drafted guys who weren't smart. "Nine of ten have failed. They never improve," Jimmy said. One prospect said, in all seriousness, that he was raised by wolves. Jimmy did not draft him.

Bob Ackles drew up a chart for the scouts and coaches headlined, "Jimmy Johnson's Five Most Important Characteristics for Draft Choices."

Each subheading was followed by a list and a photo.

Under "Intelligence" was a photo of Ackles with a hammer, and Jimmy saying, "Bob, hit me over the head the next time I want to draft a dumb guy."

Under "Works Hard" was a drawing of a weight lifter.

Under "Gym Rat" was a drawing of a rat bouncing a basketball.

Under "Character" was the question "Is he a bum?" and a photo of a Bourbon Street bum.

Under "Playmaker" was a photo of Zach beating Buffalo with an interception return.

Zach's success didn't affect just Miami; it affected the whole NFL. Scouts trekked to Appalachian State, three hours of hairpin turns and mountain roads from the nearest airport, to study 5'9" linebacker Dexter Coakley, grumbling to Dolphins scouts, "I'm here because of Zach Thomas."

He did draft Zach Thomas, even though his scouts didn't grade him that highly, because three coaches saw him before the draft, and special-teams coach Mike Westhoff begged for him. So the Dolphins ranked him higher than his numbers indicated. They considered him the top middle linebacker in a weak draft for middle linebackers, but when they checked around the league, they felt confident no one else would take him before the fifth round. And so while he would have been a good pick in even the first round, they waited until the fifth and got a steal. Jimmy's draft was all about filtering through reams of information, targeting players who fit his system, and then picking them just before someone else would, when they were good values.

Zach probably would have been overlooked by Don Shula because he didn't fit Tom Olivadotti's system and Shula used his coaches to study veteran free agents more than rookies. "Coach Johnson watches more film," Anthony Hunt said. "There's not a name he doesn't know." Another staff member told the *Sun-Sentinel* Jimmy "wants to hit on every pick. Shula wanted to hit on the first- and second-rounders and then get whoever."

Shula wasn't alone. A few teams, some successfully, others not so, did not involve their coaches at all. When Ackles went to Arizona to reverse the Cardinals' pathetic draft history, he insisted the scouts and coaches work together; the scouts had never even asked the coaches what qualities they most coveted at their positions. The great Cowboys team of the seventies and the Redskins of the eighties were built with little input from the coaches. But Jimmy came to the Cowboys and Dolphins only when it was understood the coaches would be very involved in picking their own players and he would have final say.

"That way the coach can not only put together the team he wants and that fits his personnel, he can also know that much more about the player and motivating him," Jimmy reasoned. "If the coach picks the player, then when he's got him on the field, he's going to make it work, whereas if someone else picks the player, the coach may say, 'Hey, I didn't even want this guy in the first place,' and he won't work as hard to make him successful.

"A lot of teams don't have the coaches, the trainers, the strength coaches, the security director as involved as we do. We have a lot of former college coaches who recruited and put together a lot of good teams. We're used to evaluating talent. It really wouldn't be smart not to utilize the experience our coaches have. I can pick up a phone and a college coach will be honest with me because I've known him for twenty years. They're not gonna sell me just because he's their guy. Just like Mark Duffner today. He's not gonna lie to me about Chad Scott. But if I don't know the college coach and call him cold, he's going to avoid telling me some of the negatives. You keep on grinding and you keep on grinding and someone might say something that throws up a red flag, and the more you investigate, you find it's a problem. As much as anything, this is a process of elimination. The more you find out, the more problems you eliminate."

Next, he eliminated some problems in free agency. J. B. Brown and Chris Singleton were released. Steve Emtman and Scott Miller refused pay cuts and were dropped. Charles Jordan slashed his salary and came back. Louis Oliver, Randal Hill, Michael Stewart, and Robert Bailey were also dropped. Bernie Kosar retired. Dwight Hollier, Daniel Stubbs, Bernie Parmalee, Lamar Thomas, Irving Spikes, Frank Wainright, Tim Jacobs, and O. J. Brigance re-signed. Stubbs said he rejected an offer from Philly worth $300,000 to $400,000 more because he had business interests in South Florida, loved the warm weather, loved playing for Jimmy and a winner.

Even opponents signed more because of Jimmy and Miami than money. George Teague, a playmaking free safety since his Alabama days, turned down a lot more from Baltimore because he "really wanted to play for Jimmy Johnson." Cornerback Clayton Holmes, who once ran a 4.23 forty for Jimmy's Cowboys but had been suspended a year for drugs, re-signed with his old boss. Corey Harns, who could play safety or corner, got the most money.

Two or three of those newcomers could start in 1997 alongside T-Buck in a revamped secondary. Jimmy said one of his biggest first-year mistakes was taking three fourths of the year to recognize he needed to upgrade his safeties. Now he had done so and could draft different areas. Tight end Walter Reeves and wideout Lawrence Dawsey signed as cheap backups.

Teague, Harris, and Dawsey had all played with Terrell Buckley, and T-Buck, once scorned by Jimmy the commentator and coach, once forced to take a pay cut by Jimmy, convinced them to come and persuaded Jordan to take a pay cut. Even Jordan called Teague four times a day to recruit him. T-Buck repeatedly called Dawsey, his college roommate and fellow Christian. His life had come full circle. "The Lord's blessed me," he said.

The Dolphins worked out but decided they couldn't afford veteran kicker Jeff Wilkins, opting to risk a 1997 playoff spot on unproven kickers. Joe Nedney would be challenged by young Olindo Mare, but Nedney and the coaches thought removing an inconsistent false step from his approach could boost his accuracy.

Prized linebackers Darrin Smith and Micheal Barrow were also deemed too expensive. Even middling linebackers Ron George, Mike Jones, and Jim Schwantz; defensive backs Darrien Gordon, Brock Marion, and Dave Thomas; wideouts Kevin Williams, Eric Metcalf, Nate Singleton, and Brett Perriman; guard Ben Coleman; and defensive linemen Michael McCrary and Ernie Logan proved too expensive. "Every time I look at the salaries these free agents are asking," Jimmy said, "I tell our coaches, 'Get back in the film room and start getting ready for the draft.' "

Forty-five Dolphins, including every coach, scout, five doctors, three trainers, and even their priest evaluated players at the scouting combine. They made flights and phone calls across the country. These evaluations were exhaustive. Besides the psychological, intelligence, and physical tests, players were asked for their Social Security, driver's license, and phone numbers. They not only were measured for height and weight, they paraded in front of the scouts wearing nothing but shorts, and a photographer took photos of front and rear views. "That's an experience in itself," Arizona State quarterback Jake Plummer said. "I was with Keith Poole, and we're nothing to look at. We're skinny. I could see the scouts elbowing each other and getting a laugh out of it. But come game day, I put on the pads and play my heart out. Size has a lot to do with it, but a lot has to do with heart."

The Dolphins agreed, but they looked at body structure and decided pass rushers Jason Taylor and Nicholas Lopez could put on enough weight to become good pro defensive ends, just as Tony Tolbert had for the Cowboys. They looked at calves and thighs; skinny calves usually offered speed and quickness, but a speedster with thick thighs might be better suited to running back than cornerback.

Players were measured for their times in the ten, twenty, forty, and short shuttle, for distances in vertical and broad jumps, for repetitions in the 225-pound bench press. Jimmy was more interested in quickness than straight-line speed. The bench indicated not only strength but workout dedication.

The Dolphins gave numerical grades to players in thirteen general areas: athleticism, size, durability, learning ability, competitiveness/toughness, production, work habits, coachability, consistency, citizenship/character, tolerance of pain, leadership, and positive attitude.

Then they graded players in thirteen areas specific to a position, as ranked by the position coach. For instance, at the top of the list for quarterbacks were arm

strength, quickness of release, accuracy, ability to throw on the run, touch/antici-
pation, and vision/reaction. Most important for a wide receiver: hands, competi-
tiveness/ability to make a tough catch, concentration, adjusting to the ball,
tendency to fumble, ability to take a hit, ability to get open, release off the line of
scrimmage, and speed/acceleration.

The scouts and coaches then listed strong and weak points and wrote summaries of every player they evaluated.

All this information was recorded on computer and paper. The Dolphins typically had ten to twenty pages even on rejects. They had sixteen pages in their file
on their eventual first-round pick. That didn't include notes by Jimmy, Bob, the
assistant coaches' personal interviews, and the final "director's report" sum-
mary, and it would have been more except Yatil Green had left the University of
Miami a year early. They had twenty-one pages on third-round pick Jason Taylor, even though he went to Akron, 1,200 miles away.

Jimmy loved middle-round picks, and he had five extras. The league awarded
three compensatory picks at the end of the third round for the free agent losses
of Marco Coleman, Bryan Cox, Troy Vincent, and Irving Fryar, and he picked
up a fourth for Terry Kirby and a fifth for Pete Stoyanovich. That gave him six of
the first ninety-six picks and eight of the first 123.

The league allowed him to bring in twenty players from out of town for final
workouts and interviews, and he used them all. But he could bring in as many
local players as he liked, an advantage because Florida was the nation's top talent source.

So he watched Yatil Green work out in person at UM, again in Davie, and
then, ten days before the draft, Yatil spent several hours allaying the questions of
Jimmy, offensive coordinator Gary Stevens, and receivers coach Larry Seiple.
UM coach Butch Davis, one of Jimmy's former assistants, told the Dolphins all
about Yatil: about his great athletic ability, how he had been one of three Hurricanes suspended for using a limousine paid for by an agent, how he had missed
time with a pulled hamstring, how he had taken himself out of a game, how he
liked to goof off with the guys. Yet he was a 6'2", 205-pound playmaker with 4.3
speed and a 40.5-inch vertical jump, and the 'Fins desperately needed a big-
player receiver. The 1996 Dolphins had only four touchdowns of fifty yards or
more, just one by a wide receiver. By contrast, the champion Packers had a
dozen during the regular season and three more in the Super Bowl.

A couple of weeks before the draft, Jimmy thought Yatil might be available
when the Dolphins picked, especially if they moved up a few spots. But when
the Dolphins called around the league to learn who liked whom, and then did
mock drafts the day or two before the draft, Yatil did not last until their pick in
even one scenario. Jimmy was certain the Bucs or Giants would take him.

In fact, he feared all his top players would be gone. He liked only nine guys, and since the Dolphins were picking fifteenth, chances didn't look good. The day before the draft, he thought the only top player who would fall to him would be Jim Druckenmiller, and he considered taking him even though he had Marino and Erickson. More likely, though, he figured he'd trade down to the end of the first round or the start of the second and get some extra picks.

He dotted his nine favorite players and put another dot beside the five guys he felt were worth trading up for. To move to the first, second, or third picks for tackle Orlando Pace, defensive lineman Darrell Russell, or cornerback Shawn Springs, he would have to give up most of his draft picks, and he would not do that. He would have taken Bryant Westbrook or Peter Boulware at four, and offered Baltimore his first, next year's second, and a bonus pick for that selection, but Baltimore wanted this year's second, and Jimmy said no. Baltimore took Boulware fourth, and Detroit nabbed Westbrook fifth. Seattle took tackle Walter Jones sixth, and two Jimmy favorites—linebacker James Farrior and cornerback Tommy Knight—went eighth and ninth.

But when the Giants and Saints stunned everyone by taking wideout Ike Hilliard seventh and guard Chris Naeole tenth, Jimmy started feeling better. Butch Davis was visiting, and Jimmy called him aside to talk about Yatil again. Jimmy thought Tampa would take Yatil twelfth, but when the Bucs took scatback Warrick Dunn, Jimmy figured that either Yatil or Reinard Wilson would be available fifteenth. He would have liked to slide down a few spots and take the undersized defensive end, but when Cincinnati decided Wilson could be a pass-rushing 3–4 linebacker and took him fourteenth, the Dolphins' answer was obvious.

Still, a couple of teams offered trades, and Ackles kept the best offer, San Francisco, on hold on his phone while Jimmy got out of his seat and walked to the back of his "war room," where scout Jeff Smith had Yatil and agent Drew Rosenhaus on another phone line, their lives on the line. It was a Florida native and UM receiver's dream: the Dolphins and Dan Marino.

"Tell me I'm your guy," Yatil told Smith. "Please tell me I'm your guy."

"Hold on," Smith said.

Yatil held for nine nervous minutes. Jimmy got on the phone. Yatil handed his phone to Drew. Jimmy told Drew he had San Francisco on the other line and he could trade this pick if Drew were going to give him any problems on a five-year contract.

"Coach," Drew said, "you and I have done a lot of business. Come through for me. We'll come in tonight and take care of business. You've got my word on it."

Yatil begged for the phone, and Drew gave it to him.

"If I'm going to take you, I want a hundred percent commitment to our off-season conditioning program," Jimmy said, waving his arms. "It's a nine-to-five job. I want you working here eleven months out of the year."

"Yes, sir," Yatil said.

"I don't want any hamstring or groin problems," Jimmy said.

"Yes, sir!" Yatil said.

"Congratulations on being a Dolphin," Jimmy said; and Drew screamed and pumped his fists, and family and friends went crazy cheering.

Jimmy pointed at Stevens and Seiple and said, "You wanted a big receiver who could fly. You got him." He walked over to contract guru Bryan Wiedmeier to relay what Drew said, slapped Father Leo on the butt, and returned to his chair.

Had he expected Yatil or Drew to say no?

"I want to be up front before I draft him about what I expect," Jimmy explained later in the privacy of his office. "We've got one player, Trace Armstrong, who lives in Gainesville and doesn't want to move here. He's the only one. In Yatil's case, it's not a problem because he already lives here. But I want him to verbally say what he's going to do. Then if there are any problems, it's easier for me to say to him, 'You said you'd be here and not miss a single day, and that's what I expect.' " Only one first-round pick would sign before Yatil would, nearly a month before camp opened.

As the Dolphins neared their second-round pick, the forty-fourth overall, Jimmy rejected trade offers because two players he liked remained. The Dolphins rated Louisville cornerback Sam Madison a late first-round pick, Jason Taylor a high second-round pick. Jimmy asked his coaches and scouts which one they preferred. Ultimately, he figured Houston needed a quality cornerback and would take Madison forty-sixth, so he grabbed Madison and thought about parlaying one of his third-round picks into a late second-round pick for Taylor. But he couldn't find a deal worth the cost—and wound up with Taylor anyway, with the first of his four third-round picks, seventy-third overall.

His first three picks filled his three most critical needs (pass catcher, pass stopper, pass rusher) with players rated higher than where they were drafted. "That in itself made the first-day drafting outstanding," Jimmy said. "Then when we got to the last three picks of the third round, we were able to fill roles. I wanted to get linebacker help since we were living on the edge last year with undersized rookie backups and had released Chris Singleton."

He got a pass-rushing linebacker with an unbelievable work ethic in Derrick Rodgers, a guy who could play inside or outside linebacker in Ronnie Ward, and a three-hundred-pound tackle with quick feet in Brent Smith in that third round. On Day Two, Jimmy turned into a wheeler-dealer again, turning two picks into six.

Of the players he targeted at the Senior Bowl, he ultimately drafted only Taylor. Why did the others fall by the wayside? Bryant Westbrook and Reinard Wilson could have been the Dolphins' first pick if they had not been chosen, and Jim Druckenmiller could have been a Dolphin if Yatil had not been available. The

Steelers thought Chad Scott could play corner and used the twenty-fourth pick on him; Jimmy wouldn't have taken him that high. Dexter McCleon hadn't produced as many plays as Madison and thus was rated lower. Ralph Staten fell out of favor because of off-field problems. Terry Day and Pratt Lyons were considered in later rounds but were drafted just before the Dolphins wanted to take them.

Like Daryl Gardener in 1996, Yatil Green was more a gamble on greatness than a safe, sure bet. But as Al Davis told Jimmy when he foolishly considered trading Michael Irvin, "You can't give this guy away because he scores touchdowns—and the people who score touchdowns win games." If Yatil could use his speed to get deep and his height and leap to score in the red zone, then the Dolphins' aging but still greatest weapon, Dan Marino, might turn his 1996 curses into 1997 cheers.

"When Dan went down, I was saying more [curse words]," Seiple said. "When he came back, he was saying them a little until we got Fred Barnett back. It was hard to get continuity going between wide receiver and quarterback. It was my fault we were rolling receivers in and out. We were trying to find a guy who'd step up, and no one did other than O. J. McDuffie. That's not going to happen this year."

Because he expects Yatil, O.J., Fred, and Troy Dayton to give Marino a quartet of good receivers and expects Yatil to work harder than he did in college.

"The more you talk to people, you find his work ethic isn't as bad as people say," Seiple said. "He did everything the wide receiver coach asked, everything the strength coach asked. Now, when guys were just bullshitting around, he'd join in. Our players will control that. They get in there, they don't fart around. He'll catch on quick. He better—or my ass is on the line. I'll be selling newspapers on Pines Boulevard."

Put this in those headlines: Yatil Green tore the anterior cruciate ligament in his knee in practice July 17, when his cleat caught in the grass as he turned for a pass, and was expected to miss the 1997 season. Kirby Dar Dar, the reserve receiver and special teams star, already had been lost to a torn ACL, the same injury that befell Fred Barnett the year before. And the next day, another special teams standout, Larry Izzo, suffered a season-ending torn Achilles' tendon, the same injury that struck Dan Marino and Don Shula years before. But Jimmy had drafted another promising wide receiver, Brian Manning, and several linebackers who could help on special teams, and even if this draft class contributes nothing, the coach says the 1997 Dolphins will be better because they won't endure the turmoil and transition of 1996. This year, even if Erickson has to replace Marino, he won't be so baffled by a complex offense that he has to call a time-out and come to the sideline and say, "What the fuck is P–38?"—and watch Marino and Kosar break out laughing.

"I think we'll be significantly better this year, which puts us in the play-offs. Now, if we're in the playoffs and we're healthy and we've got momentum, anything can happen," Jimmy predicted. "But I think we'll have our strongest team in '98. Then we'll have three groups of players we've drafted who know our scheme and what we want, we'll have room under the salary cap to pick up veterans, and our young players will have the experience to win it all."

About $6 million of their salary cap money in 1996 and 1997 will be "waste money," paying off bad contracts to Eric Green and Gene Atkins and all those other ignoble mistakes. But the cap slate will be clean in 1998, and the Dolphins will have $7 million, maybe $8 million, to spend on star free agents. If a new television contract raises the cap, they'll have even more room, but Jimmy hopes the cap doesn't rise because then his competition will be in serious trouble. For instance, according to an NFL study dated March 27, 1997, the 1998 Raiders would have forty-one players under contract and be $16.476 million over and the '98 Cowboys would have just twenty-seven players signed and still be $8.441 million over. Don't you know that Jimmy would just love to raid Jerry and Barry's Cowboys?

"If it stays flat, there's gonna be a lot of people scrambling for money," Jimmy said. "We've got no bullets now. We'll have plenty of bullets in 1998."

And maybe Jimmy Johnson and Dan Marino will get the ring they so desperately covet in Super Bowl XXXIII, on their home field in their beloved South Florida. And if they do not?

"I'll be the first one to walk if we don't win," Jimmy said. "No one will have to ask me. Nobody's gonna have to call in on a radio show and say, 'Hey, get rid of Jimmy Johnson.' I came back for one reason—to win. As much as I enjoyed TV, and I did have fun, I never had the great feelings or the horrible feelings that I have coaching football. And I want that. Maybe this might be masochistic, but unless you are absolutely at the depths and absolutely miserable, I don't think you can fully experience the ecstasy when you then reach the top. The misery of being 1–15 made that first Super Bowl win fantastic.

"Very few people ever feel that, and I feel sorry for people who go through life with a few bad days and a few good days. They live seventy years and they die.

"I have lots of horrible days and lots of great days. And when I lay down to rest, I'll look back and say, 'Hey, it was a hell of a ride.' "

About the Author

STEVE HUBBARD is the author of five books and an award-winning reporter who has covered the NFL for seventeen years. He covered the Steelers for *The Pittsburgh Press*, the Eagles for the *Daily Times*, and the Bengals for *The Sun*. He has written for *Inside Sports*, *The Sporting News*, and *The Washington Post*. He lives with his wife and two children in Pittsburgh.